Clairvoyant of the Small

Clairvoyant
of the Small

The Life of Robert Walser

Susan Bernofsky

Yale

UNIVERSITY PRESS

New Haven and London

Published with assistance from the foundation established in memory of
Philip Hamilton McMillan of the Class of 1894, Yale College.

Yale University Press books may be purchased in quantity for educational, business,
or promotional use. For information, please e-mail sales.press@yale.edu (U.S. office) or
sales@yaleup.co.uk (U.K. office).

Set in Bulmer type by IDS Infotech Ltd.
Printed in the United States of America.

Library of Congress Control Number: 2020948375
ISBN 978-0-300-22064-3 (hardcover : alk. paper)

Frontispiece: Klaus Dennhardt, *Portrait of Robert Walser*
(Private Collection of J. A. Hopkin, Berlin)

A catalogue record for this book is available from the British Library.

This paper meets the requirements of ANSI/NISO Z39.48-1992 (Permanence of Paper).

10 9 8 7 6 5 4 3 2 1

For Richard

Contents

Searching for Robert Walser

NOT SO LONG AGO, ROBERT WALSER (1878–1956) was the greatest modernist author you'd never heard of. Although much admired as a young writer in his native Switzerland and beyond, including by his contemporaries Franz Kafka, Robert Musil, Hermann Hesse, and Thomas Mann, he was almost forgotten in later life—and his obscurity outlived him. Only after the centenary of his birth was his work rediscovered and enthusiastically embraced by new generations of readers and scholars. A "writer's writer" celebrated mainly for his brilliant short prose, Walser is now recognized as one of the most singular and original voices of the early twentieth century. He is also revered as a literary antihero who lived and wrote on the margins of society, a romantic outsider.

The bits of Walser's life story best known today are that he trained as a bank clerk and butler when young and later spent decades as an inpatient in a psychiatric clinic, dying while out for a solitary walk in the snow. Readers in the English-speaking world might know his novel about butler school, *Jakob von Gunten,* on which the film *Institute Benjamenta* by the Brothers Quay is based, or have picked up a copy of *Selected Stories of Robert Walser* from 1982 with the foreword by Susan Sontag. Those who encountered Walser more recently may have heard first of the miniature manuscripts (microscripts) he produced during the latter part of his career—though not only while institutionalized, as is widely and erroneously believed.

Undoubtedly important elements of his story, these together create a somewhat misleading picture of the person and author Robert Walser. In this book, I aim to fill in the gaps and present a portrait of the artist as a literary professional, a master craftsman who encountered many obstacles on his path but remained unwaveringly devoted to his art. For most of his career, Walser eked out a modest living by his pen, above all as an author of the short newspaper texts known as feuilletons—brief sketches or anecdotes drawn from ordinary life, not unlike *The New Yorker*'s "Talk of the Town" section—a genre he transformed into a vehicle for spectacular feats of narration.

The misperception of Walser as a minor writer was to some extent a result of his cultivating this form and devoting his work to "small" subjects and modest motifs. Spinning tales around insignificance, he preached a gospel of appreciation for the overlooked marvels that surround us, prompting W. G. Sebald to dub him "a clairvoyant of the small." "We don't need to see anything out of the ordinary," one Walser narrator proclaims, "[w]e already see so much." For glorifying the modest and inconspicuous, Walser is cherished by many for whom this stance represents a rejection of and resistance to the pernicious commodification of contemporary life.[1]

Forced to leave school at age fourteen out of economic necessity, Walser apprenticed as a bank clerk in his native Biel while harboring dreams of becoming an actor. After moving to Zurich to work in the bookkeeping division of an insurance firm, he published his first poems and then quit his job to devote himself to writing. Soon after his first book, *Fritz Kocher's Essays,* appeared, he moved to Berlin to join his older brother Karl, an artist and stage-set designer. The two became notorious for their antics and boisterous conduct, a pair of *enfants terribles* living large among the creative spirits of prelapsarian Berlin, a hotbed of literary and cultural activity. Thanks to his brother, Walser was welcomed into lofty artistic circles. But he felt ill at ease in high society, which he rebelled against by enrolling in butler school, scandalizing his artistic peers. Even after beginning to "perform" as a writer by producing novels—three in rapid succession that were well-received by critics, including Musil—his books failed to reach a wider audience; they were too quirky, too seemingly modest, too *Swiss.* And while his short prose was admired by fellow writers (Kafka loved reading Walser aloud), the young dreamer was soon a has-been with writer's block. He retreated back to Switzerland in defeat.[2]

Robert Walser's true career begins here. As his dream of literary stardom fizzled, he began to experiment with short prose forms that, over the next two decades, developed into the high-modernist masterpieces that became his signature achievement. Taking the feuilleton-style essay as his starting point, he layered on strata of descriptive flourish and metaphor until he'd constructed elaborate edifices around the simplest topics interwoven with fictional elements, such that it was impossible to tell where essay ended and story began.

Walser's protagonists include children, social outcasts, artists, the impoverished, the marginalized, and the forgotten. All these figures have a penchant for speaking in remarkably erudite, well-crafted, and, above all, lengthy sentences whose complexity and intelligence belie the ostensible insignificance of those who utter them. An astute observer of power differentials, he writes of servants whose employers cower inwardly before them because they understand that their dominance is precarious and must be either voluntarily acknowledged or physically enforced. Thus, the powerful find themselves desiring and depending on their subordinates' goodwill. But if nurturing a desire of any sort means surrendering power, Walser describes such renunciation as a joyful, empowering act.

Irony permeates Walser's universe. Not, however, the sardonic and occasionally sarcastic sort famously associated, for example, with Thomas Mann. Walserian irony is a different Weltanschauung altogether. Juxtaposing modesty with stunning verbal opulence, Walser's words ascend from the terrain they purport to map, taking flight and sketching such mesmerizing arabesques that a sentence's ostensible "meaning" becomes the least important thing about it.

Walser's prose pieces spiral around their topics, amassing observations, thoughts, and insights until all human history appears contained in the simple act of, say, looking at a picture. The thick texture of his prose foregrounds the writing itself, his syntactical and semantic complexity reflecting the jangling, anxiety-ridden, euphoric spirit of the modern age. His later narratives are characterized by abrupt changes of topic and direction; a new phrase might be prompted by a rhyme that provokes an association or a metaphor that sparks its own subnarrative. His winding sentences parody bureaucratic German by filling its structures with disorienting phrases. The relativizing adverbs he favors—approximately, perhaps, probably, so to speak—constrict their object until the firm ground of factual assertion disappears entirely.

Reading Walser's late stories is like watching a murmuration of starlings in swirling flight. Even those who know his work well can rarely predict where his mind will go next. Echoes of his early writings can be heard in Kafka, and the influence of his later work stands out in Friedrich

Dürrenmatt, Peter Handke, and Thomas Bernhard—along with many other writers who have found inspiration in his pages.

Seen from the twenty-first century, with our lives increasingly defined by an infinitely networked and often militarized global culture—even for those of us who, unlike Walser, never performed wartime service—it is easy to identify with his ambivalent response to the jarring new technologies of his age. Of all the writers who set out to unmask the idol Progress, none understood more acutely what havoc velocity and mechanization were wreaking on the human spirit. While the inspirations of city life and its tempo are clearly visible in much of his work, he often cuts against the technological grain by nostalgically—and only half-ironically—invoking the pastoral tropes of romanticism, including some taken from the legacy of romanticism's medieval past. The stock figures of the page boy and itinerant journeyman poet appear frequently in his early writings.

The trope of the itinerant journeyman is one Walser came to regret, as it was direly overused in assessments of his work. But this figure accords well with his preferred method of reclaiming the landscapes in and around the Swiss and German cities where he lived: striding through them on foot. A prodigious walker who preferred his own two feet to any other form of transportation, he thought nothing of walking all night, traversing, say, the eighteen miles from Bern to Thun and then climbing a mountain in the morning. Many of these walks became the basis for some of his best-known stories, such as his novella *The Walk*, set in Biel. Unlike a flâneur moving through a city at a leisurely pace, obsessively noting and recording experiences in granular detail, Walser was a speedy walker devoted to swift apperception and glimpses following one another quickly.

Uncompromisingly averse to being fenced in or encumbered in any way, Walser moved restlessly from city to city (Stuttgart—Munich—Zurich—Berlin—Biel—Bern) and especially *within* these cities, inhabiting an endless succession of furnished rooms usually rented from older women. He relocated as many as thirteen times per year, his few possessions stashed in a suitcase. Supporting himself on the modest fees he received for his books and magazine and newspaper publications, he spent most of his life in straitened circumstances—which he preferred to surrendering the freedom to live and work as he chose.

By the mid-1920s, Walser was living an economically precarious existence in Bern, the Swiss capital, with ever fewer publishers—including

the newspapers he depended on for income—interested in his work the
more radical it became. He was socially isolated, drinking heavily, and increasingly unconventional in his behavior and affect as mental illness became a complicating factor in his life. In 1929—at age fifty, and at the height
of his creative powers—he entered Waldau Asylum outside Bern. He
would spend his remaining twenty-eight years in institutional confinement.
During his intake interview, he reported experiencing auditory hallucinations, insomnia, depression, and an inability to concentrate—symptoms
recorded in his medical record along with a diagnosis of schizophrenia
now considered questionable. Afraid to be alone at night, Walser turned
down the offer of a private room, preferring to sleep in a communal dormitory. It remains uncertain what his condition was, precisely, and whether it
warranted long-term hospitalization. Although he committed himself voluntarily, it was not with the expectation of making the clinic his permanent
home.

Still, the asylum was, among other things, a refuge. He had been
desperate for relief from a paralyzing isolation. As one of his final acts
before seeking psychiatric help, he tried to persuade one of his landladies
to marry him. When she refused, he asked her sister. And after that, he
asked his own sister Lisa to allow him to live with her in her small apartment. But years as an urban nomad had left him an irritable, jumpy, and
depressed companion who often comported himself in socially inappro-
priate ways, and his sister didn't feel capable of looking after him.

The asylum, then, became Walser's solution to his crippling loneliness, and he appeared satisfied as long as he remained there on his own
terms, even continuing to publish. But in 1933 he was transferred against
his will, and for reasons largely bureaucratic, to the Cantonal Asylum in
Herisau, in the Appenzell region of eastern Switzerland, an area unfamiliar
to him. The transfer upended the life he'd become accustomed to at Waldau. Only the threat of force secured his cooperation the day of his transfer, and he never published again.

In Herisau, Walser assembled paper bags and wiped down dining-
hall tables after meals. He followed the regimented life of a patient—except
that he was one of the few clinic residents allowed to take walks on the
surrounding hills on his own recognizance, a privilege he took full advantage of. Some of these walks were undertaken in the company of Carl
Seelig, his legal guardian and eventual literary executor. Seelig visited

Walser dozens of times in Herisau, joining him for long rambles through the countryside and then transcribing conversations he later published. These, along with the entries in Walser's medical record, comprise the main surviving documentation of the last years of Walser's life.

The now-famous microscripts were discovered after Walser's death in 1956. When these hundreds of tiny slips of paper covered in a pencil script just one to two millimeters high came to light, they were assumed to be written in secret code. The microscripts are astonishing objects. Written on various sorts of scrap paper including business cards, pay slips, and rejection letters, they display an incredible textual density, with the tiny pencil marks completely engulfing any original text. The manuscript catalogued as Microscript 200, for example, which became the story "Swine," measures only two and three-eighths by three and three-sixteenths inches and contains nearly six hundred words, about two pages of printed prose.[3]

Myriad questions surround these tiny documents, which, in conjunction with Walser's diagnosis, have given rise to a mystique: the mad author compelled to minimize his writing within the confines of the asylum. In fact, Walser began drafting his work in microscript form years before entering the clinic. As it became more difficult for him to publish his work in the mid-to-late 1920s, he created commensurately fewer fair copies for submission. His final novel, *The Robber* (1925), was composed in microscript form but never transcribed by its author.

As he approached the end of his career, Walser wrote for the pleasure of writing itself. He wrote out of the sense of professional identity he had developed over the decades, out of habit, and out of a desire to continue experimenting. These pages bear witness to an extreme artistic delight. In the private realm of Walser's pencil landscape, he can be infinitely witty, irreverent, and cruelly insulting with impunity, writing sentences that swoop and gambol about their subjects, sketching out narrative spaces with aplomb. But he lacked an audience. What he needed wasn't newspaper readers; it was a proper rediscovery by the literary intellectuals who had championed him during his early years. He nearly attracted their attention once more in 1925, when he published his final book, *The Rose,* with the help of writer/editor Franz Hessel, who at the time was co-translating the first volume of Proust's *In Search of Lost Time* with his friend Walter Benjamin. Then a virtual unknown, Benjamin wrote an essay about Walser in 1929 that he read on the radio, but Walser's career was as good as over by then. *The Rose* found few readers, and he was unable to publish another book thereafter. His disappearance into the asylum was a quiet exit that left no ripples in the literary community.

Writing Robert Walser's biography was the last thing on my mind when I started translating him more than thirty years ago. I quickly fell in love with his writing—the way each of his sentences takes you on a journey that so often lands you somewhere utterly unexpected. I loved his gentle wit, his sly humor, his endlessly self-effacing grandiloquence, his metaphors that shift our understanding of how the world is made. Translating him helped me understand how he pulled off his narrative sleight-of-hand again and again. All these years later, he still astonishes me.

In the fall of 1987, having just completed a bachelor's degree in German and creative writing, I traveled to Zurich on a Swiss Universities Grant to spend a year studying and translating at the Robert Walser-Archiv, then located in the rear garret of a grandly turreted building called the Red Castle on the Zurich waterfront. I enrolled at Universität-Zürich and audited some classes there—a lecture on contemporary Swiss literature with Hans Wysling, Introduction to Translation Studies with Mary Snell-Hornby, and a profoundly immersive seminar on James Joyce with Fritz Senn. But mostly I spent my days studying and reading in the room at the Walser archive set aside for visiting scholars—most weeks that was just me—with its big wooden table stained a deep forest green, nearly the same hue as the twelve linen-covered volumes of the complete edition that was my prize possession. I slowly filled volume after volume with penciled annotations, ideas about English wording, and notes on which stories would work best in translation.

Each morning, as early as I could manage, I would set out from my tiny room in the personnel dormitory of the Swiss Epilepsy Clinic, near the Tiefenbrunnen tram depot, and walk along the shore of Lake Zurich to the archive, passing swans, boats, the chestnut-lined promenade, the Le Corbusier pavilion, and the grinding gears of sculptor Jean Tinguely's strange huge *Eureka*. The Alps appeared at the far end of the long, narrow lake on clear mornings, looking much too large to hide behind clouds, as they did most of the time. It moved me to walk where I knew Walser once had. I hiked through the woods to visit the lake called Greifensee, described in his first published prose text, and took the train to see the house in Wädenswil where his novel *The Assistant* was set. But I always returned to the worktable at the archive and my dictionaries. I usually stayed until closing time, popping out only at noon to buy a cheese sandwich or slice of *Wähe* (a sort of Swiss tart) at a nearby bakery. When the cleaner quit, I jumped at the chance to earn some badly needed cash. The job came with a key to the archive's public areas, and from then on, I would translate as well as mop on weekends.

In the next room, seated at a pair of desks shoved back-to-back, Bernhard Echte and Werner Morlang hunched over thread counters—small magnifying lenses mounted on frames—peering at the tiniest manuscripts I'd ever seen. Using identical typewriters, they turned out draft after draft of their transcriptions for volume four of the six-volume edition-in-progress *Aus dem Bleistiftgebiet* (From the Pencil Territory). They passed the drafts back and forth until they were satisfied that they'd deciphered each microscript as accurately as possible. Occasionally, one of them would slip me a photocopy of a story they were especially pleased with, and a couple of these found their way into the manuscript I was gradually assembling.[4]

Over the course of translating seven books by Robert Walser, I grew accustomed to ventriloquizing him in the English-language voice I hear in my head when I read him in German. Writing his biography, I found it important to keep in mind how much of what I feel I know about him is projection, particularly as he keeps explicitly reminding me—and indeed all his readers—that, as one of his characters declares, "No one is entitled to act toward me as if he knew me." But isn't that true of everyone? Psychiatrist and author Kay Redfield Jamison writes, "When I teach psychiatry residents and graduate students about psychotherapy, I stress the respect one must keep for the abyss between what one thinks one knows and what one actually knows about another individual's mental life."[5] And of course this principle holds doubly true when the individual in question lived and died many decades in the past.

Walser's radical declaration of unknowability notwithstanding, he often writes stories that are at least in part autobiographical. Occasionally he goes so far as to explicitly invite readers to view his stories as biographical truth, as in "A Sort of Story," whose narrator opines, "The novel I am constantly writing is always the same one, and it might be described as a variously sliced-up or torn-apart book of myself."[6] But do those familiar with Walser's writings really know much at all about the life of their author?

From early in his career, Walser regularly mixed autobiographical and fictional elements in his work. His first novel, *The Tanners,* portrays the relationships between four siblings in early adulthood; the characters are transparently based on Walser's own siblings, and the structure of their conflicts is cribbed from real life as well. But none of the four is an exact portrait, and not all the events described in the novel correspond to real-life occurrences. Even so, the generally autobiographical thrust of this and many other works tempts us to assign them a documentary function. His first biographer, Robert Mächler, leans heavily—too heavily, it seems to me—on Walser's stories and novels in *Das Leben Robert Walsers: Eine dokumentarische Biographie* (The Life of Robert Walser: A Documentary Biography) from 1966. While this book is a pathbreaking work of early Walser reception—one I greedily devoured as a young enthusiast— Mächler inevitably conflates writer and work, presenting a portrait of his subject distorted through the lens of Walser's own fiction. A similar tactic is employed in Catherine Sauvat's thematically structured biography *Robert Walser,* first published in French in 1989.[7]

As Walser's first twenty-first-century biographer, I too am often faced with the choice of either quoting from Walser's own writing to bolster a claim or citing nothing at all. Documentary material becomes lamentably sparse during certain periods of his life, as this urban nomad discarded most of the paper that came his way. And so I quote extensively from Walser's work in the present volume, but always keeping in mind that masquerade and dissimulation are crucial themes in his fictional universe. In a letter to the editors of the newspaper *Frankfurter Zeitung* in 1927, Walser explained that as an essayist he took inspiration from real-life occurrences, giving them poetic form as seemed to him artistically effective. Glimpsing an advertisement for a performance of Georg Büchner's play *Leonce and Lena,* for example, prompted him to write the prose piece "The Dramatist," claiming, among other things, that he attended the performance in question—which he did not. "I love and honor facts," another of his narrators proclaims, perhaps while winking.[8]

A great deal has changed in Walser scholarship since Mächler's biography, which commemorated the tenth anniversary of Walser's death and appeared the year of my birth. In the intervening decades, many new works by Walser have been discovered—approximately one-third of his extant oeuvre—along with numerous letters collected recently in a three-volume edition. And many scholars have gathered invaluable documentary material on his life and work, foremost among them Bernhard Echte, who in 2008 published the five-hundred-page *Robert Walser: Sein Leben in Bildern und Texten* (Robert Walser: His Life in Images and Texts), an important source text for my book.[9]

Above all, though, I rely on the materials I have been collecting since my first visit to the archives in 1987. This rich trove includes articles, book reviews, letters, memoirs, and diary entries by Walser contemporaries whose lives intersected his. I delved into doctors' entries in his medical files, city registry ledgers indicating changes of residence, pay stubs, bank statements, tax forms, and recorded gossip. His numerous residences are documented in the appendix for readers inclined to undertake Walser pilgrimages of their own—following accounts of his life in these many, many abodes. Most importantly, there is the literature he left us: four surviving novels, poetry, dramatic sketches, and thousands of pages of short prose. The stories I tell about Walser's life are interspersed throughout this book with discussions of his most important works and the place they stake out for him in the literary canon. My goal in writing this biography is to show the reader a cannier and sharper-edged side of Walser as an ambitious literary artist who wielded irony as if it were made of iron; he used the pose of naiveté to unmask human secrets in all their difficulty and sadness, and had a singular understanding of how to approach, through indirection, insights that resist being grasped outright—much like this glorious shape-shifter of a writer himself.

Behind the Toy Shop

1878–1894

ROBERT OTTO WALSER WAS BORN at three in the afternoon on April 15, 1878, in a back room above a general store that specialized in toys but also sold all sorts of sewing and stationery items, leather goods, music and umbrella stands, costume jewelry, and mirrors. The shop was located in a modest-sized city in the Swiss canton of Bern that was called either Biel or Bienne, depending on whether one was speaking German or French; the town was just settling into a bilingual identity, with a rapidly growing francophone population arriving from across the Jura Mountains to the north. Along the lakefront, broad streets and generous vistas greeted travelers arriving at the train station, while the city's dense older core occupied the higher ground at the base of the foothills some distance away, in defense against the flooding that once beset the region. In between lay a newer district, the fashionable heart of town at the time of Walser's birth.

As shop owners in this area, his parents, Adolf and Elisa Walser, epitomized the city's growing middle class. The living quarters behind their shop "possessed an air of solidity," Robert would write some fifty years later with characteristic mock-formality in a prose piece titled "Childhood," "and its rooms had bright windows." The early years of Walser's childhood were framed by idyllic settings, according to the narrated memories that appear in virtually identical form in a number of his more overtly autobiographical stories and essays. The narrator of his first published novel, *The Tanners* (1907), recalls "a bright, large nursery which the sun seemed particularly to enjoy filling up with light," in a building "where my parents ran a delightful costume jewelry shop where people were always coming in to buy things." And "Childhood" describes how, as a small child, he enjoyed spinning around and around on the revolving chair at his father's desk on the second floor, from which a narrow flight of stairs "led down from the office into the shop or commercial space that was resplendent with luxury articles of all kinds."[1]

Since toys were an important part of the family business, the eight Walser children were never short on playthings. Lina Marty-Hauenstein, a childhood friend of Robert's older sister, Lisa, recalls: "We always tried out all the new toys and games at the Walsers' first; other children would get something as a Christmas present, but in that household there were new things all year round; for instance once they brought out a magic lantern, and there were always new pictures to put in it, they'd just run down to the shop to get more."[2] Alongside the dolls and jumping jacks, the shop sold the line of educational toys called Froebel Gifts, designed by the German pedagogue Friedrich Fröbel, who also invented kindergarten. Fröbel's sets of wooden building blocks in various configurations, meant to foster children's inventiveness and free play, suggest the approach to children's upbringing favored in the Walser household. The children were encouraged to run around, and their mother often joined in their games.

Robert was the second youngest of the Walser brood. Closest to him in age was Karl, one year older. The two were devoted playmates who explored the nearby wooded hills and the courtyard behind the house. This courtyard appears repeatedly in Walser's writings. In "Page from a Diary," he recalls returning to his hometown after spending many years in Berlin: "How small I felt at the sight of the tiny courtyard where Father used to stack his shipping crates. In the tile-roofed shed, we once played hide-and-seek, and the crates had such an appealing scent. Everything looked just as it had in former times, even the neighbor's little garden where we often caught a glimpse of a pretty girl, and the potter's workshop across the way." Marty-Hauenstein describes this courtyard and workshop as well: "The two boys were always 'finding' a lump of clay there, and then they would knead it and shape it into buildings, bridges etc., and they used generous portions of water when working with this clay. Then the unhappy end! Their good mama came and found her two youngest children filthy: hands and feet, faces and hair, Sunday and everyday trousers, all covered in clay; I'm sure they were properly scolded, but I never saw those two little dirty birds ever get a whipping."[3]

Happy childhoods may have their uses in the lives of writers—just think of the literary capital Vladimir Nabokov derived from the sun-dappled meadows of his beloved childhood estate. In Robert Walser's case, however, the idyll did not last long. By the time he reached adolescence, a combination of personal and professional setbacks sent his family into a state of decline that taught him all he needed to know about personal struggles, interpersonal conflicts, and the cruelty with which the world receives those who have fallen in fortune. This isn't to say he wouldn't have become an acute observer of human psychology if his childhood had ended as gloriously as it began; but the traces of early sorrow engraved on his childish heart certainly played a role in determining the sort of writer he would grow up to be.

Considerable social and economic disparity informed his parents' respective upbringings. Adolf Walser (1833–1914) came from a long line of pastors and intellectuals, and, having been born into a prosperous household of respectable, well-educated burghers, he later displayed a lackadaisical approach to money—it seemed not to worry him inordinately how much he earned and saved as long as it was enough to keep a roof over his head. His wife, Elisa Walser-Marti (1839–1894), on the other hand, grew up a half-orphan in a hardscrabble farming community, and her social and financial ambitions far exceeded her husband's.[4]

In "Portrait of Father," a piece written two years after Adolf Walser's death, Robert offers a fictionalized double portrait of his parents, framed as the remembrances of seven unnamed children gathered at their father's bedside after his passing. The parents described here differ radically from one another in temperament and sensibility. The father is a peace-loving soul who "achieved more than many a violent man could accomplish using the so-called will to power, thanks to his strength in being yielding and patient, as well as through the quiet gift of irony." As for the mother, the narrator speculates: "It is not immediately obvious but nonetheless by all means possible that it may have been our mother who wished to see our father ascend into both commercial and social heights from which—since he proved to be no match for this difficult position—he soon toppled, taking with him, of course, the so respect-worthy woman and all her ambitions."[5]

In an earlier phase of Elisa Marti's life, ambition had been key to her survival. Born in the rural Emmental region, she grew up in precarious circumstances. Her father, Ulrich Marti, had been a respectable craftsman,

a nailsmith like many of his line, but at the age of twenty-eight he fell ill
with dysentery and died several months before Elisa's birth on March 7,
1839. His widow, Anna Barbara Marti-Schürch, was left with three children to support and little means to do so; her parents' farm was not thriving, leaving her with few good local options. She packed up her young son
and two daughters and moved away—it isn't known to where at first. Eventually she settled in Biel, to which several of her eleven siblings had also
relocated; the announcement of her older daughter Fanny's marriage in
1861 names Biel as the family's place of residence. This daughter made a
good match, marrying a wealthy ironmonger, Johann David Rummel.
Shortly afterward, young Elisa began to help out in her sister's household.[6]

Fanny was often unkind to her little sister, who experienced her as cold
and haughty, but there was plenty of work to do in the shop she ran, special-
izing in silks and trimmings, and she helped her sister begin her own rise
from poverty to prosperity. When Elisa married Adolf Walser in 1868, she too
came to inhabit a higher social class, all the more so as her new husband came
into a significant inheritance just two years into their marriage. Elisa was
welcomed into the Walser family circle, especially by Adolf's mother, Maria
Juliana Walser-Hurter, who, like Elisa, had lost her father at a young age.[7]

In her new circumstances, Elisa Walser soon blossomed into "a lady
par excellence"—as Claire Zahler, a friend of her daughter Lisa, would
reminisce many years later: "She was the most important figure in the family, the axis around which everything turned. Always gracious and polite,
but there was also something resolute about her that commanded respect."[8] In the photographs taken of Elisa in the 1870s, she appears solemn, calm, and kind, posing stiffly in the photographer's studio in elegant
dresses buttoned to the neck. Her face is softer in the pictures with her
children. In one, a befrocked baby Hermann sits on her hip, while toddler
Adolf stands rather formally at her side, at his feet a toy horse that signaled
that these two well-dressed children had all a boy could want. Elisa's lips
are pressed tightly together in all of the pictures that survive from this
period, but looking at her eyes, one can easily imagine her mouth erupting
into laughter. It is as a mischievous young girl—a *Berner Meitschi* (little
Bernese maiden), to quote a dialect expression Robert would use at various points in his writing, an ironic bit of folkloric flair—that Elisa must
have smiled and flirted her way into the life of straitlaced young Adolf
Walser, the burgher-in-the-making.

Adolf's background, characterized by generations of prosperity, education, and literary and intellectual achievement, couldn't have been more different from that of his wife. The Walsers were a respected clan whose members included pastors, scholars, and merchants. Most of them settled in and around the town of Teufen in the canton of Appenzell Ausserrhoden in the northeast corner of Switzerland early in the seventeenth century. These forebears were often—as Robert Walser would himself become—tremendous walkers, known for the hardiness with which they would dash about the countryside at great speed well into old age.

There was one ancestor whose accomplishments Robert particularly took pride in: his great-great-great-grandfather's cousin Gabriel Walser-Zollikofer (1695–1776). Robert would later refer to him in a prose piece titled "A Writer" as the author of "a long historical work." Walser-Zollikofer studied theology in Basel as well as in the German university towns Marburg, Tübingen, Jena, and Halle before returning to Switzerland to lead congregations in Speicher and Berneck. He enjoyed a reputation as a man of conscience and tolerance, and advocated for the mentally ill. A stalwart walker, he was no doubt well-served by his penchant for hiking in his work as a cartographer. Walser-Zollikofer drew maps of several Swiss cantons (Luzern, Uri, Glarus, Graubünden), but he specialized in the Appenzell region, to which he devoted an entire volume that appeared in 1740: *New Appenzell Chronicle, or Description of the Canton of Appenzell.* In later life, he drew fifteen new maps of different parts of Switzerland for the 1769 *New Atlas of the Swiss Republic.*[9]

A second notable forebear was Robert's grandfather Johann Ulrich Walser (1798–1866), a prolific author in his own right. Like many of the Walser line, Johann Ulrich studied theology, but during his studies he became involved in the revolutionary republican politics sweeping Germany and Switzerland in the wake of the Napoleonic Wars. Johann Ulrich got himself thrown out of the University of Tübingen after a rivalry between fraternities representing opposing political views escalated into a battle involving cudgels and axes. Even so, he was ordained as a pastor in 1817 and took up a post in Grub, a small Appenzell town between Heiden and Rorschach.

During his studies, Johann Ulrich had begun to write and publish anonymous pamphlets such as *The Little Ledger-book in the Land of Utopia,* a parody of office life. In addition to satires, he published more serious writing, including a history of the different religions represented in the Appenzell region and a pamphlet promoting the separation of church and state, which he was the first Appenzell pastor to advocate. He wrote a satirical brochure in support of a fanatically anti-Semitic journalist (Hartwig Hundt-Radowsky) who appealed to Johann Ulrich as a pro-republican agitator fighting to strip the German aristocracy of its privilege and power. Johann Ulrich's tongue-in-cheek pamphlet *Clear-as-day Proof That Hundt-Radowsky Is the Antichrist Described in the Book of Revelations or the Beast from the Abyss with Seven Heads and Ten Horns* probably seemed funnier at the time than it does now.[10]

The republican form of governance that had briefly been imposed on Switzerland under Napoleon inspired some Swiss liberals of Johann Ulrich's generation to lobby for a modern constitution for Switzerland that would create a strong centralized government, limiting the power of the individual cantons. Beginning in the 1820s, Johann Ulrich became increasingly involved in the political efforts that would eventually result in the ratification of the new constitution. From his pulpit in Grub and in numerous newspaper articles and privately printed pamphlets, he defended the position of the republican liberals seeking political change. Along with the separation of church and state, his desiderata included a modernized school system and freedom of religion. His political activities made him a controversial pastor, with some among his congregation grateful for his efforts and others vehemently opposed to them. He nonetheless acquired a reputation for both intelligence and wit in defense of his causes.

It was Johann Ulrich who uprooted his branch of the Walser clan from its ancestral home in the Appenzell region in eastern Switzerland. In 1833 he was offered a post at a church in Liesthal, a small town outside Basel, halfway across the country, and he accepted it. But the Liesthal congregation soon wearied of being confronted with their pastor's political opinions every time they picked up the newspaper, and when Johann Ulrich's initial appointment expired in 1837, they let him go. Stripped of his post, he founded his own publishing house and began printing radical journals and pamphlets written by others along with *Basellandschaftliches Volksblatt* (Popular Newspaper of the Basel Countryside), a newspaper he himself edited. Under his stewardship, the *Volksblatt* became one of the top-circulating papers in Switzerland and an important weapon in the fight to establish a strong federal government. Because Johann Ulrich gave succor to political refugees from the revolution in Germany who had managed to cross the border—he printed their pamphlets, too—he was no longer welcome on German soil, or French soil for that matter. Even at home he was subject to attack by opponents of his cause: one night someone shot a pair of bullets through his bedroom window (not hitting anyone). In the end, Johann Ulrich was triumphant. A new Swiss constitution based on the American model was ratified in 1848, and he was elected to the new Swiss parliament before his death in 1866.

Robert Walser's father Adolf was the ninth of Johann Ulrich's thirteen children. Of the thirteen, only one received a university education (the youngest, Friedrich, who became a well-known architect); all the other sons learned trades. Adolf chose the trade of bookbinder and was sent off to apprentice in Paris. This city would later play an important role in his son's fiction, invoked as a distant land of elegance and *savoir-vivre*, a magical place where a cloud might descend to the street and lie there like a resting swan. In "Parisian Newspapers" (1925), the narrator boasts of the sophistication he's acquired thanks to this metropolis: "Since I have been reading the Parisian papers, from which the scent of power emanates, I have become so refined that I do not return greetings and, what's more, this amazes me not at all."[11] Paris is a place to which Robert Walser has many of his secondary characters travel—painters and poets alike—but never his protagonists. He himself never saw the French capital with his own eyes.

Adolf Walser picked Biel to settle in after completing his Parisian apprenticeship in 1864. At the time, this medium-sized Swiss town was just expanding into a city. Biel had been declared part of Canton Bern in the 1815 Vienna Congress and was meant to serve as a buffer between the capital city, Bern, and the Jura region that was incorporated into the canton at the same time. (Bern was German-speaking and predominately Protestant, while the Jura was French-speaking and Catholic.) Biel was granted significant municipal powers, including the right to introduce unusually favorable tax laws that led to significant growth, especially in connection with the city's increasing industrialization; the population quickly rose from around 5,600 (in 1850) to 11,700 (1870) to 21,200 (1888). During this period, Biel acquired its nickname City of the Future and boasted both a Future Street and an Imagination Street.[12] The new tax laws lured a large number of French-speaking watchmakers from the Jura region as the city continued to industrialize. By 1885, two-thirds of Switzerland's watchmakers were employed here.

Adolf's business boomed as well. Though he had started out modestly—with a workshop producing packing cartons—he was able to relocate a number of times. He did so in 1866, 1867, at least twice in the early 1870s, and twice in 1879, each time choosing a larger, more centrally located storefront. Already in 1867 he took out an advertisement in the *Schweizer Handels-Courier* (Swiss Business Gazette) announcing that he had augmented his shop with a bookbindery and *gainerie,* a workshop for producing leather goods. The shop itself, according to the advertisement, now carried "a generous assortment of writing, postal, packing and tissue paper, pencils, pens, ink, slates in four sizes from 15 to 30 centimes, rulers, notebooks, notepads as well as business and household ledgers and bound notebooks in various sizes." Also "sewing-cushions most elegant in form" and a variety of packing materials, including "round boxes for pocket watches."[13]

In the 1870s Adolf expanded his offerings to include baskets and ladies' handbags in oilcloth and leather and moved his shop to a grand street with a lot of commercial activity called Schulgasse (present-day Dufourstrasse), and from there to Nidaugasse, the town's most fashionable address. Over the following several years, he would move from one Nidaugasse address to another, including (in 1879) to a particularly fancy, newly renovated building where he started calling his shop Magazin Adolf Walser (to appeal to French-speaking customers) and advertised a much-expanded range of merchandise. One notice describes the shop as a *Papeterie- & Quincaillerie-Geschäft,* in other words, a stationery and hardware store in which all sorts of household goods could be purchased. Adolf's offerings were well-calculated to appeal to the needs and tastes of Biel's rapidly rising middle class.

The customer stepping out of the bright sunshine of Nidaugasse into the interior of Adolf Walser's shop was greeted by a profusion of objects: everything from tablecloths and petroleum lamps to walking sticks. Display cases of costume jewelry sparkled with necklaces, bracelets, cufflinks, and watch chains. The toy department was renowned for its large selection of dolls, picture books, and games of every description for both children and adults. Adolf himself could often be found behind the counter, chatting with the customers and neighbors who would drop by the shop on their way through town. He was sociable and well-liked. Unlike his own father, he never talked politics, a characteristic borrowed by his son Robert years later for "Portrait of Father": "That he intervened strikingly little in matters of state and public concern was definitely not a virtue in him, but in any case it was in keeping with his modest nature."[14]

Adolf's business had been well established by the time he married Elisa in 1868, when he was thirty-five and she twenty-nine. He was certainly in a position to support a wife by then, and his business continued to expand along with his family: the Walsers' oldest son, Adolf, was born in 1869, followed by Hermann (1870), Oscar (1872), Ernst (1873), Lisa (1874), Karl (1877), Robert (1878), and Fanny (1882). At some point along the way Elisa's mother moved in with them and stayed until her death in 1877. The rapidly growing family relocated as often as the business: the ledger books of Biel's Municipal Registry of Inhabitants show Adolf Walser to have registered at least eight different private addresses.

Robert was born at the height of his family's commercial success, at a point when the Walsers occupied a stately four-story residence joined at the rear to Adolf's Nidaugasse shop. Their home boasted a little second-floor balcony where Elisa could step out for a breath of air while tending to her children. Both buildings belonged to Alexander Schöni (1796–1880), who, like Adolf's father Johann Ulrich Walser, was a leading figure in the radical Swiss republican scene, serving in various positions in local government. Like Johann Ulrich, he took in political refugees from across the border in Baden and was so active in their support that his house was nicknamed the Revolutionary Salon, an ironic place of residence for the decidedly unpolitical shopkeeper.[15]

By the time the writer born in the Revolutionary Salon turned two, the family had moved a few doors down to a building on Nidaugasse, where as the scion of a petit-bourgeois household, Robert spent his early years in relative comfort, his principal occupation getting up to mischief, often together with his brother Karl. Walser wrote no diaries and almost no letters in which he reminisces about his early childhood, but a series of sketches from 1925—the "Felix Scenes"—describe a childhood that seems to accord well with what we know of Walser's early years. The first of these scenes is a soliloquy spoken by the eponymous character, prefaced with the stage direction "Felix in front of his parents' shop, he's four or six years old":

> How lovely it is to be so small. You're not responsible for a thing. I'm practically still a riddle to myself in many respects.

All the beautiful goods in the shop window. At the very back of the shop, facing the little alley, is my father's office: Already I have some inkling of what such an office is for. My sister, who is younger than I am, seems extremely demanding; she has a need which I have already left far behind me, she has to have a stopper in her mouth at all times, otherwise she finds the situation deplorable [. . .] My mother is always rushing about, as if she can't find the time for many things she would like to devote herself to. She'd come play with me if that were permitted her. It seems to me she has too much to do, and it almost worries me that I have no worries.[16]

In other "Felix Scenes," Walser writes of Felix and his brother lying in wait for a less prosperous companion, the son of a carpenter, whom they plan to capture and humiliate (he outwits them); of Felix being treated by a doctor after a firecracker burns his face; and of Felix losing an argument to his younger sister. The backdrop for these adventures is the elegant shop, the office, and the courtyard behind it. The scene set here is one of prosperity, with Felix and his brother feeling superior to their working-class playmate until he informs them that his father will have a word with theirs if they abuse him. Felix's family has a maid—he notes "I don't think our maid cares too much for me"—and a similar observation is recorded in Walser's 1922 prose text "Fidelio," whose narrator reports the family's maid once "threatening" him with the words, "Just you give some pious thought to that!" Many other scoldings receive literary form as well. Young Felix gets drunk on the dregs of an abandoned beer glass at an outdoor café and is spanked for it, and he trespasses to climb a tree, to the owner's horror. And the narrator of "Fidelio" recalls a teacher upbraiding him for some unspecified malfeasance with the words, "Even the Rhine can never wash that away."[17]

Was Robert as much of a scamp as all these fictional or semifictional characters? Marie Schaetzle-Ehrensperger, another childhood friend of Robert's older sister, Lisa, recalls Robert and Karl as the wild children of an otherwise decorous family:

We were always received warmly but somewhat stiffly at the Walsers'. Lisa's father would make her play the piano for us. Meanwhile Father Walser would fetch a bottle of wine and insist we drink some even though we didn't like the taste. Sometimes the older brothers would come into the parlor and greet us formally; meanwhile we could hear Karl and Robert getting up to mischief and arguing out in the kitchen. —Once, as schoolchildren, four of us including Röbi [Robert] hiked up Bözingenberg. On our way down, Röbi said: "Let's play here!" We lined up big rocks like bowling pins. Then he ordered us to knock down the big stones using smaller ones: the bigger ones were the bourgeoisie, he said, and the little ones were Socialists. Later we stopped in at a little tavern. Röbi ordered wine and rolls for all of us, as a result of which we were soon all giddy. As we were leaving, he said to the innkeeper that we didn't have any money but that his father was good for it.[18]

A major and ongoing source of drama in Robert's early childhood was his turbulent relationship with Karl. The two often quarreled, and Karl spurred on his younger brother to engage in mischief. In several fictional works, Walser writes of feuding brothers who reconcile after the younger brother begs the older one's pardon even though it was the older brother who was in the wrong. In the version of events presented in his first and most autobiographical novel, *The Tanners*, for example—in a letter written by protagonist Simon to his brother Kaspar—the quarrel has its roots in a humiliating gesture:

> Once at the dinner table [. . .] you threw a platter of sauerkraut at me, because you couldn't resist, saying: "Here, catch!"
> I have to tell you, at the time I was trembling with fury even if only for the fact that here was this lovely opportunity for you to insult me so cruelly, and there was nothing I could do about it. I caught the platter, and was stupid enough to savor the pain of this mortification all up and down my gullet. And do you remember how, one noon [. . .] someone came creeping up to you in the kitchen and asked you to be friends with me again. It was an incredible feat of self-control [. . .] to overcome those feelings of shame and defiance to reach out to you, the very figure of an enemy inclined to scornfully reject me. I did this and to this day am grateful to myself for doing so.[19]

In "Felix Scenes," on the other hand, written nineteen years later, the affront is omitted; the story presents only the moment of reconciliation:

> You can hardly be resolved to appreciate sufficiently how much
> effort this hesitant approach costs me in my proud fraternal
> soul. By no means does your face express the requisite energy
> for appreciating me and what I'm up to here by even a finger's
> length or breadth, and thus shall this kitchen bear witness to
> one of the boldest, most fearless and doubtless also the most
> daredevil feats that a person has ever wrung from himself.[20]

The writer who recorded this scene was well into his forties at the time and displays a psychological sophistication surely far beyond the capacity of the young children portrayed here. But the structure of the interaction reveals an uncanny prescience: a child apologizing, although he believes himself in the right, for the sake of attaining his brother's approval, which he desires. This is a classic example of the sort of empowerment through active renunciation of power that will appear again and again in Robert Walser's work.

As a child, Robert must have found it difficult to assert any personal power at all as the second-youngest of eight siblings—including five older brothers. Only Fanny was younger, and even she had some sway over him. Robert would later relate in a letter that as a child he was assigned the task of telling Fanny stories to amuse her, and if he rebelled against this chore, she would complain to their mother, who would punish him.[21] But childish power struggles among siblings would not remain foremost in young Robert's thoughts for long.

The family's fortunes changed drastically during the 1880s, with one trauma following another. In October 1884, Robert Walser's oldest brother, Adolf, died after a three-month-long illness, at the age of fifteen. In a fictionalized memory Robert recorded years later, he recalls playing in the courtyard with Karl as their brother lies ill and having their mother shout at them out the window, calling them "monsters." Elsewhere he writes of having been unable to weep after his brother's death and feeling like a "villain" as he watched his sister's tears flow. Still inconsolable two and a half months later, his mother Elisa wrote to her niece: "How often I sat at my child's bedside wringing my hands and imploring the Almighty:

God, my God, hear my words in mercy and restore the health of our dear child, Lord, Lord, do not take my child from me! I would have given my own heart's blood to save him."[22]

At around the same time, Adolf Walser's business began to collapse. Perhaps he had expanded beyond the point of sustainability; perhaps the tastes of the burghers of Biel had changed and were no longer reflected in his merchandise; or perhaps he was just one of the many casualties of the depression that rocked the Swiss economy in the early 1880s as the delayed result of railroad speculation in the late 1870s. In any case, early in 1885 he was obliged to give up the shop's prestigious Nidaugasse location and move to a much smaller space at Zentralstrasse 23—despite the name of the street, a far more remote neighborhood. Marty-Hauenstein recalled years later that after the Walser family's "bazaar" moved to the Neuquartier district, she would often drop by to visit: "For some reason, sales had plummeted, and you got the impression that the good, prosperous circumstances of the highly respected Walser family had taken a turn for the worse."[23]

This modest new shop closed sometime in 1886. The last advertisement Adolf published—on January 3, 1886, in the *Schweizer Handels-Courier*—offers a much more modest list of products than before: oilcloth tablecloths, "imitation tablecloths," rubber sheets for sickbeds, everything "cheaper than ever" and "below wholesale prices." The successful merchant had come far down in the world. By 1889, the family resided at Brühlstrasse 69c, in a working-class neighborhood and factory district outside the city center. In a memoiristic essay ostensibly composed by Simon Tanner in *The Tanners*, he reports, "We were now living at the edge of town in humble lodgings, the sight of which was enough to chill you through."[24]

Robert had been six years old when his brother died; the Nidaugasse shop was lost the month of his seventh birthday. At this young age, he was scarcely able to grasp the gravity of these events, at least not consciously. Worse was to come. The third major blow to strike the Walser family was the decline of Elisa Walser's mental health during this period of personal and financial setbacks. The loss of social status that accompanied her husband's business failures had stressed her psyche to the breaking point—even as he, perhaps displaying the passivity his son later described as being "patient and yielding," took these setbacks in stride.[25]

Elisa was now reexperiencing the deprivation she had watched her own mother struggle with throughout her childhood. A photograph taken around 1890 shows her dressed as elegantly as before, but her face is hard and sad, with no trace of laughter in her eyes. A letter she wrote to her son Hermann in 1889—studying in Bern thanks to a loan from a mentor—speaks of the hopes she'd had for her children's upbringing and her despair at having been unable to fulfill them: she always tried, she writes, "to awaken the ideal within all of you"; but, "How often I felt that I had so few intellectual resources at my disposal, and in the chaos of running the shop, there was no chance to develop them; and so in my helplessness I begged that my children be given the gifts of intellect they would need, even though I myself was unable to help them in this regard." In this and two other surviving letters to her son, she speaks of the strength she derived from her religious beliefs, exhorting him to keep his own faith alive and speaking of her gratitude for the blessings she had received: "So many riches have come to us from above, we can only have received this opulent blessing from higher spheres."[26]

These letters are among the few surviving documents that tell us firsthand what kind of person Robert's mother was, and how she struggled. She would write to Hermann of feeling ever less strength in her hands and legs, and of her knees buckling beneath her as she walked one day, making her afraid to leave the house. Besides these words, what we know of her comes from the portrait Walser sketched of her with remarkable consistency in some dozen texts written over twenty years. As he writes in "The Merchant" (1916): "The lack of success had destroyed the family's domestic existence. The poor woman, proud and sensitive by nature, was made ill by it all."[27] The details of her malady are always delicately circumscribed in these portraits, never shown in sharp focus, but these ailments are invariably psychological.

"Portrait of Father" alludes only glancingly to Adolf's commercial failings: "The extent to which our father may have been, shall we say, maladroit in managing his business affairs and their development, is not at all clear to us." Relatives in a position to offer financial help chose not to. The narrator notes how ungenerous it is of the children to harbor the thought that their father—who himself had enjoyed a substantial inheritance—was leaving nothing to them. But no one was more disappointed in him than Elisa. Her general unhappiness over the collapse of the middle-class life she had worked so hard to establish and her dissatisfaction with her husband's lack of ambition and commercial prowess turned her into a nag who could not bring herself to stop reproaching her husband for his failings. "Since he was forced to listen to her endless complaints," Robert has his narrator report in "Portrait of Father," "it cannot be said that our father led a pleasurable life at her side."[28]

The children, this piece goes on to note, were swayed by their mother's influence to underestimate their quiet, unassuming father—in retrospect a wrong the narrator wishes to right by establishing once and for all that the source of their mother's unhappiness was not their father's actions per se but outside misfortunes that she was less well-equipped to bear than he was. She "railed from the depths of her nobly sensitive soul—a glorious rebel—against the weight crashing down upon her and the chastisement she had by no means deserved."[29] (For what it's worth, Walser's portraits of his mother tend to downplay the psychological toll that raising so many children—and losing one to illness—must have had on her; though of course having so large a family was more common then than it is now.)

When the last of Adolf's shops closed, he began to trade in wine and olive oil—a business that kept the family marginally afloat. Tax records from the late 1880s show that the authorities estimated his income as a wine seller at 500 francs a year, only one-third his earnings a decade before. A copy of a letter of recommendation he received from the municipal council in 1889 shows that he was seeking other employment during this period. But by the early 1890s his new business began to bring in a bit more money after all, and the family moved again, twice, each time to a somewhat better address (Zentralstrasse 40, Zentralstrasse 52), though they partially financed these moves by taking in lodgers.[30] And despite the financial hardship, certain key features of middle-class life were retained: Adolf sent his son Ernst off to study in Bern, and all the children took music lessons. Robert was assigned the piano—for which, according to his younger sister, Fanny, he lacked both desire and talent, though he would later write with great warmth about his love of music.

But while Elisa's children and husband adapted to their new circumstances and went about their lives reasonably contented, something in Elisa had snapped, and she never recovered. Her nerves were constantly frayed, and her children tiptoed around her, carefully avoiding all disturbances that might send her flying into a rage. Walser's second novel, *The Assistant* (1908), contains a scene inspired by this period in which several children take their mother on an outing to the woods and are overcome with relief when they find a secluded spot that pleases her:

The children were all happy that their mother was pleased with their hollow, that she was able to sit there quietly, caressed by all the advantages of so lovely a resting place. They knew the desires and needs of their mother's spirit. [...] From time to time the children glanced over at their mother to see whether or not she was cross, but no, she was gazing straight in front of her with a kindly and otherwise reticent expression. [...] When their mother was able to smile—which was such a rare occurrence— then the entire surrounding world smiled at them as well. Mother was already ill in those days, she suffered from an excess of sensitivity. How sweet the children found the peaceful repose of this woman, who was being gnawed at by unhappiness from all sides.[31]

Other portraits Walser sketches of his mother are less placid. The mother in "Felix Scenes" gets so worked up at dinner one night that she hurls a knife at the wall despite the presence of a respected guest. A moment later she vehemently objects to having her state of mind analyzed:

ARNOLD: My mother's behavior can be attributed to unsound nerves.

MOTHER: To what can I be attributed, insolent boy?

ARNOLD: Please forgive us, Professor.

MOTHER: Heartless son.[32]

Finally Elisa Walser's profound unhappiness gave way to "a long, difficult illness" severe enough to incapacitate her. A letter Walser wrote to his sister Lisa on May 5, 1898, recalls that among all the siblings it was Lisa who spent the most time tending to their mother "during the period when she was suffering." Nowhere in Walser's writings or extant letters is her final affliction named, but an entry in his medical record decades later indicates she was "apoplectic," that is, had suffered—or was thought at immediate risk of—a stroke.[33] She died on October 22, 1894, when Robert was sixteen years old. By then he'd left school and was well into an apprenticeship as a bank clerk. Despite his young years, his childhood was over.

TWO

From the Bank to the Stage

1885–1896

ROBERT WALSER'S EARLY DEPARTURE from school notwithstanding, the primary- or secondary-school pupil is one of the most frequently encountered figures in his work. His first book-length publication—*Fritz Kocher's Essays* (*Fritz Kochers Aufsätze*), which appeared in 1904 when its author was twenty-six—features a collection of twenty short prose pieces masquerading as the homework assignments of a boy who died shortly after leaving school. The arch, suppressed-smile cautiousness with which this narrator addresses Christmas, friendship, music, "the fatherland," and school itself points the way to a persona—the precociously insightful child—that will appear again and again in Walser's books.

Robert himself was a good and diligent pupil although stories abound in his later work of being reprimanded as a child both at home and at school. Certainly, he and Karl enjoyed pulling pranks and inventing games, and Karl—in many ways Robert's role model—did not do well at school. Karl's grades were weak, and both his parents and his teachers considered him lazy, at least until he entered *Progymnasium* (roughly equivalent to junior high school in the United States) and started taking art classes with Jacob Häuselmann, an engraver, photographer, and landscape painter who inspired him to pursue a career as an artist.[1] Robert studied with Häuselmann as well.

School also served as a refuge for this seventh of eight children whose mother didn't have much time for him even before her devastating final illness. Walser has novel protagonist Simon Tanner describe his envy of other children who were lovingly cared for: "I had a need to be treated with affection, but this never happened. [. . .] I had a reputation for being a scallywag—not without cause, as I recall—but it was nonetheless sometimes

hurtful always to be reminded of that. I would so have loved to be coddled."
School provided a "compensation for the minor affronts" suffered at home
for a pupil who "took great satisfaction in bringing home good grades."
The narrator of Walser's "The Poet" reports: "History lessons excited me.
Studying Jesus Christ in religion class was a sweet pleasure. I approached
the subject not with reluctant diligence but almost with enjoyment, finding
it entertaining." And the narrator of "The Young Poet" remarks: "Since he
wrote a clean, tidy, nimble hand and apparently took particular pleasure in
tracing out his letters, the writing teacher once told him he should aspire to
become an office worker." Robert's school record covering the years 1885
to 1892 includes row after row of perfect grades. There is only a single year,
1889, when his grades in all categories except "drawing" sank a little, and a
particularly high number of absences (twenty) was recorded; this is the year
the Walser family moved from their prosperous neighborhood to working-
class quarters.[2]

One of Robert's teachers, Pastor Harald Marthaler, had a particularly powerful impact on him. News of Marthaler's death in 1925 prompted
Walser to write about him in several different works. "The aforementioned
pastor," one narrator reports, "was something like a friend to me who
made a friendly impression already simply by now and then running into
me in the crowd out in the open air, in other words, I liked him." In "Felix
Scenes," Walser speaks of a religion teacher interrupting his lesson one
day to tell his class how concerned he is about the possibility of war with
Germany. Robert may have worried about not living up to this teacher's
expectations. In his novel *The Robber* (1925) an interlocutor claims that
the title character's performance in religion class was disappointing. But
in *The Tanners,* Simon recalls, "In religion class I once delighted one of
my teachers by finding just the right word for a certain feeling."[3]

Except for Marthaler, there is no mention anywhere in Walser's work
of any teacher or similar mentor who might have encouraged the young
pupil to read great works of literature, much less try writing some of his
own. Nor does he ever speak of books being read or discussed by his parents, though the family did subscribe to two popular journals, *Vom Fels
zum Meer* (From the Cliffs to the Sea) and *Die Gartenlaube* (The Arbor).
When Walser writes about his childhood enthusiasm for reading, it is usually in connection with the often sensational stories he read in the pages of
these magazines. In one piece, for example, he enumerates two pages'

worth of hideous forms of torture, each presented in disturbingly voy-euristic detail, before dryly remarking, "As a boy in my childhood home, I enjoyed reading and therefore did quite a lot of it." Some of the cruel acts young Robert read about apparently included sawing people in half (a lot of work for the "two strong, sturdy men doing the sawing") and "being slowly roasted or braised in a frying pan like a fish or a piece of juicy meat and thereby being rendered suitable for admission into Heaven, as it were, with the most delicate precision."[4]

Perhaps literary inspiration arrived in Robert's life by way of his older siblings. Lisa and Ernst (four and five years Robert's senior, respec-tively) were bookish. Lisa organized a reading group with several of her friends, led by a young teacher. And Ernst, having decided to go into teaching himself, was attending a *Gymnasium* (high school for pupils with academic aspirations) at the same time Robert was scallywagging his way through grade school. When Ernst left town to enroll in the Teachers' Seminar at the University of Bern, he bequeathed his standing desk to Robert. In *The Tanners*, Simon recalls his older brother teaching him "to have a sense for the beautiful and noble": "From his eyes we imbibed the fire that filled them when he spoke to us of art."[5]

Other sorts of imbibing played a role in Robert's childhood exploits as well, even beyond the incident related by Schaetzle-Ehrensperger when he ordered wine for his companions and himself. In several of Walser's later stories describing schoolboy misadventures, groups of children—invariably including the protagonist—are caught and punished for consuming beer. The narrator of "Knocking" reports: "An instructor once took several pu-pils over his knee and spanked them thoroughly, to impress upon them that bars exist only for adults. I also was among the group beneficially beaten." A similar tale is recounted in the story "In Junior High." And indeed the records of the *Progymnasium* Robert attended cite an investigation—conducted when he was eleven—that found twenty-three pupils to be regu-lar visitors at a pub apparently not particular about the ages of its patrons, though Robert may not have numbered among the youthful delinquents caught in that particular sting. Another Walser story, "The Weibel Boys," tells of a pair of brothers, aged ten and eleven, who get punished for helping themselves to their father's supply of wine.[6]

When Robert left school at age fourteen, he was one year shy of com-pleting his *Progymnasium* studies. A pupil of his abilities might have been expected to continue on to *Gymnasium,* but instead, Robert began an apprenticeship. Given the family's straitened circumstances—and the fact that the state of Elisa's health made her incapable of giving the adolescent boy the supervision and guidance he needed—Adolf wanted Robert to become financially self-sufficient as soon as possible. He took advantage of a personal connection to the director of the Biel branch of the Bern Cantonal Bank—located at Nidaugasse 27—to secure an apprenticeship for his youngest son.

The young apprentice performed well. Even before the official completion of his training three years later, he was issued a certificate on January 3, 1895, confirming "that Mr. Walser [. . .] has been trained in various office tasks, that he writes a beautiful hand, and that with regard to his conduct and industriousness we can declare ourselves thoroughly satisfied."[7] To be sure, Simon Tanner reports a quite different apprenticeship experience:

> During the first year I acquitted myself splendidly; for the novelty of what I encountered in this world filled me with timidity and fear. The second year found me a model apprentice, but in the third year of my apprenticeship the director cursed me to the devil, keeping me on only as an act of mercy, in deference to my father, whose close acquaintance he'd been for many years. I'd lost all gusto for work of any sort and spoke insolently to my superiors, whom I considered unworthy to order me around.[8]

The protagonist of *The Tanners* clearly displays a penchant for insubordination, which reveals itself already in the novel's opening scene, in which he quits a job in a bookstore not long after coaxing the proprietor to take him on. Many of Walser's other fictional personas display similar proclivities, taking on work beneath their abilities and then surreptitiously mocking their employers. Writing such characters and exploring their misadventures may well have been vicarious rebellion on Walser's part, perhaps a wish to be more like his bolder, more audacious older brother. There is no record of Robert ever having been anything but a model employee. In one late prose piece, in fact, the narrator confesses: "During my apprenticeship, I behaved stiffly, in a tight-lipped manner as it were, as

though a never-before-seen astonishment at myself and the world was holding its hand before my lips, obviating all possibility of my expressing myself
suitably." And "Felix Scenes" contains a dialogue between Felix and his
father in which the father reports that the boy's boss at the bank has been
complaining of his taciturnity though he was otherwise satisfied with him.[9]

Around the same time as Robert started his apprenticeship, he saw
his first play. Seats in the third balcony of the Biel Municipal Theater were
modestly priced at half a franc. During the winter season, the theater
would host various visiting productions, including—on February 18,
1894—Friedrich Schiller's classic play *The Robbers*, starring Karl Broich
and directed by Peter Hain.[10] This play, and especially its tragic hero, had
a profound effect on young Robert and provided a key motif that occupied
him throughout his literary career.

The Robbers tells the story of two rival aristocratic brothers. Karl
Moor is handsome, idealistic, and kind, while his younger brother, Franz,
is an unattractive schemer. As the elder son, Karl is in line to become his
father's sole heir, but while he is off at university, Franz succeeds in persuading their father to disown him. Karl, shocked at the betrayal, joins a
band of Robin Hood–style bandits whose leader he soon becomes, swear-
ing eternal fealty to the group. But he is unable to control his robbers,
some of whom begin to commit increasingly heinous acts for which he is
forced to take responsibility, and when he orders the band to attack the
castle where his wicked brother has had their father imprisoned, the plan
backfires irredeemably. The tragic story pits intellect against feeling, the
rule of law against the true meaning of freedom—heady topics for a boy of
fifteen.

Robert, spellbound, began dreaming of the theater. He acquired a
copy of Schiller's play and set to learning Karl Moor's lines. He even assembled a robber costume to wear when reciting the role—a costume im-
mortalized by Karl in an 1894 watercolor portrait demonstrating the future
artist's already considerable talent. This painting survives today—in the
collection of the Robert Walser Archive in Bern—as do Walser's descriptions of it in fictional contexts, such as in the story "Wenzel" (1909):

> This young man of sunny disposition dons a velvet vest his
> father once wore to weddings. Across his shoulders he flings
> an old avuncular cloak once bartered for in a town on the

Mississippi, and around his hips he wraps a sash from the
Glarus region. The head receives a suitable covering, a sauce-
pan made of felt and trimmed with a mallard feather. The hand
has managed to procure a fear-inspiring pistol, and forest-
ranger boots adhere to the legs.[11]

A similar description can be found in Walser's novel *The Robber* (its title
a reference to Schiller's play).

As a teenager, Robert was not yet interested—as he would be later—
in teasing out the writerly complexities of Schiller's verses; he wanted to
speak them onstage, in costume and in front of an audience, never mind
that he was awkward and shy, a coltish, long-limbed adolescent. "Wenzel"
describes a young wire factory apprentice's sudden infatuation with
the theater. After seeing a performance of *The Robbers,* the protagonist so
fervently wishes to become an actor that he runs to the nearest bookstore
to fill his arms with volumes of plays by Schiller, Goethe, and Shakespeare
and immediately starts learning his lines by heart while also studying the
biographies of actors and playwrights printed in the popular magazines
his family subscribes to. He then joins an amateur theater. As a skilled
copyist, he is asked to produce individual acting scripts for the company's
next production, the play *Klaus Leuenberger.*[12] This copying is paid work,
but Wenzel's father is horrified at even a tangential brush with thespian
depravity and threatens to throw the manuscript in the fire.

Fictional Wenzel's sister advises him to replace acting with poetry, as
he is far too shy and clumsy to be an actor. The protagonist nonetheless
decamps to "a distant larger city" and takes acting lessons from a "recognized stalwart performer of heroic roles": "He performs lung, tongue, lip,
and breath exercises and learns to pronounce vowels and consonants
properly and clearly."[13] His lessons go well until the actor teaching him
receives an angry letter from Wenzel's father ordering that the lessons
cease; the two aunts Wenzel is boarding with have spilled his secret.

We don't know whether Robert's father reacted as harshly to his
son's theatrical aspirations as Wenzel's. Adolf had already been confronted
with the prospect of having an artist in the family well before his youngest
son was bitten by the theater bug. And in Robert's case, there were the
reassuring facts of his excellent record at school and in his apprenticeship.
But the "Felix Scenes" register significant paternal discomfort with the

son's newly blossoming passion for the arts (in this case, literature). A letter Felix receives from his older brother notes that "reading is absolutely
not as superfluous as some people believe" and advises him,

> above all, do not let yourself be intimidated by Papa. Of course
> he means well by you, and when he urges you to avoid all con-
> tact with intellectual matters, it is your duty to understand him,
> but you most certainly do not have to follow his advice. In his
> kindheartedness, he fears all sorts of possibilities, for example
> that his sons might not sufficiently prosper. He considers
> dwelling on *belles lettres* a mere diversion, something that dis-
> tracts one from many useful matters, whereas in fact it's educa-
> tional, not at all a dissipation of energies.[14]

A father struggling with his own increasingly limited ability to support his
family might well appreciate practical career choices such as would give
his children lives of financial stability. And if indeed Adolf Walser was as
worried about Robert's future as "Wenzel" and "Felix Scenes" suggest, his
fears were justified, and he would eventually live to see Robert's hopes of
a financially successful literary career dashed.

Half a year after Elisa Walser's death, in April 1895, Robert left his apprenticeship at the Biel branch of the Bern Cantonal Bank to take up a position
as a *commis* or clerk at the venerable banking and shipping establishment
Speyr & Co. in Basel, the town of his father's birth. The French word
commis today summons up images of clerical servitude akin to those
found in Dickens or in Melville's "Bartleby, the Scrivener." The *commis*
populated offices throughout the Helvetic Confederation, buttoned up
to the Adam's apple in the stiff high collars that were obligatory office
wear at the time, with backs stooped and fingers cramped from filling
page after page of ledger books with copperplate script. In an era when
typewriters were a new technology and far from ubiquitous, bank records
were kept by hand. Most business correspondence—down to the addresses on envelopes—was handwritten as well. As an author, Walser
invoked the figure of the *commis* again and again, a fruitful object of study
for his explorations of the hidden power of the subservient. Robert was by
all accounts the model of a dutiful, diligent employee. But even as the

young clerk was obediently dunking pen into inkwell, his brain was filled
with fantasies of striding across Europe's finest stages while declaiming
heroic roles.

In Basel, Robert rented a room in the home of his father's oldest
sister, Juliane Haller-Walser, at Bäumleingasse 10, a tiny house tucked
behind a book shop on a block dominated by imposing court buildings
that gave the street a somber appearance. Basel was somber in general, as
the fortifications erected to guard against flooding from the Rhine flowing
through it had led to streets and alleyways so intricately crabbed that it
was difficult to get a view of anything from anywhere. The city was the
opposite of sprawling, open Biel, and further industrialized—above all in
its growing chemical industry—with the attendant prosperity.

The young *commis* remained employed at Speyr & Co. until the end
of August. The firm occupied an ornate neoclassical edifice of white stone
with a grand carpeted staircase inside an entryway illuminated by a large
ornamental skylight suspended between Ionic columns. Everything about
the building bespoke the prosperity to be safeguarded there, a place where
even a lowly clerk was an important cog in the system. A Speyr & Co.
personnel ledger from late May 1895 lists Robert as a correspondence department employee, and biographer Robert Mächler reports that by the
end of his stint there, he was working as private secretary to one of
the firm's partners and one of Switzerland's most influential financiers,
Johann Jakob Schuster-Burckhardt.

Whether or not Robert moved out of his aunt's apartment for reasons similar to those depicted in the story "Wenzel," by early June he was
residing at Theaterstrasse 22, conveniently located right across from the
theater. Though only a five-minute walk from his previous digs, his new
attic room put him smack in the center of Basel's Old Town district. He
remained there until late August, when the pursuit of his theatrical dreams
prompted yet another move, this time across the German border to Stuttgart. He was seventeen years old.

Karl had moved to Stuttgart in 1894 to apprentice himself to Gustav
Kämmerer, a respected stage-set designer. This was his second apprenticeship. In 1893 Karl had begun to study draftsmanship with an architect
in Biel (a concession to his father's desire to see his son's talent put to
practical use) while studying applied arts at Biel's Cantonal Technical
College with sculptor Ferdinand Huttenlocher. It must have quickly be-

come clear to him that he would rather paint pictures of buildings than assist in their construction. After his mother's death, Karl set out for Stuttgart to spend two years apprenticing in a field more to his liking, one in which he would eventually become far more famous than his teacher.

During his apprenticeship with Kämmerer, Karl helped his teacher paint stage sets for Stuttgart's Royal Court Theater, giving Karl tremendous status in his younger brother's eyes. Robert arrived dreaming of a theatrical apprenticeship himself. According to his 1916 prose piece "The Brothers" (the only extant account of this period in their lives), Karl and Robert shared a room in a lodging house called Herberge zur Heimat on Gerbergasse. A photograph of the Herberge's dining room taken around 1900 shows more than four dozen men crammed around small tables or seated upon wooden benches at long, narrow dining tables. Though bright light streams in through the windows, the interior is dim. It is clearly a working-class establishment catering to a public that needs to eat cheaply and heartily.[15]

If the possibly fictionalized account in "The Brothers" can be trusted, Karl and Robert got up to their usual mischief at the Herberge. One day, in a fit of youthful spontaneity, they sent their hats sailing out the open window of their room, startling passersby. For this they received a stern scolding from the innkeeper. On another occasion, a pastor paying an unexpected visit flung open their door only to discover Robert stark naked in the middle of the room, posing as Mark Antony weeping over the corpse of Caesar. The visitor "immediately beat a retreat that soon became a panicky flight." The sight of the fleeing pastor was apparently sufficiently risible to keep the brothers in stitches for the rest of the year they spent together at the Herberge. Another prank dating from this period, described by a friend who heard the story second-hand, involved Karl's threatening a "bourgeois gentleman out for a stroll" with a sturdy stick and so convincing a show of ire that the poor man ran away from him "till he was nearly dead."[16]

Both exuberant young Walsers had many opportunities to pursue their love of the theater. The narrator of "The Brothers" reports that the two protagonists were frequently slipped a pair of free tickets by a generous director, allowing them to see performances like *Othello* with Gertrud Eysoldt and Adalbert Matkowsky. These tickets would be in the "standing parterre," where the less affluent members of the public would watch plays over the heads of the better-heeled. Perhaps the brothers saw the production of Schiller's play *William Tell* that was put on in Stuttgart during this period—an obvious choice for them given the play's Swiss setting and Robert's infatuation with its author.[17]

The legendary hero William (Wilhelm) Tell looms large in Swiss folklore, and in Switzerland's self-understanding. First recorded in a late-fifteenth-century Swiss chronicle, the legend of Tell relates how this expert marksman and freedom fighter assassinated the Austrian tyrant Albrecht Gessler, leading to the founding of the Swiss confederacy in the early fourteenth century. Schiller's 1804 play about the hero contains famous lines that every Swiss schoolchild knows by heart, such as when Tell lies in wait for his villainous quarry: "Here through this deep defile he needs must pass." Walser later spoofed this legend and the sanctimony surrounding it by inserting an aside that undermines the self-assurance of Tell's declaration: "Here through this deep defile, I think, he needs must pass."[18]

Robert also took frequent walks out into the beautiful countryside surrounding the town, often visiting Solitude Palace with its rococo façade.[19] The palace had once housed an elite military academy, Karlsschule, that counted a young Friedrich Schiller among its pupils, making the place an object of fascination for Robert. Solitude is only about five miles from the center of Stuttgart and can be reached on foot by meandering through wooded hills filled with sunlit cathedrals of yellow beech leaves and gray trunks on a bright autumn day.

Much of the Stuttgart Robert Walser wandered through no longer exists. As an industrial center, it was heavily bombed during World War II, destroying nearly half the city, which is now dominated by a pedestrian zone lined with commercial buildings dating mostly from the 1950s. But even today, the avenue Hauptstätterstrasse remains part of the large ring enclosing the city center. From the Herberge zur Heimat, Karl and Robert could stroll along Hauptstätterstrasse—six carriages wide, with a central track for horse-drawn trams—all the way to the elegant arches framing the entryway to the Royal Court Theater. Robert had secured employment as a *commis* in the advertising department of the publishing house Union (also on Hauptstätterstrasse). After that, he took a job at the Cotta publishing house in the same building.[20]

While Karl's theatrical star rose ever higher, Robert's fizzled before achieving any altitude at all. Several of Walser's stories depict—always in quite similar terms—a young man asking an actor for career advice. In "The Audition," the protagonist requests acting lessons from one Frau Benzinger—inspired by real-life actress Eleonore Benzinger-Wahlmann, then an aging doyenne of the Stuttgart theater—who distracts him with an unnerving flash of petticoat. After he speaks his lines—poorly—she responds: "You should thank God that you have fallen into the hands of a person who means well enough by you to tell you the truth. . . . You possess not the faintest trace of theatrical talent. Everything about you is hidden, veiled, buried, dry, and wooden. You may be the most ardent of human beings on the inside, churning with the most fervent passions, who knows?, but none of this can be seen when looking at you, nothing is expressed."[21]

In "Wenzel," too, the protagonist is granted an audience to recite some lines for an actor whose verdict disheartens him: "Young man, whatever your lineage, whether properly respectable or not, you lack the divine spark!"[22] There's a legend of uncertain origin, circulated among generations of Walser scholars, that this real-life thespian was Josef Kainz, one of the most prominent actors of the day, although there is no evidence Kainz ever set foot on a Stuttgart stage.

In any case, the demise of Robert's theatrical aspirations made room for aspirations of another sort. At some point during his year in Stuttgart—approximately by the time he turned eighteen—his passion for words shifted from lines spoken onstage to lines on the printed page. This shift would later be embodied in a pun that appears again and again in Walser's work: the expression "the boards that signify the world," a metaphor for the stage originating in Schiller's poem "To My Friends." In a number of Walser's later stories one finds the phrase "the pages that signify the world," referring ironically to influential newspapers and journals while still preserving the allusion to Schiller through the rhyme of "boards" and "pages" (*Bretter/Blätter*). The aspiring actor became an aspiring writer. "There isn't going to be any acting career," young Robert wrote to his sister Lisa that year, "but if God so wills it, I am going to become a great writer."[23]

"The Brothers" makes no mention of dreams of appearing onstage. Instead, it speaks of poetry: "Did we not spend entire lovely Sundays and other days as well wading about in the voluptuously green grass of the

landscape and in the soft, dreamy landscape of May, only to rest then here
and there most deliciously beneath blossoming apple and pear trees from
our wanderings and 'landscapes,' from the difficulties of painting and writing verse, whereby we often deigned to fall into deep slumber like counts
and dukes, only to awaken later on like princes?" The brothers, Walser
writes, "were not yet reading Verlaine, but we read Heinrich Heine and
Uhland, and found their taste and savor very much to our liking."[24] Both
these writers were known, like Schiller, to infuse their work with a desire
for republican reform. So the shift from drama to poetry, like the shift from
stage to page, still spoke to the same fervent desires in the souls of these
young enthusiasts.

The roommates took leave of one another in autumn 1896. Karl had
been offered a fellowship to study at the School of Applied Arts in Strasbourg, and it made little sense for Robert to remain in Stuttgart without
him. Robert set off on foot, walking along country roads and woodland
trails that took him first to Tübingen, then to Hechingen, then back across
the Swiss border to Schaffhausen. On September 30, 1896, he visited the
registry office in the town hall of Zurich to report his new address. The
fledgling Swiss writer was back in Switzerland again.

THREE

The Young Poet

1896–1899

FOR A WRITER TO CHAFE AGAINST the necessity of a day job is nothing new. In Robert Walser's case, deciding that regular employment was incompatible with his artistic aspirations was particularly daring, as he'd experienced as a child what precarious finances could do to a family's well-being. His father had done his best to offer Robert a financially secure future, apprenticing him in a field chosen for its promise of stability. But during his years in Zurich, Robert realized that pursuing the arts would require all his energies, precluding a professional career in the banking sector. He wasn't romanticizing poverty. Dreaming of a life devoted to creative pursuits, he fantasized not of struggle and impecuniousness, but of acclaim and honor, the just rewards of the successful artist. He would claim this success in exchange for honest work and artistic achievement. Watching his older brother reject a career as a draftsman to pursue painting inspired and encouraged him.

The transitional years that began when Robert struck out on his own in 1896, parting from Karl and taking up residence in Zurich, the commercial and artistic capital of German-speaking Switzerland, were crucial in his development. This was when he set the goals and standards for his artistic production that he would adhere to for the rest of his career. Describing this period in retrospect in a biographical note written in 1920, Walser reports that the young man he had been in those days worked "now in the insurance business, now in banking [. . .] and wrote poems, whereby it must be stated that he did not do this on the side but instead always first rendered himself jobless for the purpose, apparently in the belief that art was a noble thing. Indeed he considered poetry almost sacred."[1]

When he first arrived in town, though, gainful employment was still a priority for him, and he accepted a job in the bookkeeping division of the cargo insurance firm Schweiz for an annual salary of 1,500 francs (roughly $19,500 in today's dollars)—three times the profit his father had reported to the Biel tax office from his business the year before.[2] To eighteen-year-old Robert, it seemed a fortune. The detail of this generous salary remained lodged in his mind; seventeen years later, writing a story based on his experiences in Zurich that year ("Johanna," 1913), Walser recalls that princely sum: "I was, I remember, nineteen years old, wrote poems, still wore no proper collar, ran around in the snow and rain, always arose early in the morning, read Lenau, considered an overcoat a superfluous item, received a monthly salary of one hundred twenty-five francs, and did not know what I should do with all that money."[3] The narrator of this story rents a room from "package man Senn," who took in several lodgers in the rooms of his large apartment not occupied by his cowering wife and two sons, "Theodor and Emil Senn, [whom] he thrashed." Zurich Registry Office records from this period show that Robert Walser—aged eighteen, not nineteen—did indeed rent a room from a post office employee by the name of Caspar Senn at Zeughausstrasse 3 for several months beginning September 30, 1896. The records also document a second tenant who moved in around the same time: Johanna Lüthy, twenty years old and born in Biel; she lists her profession as "shopgirl." Walser's fictionalized reminiscence describes a heady romance with this young neighbor, or at least her fictional counterpart:

> I wrote a poem in her album, a bold, extravagant firstborn—she showed it to her mother, and the mother warned her little daughter about me[. . . .] We lived four flights up. Should Johanna, standing downstairs at the front door, have forgotten her umbrella or handkerchief or something else, I would receive the commission to dash upstairs and fetch the forgotten item. [. . .] Her hands were voluptuous and soft and as white as snow, and kissing them—how it intoxicated and enchanted me. Senn was furious with us, because we would study English together until deep into the night in Johanna's room. He no doubt heard through the wall what a caressing, amusing sort of English we were up to.[4]

Which isn't to say that Robert necessarily enjoyed a romance with his fellow lodger in real life. The story might, after all, have been a case of wish-fulfillment. Or did he creep into her room at night, taking care that the floorboards not reveal too much about his destination, and did they perhaps giggle together over a language textbook like a modern Paolo and Francesca? A photograph of Johanna Lüthy shows a happy- and healthy-looking girl, with a glowing complexion and thick hair tied back in a loose chignon, smiling with a mischievous air.

Lodging in a private apartment was a financially prudent choice for the young clerk newly arrived in Zurich, where the cost of living was higher than in Biel. Zurich isn't the capital of Switzerland, but it felt and feels like a capital city: prosperous and bustling, the locus of Switzerland's banking and insurance industries. Nestled in a valley on the northern shore of the lake that bears its name, it is bisected by the Limmat River. Parallel to the river, the city's famous Bahnhofstrasse—Zurich's one grand boulevard and central artery, nearly a mile long—connects the lakefront to the main train station. A popular destination for Sunday-afternoon strolls, Bahnhof-strasse is lined on both sides with some of Zurich's most elegant shops.

Compared with Biel—which Walser once called "a very very small metropolis"—Zurich displayed its wealth ostentatiously.[5] The insurance company in whose offices Robert spent his days copying out ledgers by hand was located in a grand building occupying one edge of Paradeplatz, a large square. Directly opposite was Sprüngli, an elegant confectionery shop and refreshment room. In 1897, construction began on a second major bank building along the square's western edge, establishing it as a center of finance (and chocolate). Paradeplatz was still crisscrossed by horse-drawn streetcars, but the first electric tram line began to circulate there the year of Robert's arrival, and by the turn of the twentieth century all the streetcars passing through the heart of town were electrically powered. Arriving each morning at Paradeplatz, surrounded by Zurich's most comfortable burghers hurrying to other, grander jobs in the banking and insurance sectors, Robert was confronted by the vast financial disparities between different social classes in this large city. These disparities were even more striking because he had chosen an extremely modest neighborhood to live in.

The district where Caspar Senn rented out rooms to tenants was known as Aussersihl because it lay outside the Sihl, Zurich's second river, which curled its way along what had been until recently the city's western edge. Aussersihl was the outskirts, the industrial edge of town, home to a working-class population with far fewer financial resources than most people in the city center. The building at Zeughausstrasse 3 was just around the corner from the barracks where the young men of Canton Zurich did their military training. The Sihl is sunk deep below street level here in defense against flooding, which makes the neighborhood feel cut off from the city on the other side as if by a moat, even though Zeughausstrasse is just a few minutes' walk from Zurich's main train station. Robert was a speedy strider; his walk to work took him fewer than fifteen minutes.

Robert's official position at the Transport Insurance Company Schweiz was assistant bookkeeper, a job that involved keeping ledgers, making the clerk's responsibilities graphic as well as mathematical. Using a straightedge aligned exactly parallel or perpendicular to the edge of the page, he inked in lines of various sorts—dotted, plain, double, extra-thick—at the appropriate points. Clerks were at the bottom of the administrative hierarchy. The only place for a promising young man of Robert's intelligence to go was up. Although he could never advance to the sort of position Franz Kafka, with his doctorate in law, would hold at the Workers' Accident Insurance Institute in Prague a decade later, levels of advancement were still accessible to him. The main problem, it turned out, was that he hated the work. A life devoted to money and its management could hardly bring fulfillment to a soul still resonating with the passionate revolutionary words of Karl Moor.

Five months after moving to Zurich and taking up a post in the Schweiz company offices, Robert felt so unfulfilled by his labors that a decisive measure seemed in order. He decided he wanted to work to support the cause of the workers, the eternally laboring underclass, and to this end he sought employment in an organization devoted to the principles of socialism. On March 3, 1897, he mailed a letter to Robert Seidel, the German-born journalist, poet, and teacher who served as editor-in-chief of the Swiss socialist weekly newspaper *Arbeiterstimme* (Voice of the Worker), published in Zurich. "Highly revered sir," Robert wrote,

> Might you possibly require an employee in your esteemed of-
> fices as a copyist or something of the sort? If so, I would like

herewith to offer my utterly devoted services and should consider it a stroke of good fortune and be grateful if you would
make use of my offering.

I am 19 years old, have completed a commercial apprenticeship and been active in various trades, as you will be so good as
to confirm in the attached letters of reference. At present I am
working here in an insurance firm, but I don't like it, I feel a
powerful urge to leave. Please understand, this work simply
does not interest me, it leaves me cold; I have no idea what I am
working for, but I do have a fairly clear notion that I am of little,
terribly little use here. It seems to me that if I came to work for
you, even in the most trifling capacity, I should nonetheless
know that these labors had a value and merit. In short, I should
so dearly love to serve a party to which my entire heart belongs,
and should most certainly succeed in gaining your approval
through my loyalty and industry and zeal. My expectations are
modest, and I know 2 foreign languages, one of them more or
less perfectly, the other fairly well.

Please be so good as to accept the assurance of my utmost
esteem.

Your devoted Robert Walser[6]

This high-flown epistle fell on sympathetic ears. Seidel responded
with a friendly if businesslike letter ten days later, regretting that he was
unable to offer Robert employment but saying that he admired his youthful enthusiasm ("You are full of drive and want to be of use to the world")
and inviting him to pay a visit during his daily office hours. He would be
happy, he said, to assist Robert in his search for "a sphere of activity that
will bring you satisfaction and be of service to mankind." The visit took
place and must have been inspiring, because when Robert next wrote
to Seidel, wishing him a happy International Day of Labor on the eve of
May 1, he sounded both encouraged and grateful: "I shall never forget how
amicably you received me and how kindly you advised me, and I intend to
work following the path you have shown me."[7]

Six weeks later, Robert wrote again, this time to submit a poem, asking Seidel to consider publishing it in *Arbeiterstimme*. In the accompanying letter, he reports that he is continuing in his efforts:

In my work I am making progress very slowly, but still it is steady progress. I accomplish what I can. Now I want to read a great deal more than I used to—to read good books and read them slowly, isn't that right, esteemed sir?

I take pleasure in immersing myself as deeply as possible in some matter, and getting properly to the bottom of things, and I can't help laughing—madcap laughter—when the bottom proves to be rotten, or when it gleams like the clearest sky.

Above all I am making an effort to always fully and completely grasp and use each moment. This is the golden kernel of reason. It's just that my heart keeps ringing out over-poweringly.[8]

Seidel must have called the young enthusiast to account, challenging him to develop a more analytical and less impulsive approach to both literature and life.

Robert's three letters to Seidel are revealing even in their handwriting. The first letter, written as a self-introduction, is penned in a flawless, regular *Kurrent* script—the old German cursive handwriting still in wide use at the time. The second letter with the May 1 greeting is written in the more modern roman script—perhaps Robert decided that the copperplate formality of *Kurrent* was too office-dusty for an exchange between fellow lovers of progress and verse. He wasn't necessarily imitating Seidel's handwriting—Seidel had written to him using a typewriter—though Seidel probably favored roman script in general.[9] Robert's third letter to Seidel was written in a much looser hand, a more fanciful version of roman script, making an even more informal impression (the same handwriting he used later that year writing to his sister Lisa).

Either before or after meeting with Seidel, Robert read his book of poems that had appeared two years before—*Amid the Frenzy of the Battlefield and Loneliness*—a work that sold enough copies to go through a good half-dozen subsequent printings, though Seidel is now remembered only for his work as a journalist and editor, not as a poet. These works are the rhyme-and-meter representation of revolutionary strivings, full of lines like "My belief is Progress's messenger" and "Only in freedom can I love my homeland." Seidel was working in a poetic idiom in which political slogans rhymed with the passionately inflamed hearts of young men striving for a cause.[10]

"Future!," the revolutionary poem Walser sent to Seidel for consideration, displays a similar fervor.

Future!

The wonderfully fair age is nigh
When in the royal halls
Freedom's new faith will resound
Against the marble walls.

Where people, loving, stroll upon
the avenues, up and down;
Where unfettered progress blooms—
And a thousand songs bloom too!

Where men are nothing more than men
and infinite in their love,
and where Labor, which now is weeping,
will be raised to highest joy.—

Where passion and where noble deeds
are intimately conjoined.
The happiness of this free age
portends a free race of men!

The wonderfully fair age is nigh
of which we sing our songs.—
Already I hear the royal eagle "Spirit"
boldly spread its wings.[11]

Just as "bold" and "extravagant" as the "firstborn" Robert and/or his fictional doppelganger penned in Johanna's album, this poem has little about it to suggest greatness. Conventional in imagery and sentiment, and alternating between clichés and awkward locutions, "Future!" speaks of a coming age in language cribbed from days of yore. Its one moment of appealing oddity—appealing despite the hopeless clunkiness of the lines—comes at the end of the final stanza, with the conceptually complex image of Spirit appearing in the guise of an eagle flapping its wings loudly enough to be audible to the poem's speaker. The poem strongly displays the influence of Seidel's work, down to the overuse of exclamation points. The idea to write a poem titled "Future!" may have come to Robert after reading one of the oddest and most striking poems in Seidel's book, a poem about miners titled "Deep in the Earth's Womb!" that ends with the image of a giant identified as "the Destiny of the Future" emerging from the depths of a mine to stamp out injustice with mighty feet.[12]

Robert's poem isn't much worse than Seidel's, so it's a shame Seidel declined to print it. But the poem marked a breakthrough even unpublished: it was the first time Robert had submitted work of any sort for publication, and it is clear from his third letter to Seidel that writing poems and thinking about literature was becoming what he referred to as his "work." His encounter with the older, politically engaged poet had provided him with both the permission and the inspiration to set out on his own path of exploring the revolutions that could be wrought with words. Actual political fervor, on the other hand, proved to have a far less sustained impact on him—though, as we will see, the basic principles of socialism would play a significant thematic role in his work later on. The thought that it was in the interest of some members of society for others to live in poverty continued to gnaw at him.

In a fictionalized account of the Seidel episode Walser published in 1917, as part of a story titled "Luise," the letter Robert received from Seidel (now described only as "a respected journalistic personality") appears in dramatically inflated form:

> "Youthful and tempestuous admirer," the man wrote back to me quite soberly, "it is not so easy as you apparently believe to perform duties and render sacrifices in a place where Meyer's *Encyclopedia* no doubt enjoys a foremost and also finalmost significance. That you look up to me meets with my understanding and approval, for you have every cause to consider me a great man."

An impressionable youth no longer, the author looking back at the young clerk's admiration for Seidel found humor in his own erstwhile reverence for a man whose literary accomplishments Walser the writer had long since outstripped. He also chuckles at the short life span of his passion for the socialist cause:

"This noble repudiator of all things selfish, this representative of all that is altruistic and modest must surely be a quite odd individual," I said to myself, and my desire to champion and exert myself for the lofty goals and causes of mankind dwindled with remarkable speed.

The liberties Walser takes in reporting on his early interactions with Seidel are matched in his descriptions of other parts of the young man's trajectory. For example, the narrator writes that in response to his disappointing exchange with the "respected journalistic personality," he decided it was time to "infiltrate the educated and elegant circles of society that until then I had merely admired, marveled at and worshipped from afar." He describes a move to a furnished room in the apartment of a professor's widow in swanky surrounds that prompt him to think of the story's title character, Luise, his once-admired friend, as "proletarian."[13] In truth, nineteen-year-old Robert relocated from working-class Aussersihl to one of Zurich's fanciest neighborhoods some weeks *before* writing his first letter to Seidel: the return address on the letter shows he was already living in Hottingen, a chic district of upper-middle-class villas built high on a hill above the city proper.

The elegance of Robert's new Hottingen abode is difficult to imagine in retrospect since the building at Zeltweg 64 no longer stands. Directly next door, though, is the imposing edifice built in 1877 as the home and studio of celebrated sculptor Louis Wethli, its stately façade adorned with decorative arched windows with sculptural insets and a Juliet balcony. Robert's landlady, whose fictional counterpart in the story "Luise" is named Frau Professor Krähenbühl, had an apartment on the third floor, so Robert may have occupied a maid's dormer-windowed attic room with an agreeable view of treetops. Although Robert was still just a subtenant—a "furnished gentleman," as the expression went—this was the fanciest place he'd ever lived, even at the height of his parents' middle-class prosperity in Biel.

The young poet held out in these elite surrounds for only about a month before looking for change again. The narrator of "Luise" reports that life in the elegant villa district soon comes to seem unbearable to him ("all that refined behavior and all those lovely, witty turns of phrase and conversations fortunately soon filled me with apprehension and fear"), prompting him to petition his landlady for permission to depart. After he secures new lodgings in the "workers district," he reports feeling right at home among his largely indigent neighbors. His new landlord, he relates, is a carpenter.[14] Robert himself moved for reasons not documented beyond their fictional portrayal to a furnished room at Zurlindenstrasse 49.

Robert's new proletarian lodgings were located in the Wiedikon district, significantly farther away from the city center than he had been before, and only a few blocks from one of the five large brick-producing factories scattered along the edge of town. Indeed, the apartment house was made of brick, as were many in the neighborhood—still quite thinly settled in parts—with plenty of light and air and open fields providing patches of green between the buildings. Wiedikon had a streetcar line he could take to work in the mornings if he didn't feel like walking; it was a ramble of perhaps forty minutes, partly along the Sihl.

Living on the outskirts appealed to Robert in several ways. For one thing, every day he spent amid the pomp and bustle of Paradeplatz was automatically countered in the evenings by his return to Wiedikon's villagelike (though also industrial) surrounds. From there, a few minutes' walk took him to open fields, then to the forested foothills of the Uetliberg. The crest of the mountain could be reached by funicular even then, though it was easily enough ascended on foot. He would remain in Wiedikon for half a year.

One of Robert's earliest surviving letters, written to his sister Lisa in two sessions, on July 30 and August 3, 1897, was sent from Zurlindenstrasse. It is remarkable in showing how Robert was beginning to develop the characteristic voice that would enliven his narrative prose. In the first half, he declares that he is hungry and that this hunger is prompting his desire for letter-writing, since when his belly is full, he thinks only of himself and not of distant others. This association ("It is certainly not happiness to long for something far away!") launches him into an entire mini-essay on longing:

> Where longing is concerned, it is first off superfluous, secondly comprehensible, and thirdly incomprehensible!—It's superfluous because it merely burdens one; comprehensible the way an illness is comprehensible, or a sin; but incomprehensible because so many people are unable to live without this superfluous thing, because so many people engage in longing, wasting

away in longing and finding themselves unable to extricate themselves from it, indeed they even find a certain sweetness in longing. That people so often, so willingly engage in something so burdensome, something so wistful as longing itself—that's the pathological condition afflicting us. Christianity is the religion of longing! For this reason alone, this religion is so unnatural, so unworthy of human beings! A person who has shaken off longing has done better than another who has written 100 very nicely rhymed but also longing-ridden songs. Songs of this sort should not even be printed. The police should most definitely intervene in such cases. O Uhland and his ilk! But enough for today![15]

Several things about this letter now appear quintessentially "Walserian." First there's the overall irony of the writer's central conceit: his argument against longing belies the fact that he himself is filled with it, and indeed he begins the letter by noting that receiving a letter from his sister has made him sigh; he even asks her to consider moving to Zurich rather than Bern to continue her studies. Then there is the juxtaposition of opposites—longing declared simultaneously superfluous, comprehensible, and incomprehensible—without any acknowledgment of the contradiction, which has a humorous effect; excessive repetition of the word "longing," almost to the point of absurdity; and mock-philosophical musing ("That people so often, so willingly engage in something so burdensome, something so wistful as longing itself—that's the pathological condition afflicting us") that soon gives way to a straight-faced and surprising observation: "Christianity is the religion of longing," on the basis of which he declares this religion "unnatural" and "unworthy of human beings." If Christianity is unnatural, does that mean other religions are natural, or indeed that naturalness is a natural expectation? Would a "natural" religion be worthy of humans? These two sentences in the letter evoke a maze of questions and suppositions, which Robert leaves serenely unanswered, moving on to praise the person who has "shaken off longing." He himself, though, is clearly in its thrall, as was the German poet he cites a few lines later, Ludwig Uhland, whom he had read with Karl in Stuttgart.

Many of this letter's literary features will come to characterize the speeches delivered by characters in several of Walser's stories and novels.

His true beginnings as a writer, I would argue, lie less in the stiff, cribbed lines of tendentious verse he considered his "work" than in this friendlier, playful mode of writing intended to give pleasure—both to himself, as he wrote, and to his sister, whom he loved. The generosity of spirit in these lines far outshines the grandeur of the "royal eagle Spirit" boldly spreading its wings in "Future!" Young Robert is far more philosophical when he dons the mask of unseriousness.

At the end of the letter, Robert promises to speak the next time he writes of something more useful: "the deed." And indeed, in the second part of the letter written four days later, he recalls this promise, but instead of the expected discourse he notes only that addressing the topic would require "an essay of many pages, which I prefer to leave unwritten for the moment," though he adds: "This much I can remark in any case: the world is practically suffocating beneath a lack of deeds. And so a single person can achieve an enormous amount with a deed!" What sorts of deeds he has in mind he doesn't say, though his correspondence with Seidel suggests that sitting day after day in an insurance office copying out ledgers isn't what he has in mind. He may be recalling Goethe's *Faust,* in which "deed" features prominently as a possible interpretation of the Greek word *logos* in the Gospel of John. Or perhaps he has already dipped into the letters of Heinrich von Kleist—we know he read them before 1898 in any case—and happened on the one in which Kleist famously reports to his sister Ulrike (on May 1, 1802) that he has "no other wish than to die after having produced three things: a child, a beautiful poem, and a great deed."[16]

Recalling this period of his life years later, Walser remembered the sense of longing for some meaningful activity that so powerfully moved him. "Nineteen years old and still you haven't done a thing for posterity!," his narrator exclaims with impatience in "Luise."[17] His employment at the insurance company was no help. Although it paid well, at least for a young man's needs, it was a drag on him emotionally and spiritually, and he sensed that year after year of bending his back in the service of other people's wealth would get him nowhere. He needed to get away from this world. But how would he live? All around him in Wiedikon, he saw his working-class neighbors struggling to make ends meet; were they any freer than he was? Was living among them a source of inspiration?

Luckily for him, fresh inspiration soon arrived in the form of his brother Karl. In his August 3 letter to Lisa, Robert had mentioned that he would be spending his vacation with Karl in Stuttgart and that Karl would then come to Zurich. Karl had been studying for the previous year at the School of Applied Arts in Strasbourg, where he had distinguished himself as one of the most talented students and had been chosen by the painting teacher to assist him in creating stage sets for a performance at Strasbourg's Municipal Theater.[18] Karl's studies there complete, he chose Zurich as his next way station, arriving on October 17. In preparation for Karl's visit, Robert gave up his room on the outskirts and moved to more central quarters at Neumarkt 3, situated in the very heart of the Niederdorf neighborhood. The Limmat's east bank was decidedly less prosperous, featuring tiny crooked alleyways snaking up the hill away from the river. The buildings that lined these alleys didn't get much light.

Karl's arrival in Zurich meant a great deal to Robert. It brought him a conversation partner who understood his artistic ambitions and had followed them since their earliest stirrings. As much confrère as frère, Karl responded meaningfully to Robert's early poems, critiquing and encouraging. And serving as host to Karl in Zurich, where Robert had lived and worked for a year—and where he earned a salary that allowed him to pick up the tab when the brothers went drinking in Niederdorf's bars—for once reversed the balance of power between the two, at least temporarily. (Karl was on such a tight budget that a fellow art student remarked that he lived "mainly on water, bread, and apples.")[19] Robert also introduced his older brother to his Zurich friends, which, however, instantly produced complications.

Thanks to research by Walser scholar Bernhard Echte, we know that Robert's associates in Zurich included two women whose portraits Walser would repeatedly sketch in various works of fiction: Rosa Schätzle and Louisa Schweizer.[20] The two were close friends—they sometimes even cohabited in Louisa's Aussersihl apartment at Badenerstrasse 257—and a fair bit older than Robert, by seven and eight years, respectively. Schätzle was from Biel, the daughter of a stationery shop owner. Both women had complicated romantic histories they were delighted to relate to this rapt, charmingly inexperienced listener.

Schweizer, a strikingly beautiful woman who worked as a bookkeeper and photographic retoucher, had been seduced and impregnated

by her adulterous boss. After giving birth (on September 5, 1897), she resolved—at least according to the story "Luise"—to raise her son without
the help of the child's father. Her predicament features in several other
Walser texts as well, including the novel *The Assistant*, in which Louisa's
story is attributed to a character named Klara. The strength and determination of this woman who, though in a socially weak position, rejected the
wealthy man who might have supported her made a powerful impression
on Robert. In *The Assistant*, the young protagonist, Joseph Marti, credits
Klara with introducing him to the ideas of free-thinking nineteenth-
century writers like Heinrich Heine and Ludwig Börne; she shares his
enthusiasm for socialism. In "Luise," the narrator repeatedly mentions
Luise's self-identification as a proletarian and says that eventually, "living
as a proletarian among proletarians," she became the "Queen of the Poor,"
an inspiration to her struggling neighbors. Real-life Louisa was no doubt
delighted to hear of young Robert's correspondence and meeting with
Robert Seidel; perhaps she even encouraged it.[21]

Like Schweizer, Schätzle would serve as a model (often under
her own name, Rosa) for characters in a number of Walser works, including the novel *The Tanners* and several stories. Walser's fictionalized
portraits of Schätzle depict her as passionate, temperamental, impulsive,
and inclined to melancholy. Photographs from the time show her with
an intense, almost hungry gaze, eyes bright in her open face, and with a
flair for dramatic outfits and theatrical hats. In one fictional portrait, she
dances around her room with castanets. Schätzle was a translator with
literary aspirations and ties to Zurich's avant-garde. In a letter thirty
years later, Walser recalls witnessing a scene in which her characteristic
spunk was on display. Maurice Reinhold von Stern, editor of the journal
Stern's Literarisches Bulletin, made the mistake of addressing Schätzle as
"dear Fräulein," prompting her to reply indignantly, "I'm not your dear
Fräulein."[22]

By introducing Robert to her art- and literature-loving friends,
Schätzle did him a service. He reciprocated by introducing her to Karl,
with whom she promptly fell in love. Karl in those days was dashing: tall
and slender, with a bright shock of red hair crowning eyes that looked either perpetually sleepy or like those of a daydreamer. He wore an artfully
curved thin moustache to set off his sensual lips and carried himself with
the aplomb of one already convinced as a young man that he is destined

for greatness. It isn't known to what extent he reciprocated Schätzle's feelings, but he did present her with one of his pictures, a landscape done in pastels. Their mutual friend Flora Ackeret in Biel would later report that Karl's behavior toward Rosa was generally inconsistent and sometimes even insulting, as when he gave her a book about the painter Karl Stauffer-Bern as a gift and later demanded its return. Schätzle seemed disastrously attracted to handsome younger men who treated her dismissively. Even her lover Paul Renfer, a childhood friend of Robert's and a photographer in Biel, betrayed her trust and also had a serious drinking problem, at least according to Walser's fictional portrait of him.[23]

Karl remained in Zurich until January 4, 1898, living first with Robert and then moving to quarters of his own in a section of Aussersihl far more distant from the city center than any of Robert's addresses, but no doubt in keeping with his budgetary limitations. It was also a good location for a painter in need of the time and space to devote himself to his art. The house stood at the edge of town, across the street from the large Sihlfeld cemetery filled with quiet neighbors. Karl remained there for one month before accepting a job painting decorations on the walls of a dancehall in the little town of Sursee outside Lucerne, about halfway between Zurich and Bern.

Robert, meanwhile, made a far more dramatic move. Prompted perhaps by the same desire for meaningful change that had caused him to write to Seidel half a year earlier, and now inspired as well by his brother's artistic strivings, he gave notice at his insurance agency. An internal memo dated November 19, 1897, gives instructions for the hiring of his replacement (at a maximal salary 33 percent higher than Robert had been paid). The memo specifies that Robert resigned from his position, so we know he wasn't fired. The letter of reference provided to him affirms that the assistant bookkeeper "is leaving us today of his own volition" and that "Herr Walser has proven himself a capable, hard-working, and reliable employee & we sincerely wish him all the best for his future career."[24] It isn't clear what sort of "career" the writer of this reference letter had in mind, but for Robert it must have been clear enough, because just a few days later he set off for Berlin.

Then as now, Berlin was an important destination for young German-speaking artists and writers, already enough of a metropolis to make Zurich seem more a town than a city. It wasn't the sort of place you

went to further your training as a copy clerk. For Robert, traveling to the
German capital was a grand gesture, a big adventure—he was visiting
the epicenter of art and culture, leaving his homeland behind. It was
also an experiment, a testing of the waters to see whether he might find a
place for himself there. Perhaps he'd been encouraged in this venture by
Renfer; a fictionalized account of the journey he wrote a quarter of a century later ("The Poems") reports, "At the age of nineteen, I traveled to
Berlin on the advice of a photographer and learned there what it meant to
be homesick." What exactly Robert did and saw on this journey is not
recorded, though more than one Walser story set in this period refers to
"a disappointment" experienced in Berlin. He must have been expecting
to stay for a while: before leaving he applied for a deferment of the military
service he would have been expected to show up for after his twentieth
birthday the following spring. What happened to him in the German
capital? Had he hoped to be welcomed into a community of writers, only
to find the Berlin intelligentsia unreceptive to him, with his strong Swiss
accent and his lack of a formal education? Twenty days later he was back
in Zurich, where he moved in with Karl, sharing his room until Karl left
for Sursee.[25]

But although his plan to become a literary Berliner had apparently
come to naught, Robert had made a decisive step, one establishing a pattern that persisted throughout his professional life: "rendering himself
jobless" (as he would put it in that 1920 biographical note) for the purpose
of writing. He adopted a parsimonious lifestyle, living in furnished rooms
and taking his meals in inexpensive restaurants, just as his father, the impoverished widower, was doing back in Biel. Living this way meant that
temporary employment was enough to permit him to devote months at a
time to writing alone. The most important thing he earned each time he
took a job was a subsequent period of freedom.

Defining his clerical employment as a "day job" unconnected to his
true aspirations took courage since he would be starting each new job at
the bottom of the office hierarchy. Or maybe he hoped, each time he left
one of these jobs, that it would be the last he would ever need. He wanted
writing to be his *professional* form of existence; he didn't want to be a hob-
byist. Just as his brother drew and painted all day long, developing his
skills, Robert wanted to pursue writing with all his energies, to give himself space for contemplation and dreaming.

Still, several of his stories feature aspiring young poets who display far less swagger. The narrator of "The Poems" (1919), for example, backed himself into a corner by impulsively giving up his job to run off to Berlin:

> I gave up a quite acceptable position and set out to make the acquaintance of Life; but what goes by the name of Life frightened me, and I experienced a disappointment; I wept on foreign soil about my error and returned home. Here at first I was in difficult straits, finding myself unemployed, yet at the same time I was unspeakably courageous and had the feeling that things would go well for me.
>
> I myself don't quite know how I started writing poetry. I read poems, and this gave me the idea to write some of my own. [. . .] I wrote poems out of a mixture of bright-golden prospects and anxious prospectlessness, constantly half fearful, half almost bubbling over with exultation.[26]

According to this account, long-term intentional unemployment-for-the-sake-of-art, so romantically described in his 1920 biographical note, isn't quite how things appeared to him at the time: "Since I was jobless, I wrote letters of application to commercial firms and took a secret pleasure in this as well. Everything gave me pleasure." And he held more jobs than we now have records of. In a letter to his sister Lisa from May 5, 1898, he writes, "As for me, I am valiantly studying French, I go to the office every morning, return home insane, expect letters, don't write any but nonetheless expect every evening to find at least three letters."[27] We don't know what office he was going to at that point, but no more than half a year may have passed between when he left the insurance firm and went looking for his next day job.

Meanwhile, he had spent the better part of the winter writing and by spring had assembled some forty poems that he carefully copied into a notebook and mailed to Josef Viktor Widmann, literary editor of the important Swiss newspaper *Der Bund* in Bern. Perhaps Robert had grown up seeing his father reading *Der Bund;* one photograph depicts Adolf Walser immersed in a copy. Widmann was considered a Swiss literary authority, an eloquent critic who wrote in several genres, and a personal friend of cultural luminaries Gottfried Keller and Johannes

Brahms. His son Max had run the amateur theater club in Biel that Robert perhaps had joined. Widmann had also been printing travelogues and essays on geography by Robert's older brother Hermann—now a geography teacher at a *Gymnasium* who had recently (1896) completed his doctorate. Little is known about Robert's relationship to this brother, eight years his senior. There's no evidence that Hermann introduced Robert to Widmann.[28]

Exciting news arrived that spring: Widmann accepted six of Robert's poems for publication. When they appeared in May 1898 in *Der Bund*'s Sunday literary supplement, only the initials R.W. identified the poet (by whose choice is unclear), and they were prefaced with an account of how the poems came into the hands of their editor: "A twenty-year-old commercial employee in Zurich, R.W., who left school for the office at the age of fourteen and so had no opportunity to pursue a course of higher education, recently sent the editor of this supplement a notebook containing approximately forty lyric poems, his 'firstborns.' " Widmann goes on to discuss the poems' strengths and weaknesses, as he sees them, singling out certain lines for praise. He writes how pleased he was by the absence of "banal love poetry" in the selection, finding instead "something elemental and authentic and at the same time something very delicate" in the moods summoned up by the poems, along with a "curious surefootedness, almost that of a sleepwalker," which allows the poet to move "at the outermost borders where one can so easily tumble from the standpoint of the sublime into the abyss of the ridiculous."[29]

Robert's first published poems show how much he had learned since writing "Future!" only a year earlier. Gone was the disastrous combination of solemnity and clichéd rhymes. He was still using rhymes, but they were now light and quirky. Two of the six poems invoke the "longing" he had written about so extensively to his sister the previous July. "Gloomy Neighbor," on the subject of poverty, still shows a concern for social justice, but—formally shaky and marred by inconsistent rhythm—it is the weakest of the batch and the only one of the six Robert would discard when assembling his first book of poems. Others are quite strong. He later referred to "A Little Landscape" as his first poem.[30] It sketches a landscape using a strategy of strict repetition, with a surprising swerve in the final two couplets:

A Little Landscape

There stands a little tree in the meadow's ground
and many more nice little trees as well.
A little leaf freezes in the frosty wind
and many more single little leaves as well.
A little snow heap shimmers on the bank of a brook
and many more white little heaps as well.
A pointy little mountain peak laughs down into the depths
and many more rascally peaks as well.
And in all these things the Devil lies
and many more poor devils as well.
A little angel averts his weeping face
and all the angels of heaven as well.[31]

Although written before the end of the nineteenth century, this poem seems like a work of early expressionism with its landscape abstracted into discrete features of the natural world, each of them presented in isolation from their context and then curiously multiplied. The sudden swerve to devils and angels takes this poem unexpectedly into the religious realm, with the twist that it appears the angels are horrified at the hidden devilry of all these seemingly harmless natural phenomena (trees standing, leaves freezing, snow shimmering, mountain peaks laughing). Just as quickly, the "Devil" turns into a human unfortunate with "poor devils." Most of the landscape poetry crossing Widmann's desk must have been far tamer than this strangely psychological vision of the natural world.

The strongest poems in the group, "Brightness" and "Always at the Window"—both landscape poems as well—are thickly lyrical, with musically integrated rhymes and gently disjointed imagery. The latter poem (from whose title Walser later dropped the "always") repeats the atomizing strategy from "A Little Landscape."

Always at the Window

The heart-warm brown of the earth,
the childish white upon it,
the silver-green meadow now
have sent a dream into the world,
the dream of a smile.

My cheeks are being stroked,
stroked by a good person's hand;
my eye is blind with bliss,
and so I cannot say
whose tender hands these are.

This dream of a happy smile
was sent out into the wide world
by these colors, delicate and womanly,
nodding in assent:
I stand at the window now.[32]

In this poem, the landscape—whose colors have become animated, psychological—conjures up a dream that is then experienced by the speaker in the second stanza. The poem's lightheartedly skipping rhythms in German and sparing use of rhyme show a mastery of the form that is a far cry from the forced and lumbering lines Robert was writing just a year before.

The publication of these poems brought Robert to the attention of yet another powerful literary figure, Franz Blei, who was to play an even more important role than Widmann in launching his career. Seven years older than Robert and the scion of a wealthy Viennese family, Blei had already published two plays and a number of essays. He'd come to Zurich to complete his studies of political economy and literature, his dissertation (1895) a translation-with-commentary of Ferdinand Galiani's *Dialogues on the Grain Trade*. Blei was well-connected in Zurich's literary world. One of his friends, a German psychiatry and literature student named Otto Hinrichsen (remember that name), read the poems by Widmann's latest discovery in *Der Bund* and brought them to Blei's attention. Blei dropped Robert a note inviting him to call.

In a portrait written decades later, Blei provides the most complete physical description we have of young Robert:

A few days later, he stood there in my room and said, "I'm Walser." A tall, rather gangly fellow with a bony, reddish-brown face, over which fell a thick blond shock of hair that had successfully resisted the comb, gray-blue dreamy eyes and well-fashioned hands that stuck out from the too-short sleeves of his jacket and did not know where to go and would have liked best to have sought refuge in his trouser pockets so as not to be there at all. That was Walser, half itinerant journeyman, half page-boy, and all poet.[33]

Blei, self-possessed and already quite the man of the world, must have appeared an impressive figure to inexperienced, self-conscious Robert. Blei was highly educated, articulate, and comfortably natty in the tailored suits that came with his social standing. His open, friendly face was adorned with a pince-nez and a pointy little beard. Walser later described his visit to Blei's home, and the circumstances leading up to it, in "Dr. Franz Blei":

> I was twenty years old, living as a commercial employee in Zurich and residing there in an old house on the mountainside, in a room that had been occupied just before by a painter, namely my brother. [. . .] This was in May, and Widmann in Bern had published several of my poems in his Sunday supplement. For the first time in my life, I saw myself in print, which made me almost mad with pleasure. [. . .] One evening [I received a letter from] Dr. Franz Blei, who asked me to be so good as to visit him, as he wished to make my acquaintance. The next day, at six in the afternoon, I went to see him. [. . .] He gave an extremely friendly smile when he caught sight of me, and with visible courtesy and graciousness ushered into his home a young person who had as yet in no way acquired the art of presenting himself in a self-assured manner.[34]

According to this account, Blei drew Robert's attention to the work of Lenz, Büchner, Brentano, Novalis, and other canonical authors (a circumstance registered without irony, suggesting these were names with which the young poet was previously unfamiliar). Blei also gave him some books and invited him to a party.

Overall, the tone of "Dr. Franz Blei" recalls Walser's account of visiting Robert Seidel, with a narrative voice prone to hyperbole. Both texts were written in 1917, during a period when Robert was mining his Zurich experiences for material. (Unlike the Seidel story, however, we can't check his account of these conversations against actual documents.)

In this telling, Blei asks the narrator about his plans twice. At first, the young man affirms that he intends to keep working as a clerk while he pursues his writing—a response Blei is said to accept respectfully and without a trace of arrogance. But when they meet a second time and Blei asks whether he wouldn't like to travel to Munich, the narrator says he doesn't wish to. When asked to elaborate, he explains:

> This coming fall, I shall resign from the position I currently hold and as a result shall be without employment and work, whereupon it is my intention to go into seclusion. I shall lock myself away in the remoteness of some room on the outskirts of town and there continue to write poems. This is a quite simple plan that—if I am not terribly mistaken—I can definitely carry out, realize, and bring to life. When I have then written a few acceptable things, I shall look for and find a new suitable position, shall return to an office and be the same sensibly and purposefully working individual as before.[35]

Assuming that Walser's later account of the conversation is accurate, his intention to fund his writing with office work had already been formed by 1898.

Robert's acquaintance with Blei proved crucial in advancing his nascent career. The June 24, 1898, entry in Blei's diary indicates how much Robert impressed him from the start: "Robert Walser, a young man from Bern who is working as a clerk here, recently paid me a visit. He will achieve extraordinary things." And on July 1, Blei wrote, "Walser brought me his poems, of which I am copying these"—he then copied out between five to eight poems; the exact number is unclear since he later tore out one of the pages. (These are the only poems included in this entire two-hundred-page diary.)[36] One poem was among those printed by Widmann while another was mentioned in his introduction.

Franz Blei's prediction that Robert would "achieve extraordinary things" was self-fulfilling to the extent that Blei not only encouraged the younger writer but also helped him continue to publish. The following spring, he suggested that Robert send his work to Peter Altenberg; the master feuilletonist and key figure in Vienna's bohemian coffeehouse scene was also an editor at the respected bimonthly journal *Wiener Rundschau*.

Robert did as he was told, sending his poems and a letter on April 15, 1899. Altenberg's magazine published eight of the poems in its August 1, 1899, issue under Robert's full name. These poems were similar to those Robert had sent Widmann and Blei; one of them ("Brightness") was even among the group published in *Der Bund*. The last and shortest among them was the rhyming quatrain "Adage," which, under the revised and difficult-to-translate title "Beiseit" (off to one side, in seclusion, discarded, shelved) has become one of the most beloved of Walser's short poems:

Adage

I go out for my walk,
it leads a little way
and home. Then without sound
or word I'm set aside.[37]

An editor's note accompanying the poems in *Wiener Rundschau* praises their author's "honest talent" and "highly original feeling for nature" despite a certain "awkwardness." It also quotes Robert's accompanying letter to Altenberg: "While I do hope that this delivery does not come as a surprise to you, might I also at the same time hope that no disturbance lies herein. If this should nonetheless be the case, I should like to ask your forgiveness. I should like to leave all directives regarding this matter entirely to your benevolence, to which I most thankfully and calmly bow."[38] As letters of submission go, this one—sent on Robert's twenty-first birthday—is remarkable for its submissiveness. While the editor's note cites these lines as evidence that the poet is "free from all posing," I would argue the opposite. In their highly mannered humility, these lines *perform* modesty more than exemplify it. They are markedly different from the genuinely humble letter Robert wrote to Robert Seidel two years earlier. Unlike its predecessor, this letter was written by a young man convinced of his literary talent and eligibility for publication.

Although few of Robert's letters from this period survive, the ones that do—particularly those written to Lisa, which are playfully essayistic as early as 1897—show him developing a unique voice characterized by tongue-in-cheek mock-solemnity, rhetorically strategic repetitions, and a gentle humor that does not detract from his respect for, say, his sister's loneliness or writer Peter Altenberg. Robert works hard at crafting his poetry and "plays hard" in letters that entertain both writer and recipients. Admirers of his early poetry emphasized that these works show talent while being interesting, quirky, and a little awkward; no one considered them great, and in fact they aren't. If such poetry was all Robert Walser ever wrote, he'd be forgotten. It was as the author of letters that young Robert was teaching himself to write.

FOUR

Drama

1899–1900

IN LATE JANUARY 1899, Robert decamped to Thun, an idyllic little town at the gateway to the Alps some forty miles south of Biel. He was feeling shaken-up and out of sorts after troubling events that winter involving his brother Ernst, five years his senior. The family drama had taken place shortly before Robert returned home for Christmas—if "home" was the right word for it now. Family holidays were a reminder of how completely lost his childhood world was. Ever since 1897, the Walser homestead had been a modest apartment at Neuhausstrasse 18, where Adolf Walser lived with his two daughters. The building was located near the chic addresses where he'd formerly done business, but that era was receding into memory. Having closed the last of his shops the year before, Adolf was now trying to keep himself afloat as an importer of Italian wine and oil.[1] Quarters in the new apartment were cramped enough that making room for visiting sons to sleep was a challenge. Karl was staying with Ferdinand Huttenlocher, his former teacher.

Papa Walser's landlords were the prosperous Schumacher family, who owned a foundry; their daughter Flora occupied one of the other apartments along with her husband, Henri, a postal clerk. Flora Ackeret was a vivacious hostess with a flirtatious air who loved filling her drawing room with Biel's young intellectuals. She wasn't much older than the Walser siblings and welcomed their company when it was available. Fanny was sometimes at home, sometimes off at a residential school, and Lisa—studying in Bern—was around mostly on weekends. Their brothers came and went, occasional visitors. To her friends, Ackeret's door was always open. Neighbors were encouraged to drop by too, including the many children of the Schätzle family. Ackeret's other associates included the wealthy young art collector Otto Ackermann, now living in Zurich, where

Robert met him through Rosa Schätzle. To Karl Walser's disgust, Ackermann was buying up the work of impoverished and as-yet-unknown young painters there at bargain-basement prices. Soon he would open a gallery in the ground-floor storefront of the Schumachers' apartment building. He had literary connections as well and helped Ackeret publish some of her fanciful texts about social equality.[2]

This convivial atmosphere was disturbed in the summer of 1897 when Ernst Walser returned to Switzerland after six years abroad. Ernst had wanted to be a *Gymnasium* teacher like Hermann but had been prevented from pursuing a graduate degree by his father's declining finances, so, for want of better options, he'd taken a post as a private tutor in Naples. Although one position had led to the next in Italy, none seems to have suited him. Mächler reports that he also suffered a head injury after a riding accident.[3] Back in Switzerland, he was called up to complete the obligatory military service he'd deferred during his time abroad, and that wasn't to his liking either. Insulted by his commanding officer's tone of voice, he was demoted for knocking the cap off his head. Then he was caught attempting to falsify his service record to conceal the demotion and was sentenced to jail time. Meanwhile, he began to write Ackeret missives that were halfway between love letters and cries for help. His letters began, "My dear Frau [Mrs.] Ackeret," except that he drew slashes through the letters of her last name, making the line secretly (or not so secretly) read, my dear woman/wife (the other meaning of "Frau"). He borrowed money and books from her, asked to stay in her apartment (she sent him to the inexpensive Hotel Blaues Kreuz nearby), and wrote to her from his barrack in fall 1898 that the question on his mind was "whether I should come home, to live with you, or instead go far, far away so as to be able to report to you shortly afterward that thanks to you I have become a writer and poet. That last part is really true, you've made me these things."[4]

Over the course of that autumn, Ernst's mental state deteriorated so dramatically that Ackeret and one of her brothers discovered him attempting suicide:

> Hermann and I found him—I can't remember by what coincidence—just as he was about to drown himself. Now I asked my parents to give him a room, and he remained for the three weeks before he had to go back to the army. Sometimes

he would turn on the lamp in broad daylight and write muddle-
headed newspaper articles that were always rejected. [. . .]
Once he turned up wearing one patent-leather shoe and a hob-
nailed boot held together with twine; when I drew his attention
to this, he said how astonished he was to find me so concerned
with appearances.[5]

On December 16, 1898, at the age of twenty-five, Ernst Walser was committed to Waldau Asylum outside Bern, having been transported there
directly from the military jail where he was serving time for his act of insubordination. The clinic intake form notes that the patient had been suffering from general irritability exacerbated by persecution mania over the
previous year and declares him incapable of "coping with disagreeable
situations." Ernst told the Waldau staff that he had long been experiencing
difficulties in professional contexts. He'd quarreled with his employers,
changed households repeatedly, and disciplined his pupils more harshly
than appropriate; general nervousness and quickness to take offense gradually escalated into full-blown paranoia. The admitting physician sum-
marizes: "Depressed and anxious. Apathetic and irritable."[6] After an
escape attempt that January and an apparently quite serious suicide attempt the following October, Ernst became a long-term resident of Waldau, his official diagnosis *dementia praecox,* a form of schizophrenia.

For Robert, news of Ernst's hospitalization came as a shock. This was
a brother he'd long been in the habit of looking up to, a man in the prime of
life who'd enjoyed an education. The entire family was justifiably distraught
and confused over Christmas 1898 when they gathered in the Neuhausstrasse apartment. Ernst's fate cast a pall over any festivities, though it
wasn't yet clear his hospitalization was anything but temporary. To add to
their distress, his disciplinary imprisonment and subsequent internment at
Waldau soon became public knowledge, producing enough of a scandal that
Adolf decided to move himself and his daughters out of the heart of town,
the ground zero of gossip, to rooms in the quiet suburb of Nidau.[7] Ackeret
was upset too. Ernst had been one of her protégés, and she'd encouraged
his literary ambitions. Now she felt worried for him, and a little guilty: Had
she led him on, and could disappointed love have driven him to madness?

Flora Ackeret is an important source of information about the
Walser siblings during this period. Years later she would write a long

reminiscence, including detailed portraits of several young Walsers, in a letter to Hermann Hesse. In these notes, she confessed to a painful and humiliating episode from that spring. Apparently, she'd proved to be one of the many women incapable of resisting Karl Walser's charms. Though she was eight years his senior and married, it seems that Karl began to court her during the early months of 1899. He had decided to stay in Switzerland all spring to paint while living in various villages outside Biel and Solothurn. Perhaps the presence of the oh-so-annoying Otto Ackermann at Christmas had ignited his jealousy, making him take Ackeret and her artistic dabbling more seriously. He offered to redesign her wardrobe in colors that would suit her better (the ever-seductive tactic of cloaking criticism in compliments) and sent her an envelope filled with colorful little pictures he'd drawn of scenes they'd experienced together. Though as late as March 1899 she was still reading his letters aloud to her husband, she soon fell passionately in love with Karl, overcoming whatever misgivings she must have had after hearing about the unfortunate experiences of Rosa Schätzle, who'd warned her in a letter that both brothers were "spongers." Ackeret distrusted Schätzle and found distasteful what she saw as her tendency to overshare; but these were serious warning bells and not so easy to dismiss, so Ackeret must have had a talent for denial.[8]

Robert, meanwhile, was in Thun. He'd arrived in late January and found lodging at Obere Hauptgasse 39, just steps from the river Aare. This street with its double row of shops—some with entrances at street level, others facing a raised walkway half a flight above—led directly to the main square and Town Hall, which was crowned by a clock tower whose bells Robert could hear while reading in his furnished room late at night. From the main square, stone steps with a wooden canopy zigzagged up the hill to the church and castle that loomed above the town. Thun was quiet, picturesque, and small, its population a scant ten thousand. It was also only a short train ride from Bern.

It isn't clear what prompted Robert's move from Zurich to Thun. A nostalgia-tinged essay he wrote a quarter of a century later reports: "[I] quietly hid myself away [there], so to speak, as a clerk in a savings bank."[9] Was he hiding? Perhaps Ernst's hospitalization—and his family's distress over it—had made him want to be closer to Biel and Bern in case his help was needed. Karl was now back in Biel too. Robert was writing more and more, and showing his work to his closest confidant was important to him, although he was uncomfortable watching the romance between his brother and Ackeret unfold. He had complicated feelings about it: jealousy, envy, sexual confusion. He too had noticed Ackeret's beauty and later wrote of it several times.

Perhaps Karl sent a letter updating him on the progress of his clandestine love-suit; two Walser stories written in 1919—"The Comrade" and "An Epistle Sent in Friendship"—portray characters confused and disturbed by the contents of letters they receive describing such a love affair ("Feverish, I crept to and fro. Bright sunshine inspired me with chills and whirling dizziness"). One narrator is so discombobulated that he gets himself fired from his job. The lover, meanwhile, is described with expressionist panache: "The wind flutters your hair. Trees bend down beneath the tempest. How magnificent is happiness so lofty in nature."[10] In short, the older writer was reflecting, not unironically, on his younger self's glorification of his brother's romantic conquest.

Meanwhile, this love story was taking place against the backdrop of the family's concerns about Ernst. The onset of his illness had been so gradual that no one had understood what was happening until he became seriously afflicted. What if Ernst wasn't the only sibling touched by madness? Most of the Walser children were eccentric in one way or another, with the notable exception of Oscar, the bank clerk industriously climbing the career ladder, whom Karl and Robert used to tease for being such a well-adjusted, upright individual. And Hermann—their oldest surviving brother—was certainly a role model. A respected teacher with a doctorate, he would eventually hold a professorship in geography at the University of Bern. He regularly sent his father money, helping to support his younger siblings.[11]

So that made two Walser siblings with apparently stable lives.

As for the rest of the family, Ernst wasn't the only one who had difficulty "coping with disagreeable situations"; that also applied to both Robert and Karl, while Lisa exhibited her own moody mixture of ambition and resentments. As the oldest daughter, though the middle child among the seven, she had run the household during her mother's illness. It wasn't until three years after Elisa's death that Lisa was able to enroll in the three-year course of study that would prepare her to become a schoolteacher. Karl and Robert, by contrast, had begun their apprenticeships while Elisa was still alive.

Ackeret's portrait of Lisa, six years her junior and considered a great beauty, is hardly flattering; there must have been rivalries or other tensions between the two. Ackeret writes in her letter to Hesse that she very much enjoyed Lisa's friendship and was always happy when she was in town, but then she details a long catalogue of slights and grudges. She recalls Lisa inviting her on outings and then running into other friends she was clearly happier to spend time with; reports her borrowing and losing various small items belonging to Ackeret (a lidded basket, her best gloves) while never misplacing any of her own things; and accuses Lisa of talking constantly about "living for the moment." Lisa's apparent dislike of her maternal aunt annoyed Ackeret, as did the way she complained about her father's brother in Basel, who was always sending them money—she didn't want to see herself as a charity case—but never came to visit. When he did come to town, Lisa made no effort to see him, or so Ackeret reports, also recalling that this uncle's money paid for deposits on apartments, university fees, and the like.[12]

As for Robert, who began to pay visits to the Ackeret household beginning in 1897, Ackeret remarks:

> of all of them, he was the only one I took an immediate liking to just as he was. Back in those days he was certainly neither spiteful nor unjust [he would later displease her by writing about her affair with Karl]. I'm sure of it, it's just that he kept running away all the time, because without realizing what he was doing, he was avoiding all the ugliness. I can still call to mind his lost expression and that peculiar way he had of withdrawing. [. . .] Like Papa W., like Ernst, like *all of them* with the exception of Oscar and Lisa, there was something actually rather dull about him. A certain dry, diffident manner, slow to open up.

Ackeret described Robert and Karl as being "like twins without the physical resemblance, but in their opinions and gestures," both of them "young, proud, high-spirited louts" who "at the time were still marvelous and handsome."[13] She disapproved of the pranks they got up to, their way of sharing private jokes at the expense of everyone else. A mutual admiration society, though not without its tensions, they made her feel insecure, as if the petit-bourgeois security of her life were somehow an intellectual or even moral failing. Neither one of these artistic strivers seemed quite cut out for the life of a solid citizen, which was perhaps what drew her to them, especially to dashing, self-assured Karl.

In the spring of 1899, Karl's affair with Ackeret reached a tumultuous conclusion. As Ackeret relates the story two decades later, Karl began pressuring her to leave her husband and run away with him, and soon she wanted nothing more. One night in early May he pulled her into his bed in the dark maid's garret when she came to say goodnight—not exactly how she would have chosen to consummate their love—and the next day she gathered her courage and announced to her husband that she was leaving him. Instead of the painful collapse she'd expected, he became enraged and shouted accusations of adultery before summoning Karl to berate them both. Karl's response, Ackeret writes, was to quietly gather up his drawing board and books, say "Adieu," and walk out the door.[14]

Amid all this real-life Sturm und Drang, Robert found himself drawn once more to the literal drama that had so infatuated him as a teenage theater-goer. In Thun, he embraced a new hero very much in keeping with his mood: the brilliant but ill-fated author and playwright Heinrich von Kleist (1777–1811). Kleist came to Thun in February 1802 at the age of twenty-four, having hatched a plan to escape the life of officialdom that was his birthright as the scion of Prussian military nobility by becoming a farmer in rural Switzerland. His plan was foiled first by his fiancée's unwillingness to follow him, then by ever-louder rumors that Napoleon was planning to invade Switzerland. To wait it out, Kleist rented a small house on a tiny island in the Aare outside Thun and for the next few months wrote himself into a frenzy while isolated from all human society except that of his young housekeeper. In short order, he wrote the initial version of what would be his first major play (*The Schroffenstein Family*) and the beginnings of two others (*Robert Guiskard*, only a fragment of which survives, and *The Broken Jug*). In the few letters sent during this period—including the one quoted in Chapter 3—he sounds increasingly unhinged.[15]

Kleist's passionate approach to both art and life was well-suited to inspire twenty-one-year-old Robert. The young poet whose heart had been inflamed by socialism just two years earlier couldn't help but be moved by the potent cocktail of Kleist's patriotism and desire to live the honest, simple life of a farmer—"simple" at least as understood from the perspective of his elite background. Like Schiller's *The Robbers,* which captivated Robert as a teenager, Kleist's work glorifies loyalty, principles, and heartfelt sentiment over scheming, crafty intellectualism. Kleist also loved historical material that could be employed allegorically to comment on contemporary affairs. One bit of history that interested him particularly was the 1386 Battle of Sempach in which Swiss peasants successfully fought off an attack by heavily armed knights defending the interests of the House of Habsburg. In Walser's 1907 story "Kleist in Thun," recounting this episode in Kleist's life, the writer is hard at work on a play inspired by this battle. Walser himself later published a story with this subject matter.[16]

Kleist was to remain a recurring figure in Walser's work.[17] He also had a powerful impact on him as a literary craftsman: in the muscular lines of *Robert Guiskard,* features emerge that clearly influenced the young writer's style, above all a linguistic compression that gives the text its vehemence and force. The first speech of Kleist's play contains the neologistic compounds *angstempört* (indignant with fear) and *Entsetzensschritte* (footsteps of horror), the sorts of words Walser would soon draw on for effect.

If Thun was a refuge, Robert presumably also moved there intending to write. He knew no one there, rents were cheaper than in Zurich, and he was spared the constant whirl of commerce and competition that dominated life in the big city. In Zurich, where the haves and have-nots crossed paths daily in the city center, one was always being reminded who one was, or being asked who one was, or asking oneself. In Thun, no one was expected to be anything much, and Robert was free to take a job, not take a job, take one and drop it for another, or do nothing but write all morning and then gaze into the limpid waters of the Aare until his mind became one with the reflected sky. In his later stories about the period, Walser gave differing accounts of the positions he held there. Two stories—"Kleist in Thun" and "Apollo and Diana" (1913)—mention a brewery as their narrators' place of employment, while two later ones ("Back then, oh, in those days" [1925] and "Notebook Excerpt" [1927]) speak of a "savings and loan."[18]

And, of course, he was writing poems. He remained in touch with the mentors who had supported and encouraged him as a poet while he lived in Zurich. A 1917 story titled "Widmann" recalls a walk he made from

Thun to Bern (an eighteen-mile trek) one rainy Sunday in March to visit
Widmann in his villa. This account describes the walker's garb as a
"wretched bright yellow midsummer suit, light dancing shoes, an intentionally vulgar, insolent, foolish hat, and certainly there was no trace of a
proper collar anywhere on my person."[19] The conversation between mentor and protégé isn't reproduced in the story; the text merely describes a
friendly reception in an elegant but comfortable setting, with a dog crouch-
ing on the rug at his host's feet, a visit that the young guest interrupts after
half an hour, not wanting to overstay his welcome. This fictional visit must
have corresponded to a real-life one, because it was followed by a real-life
letter Robert mailed to Widmann from Thun on May 2, 1899, along with
some books Widmann had loaned him and an apology for having held on
to them so long.

He kept in touch with Blei as well. Shortly after meeting him the
previous year, Blei had sent Robert's notebook of poems to a group of
young writers in Munich planning a new journal. Otto Julius Bierbaum
responded on July 2, 1898: "I read the Walser poems with astonishment—
and was moved by them. He just has to find his form, and then we shall
have one more true poet among us." In the end, the new magazine never
materialized, but a year later Bierbaum was recruited by a pair of twenty-
one-year-old step-cousins, Rudolf Alexander Schröder and Alfred Walter
Heymel, who'd just inherited a fortune and wanted to found a large-bud-
get monthly. On March 15, 1899, Bierbaum wrote to Blei that the team was
accepting a Walser poem, "Brightness" ("Helle"), for the inaugural issue
of *Die Insel* (The Island).[20]

Brightness

Gray days on which the sun
has been behaving like a pallid nun
are now gone by.
Blue skies now shine blue above,
a world has freely risen up,
with sun and stars ablaze.

Silently this all transpired,
noiselessly, an act of will,
without ado.

Smiling, the miracle unfolds,
no need of fuse or rocket,
just the clearest night.[21]

Here was a nature poem, a song of praise made strange by the idiosyncratic first image of the pallid nun and the personification ("smiling") of the landscape. Delighted at the news that *Die Insel* would publish it, Blei tracked down Robert in Thun to ask whether he might have more work to share. Robert obliged, sending him a bound notebook of twenty new poems, "one more beautiful than the next," as Blei wrote to Bierbaum.[22] Blei must have sent along these poems to Bierbaum as well, because when the first volume of Munich's brand-new "aesthetic-belletristic monthly journal with illustrated supplement" appeared in October 1899, it contained not only "Brightness" but four newer Walser poems as well: "Rocking," "Dreams," "Calm," and an untitled quatrain:

Smiles and laughter
Come over me.
What does it mean?
It's just one of those things.

The almost flippant charm of these unabashedly slight lines coupled with their offhanded refusal of importance or explanation—and all of it tied up in a handy rhythmical little package that rhymes in German—exercised an intriguing appeal.[23]

The new magazine was gorgeous, too—all elegant typography with ornamental elements strewn about its pages, plentiful illustrations by old and modern artists, and a stylish sailing-ship colophon designed by Peter Behrens. Its first edition contained work by Clemens Brentano, Paul Verlaine, Hugo von Hofmannsthal, Paul Scheerbart, and others in whose company Robert was proud to appear, including his mentor Blei, who was represented with a selection of translated letters by Abbé Galiani. *Die Insel* soon established itself as one of the most important organs of German early modernism, publishing the work of established figures like Rilke, Poe, Gide, Nietzsche, Yeats, Wilde, and Whitman along with carefully chosen newcomers.

While the inaugural issue of *Die Insel* was still in press, the poems Blei had encouraged Robert to send to Peter Altenberg back in April appeared in the August 1, 1899, issue of *Wiener Rundschau:* eight poems, including "Brightness" (apparently everyone's favorite Walser poem and published thrice so far).[24] *Wiener Rundschau,* one of the finest literary journals of the era, had been around for four years at that point, publishing some of the same writers as *Die Insel,* but also Karl Kraus, Baudelaire, Dostoevsky, and Chekhov. In the August 1 issue, Robert shared billing with Remy de Gourmont, Poe, and Tolstoy. So now, little more than a year after getting his first break in *Der Bund,* Robert found himself published in leading Austrian and German magazines. The international recognition helped relieve his feelings of uncertainty, unworthiness, and fear after the turbulent winter and spring of 1898–1899. He was a writer. He could live where he wanted, do what he wanted—as long as he continued to write, a writer he would remain.

In the course of 1899 and/or 1900, he filled a new notebook—a fatter one—with fifty lovingly copied-out poems titled *Book Three: Plucked String and Longing* (*Drittes Buch: Saite und Sehnsucht*).[25] This new manuscript felt like a book and contained enough poems for themes, motifs, and characteristic rhetorical gestures to emerge. Walser makes frequent use of repetition in these poems, often boldly employing different forms of the same word as rhyme-words. The poems stake out a domestic terrain that extends tentatively into nature, leaning hard on strategically deployed vocabulary items: room, bed, window, curtain, night, snow, longing, sleep. Most of the poems rhyme, some are organized into stanzas. Certain turns of phrase recur too, lending the volume a sense of unity. All the poems display a real or feigned naiveté on the speaker's part, a stance that prizes honest wonder while at the same time presenting enough quirky observations and invented words to skew the poems ever so slightly into oddity— including strange compounds that display a Kleistian influence: *aus bangverwühltem Himmel* (from fearfully disheveled skies) and *erinnerungsheißes Rot* (a crimson hot with remembrance). A few of the poems— some of the weakest in the collection—are crossed out in pencil. In the end, only fifteen of the fifty poems ever saw print. Robert eventually gave the notebook to his sister Fanny for safekeeping, and it was found among her effects following her death many decades later.[26]

In the volume's strongest poems, the stanzas develop an incantatory reiterative force that drives them forward even as their subjects and words insist on a chilly nocturnal peace—this tension gives the lines energy and

power. Even some of the simpler unpublished poems display a strange
energy, such as "Winter Rain" ("Winterregen"):

> I behold soft rain
> falling on hard meadows,
> falling on angry trees,
> falling on dark houses,
> from skies disheveled with fear,
> falling on the slumbering earth,
> sleeping its winter slumber.
> Now all of this must change.
> The earth now must awaken,
> the meadows have to swell,
> the trees must kindly gaze
> upon familiar houses,
> for a weak and kindly rain
> from skies disheveled with fear
> now visits the wintry earth.[27]

Here the natural world is imbued with human psychology, but not as a
reflection of a particular person's mental state; rather, nature itself exhibits
sentiment and intention. It's a little unsettling, which provides an interesting contrast with the poem's "light" repetitive structure and lyrical vocabulary and tone.

This *Book Three* also contained what has become one of Walser's best-
known poems, "World" ("Welt," originally titled "Happiness" ["Glück"]):

> Laughing there arise
> in the comings and the goings
> of this world many deep worlds
> that all go roving onward
> and fleeing past each other
> display ever greater beauty.
>
> Their being is in motion,
> their greatness lies in fleeing,
> disappearance is their life.

I feel no longer worried
for I can, still unshattered,
a world, strive through this world.[28]

In this poem, the many worlds that make up the world are constantly mul-
tiplying, constantly in flux. This study of motion carries a sense of mo-
mentum in its driving rhythms, particularly in the first stanza. Strangeness
arrives when the narrator asserts at poem's end that he too is a world
among all the other moving worlds, which he experiences by "striving
through" them "unshattered," a participle that seems to imply imminent
danger. The image is mysterious, the rebelliousness of the claim disarm-
ing. Walser has hit his stride as a poet—an odd stride, to be sure, but one
with a voice uniquely his own that justifies the warm reception his work
received from other writers.

Robert was eager now to meet and interact with the band of poets in
Munich who'd been supporting his work. Karl had been moving among
circles of artists for years, even spending some months in Munich as an
apprentice to stage-set designer Adolf Lentner in 1898. Now it was Robert's turn. A letter enclosed with books he returned to Widmann on May
2 announced his intention to "go to Munich in order to learn something
and see how long I can bear it." Robert registered his departure from
Thun that same day.[29]

No evidence suggests he made it past Zurich, however. On July 2,
1899, the Sunday supplement of *Der Bund*—in which his first poems had
appeared just over a year before—published his prose debut, "Lake Greifen" ("Der Greifensee"), the very first "walk story" of his career:

It's chilly this morning, and I set out at a march from this large city
with its large, famous lake for a small lake known almost to no one.
On the road I find nothing any ordinary man might not find on
any ordinary road. I wish "Good morning" to a few hardworking
reapers, that's all; I glance attentively at the lovely flowers, again
that's all; I cosily start chatting to myself, once more that's all.[30]

About three miles long and about four miles southeast of Zurich, Lake Greifen is nestled in the farmland beyond the mountains on the city's eastern

edge. It's a strenuous walk from Zurich through the woods and inevitably involves hustling up and down some hills. The pastoral scene described here—the presence of the reapers cutting the tall grass or grain suggests the month is June—is something Walser might, of course, have written from memory while still in Thun. But given all the beautiful walks he took during his time in the Bernese highlands that he might have described instead, it seems more likely he is describing a recent walk taken while in Zurich.

This descriptive prose text of some seven hundred words is already quintessentially Walserian and displays many characteristics for which he would be known in his later work. The self-assured rhythm and flow of his long sentences mimics the walker's stride. He lists the things he does and sees in a narrative concatenation almost expressionist in its movement: assorted glimpses of this and that coalesce to form a landscape. Typical of a feuilleton work, this piece is neither fully story nor essay; it's what Walser would later refer to simply as a "prose piece." Nothing happens other than the walk itself and the perceptions it occasions, yet the narrative carries one along with a sense of propulsion. Walser plays with the form as well, for example by personifying the very description he's writing:

> You, too, dear reader, will see how and why I feel drawn [to the lake] should it interest you to keep pursuing my description, which takes the liberty of skipping over roads, meadows, forest, stream, and field, thus arriving on the banks of the little lake itself where the two of us, I and it, stop short and cannot get over the lake's unexpected beauty, of which we had only a secret inkling.[31]

A moment later, the description is invited to speak and does so in the first person. It sketches the scene in ecstatic tones until the narrator takes over again, giving us occasion to ponder the relationship between these two first-person entities. He ends the piece by describing a swim in the lake, a duck, and an ancient castle before anticipating the evening and night he intends to spend here.

If this sure-footed debut received much notice, there's no record of it now. But the apparent ease and self-assurance of this writing, in contrast to the often labored poems, suggests that the young author had found his form. It was a triumph, even though this "small form" resided at the bottom of the literary food chain somewhere below novels and poetry.

Around this time, Robert made his first and only trip to visit his mother's birthplace in the hilly countryside of the Emmental region northeast of Thun. The journey is memorialized in "The Aunt" ("Die Tante"), published in 1915: "Under various conditions and circumstances, I set out in the best of spirits early one morning in fall from the small town where I'd been quite well employed." The walk takes an emotional turn when the narrator reaches his destination:

> Above the fields, hills, farmland, and woods, there smiled, danced, and dazzled the loveliest morning sun. Gradually I came into the mountains and soon reached an isolated village ringed all around by high crags; this was the birthplace of my mother. It seemed strange to me, yet also familiar and familial. The whole world, and I as well, appeared wonderfully old and young; earth and earthly life were suddenly a dream; I felt everything was perfectly comprehensible, yet also utterly inexplicable.[32]

At a remove of fifteen years, it's impossible to say whether Walser's feelings are being recollected or retrospectively conjured. But he must have felt something while walking through his mother's native landscape for the first time. The fifth anniversary of her death was approaching, and the closer Robert came to Schangnau on this foot-journey, the more people spoke in her rural Emmental accent.

It had been a complicated year, and a mother's comfort would have done him good—not the criticisms his mother was known to utter in one of her severe, disapproving moods, but the softness of those moments when she smiled on her children in love. The remembered sound of his mother's voice mixed with the colors of the falling leaves filtering through the woods she'd played in as a girl. The narrator of "The Aunt" reports, "The thought that my dear mother had spent her youth here, had been born here, moved me deeply." At a local inn, he asks the proprietor's wife if she can tell him anything about his mother's family and is coldly rebuffed. But after arriving at the small town of Burgdorf, he is delighted to cross paths with a cousin who immediately takes him to her mother. The story's title figure introduces him to "different, additional people." The rest of the story is a sort of deflection: rather than enjoying this family reunion, the narrator instead chronicles his annoyance that his aunt finds his traveling garments ("forest green trousers and a blue and white jacket") unsuitable, even offending him rather badly with a forceful offer to give him new clothes. Performing incredible feats of perambulatory travel while dressed in outlandish—foppish, perhaps impractical—clothes will become a recurring motif in Walser's work and perhaps in Robert's young manhood as well. He enjoyed fanciful garments and the sense of freedom they allowed the otherwise shy and awkward young writer. He had covered forty hilly miles on foot in less than a day and a half of walking in his clownish outfit, after all.[33]

From Burgdorf, it was only another thirteen or so miles to Solothurn, where Robert registered as a resident on October 13, 1899. He was greeted by the same jade-green Aare that flows through both Thun and Biel, and by a backdrop of the Jura Mountains. "The mountains behind the city," Walser would write more than a quarter-century later, "look like the stage set for a play being put on by all these contemporary petit-bourgeois days that at the same time draw their strength, as it were, from the gleaming relics of the past."[34] Robert rented a room at Gurzelngasse 34, a few doors down from one of the old gates once part of the city's medieval fortifications.[35] The building was one room wide—the shutters of the two windows on each floor overlapped—and filled with the sounds of a nearby fountain and church bells marking off the quarter hours all day and night.

Solothurn was both removed from and close to Biel, and it was a simple matter for Robert to catch a train to visit his family or just walk the fifteen miles, barely a middling promenade for him. A letter sent to Fanny on March 1, 1900, announces a visit during which he plans to "take a stroll or not take a stroll in your company, drink tea or not drink tea, have a chat and observe the progress of your new coiffure"—more a casual dropping in than a journey.[36]

Robert quickly found employment at a local bank whose windows overlooked the Aare, and set to work both clerking and writing. He still had Kleist on his mind, and it is probably here that he began working in earnest on his first dramatic sketches. According to a later, possibly fictionalized, account of this period, he considered writing a play about the Battle of Sempach but was dissuaded by a mentor (Widmann? Blei?), who counseled him instead to write something that "came from within." The first short play he wrote, *The Lads* (*Die Knaben*), describes a casual hiking excursion involving three friends and one possibly younger boy ("small as a rabbit") who tags along behind them like a little brother, though it's unclear whether any of the characters are related.[37]

Franz, the play's most assertive character, speaks as philosophically as a figure out of the German classics; he even quotes from Goethe's *Faust* in one of his gravely highfalutin speeches. Franz dreams of becoming an actor, but his hopes are dashed when—you guessed it—he auditions unsuccessfully before a well-known actor who tells him he "lacks a divine spark." Since Franz possesses more passion than he knows what to do with, he resolves to become a soldier—"France is recruiting," he says, raising the question of what era this play might possibly be set in.[38]

Hermann, a budding violinist, has had a similar experience: he auditioned for Paganini (!) and failed just as miserably. The third friend, Heinrich, wishes to become a page boy, to which end he petitions an elegant woman on the street in iambic tetrameter, a fact remarked on ironically by his eavesdropping friends. There's a homoerotic ambiguity to these male friendships, as when Heinrich confesses to Hermann, "I've never been as fond of anyone as I am of you," to which Hermann replies, "with girls it's all so empty, so loveless."[39] The last words of the play are spoken by rabbit-sized Peter, who arrives onstage only when the others are out of sight. He misses his dead mother so badly, he says, that he wants to die—which, at the play's conclusion, he does. Was this Robert's "something from within"?

Robert's far more stylized and mannered second dramatic effort, *Poets* (*Dichter*), depicts five poets who respond in five different ways to the news that one of their number has died. The sole female poet, a sort of grand dame—a similar figure appears in *The Lads*—relates a dream in which an "attractive, slender youth" appears to her and begins passionately kissing her hand page boy–style, with "his red lips that laughed in his face like two pages of an open book," an image that is repeated a moment later when a group of hundreds of lads buzzes around her, kissing all available parts of her body, with the same open-book lips.[40] Walser reprised this image in later works, such as "Simon: A Love Story" (1903), presenting an Ackeretesque love triangle.

Though not among Walser's finest achievements, *Poets* stands out as an example of fin-de-siècle proto-expressionist veneration of art and the artist, with its sweet, often schmaltzy figures of speech always buttressed by the earnest conviction that the pursuit of poetry and art is a noble enterprise worth suffering for, albeit one that endangers its practitioner. Oskar, the most earnest of the poets, declares, "What can I do with feelings but let them thrash and die like fish in the sand of language?"[41] What indeed?

Cinderella (*Aschenbrödel*), another short play, soon followed, adding a new twist to an old fairy tale. There's no ball; instead, the prince glimpses Cinderella in her servant's garb and falls in love with her just as she is, scorning her two haughty and unkind sisters whose beauty is marred by their unpleasant characters. This Cinderella is a clever, complexly argumentative girl who insists she cannot marry the prince because if he gives her every luxury she might wish for, he will take from her the pleasure of being able to dream of these things. In lieu of a fairy godmother, a mysterious character makes a grand appearance, announcing, "I'm Fairytale, out of whose lips / Comes forth all that is spoken here."[42] Fairytale gives the girl an elegant gown and shoes, cautioning her not to put on airs with them. Cinderella's power is one of renunciation. By submitting cheerfully to her sisters' bad treatment, she asserts her right to determine her own experience; and when she acquiesces to the prince's marriage proposal, she weeps both because she is being compelled and because she is happy to comply. A gender-bending trio of girls dressed as page boys exclaim how titillating they find their garb. The play's metrical verse and archaic vocabulary (*wohlan, frägt, ein lustiges Jagdgefild*, etc.) recall the language of Goethe, Schiller, and Kleist, making the work feel linguistically top-heavy.

Walser's *Snow White* (*Schneewittchen*) is more successful in its playfulness, presenting a medley of self-reflexive variations on a theme and displaying intertextuality with, among other works, Kleist's play *Penthesilea*. Walter Benjamin would proclaim it "one of the most profound compositions in recent literature."[43] The play opens with the Queen asking a freshly back-from-the-dead Snow White whether she's feeling ill. This Queen is the girl's mother (no stepmothers here). Soon the Prince, enflamed by the sight of the Queen and Huntsman embracing, decides to court the Queen himself. The characters retell their stories several times, trying out different versions. In one, Snow White denies the Prince ever kissed her; in another, the Queen coaxes the Huntsman to reenact the scene of Snow White's attempted murder, demanding the girl's slaughter so vehemently it seems more than make-believe. Several characters later conspire to persuade the King he hasn't been cuckolded. As in *Cinderella,* the original tale is repeatedly and self-reflexively referred to and subverted. As the Huntsman declares:

> The poisoned apple is untrue,
> Poison the lie which so asserts.
> This venomous assertion is
> Plump and enticing like a fruit
> Swelled with seductive glamour, but
> So made inside that he who dares
> To taste of it is stricken ill.[44]

Both fairy tale plays were accepted for publication in *Die Insel*—which had continued to publish Robert's poetry—in 1901. *Cinderella* appeared in the June issue, and *Snow White* in September, followed by *The Lads* in June 1902. *Cinderella* was the first Walser work to be reviewed. Robert may or may not have known that the anonymous reviewer for the August 4, 1901, issue of the Sunday supplement to the *Allgemeine Schweizer Zeitung* was Otto Hinrichsen, the German medical student and aspiring writer he'd met through Franz Blei—and apparently had some sort of tiff with. The review praised the "lovely little work" for the "out-of-the-ordinary talent" expressed in its "uncommonly delicate, quiet lines" while also remarking that the work did not suggest the author's gifts extended beyond poetry to playwriting.[45]

In a letter that Robert—for the moment back in Thun—sent to Karl on September 22, 1900, he vows to do more serious play-writing in the near future: "I want to dramatize again very powerfully and very much and very soon. The droppings that fall from the arse of my imagination belong to you, if droppings of this sort are to your liking. I'm telling you, my imagination has the runs, maybe even the clap!!" He demonstrated his resolve with a dialogue between "Question" and "Answer" inserted in the letter. His handwriting is playful too: big curlicue letters sprawl all over the back of a photograph taken by his old friend Paul Renfer in his atelier in Biel. It shows Robert seated on a chair in a necktie and a three-piece suit perhaps not made for him: the sleeves seem too short for his long arms.

He hunches over, gazing inquisitively at the photographer with bright dark eyes rimmed by unusually heavy lower lids. His hair is cut straight across his forehead and sticks up at the crown in a cowlick. Robert used this as his author photo well into the 1920s, describing it as "the photo with all the hair" and "spectacularly well photographed." It's the first extant photograph we have of him since his confirmation picture. He looks very much the young poet, his gaze grave, his posture vaguely awkward.[46]

At some point between 1899 and 1902, Robert attempted a play that "came from within" even more than *The Lads*. *The Pond: Scenes* (*Der Teich. Szenen*)—which he never published—is Walser's only surviving work written in his actual mother tongue, Bernese German (the variety of Swiss German spoken in Biel). As an old man, he would remark to Carl Seelig that he "deliberately never wrote in dialect," which he saw as "an unseemly way of ingratiating oneself to the masses"; this one experiment was enough for him. In its language and subject matter, *The Pond* couldn't be more personal. Its child protagonist, Fritz Marti, is so convinced he is unloved by his mother, who frequently thrashes him for getting up to mischief, that he decides to put her to the test by faking his own suicide by drowning. His ruse succeeds: when he returns home, he finds his entire family in mourning. He expects a beating, but instead experiences a loving reconciliation with his mother, who regrets the "great, great injustice" she's done him. What a stunning feat of wish-fulfillment! Fritz has only two siblings in the play, Paul and Klara, but Walser gives the family his mother's maiden name (Marti) and the father the name of his own father, Adolf. And to his protagonist he gives his boyhood fear of being unloved by his mother.[47]

Shopping his short dramatic works around to book publishers more than a decade and a half after their composition, Walser referred to them as "short prose pieces in dialog form" and "theatrically fantastical plays, part in prose, part in verse." He never used the term "dramolette" now customary among Walser scholars. Instead, as he writes in 1918, describing a proposed volume of his collected plays, "It's an original work—saucy in parts, and daring, no doubt because of its youthfulness. Above all, it's full of verve and style and 'came from within.' Might you be interested?"[48]

He was learning new ways of withdrawing to safety when distress threatened, and his ever-more-distant childhood must have seemed as good a place as any to retreat to.

FIVE

The German Cities

1900–1903

IN NOVEMBER 1900, Robert set out by train for Munich, the grand capital of Bavaria in southern Germany, to meet the publishers of *Die Insel* who'd been so supportive of his work. He was excited to see this city he'd heard about from Karl. Unlike Protestant Zurich, where even the grandest buildings displayed their luxury with tasteful tact, Munich was home to the most elaborate palaces, fountains, pavilions, parks, and promenades designed on a regal scale. Once the seat of dukes and kings, Munich was relegated to secondary status in 1871, when the power of the new German Empire was consolidated in Berlin. It rebranded itself as a *Kunststadt,* or city of the arts. King Ludwig I had founded several museums, including the Glyptothek, for ancient sculpture, and, for art from the Middle Ages to the mid-eighteenth century, the Pinakothek.[1] His son Maximilian, a champion of the new iron-based architecture, bankrolled the Glass Palace, an enormous glass and metal structure large enough to house a full-sized fountain inside, and invited the public to experience the new building style of the industrial age.

Though much smaller than Berlin, Munich boasted a population of half a million by 1900, including as many as thirty thousand arts professionals. The painters and writers who flocked to the city around the turn of the century included Wassily Kandinsky, Paul Klee, Frank Wedekind, Thomas Mann, Stefan George, and Rainer Maria Rilke. In 1892, a group of modern-minded artists organized the breakaway Munich Secession—so influential that when the Berlin Secession assembled its first show in 1898, more than half the artists were from Munich.[2]

The new journals of literature and culture catering to these communities included *Jugend* (Youth), emphasizing the aesthetically pleasing aspects of modern culture; *Jugendstil,* the German equivalent of art nouveau, is named for it. The fiercely satirical magazine *Simplicissimus* took its title from the Baroque novel by Grimmelshausen. The cover of the February 13, 1897, *Simplicissimus* shows a large group of artists throttling, bludgeoning, and stabbing one another over a tiny sprig of laurel with the caption "Munich International Art Exhibition in the Glass Palace." A satirical poem about German kaiser Wilhelm II published in the journal by Wedekind under a pseudonym resulted in a six-month jail sentence on a charge of lèse-majesté.

The epicenter of all this literary activity was the tony bohemian Schwabing district, where Robert rented a room on Amalienstrasse. This was just around the corner from writer/artist hangouts Café Simplicissimus on Türkenstrasse and Café Stefanie (nicknamed Café Megalomania) at the corner of Theresienstrasse. In the cafés of Schwabing, impoverished writers brushed shoulders with the town's ubiquitous aristocrats, many of whom wore their wealth with unnerving self-assurance.

The editors of *Die Insel,* too, were part of Munich's comfortable classes, as quickly became clear when Robert set foot in the palatial four-story villa on Leopoldstrasse that housed *Die Insel*'s offices. Rudolf Alexander Schröder and Alfred Walter Heymel, both Robert's age, had rented the entire ground floor and were sharing an enormous apartment there financed by Heymel's inheritance. Their tastes extended to fancy modern sconces and custom-designed silver and chandeliers. They used English stoneware for appetizers, Sèvres or Bavarian porcelain for the main course, Venetian glass for white wine, and for red, silver renaissance goblets with gold-plated interiors. Furnishing their new digs cost them 115,000 marks, around $900,000 in today's dollars.[3]

Robert was certainly the odd man out in this circle. Franz Blei (who'd moved to Munich earlier that year) reports on a gathering in his apartment whose guests included Wedekind, who'd written a scandalous and as-yet-unperformed drama, *Spring Awakening.* Robert was seated across from the rocking chair that held the Blei family governess, a shy young Englishwoman. Suddenly Robert exclaimed to her, "You have the most beautiful feet," and no sooner had the words crossed his lips than he was cradling a foot in his hands, to the consternation of the girl as well as the rest of the party. Walser would later recall in two separate retellings that Wedekind took a lively interest in the young poet's cheap checked suit. And according to Blei's subsequent recollections, Robert asked Heymel whether he wouldn't like to hire him as a servant, but the petition came to naught since—as Blei reports—"it turned out he didn't know how to polish silver or press a top hat." In "Munich," a brief fictionalized account of his time in that city published in 1921, Walser writes of a "studio party" featuring storytelling and costumed guests ("a yodeling Tirolean," "a dagger-wearing Venetian"). Instead of participating in the festivities, the narrator reports, he busies himself with "kissing practice on the back of an artist's neck, to which she calmly submitted."[4]

Heymel took an immediate shine to the talented but roughhewn newcomer, while Schröder never quite warmed to him. Robert's pointedly unconventional behavior—compounded by his love of gaudy clothes—got on Schröder's nerves. He took it as an affectation, a way for Robert to make an impression in these intellectual and artistic circles despite his lack of education, money, and social graces. But even Schröder clearly admired Robert's work, as he wrote to Otto Bierbaum:

> In my opinion the most important material—by far the most important—we have published to date. The person himself [is] loathsome [. . .] but there's something here of what made Dante and Shakespeare great, a dark something [. . .] it's like a sort of beast of prey, the way he drives his words like claws into the thing he means to proclaim. [. . .] And in a mere 10 pages [he] manages to make great hearts admire and noble individuals adore him. If you or I ever succeed [. . .] in putting so much soul and so much greatness into a poem, then we'll have something to rejoice over.[5]

Others in the circle were better disposed toward Robert. Bierbaum was friendly from the start, and Robert hit it off with writer Max Dauthendey, a decade his senior, and his wife Annie; the couple invited him to visit them in Würzburg. He palled about a bit with illustrator and writer Alfred Kubin, with whom he visited Oktoberfest. Marcus Behmer, another *Insel* artist who'd befriended Karl during his stay in Munich, met Robert as well and found him far from eccentric:

> A tall, thin young man whose outward appearance, clothing, etc. made a thoroughly bourgeois-proper impression, and his

entire person and conduct displayed no sign of extravagance.
Friendly, engaging even, reticent, modest. I saw nothing of the
"Shakespeare enfant" that Bierbaum liked to refer to him as,
adopting Victor Hugo's epithet for the young Rimbaud, and
everything I felt for him in terms of personal liking and sympa-
thies might be a matter of my transferring the friendship I felt
for Karl to Robert. After all, I was well aware of the unusually
warm, intimate attachment between the two brothers.[6]

According to Walser's own literary representations of his time in Munich,
he was well-received in artistic society. The story "Munich" has its narrator
strolling contentedly about the English Garden with a walking stick and
spending time at the *Insel* offices where "surely from time to time baron-
esses put in an appearance, which I found fabulous. Alfred Walter Heymel
seemed to me the very model of elegance, and Rudolf Alexander Schröder
was, on the one hand, very kind, and on the other played the piano with all
conceivable elegance."[7] The narrator reports encounters with Kubin and
Behmer and that he read aloud six short stories at an *Insel* party to applause
from Bierbaum and criticism from others.

The 1915 story "Würzburg," however, registers a bit more discomfort:
"In Munich I'd gotten to know several literary personages of importance
quite well, but I experienced odd, oppressive feelings during their artistic
and literary gatherings, for which I was not in fact well-suited." It's certainly
true that the high style and general pomp in which Schröder and Heymel
lived contrasted starkly with Robert's own circumstances. Then there was
the fact that the taste of his new friends was not infallible. Yes, they printed
him, and other writers he admired, but they also published a great deal of
work he disapproved of. And he couldn't help but notice that others agreed.
The Berlin satirical journal *Lustige Blätter* (Funny Pages) published a parody of *Die Insel* in 1901 titled *Die Insel der Blödsinnigen* (The Island of
Idiots) containing spoofs of various authors published in the magazine, including Robert: one satirical poem compared a poet dreaming of immortal
fame while staring out a window to a dog dreaming of a sausage or a bone.[8]

"Würzburg" also describes a visit to Dauthendey. Despite the 175 or
so miles separating Munich from Würzburg, the story's narrator decides
to make the trip on foot. Most of what he tells us about the visit, though,
concerns clothes. His are frivolous-looking, and Dauthendey insists, after

some scolding, on supplying him with a high-collared shirt and suit from his own armoire.[9] This is followed by other acts of generosity on the part of this fatherly friend. At the end of the story, the narrator hits him up for train fare to Berlin.

Robert headed to Berlin in the summer of 1901 in real life as well. The city was still the elusive dream he'd attempted to chase in 1897, when he'd traveled there with big hopes and schemes, only to retreat in fewer than three weeks' time, finding the metropolis inhospitable. But now things were different. He was no longer just a young clerk with artistic ambitions; he was a published poet, one whose work had appeared not just in his native Switzerland, but in Austria and Germany as well, including in one of the most fashionable new journals of the day. His Swiss accent still signified "hayseed" to Prussian ears, but now he had an ace up his sleeve: Karl was in Berlin, and his brother was a master at making contacts and connections wherever he went.

Berlin was hopping. The city had undergone a period of intense growth during the final decades of the nineteenth century—its population swelled to two million by 1900—and was the site of one of Europe's liveliest high societies. While factories had bred slums in the city's northern and eastern districts, the elegance of several of its neighborhoods rivaled that of Paris. Like Paris, Berlin sported grand avenues swirling with activity. Potsdamer Platz, Berlin's busiest square, was a tangle of pedestrians, horse-drawn carriages, automobiles, omnibuses, and electric streetcars. There were theaters everywhere—thirty-seven by the 1920s—not to mention the cabarets for which the city would become famous. People hurried in and out of newfangled restaurants designed for rapid service where one ate standing up. In 1902, Berlin got its first subway line two years before New York. Industrialized modernity soon became the city's trademark.[10]

Karl had been in Berlin on and off since late May 1899. After several years of apprenticeship as a theatrical set designer, it made sense that he should move to a city full of stages, particularly one where he wasn't already known as another designer's factotum. His first professional opportunity, however, turned out not to be in theater: he started designing book covers for publisher Bruno Cassirer in 1901. Meeting Cassirer and his cousin Paul was the stroke of luck that set Karl on the path to the career success he'd been dreaming of when he headed north.

Bruno and Paul Cassirer belonged to an extended family of industrialists; their fathers co-owned a factory that manufactured electrical cables. They went into business together in 1898, opening a publishing house and gallery that showed the work of the Berlin Secession artists (including Max Liebermann, Lovis Corinth, Max Beckmann, Max Slevogt, Käthe Kollwitz, and Walter Leistikow). The cousins parted ways in August 1901 following a quarrel, with each taking half the business. Paul, now running the gallery on his own, became Germany's first art dealer to display the work of the French impressionists, bringing him to the notice of Kaiser Wilhelm, who expressed his displeasure at "this Cassirer who wants to bring us that filthy French art."[11] Bruno, meanwhile, was making his way in publishing and in 1902 began printing the influential art journal *Kunst und Künstler* (Art and Artists). Karl Walser book covers soon became a signature of his publishing house. Karl's work was also shown in the Secession's spring 1902 exhibition, and he became a full member the following year. But most of this hadn't happened yet when he welcomed his younger brother to Berlin in the late summer of 1901.

The Berlin Secession's third annual exhibition, which Karl took Robert to see, was an impressive show wild enough to scandalize art lovers with classical tastes. It included five paintings by Vincent van Gogh, a pair of Pissarros, a portrait study by Franz von Stuck, two paintings by Käthe Kollwitz, two by Lovis Corinth, eight by Swiss painter Arnold Böcklin, and a plaster cast of one of Rodin's citizens of Calais. Decades later, Walser wrote a poem titled "Renoir" in which he recalls visiting this exhibition and describes Renoir's painting *Lise with a Parasol* as "possess[ing] an enchantingly mellow tone."[12]

Robert took in both the art and his brother's excitement over it. He also observed how hard Karl was struggling to find a professional foothold in the German capital even as he amassed an impressive body of work. And Karl had so much more to show for himself than Robert did. To be respected as a writer in Berlin would clearly take more than just a few published poems and short plays. It would take a book. By November 1, Robert was back in Zurich writing one.

Fritz Kocher's Essays is a collection of short texts masquerading as the school assignments of a boy who died tragically young. The concept had a great deal to recommend it. For one thing, it was material that "came from within": Robert had been a master of the school essay as a pupil;

indeed, he is said to have written essays "on commission" for classmates of Lisa who were several years older than him.[13] And so the feuilleton path he had set off on when he wrote "Lake Greifen" was essentially a continuation of his earliest essayistic practice. For someone who'd only ever written short pieces, this was a perfect way to compose a coherent book one section at a time.

For his writer's abode, Robert chose a Zurich alleyway, renting a small apartment facing the rear courtyard at Trittligasse 6, where the south-facing windows let in a bit of light. Channeling the persona of young Fritz Kocher for this mischievous and appealingly lighthearted book was not without its ironies. The young author of these essays—as Walser reports in a preface, posing as the book's editor—died shortly after leaving school. Unlike Robert, who began an apprenticeship at age fourteen, Fritz is a wealthy lad who "wouldn't want to be poor, I'd be ashamed to death," and boasts that his father owns carriages and horses. Poverty, in his opinion, has no positive attributes at all, not even that of softening the hearts of the rich—on the contrary, it only makes one "hard and cruel."[14] Walser takes pains to create a teenage persona distinct from himself, an ironic reflection on the realities of his own childhood.

Young Fritz has an unapologetically fanciful imagination and cultivates an earnestness that at times appears risibly overblown. "The teacher sits at his desk like a hermit between high cliffs," he writes, describing his schoolroom; "the blackboards are black, unfathomable lakes." He can also wax playful, as when he remarks in an essay titled "Autumn," "When everything's so white, we write our lessons so much better," taking advantage of the German homonym *weiss* (meaning either "white" or a conjugation of "to know"). Besides his love of a good turn of phrase, young Fritz shares other characteristics with his author: he's from Biel and mentions not only going to see Schiller's play *The Robbers* ("a wonderful play, full of fire and gorgeousness") but discussing it with his brother. Fritz's name is borrowed from a classmate of Robert's at the *Progymnasium*.[15]

Robert spent all of November in Zurich writing and rewriting these essays. He tried out a range of styles and formats, with topics ranging from the meaty ("Poverty," "Music," "Nature," "Friendship," "The Fatherland") to the slight ("My Mountain," "The Classroom"). One piece, titled "Instead of an Essay," purports to be a letter received from the narrator's brother. Others (e.g., "The Fire") are as self-reflexive as "Lake Greifen."

Displaying a penchant for precision that might be cultivated by one who has spent long months filling ledger columns, Robert made the book's twenty sections almost exactly the same in length. He copied out each section in a tidy hand, stacking up the pages on his table until the manuscript was three-dimensional. A short book, yes—each of the essays was only two pages long—but a book all the same. In early December, he put the pages in a suitcase and bought a train ticket back to Berlin to sell it.

Given Karl's relationship with the Cassirer cousins, it was a natural first step to offer *Fritz Kocher's Essays* to Bruno Cassirer, sweetening the deal with the promise of illustrations by Karl. Cassirer, however, proved unreceptive. Perhaps on Bierbaum's advice—he was in Berlin working on a literary cabaret project—Robert fired off a letter to Rudolf von Poellnitz, newly in charge of the publishing house *Die Insel* had launched that October. "I unfortunately find myself in rather grievous financial straits," Robert writes, offering *Die Insel* the rights to his complete works to date for 200 marks (roughly $1,500 in today's dollars).[16] But Poellnitz wasn't interested, and neither, apparently, was anyone else. With no one willing to invest in his career on the basis of what he'd written so far, Robert turned tail and retreated back to Switzerland—for the third time since he'd started seriously pursing this plan to become a writer.

Back in Zurich, Robert sounded discouraged in a letter he addressed to Widmann on February 3, 1902, saying that his trips to Germany had taught him that he couldn't possibly be a writer given his faulty education. He asks Widmann to hire him for clerical tasks like copying manuscripts. Writing a bit passive-aggressively, Robert adds that he would greatly prefer this sort of occupation over "going around hitting people up for money." Fortunately for Robert, Widmann had other ways of helping and was still interested in doing so. Beginning in March 1902, Widmann began publishing the Fritz Kocher essays six or seven at a time in the Sunday supplement of *Der Bund,* eventually printing all of them. His support gave Robert both the resolve to continue writing and a little something to live on meanwhile. That spring, Robert produced a new series of ten short essays, collected under the title "The Clerk," that Widmann published in June, followed by Robert's first proper story (published in July/August), "A Painter" ("Ein Maler").[17]

Like the Fritz Kocher essays, "A Painter" begins with the artifice of a disclaimer: "These pages from a painter's notebook chanced to fall into

my hands, as the saying goes," the "editor" remarks, after which the
painter himself declares, "When I have finished filling these pages, I shall
burn them." Seemingly inspired by Karl's romance with Flora Ackeret, the
story is narrated by an artist who has been invited by a countess (!)—"an
exceptionally kind, cultivated woman whose acquaintance I made in the
capital"—to paint in solitude in and around her villa, which stands far
removed from society amid a mountainous landscape.[18] He paints her and
they fall in love, until being loved comes to feel oppressive and he hits the
road. The story was both a departure from Robert's previous work and a
step beyond it. His first extended narrative with (albeit minimal) plot and
structure, it was also the first to contain detailed character studies. The
painter analyzes himself, his patroness, and a sickly poet who comes to
stay with them—the narrator paints his portrait too, both literally and
figuratively—while musing on the interrelation of nature and art. Like Fritz
Kocher, this narrator has an idiosyncratic, often mock-naive way of speaking. And the story is oddly episodic, a series of present-tense reports and
tableaus suggesting that the actual story is taking place behind the scenes.

Robert sent Widmann "A Painter" not from Zurich, but from the
return address "Schoolhouse, Täuffelen on Lake Biel." Lisa had been
teaching in this rural lakeside village since the fall of 1900. Having virtually
raised her younger siblings during the years of their mother's illness, she
had now completed her formal training for a job that was, in a sense, a
continuation of that labor. The maternal role she'd assumed from an early
age gave her a gravity and dignity that Robert revered. A fellow teacher
described her as a "pretty little sorceress from Biel," saying she always
took things hard but liked it when you succeeded in teasing a laugh from
her.[19] Even though Lisa and Robert were only four years apart in age, their
relationship was shaped by the role she'd played in his upbringing. She
was one of a series of women in his life who fascinated him with their authority and the gentleness with which they asserted it, a potent combination of grace and power.

When Lisa invited Robert to share her small two-room apartment in
the rear of the schoolhouse, it meant fixing a makeshift bed with a borrowed straw mattress in what had been her sitting room and kitchen, allowing for little privacy in the evenings. During the day, on the other hand,
while she was busy teaching, Robert was free to sit in her rooms and write,
or go for walks. Life in the country was cheaper than in town, so it didn't

matter so much that he had almost nothing in his pocket, and the payments Widmann sent for his essays seemed a windfall. Half a dozen years later, when Walser published his first novel, *The Tanners* (*Geschwister Tanner*), he included three chapters in which a young man at loose ends moves in with his older sister, a teacher, in a schoolhouse much like the one in Täuffelen.

In the novel, it is winter when Simon Tanner appears. Then spring arrives and the schoolchildren bring so many bouquets of snowdrops to school that his sister, Hedwig, runs out of containers to place them in. Simon has offered his clerical services to several notaries, but none of them needs a copyist, so he is left to idly wander the region, daydream, and finally write an essay, "Life in the Country," that he sends off for publication. He helps Hedwig around the house, preparing their cocoa in the mornings and tea in the evenings, and the two become so close that she confesses to him how much of a burden her life as a teacher has become to her. She's desperate to escape and eventually does.

After three months with Lisa, Robert returned to Zurich, taking a room on Spiegelgasse, one street over from Trittligasse where he'd lived in November. This time, short on funds (he'd borrowed money from Lisa), he took a furnished room for 18 francs a month, lodging with the family of a cobbler to whom he soon took a dislike. He urgently needed a new day job to shore up his finances, but, dismayingly, he couldn't find one. This experience was new to him. The unemployment rate in Zurich had been rising, and with his now-spotty employment record, he was less employable than when he'd first arrived in town two years earlier. He even placed a classified ad in *Neue Zürcher Zeitung:* "Young writer seeks position as secretary, travel companion, or for reading aloud," but nothing came of it. He wrote to Lisa asking her not to return the straw bed he'd slept on in Täuffelen, saying he wasn't sure how much longer he'd be able to hold out in Zurich.[20]

Then he discovered the Copyists' Office for the Unemployed, a bureau where jobless scribes could be hired by the day to perform tasks like hand-addressing stacks of envelopes for a bank's correspondence. The office had opened in December 1901 to address unemployment and because a number of firms had discovered that it was cheaper to contract out this labor than hire full-time clerks. For the rest of that spring and summer and into the fall, Robert was a frequent presence there, copying out "mountains of addresses." He briefly held other short-term positions during this period—including a few weeks in the business office of the Escher-Wyss turbine and machine factory and a stint as a domestic servant for an "elegant Jewish lady"—but these were temporary positions, odd jobs. At least he soon found somewhere better to live: a friendly neighbor in his building, Ida Weiss, had a room to let, allowing him to abandon his cobbling landlord. Weiss, a widow, indulged the young writer and was patient when he fell behind on his rent.[21]

Meanwhile, he went on writing and regularly publishing short pieces in the Sunday supplement of *Der Bund* while pursuing other opportunities. He responded to a query he'd received while still in Täuffelen, sent by poet and *Insel* contributor Richard Dehmel, who was editing an anthology of literature for children. Robert wrote to him in May, sending him one short piece and apologizing that he didn't have more to offer. In August he sent three more, and Dehmel accepted two: "The Maid" and "The Man with the Pumpkin Head," to be published together as "Two Strange Stories about Death." Both gruesome little tales end with the deaths of their protagonists and the (perhaps more cruel than comforting) reassurance that life goes on even after someone has died.[22]

Robert requested 50 marks for these stories—in line with what he'd been paid by *Die Insel*. That sort of sum didn't go far. On October 5, 1902, he wrote to his younger sister, Fanny, complaining of being "unemployed, accursedly unemployed" and saying he'll probably have to "become a servant again and beat carpets and serve the grub. Much better than being a clerk anyhow." He reports that he's stopped writing since he's been unable to get anything published recently. "At present," he adds, "I'm pretty much living on nothing at all. Which at least is interesting." Asking her to lend him something to read, maybe some Zola, he promises to buy her something later in return, "a cloak for the theater or a pair of Parisian shoes."[23]

Unlike other archived Walser letters, this one's lines do not extend to the margins of the page; instead, a tidy rectangle of text floats in the middle, nicely centered and written in smaller handwriting than was usual for him. It's the first surviving example of Walser focusing on the graphic/ geometrical presentation of a handwritten text. He seems to be trying to produce a perfectly symmetrical block of writing. When his final greeting doesn't quite reach to the end of the last line, he adds two extra words, "grüsse Hermann" (greetings to Hermann)—Fanny was now living with their brother—before signing his name.[24]

The following February Robert landed a temporary position he decided to leave town for, even though the job—in the office of an elastic factory in nearby Winterthur—was poorly paid. The monthly salary, 125 francs, was exactly what he'd earned when he first moved to Zurich seven years earlier. But he needed the money, so he took it. He was now almost twenty-five years old and still at the bottom of the office hierarchy. Meanwhile, his older brother Oscar, whom he and Karl had always teased for his petit-bourgeois demeanor, had been steadily working his way up the banking ladder. Oscar's success made Robert wonder whether he'd made the right choice by abandoning financial security to be a writer. How could he continue to write if he couldn't afford to live? He hadn't managed to establish himself in Zurich, a city whose cultural community he wished to belong to. Winterthur had less to recommend it other than a landscape of rolling hills perfect for Sunday walks. Robert was once again lodging with an older woman while taking his meals at a hostel that catered to young pupils at the Technical Institute.[25] It wasn't ideal, but was acceptable in the short term; and when this position ended, he had a temporary reprieve from making plans, courtesy of the Swiss government. It was time for his military service.

All male Swiss citizens at that time were required to undergo military training followed by periodic "refresher courses"; if the country were to be attacked, more than one-third of the population could be mustered rapidly for its defense. Ordinarily Robert would have been called up for his initial forty-five-day training at age twenty. But with his various well-timed trips abroad, he had been able to defer his stint at "recruit school" until after his twenty-fifth birthday. Now he presented himself at the army barracks on the northern outskirts of Bern on May 15, 1903, where he would train as an infantryman until June 30.

An athletic walker, Robert found the physical exertions of military training less stressful than some of his fellow recruits did. He was older than most, though, and many of the calisthenics were new to him; so were digging trenches, carrying out maneuvers in formation, shooting, and of course being required to live in barracks, subject to the army's many rules.[26] Some aspects of this training—such as the long hours, the endless repetition of the same tasks, and the insistence on regularity and accuracy—resembled his apprenticeship at the bank. But the exigencies of a clerk's life were no match for the army's constant observation and instruction in every aspect of the work, with the goal of subtracting every last trace of individuality that might mar the smoothly functioning whole.

At least Robert encountered an acquaintance who quickly became a friend: Fritz Probst, Lisa's fellow teacher in Täuffelen. Unfortunately, Fritz fell ill three weeks into training and was sent home. But until then, Robert had a proper companion in the barracks who frequently met him in the evenings after dinner in the mess hall. Militärgarten, the restaurant directly opposite the barracks, had a garden where one could sit outdoors on warm spring nights eating slices of apricot tart and smoking until it was time to run back across the street for lights-out.[27]

Robert was good at military service in spite of himself. When he completed the training session, his name was added to a list of candidates recommended for noncommissioned officer training, though he never pursued the opportunity, which would have made even less sense to him than a banking career. He would have ample opportunity to play at soldiering in any case: under Swiss law, he still had four sixteen-day refresher courses ahead of him over the next two years.[28]

After the completion of his military training at the end of June, Robert joined his brother Hermann for what was described in Hermann's diary as a hike "across the hills of Arni-Landiswyl for the dedication of the Leuenberger monument in Rüderwyl."[29] Hermann had just published an informational booklet on Swiss geography that was being distributed to schools across the country along with the official government wall map, and he was every bit as enthusiastic a walker as Robert. During their hike, Hermann shared stories about the regions they passed through as they rambled up and down the hilly Emmental countryside. Perhaps their conversation inspired Robert's prose piece "The Forest," which he published that August in the Sunday supplement of *Der Bund*. The young narrator of "The Forest" resembles Fritz Kocher as he ponders the relation of topography to social development: "At school we had an old teacher with an enormous head who told us that in a relatively very short time all of Central Europe would become one huge forest if civilization were to retreat."[30] Was Robert imagining what it would feel like to sit in a classroom where his brother was lecturing?

Robert certainly understood that Hermann disapproved of his impractical—not to say frivolous—life choices. Who in his right mind would
give up steady employment at a bank, during a period when entry-level
jobs were becoming rare commodities, and instead devote his life to writing? Robert knew it was difficult for Hermann to understand why he was
content to live like a pauper in squalid furnished rooms. But perhaps the
dutiful teacher and geographer who was still helping to support his father
and youngest sister secretly envied Robert the freedom that came with not
worrying so much about security and the future. Robert spoke with pride
about all the works he'd been publishing, and those he intended to write.
He didn't need to be a banker or even a bank clerk to be happy. He might
be content to be a servant—should it come to that—if it meant he could go
on writing. There was a joy and strength to not expecting, or even desiring, too much.

SIX

The First Published Book

1903–1905

HAVING TURNED TWENTY-FIVE just before reporting for basic
training, Robert was no longer a young man, as the difficulties he'd experienced job-hunting had brought home to him. He would no longer have
the luxury of hopping easily from one position to another while taking
time off in between to pursue his literary endeavors. As for those endeavors—a handful of stories and essays in literary journals along with various
poems—what did they add up to? Without a book to his name, it was hard
to see how he could escape this endless cycle of debt and worry. He'd sa-
vored his "sweet freedom," as he wrote to Fanny when his military training
came to an end ("Only in freedom do our thoughts blossom"). But now
he'd taken a new furnished room on Froschaugasse in Zurich and
was going to have to pay rent on it. In a letter to Lisa, he described his job
hunt as "frenetic." He was again spending many of his days at the Copyists' Office for the Unemployed. So, when an opportunity for salaried employment presented itself, he quickly accepted.[1]

On July 28, 1903, Robert boarded a train that meandered along the
shore of Lake Zurich for the better part of an hour before stopping in
Wädenswil. The once idyllic lakeside village surrounded by orchards and
vineyards had grown into a town of seventy-five hundred when industrialization arrived in the form of a large textile mill and a housing development
for workers.[2] Soon, manufacturing outweighed agriculture as the main
source of wealth—a prosperity visible in the elegant villas that sprang up,
some as grand as those in Zurich. One in particular, the Villa zum Abendstern (Villa of the Evening Star), stood high on the hill overlooking the
town. It was set in a lovely garden, and a copper cupola had been added to
its distinctive square tower by the man who purchased the villa in 1902.

97

Carl Dubler-Grässle—an ambitious thirty-two-year-old mechanical engineer and inventor who'd come into an inheritance—started his own business in the villa's basement offices. The private room designated for use by his live-in assistant was at the top of the tower, its windows in three directions providing excellent views of the lake and the wooded hills on its opposite shore. Robert was to remain a member of this household and commercial enterprise for nearly half a year.

The novel Walser wrote about this episode in his life—*The Assistant* (*Der Gehülfe*), published in 1908—features many details drawn from Dubler's life and career. Mechanical inventions attributed in the novel to the character Carl Tobler correspond to real-life patents filed by Dubler. The "Advertising Clock," for example, designed to be displayed at train stations, consisted of a clock-face framed by a pair of stylized wings upon which slogans or the names of businesses could be painted. But while the fictional Tobler is unable to find investors for his clock, much less sell any, Carl Dubler successfully marketed his invention, which was installed at stations along the Wetzikon-Meilen electric tramway. Other Dubler inventions included a vending machine for bullets (for use at Switzerland's many marksmanship competitions) and a steam-release valve—both described in the novel.[3]

The Assistant is a story of decline. All of Tobler's inventions result in failure, and Tobler's wife repeatedly expresses her sadness at the prospect of having to leave behind the family's life of bourgeois comfort. Joseph Marti, the assistant of the novel's title, has his hands full writing and publishing classified ads in search of "capitalists" willing to invest in Tobler's enterprises (such ads were often found in newspapers of the time) and brushing off angry creditors. The novel's dramatic arc follows Tobler's rapidly approaching bankruptcy. He never pays his assistant's wages, threatening him angrily instead, and Joseph departs after nearly half a year in the villa—as did Robert, just after New Year's Day, the Dublers' financial collapse echoing his own parents' descent into poverty.

The novel departs decisively from reality in one important aspect, however. The assistant in the book lacks ambition. Like Robert, he is a young clerk (Walser subtracted a year from his own age to make him twenty-four) who takes refuge in the same Copyists' Office for the Unemployed. Being referred to Tobler by the director of this office represents a serious professional opportunity for him. Tobler's failure to pay Joseph's salary bothers him mainly because he owes back rent to a kind Zurich landlady. Otherwise, we learn little about his aspirations beyond his hope to someday achieve financial stability. He does appear to have inchoate literary inclinations, though: he loves to read and, on one occasion, composes a little essay out of boredom. The essay's subject is "Bad Habits"— the worst of which is thinking too much. After half a page, he throws away his draft and sets off in search of better entertainment.[4]

By contrast, Robert's literary ambitions remained unchanged during his stay in Wädenswil. His story "The Forest" appeared in the Sunday supplement of *Der Bund* shortly after he took up his new post. We don't know whether the Dublers realized there was a writer in their midst. While Robert spent his days down in the "technical office" taking dictation from Carl Dubler, at night, in the privacy of his tower room, he worked to further his writing career. He renewed his correspondence with Franz Blei in hopes of writing for a new journal, *Der Spiegel* (The Mirror), that Blei had spoken of wanting to start now that *Die Insel* had folded, foiled by its production costs. The new journal never came about. But, on Blei's recommendation, Robert submitted a book proposal to Rudolf von Poellnitz, who was still running the Insel publishing house in Leipzig even after the demise of the journal that had inspired it.[5]

Robert's proposed collection comprised a few short plays, a selection of thirty to forty poems, "Fritz Kocher's Essays," short prose pieces that had appeared in *Die Insel,* and several newer stories: "Countess Kirke: A Fantasy," "Brentano: A Fantasy," "Simon: A Love Story," "Mehlmann," and "Strange City." Poellnitz declared himself willing to consider a collection of short prose pieces, to appear in April 1904, and Robert promised to send him "Fritz Kocher's Essays" and "two other small things" (possibly "Two Strange Stories about Death") directly from Charlottenburg— meaning that he'd left them with Karl for safekeeping—and also suggested that the drama *Cinderella* might fit well in the collection.[6] He excluded his more experimental *Snow White* as well as "Lake Greifen."

Several weeks after Robert's departure from Wädenswil, Carl Dubler filed for bankruptcy. The name Robert Walser appears on the list of seventy-six creditors to whom Dubler owed money, but the former assistant never submitted a claim for repayment of this debt. "He loved this man with all his heart," Walser wrote in *The Assistant* to explain why his protagonist stayed so long in Wädenswil despite Tobler's mistreatment. Perhaps Robert

felt the same about Dubler. Perhaps Dubler was—like Tobler—an overdra-
matic bully, but he demonstrated what could be achieved by determination,
at least in the short term. Life was not kind to Carl Dubler, however. After
the collapse of his business, his wife filed for divorce, and his children became wards of the state. Dubler moved back to Zurich, took a job as a ma-
chinist, and died in his early fifties.[7]

Back in Zurich at the beginning of 1904, Robert restarted his job
search and this time found a position as a clerk in Zurich Cantonal Bank's
elegant offices on Bahnhofstrasse. He was one of approximately forty
clerks at the bank, where he toiled in a large room with dozens of desks
crammed together side by side, all occupied by overworked scribes. He
applied the bank's official rubber stamp to a sheet of paper on which he
wrote a letter to his sister Fanny, framing the circular impression with the
words, "Behold this sun! But it is a sun that makes one cold and unhappy!"
At least the pay was good: 2,000 francs a year (roughly $25,500 in today's
dollars). He wasn't the best-paid clerk, nor the worst. In fact, his salary was
only 300 francs a year less than his brother Hermann would receive as a
low-ranking professor five years later. He seemed to have succeeded in
inserting himself back into the ranks of regularly employed individuals. He
was even able, after beginning this job, to rent a small apartment of his own
again on Trittligasse: two small rooms comprising (as he later reported in
a biographical note) a "most charming, summerhouse-like apartment."[8]

If nothing else, Walser's stint as Dubler's assistant appears to have
taught him how to advocate for himself more forcefully in the letters he
wrote to potential publishers. He still needed a published book to advance
his career and escape the mindless drudgery of the copyist's desk. When
Poellnitz didn't respond promptly to his proposal, he sent several follow-
up notes, eventually also suggesting that his book might be illustrated by
his famous brother, who "writes to me that he intends to 'do the very best
work he has done up till now.' "[9] The hard sell was effective, and when
Poellnitz asked to see a sample drawing, Robert got Karl to submit an illustration for "Simon: A Love Story" depicting a young man serenading a
woman on a balcony.

It was admittedly awkward that Robert still needed the boost Karl's
name could lend. Karl was now working on a project that would take his
career to new heights: creating sets for Berlin's top theater director, Max
Reinhardt, for a production of Johann Nestroy's 1842 comedy *He Wants*

to Go on a Spree. Karl was also designing most of Bruno Cassirer's book covers—including, that year alone, volumes by Flaubert, Gorky, and Wedekind—along with having his work featured in the journals *Das Theater* and *Kunst und Künstler* (both published by Cassirer) and *Die Neue Rundschau* (The New Review, published by Samuel Fischer). He was nonetheless willing to help out his little brother.[10]

After Robert offered up Karl to Poellnitz on February 24, 1904, he waited and waited for a response. March came and went; he trudged impatiently across the river every morning, heading for a workplace he found stultifying, where everyone assumed he had a copyist's heart. The snow melted atop the Uetliberg and rain showers drenched the city, soon giving way to the desiccating, headache-inducing foehn wind blowing off the Alps. April arrived, and still no word. Robert's mood darkened as yellow and purple jonquils poked out of the mud in family gardens. On April 11, he wrote Fanny a chirpy letter about writing fairy tales to be published by a fairy-tale press, adding that "Robert Walser is weak and unhappy, because he's a fool." Two days later he wrote a much gloomier postcard to Flora Ackeret saying he wasn't doing particularly well and adding the glum postscript, "Well, be in good health, or at least stay alive."[11]

By the end of April, still not having heard from Poellnitz, he sought the assistance of Franz Blei, who suggested he get in touch with his old friend Alfred Heymel. Heymel owned the majority of Insel's shares and was officially the outfit's publisher, with Poellnitz its managing director, making Heymel Poellnitz's boss. Just as Robert had learned to do when courting investors for Carl Dubler, he fired off a pair of carefully worded letters. The first, addressed to Poellnitz, asked whether he couldn't give at least some sort of provisional answer, or at the very least confirm receipt of Karl's drawing. A postscript noted that he was also writing Heymel at Blei's suggestion. He wrote far more cordially to Heymel, asking whether Heymel agreed that the addition of Karl's illustrations would be quite an asset.[12]

Going over Poellnitz's head did the trick. On May 14, Poellnitz wrote to Robert apologizing for the delay and explaining that he hadn't yet found the time to read all the pieces Robert had published in *Die Insel*. He asked Robert to send him a list of all the pieces he'd like to include in the volume—something Robert had already done six months earlier, but never mind. Robert prepared a revised table of contents; the volume he now envisioned contained short prose and the two short plays *Poets* and *Cinderella*. Soon Poellnitz replied with an even more favorable counteroffer: Insel would print a 240-page volume of short prose priced at 3–4 marks, to be followed by a slimmer book of poems and then one of plays. The initial volume would contain "Fritz Kocher's Essays," "The Clerk," "A Painter," and "The Forest." Robert enthusiastically concurred. The book's length, he pointed out, would be easy to calculate once the typesetter began work, as all these pieces were composed of sections "exactly the same length": "Fritz Kocher's Essays" had twenty sections, "The Clerk" ten, "A Painter" fifteen, and "The Forest" ten.[13]

In June, Karl came to Switzerland for two weeks and spent some of this time visiting Robert to hash out plans for the volume. On his advice, Robert wrote to Poellnitz requesting a smaller format and for the book to be set in very small Fraktur (black letter) type. This was the start of a long series of design conversations Walser would engage in with his publishers over the years. Eventually they compromised on a midsized Fraktur, as Poellnitz was afraid the "eye dust" Robert proposed would put off readers. Robert may have hoped that each of the book's sections would fit precisely on a two-page spread, the same design-conscious impulse that made him ensure that a letter to his sister formed a perfect rectangle.

November came, and Robert returned to Bern for the first of the refresher courses that would remain part of his military training for years. At least it got him out of the office and outdoors for a while. He was all impatience by the time the book *Fritz Kocher's Essays* finally appeared in late November 1904, just in time for Christmas. Insel had decided to make a splash with this authorial debut by publishing it in three different beautifully designed editions: a leather-bound, gold-stamped "luxury edition"; a soft-cover volume with a Karl Walser landscape on the cover; and a less expensive paperback that mimicked the leather-bound copy's design. The book featured eleven illustrations by Karl, including a portrait of a Robert-like clerk gazing out an office window, a classroom with a map on its front wall, and an elegant woman sitting for her portrait.

Widmann quickly chimed in with elaborate praise for both the essays and Karl's drawings in the Sunday supplement of *Der Bund,* though he ended his review by noting that the book's author was not "in Berlin, working on becoming a salon poet" but instead was "employed as a bank clerk in Zurich and is by no means acting the Pegasus snorting impatiently in his yoke but rather is perfectly content, in the manner of people who can wait until their time comes." What was that supposed to mean? The unnecessary remark, misrepresenting Robert as a writer devoid of ambition, detracted from Widmann's praise of the "revelations—both delicate and filled with life—of an incredibly fine-turned sensibility that responds to every stimulus" and uses artfully feigned naiveté to "ironize the poetry of pathos."[14]

Just before Christmas, *Neue Zürcher Zeitung* included the book in a column of recommended holiday gifts, with a review signed "F.M." that was less than insightful, calling the "thin fiction" of dead pupil Fritz Kocher a "somewhat naïve attempt at hiding on the author's part." But the reviewer praised the book's accomplished nature descriptions and sharp observations and commentary and recommended this work by a "talented beginner." The next review that came in, on January 21, was even less helpful. Johannes Schlaf wrote in *Das Neue Magazin* that the book didn't work because he could see through the conceit and conclude that the essays weren't written by a child.[15] This was the beginning of a long tradition of reviewers overlooking Walser's ironic position that invited readers to enjoy the fiction of the child narrator while at the same time seeing through it.

Publishing *Fritz Kocher's Essays* in late 1904 made Robert reconsider his circumstances once more. Insel had paid only 250 marks for the book (about $1,800 in today's dollars), including the fee for Karl, who generously declined his cut. This was less than two months' salary at the bank. On the other hand, if he was going to be a writer, he had to write—and not just to disprove Widmann's remark about his supposed complacency. *Fritz Kocher's Essays* contained only pieces written more than a year earlier. Recently he hadn't found enough time to write. Spending all day mindlessly copying out financial nonsense at the bank was grinding down his wits and psyche. How long could he make his savings last? In January 1905, as his one-year anniversary at Zurich Cantonal Bank approached, his supervisor offered him a long-term contract and was astonished when Robert, instead of signing, gave notice on February 1. He was choosing his path.[16]

The prospect of having two more books forthcoming from Insel—the short plays and the poems—had made it easier for Robert to make this leap and commit to the profession of writer. Unfortunately, a setback arrived soon thereafter. Poellnitz had fallen ill that December, and on February 14,

1905, he died, apparently without having finalized plans to publish any additional Walser volumes.[17]

Writing to Flora Ackeret the previous July, Robert had playfully asked whether she could put him up, "just in case I were to go mad here and commit mad deeds and have to flee like a modern Rousseau."[18] She and her husband Henri had purchased a building at Quellgasse 17, where Adolf Walser was now an upstairs tenant. Lisa had been living there too while teaching primary school in Biel. The closeness the two siblings had established during their brief period of cohabitation in 1902 had faded somewhat. Robert's letters to her were still warm and filled with concern for her well-being, but he didn't write as often now.

Things had gone badly wrong in Lisa's life during the summer of 1904, leaving her drastically, desperately unhappy. According to a later report by her schoolmate Marguerite Chavannes, her heart had been broken. The object of her affection was a young legal actuary and artist, Hans Rudolf Moser, who apparently returned her love but said he wouldn't marry her because of his family's history of mental illness. Her misery was profound. She wrote to Robert of wanting to flee Biel, and he responded warmly, encouraging her to come live with him in Zurich, "such a wonderful, light-hearted city. Here, weeping is beautiful and sweet." They could take an apartment together, he wrote, expressing confidence that his salary would be enough to support them. He'd work, and she could run their household. He promised to pamper her, assuring her he knew very well how this was done. Or else, he added, "we can both go and become servants in an elegant household for the rest of our lives, you'll be the housemaid and I the dog."[19]

The siblings were not properly reunited until March 1905, however, when Robert—liberated from the bank—sent Ackeret a postcard saying he was "jobless, penniless, and had no address" and requesting an invitation to visit. He'd put off making plans until after his last day of work—perhaps hoping for an invitation to visit Karl in Berlin? He signed the note to Ackeret "Your servant + Robert," adding in a postscript that he didn't mind sleeping on a mattress on the floor if his father didn't have room for him.[20] Perhaps to remind her how much fun it was to have a writer beneath one's roof, he added a four-line playlet in which Hermann, Robert, Fanny, and Flora ask one another to affirm their happiness.

Many of his possessions were already under her roof, anyhow, too heavy to fit in his "paltry, shabby, brittle, and small [. . .] cabinetmaker's valise." He'd begun to employ an offloading technique—sending books and magazines to Lisa for safekeeping to lighten his load—with some regularity. He was already storing his army-issue rifle and sidearm with his father. The baggage he now jettisoned in Zurich may have included a cabinetmaker's widow; decades later he would refer to a mustachioed widow he once kissed in Zurich who "missed him a great deal" when he left town.[21]

In short order, Robert moved into an attic room in the Ackerets' building that belonged to his father's apartment. The building featured a terrace where Ackeret liked to sit with a book or host visitors. One photograph depicts her there with her foster daughter along with Henri, Fanny, and handsome young poet Hans Mühlestein, who was courting Fanny. (Robert found him insufferable.) Robert wrote upstairs while his now seventy-two-year-old father read the newspaper and drowsed in his armchair one floor below. Ackeret, now older and somewhat more staid and conventional in her tastes, still enjoyed conviviality and surrounding herself with writers. She was continuing to write as well as translate from Polish. Later, from Berlin, Robert would offer to help get her work published, but that could only have been out of personal loyalty rather than respect for her literary output. The feuilleton she published in the newspaper *Zürcher Post* on March 9, 1904, "The Confirmation Suit," had given him the awkward obligation of complimenting her work politely despite its banality and reliance on stock phrases.[22]

In 1915, Robert would sketch Ackeret's literary portrait in less-than-flattering terms in a story titled "Marie," in which the narrator comes to live in the house of one Frau Bandi after having "just escaped from a truly splendid career" by being "impertinent enough to turn down a binding contract of employment presented to me in the expectation that I would sign it with the utmost and greatest pleasure." This Frau Bandi, as he describes her, is a literary dilettante who "couldn't really be called beautiful any longer," but was witty and, "like all witty people, [. . .] sometimes a bit unkind." He speaks ironically of her tearfulness and penchant for indulging melancholy thoughts, suggesting she willfully chose to dwell upon and cultivate her own unhappiness. At the story's climax, she asks the narrator to pity her in her grief "over a lovely, lost dream" and come to her rescue by joining her in a double suicide.[23] He begs off.

Ackeret must have been mortified upon reading this fictionalized remembrance of Robert's visit to her household published in the May 1916 issue of the journal *Schweizerland*—how poorly he repaid her kindness to him when he was young and impoverished. Things had been so different between them back then. In 1904, he'd written a little poem about disappointment for her album with a variation of the word "unforgettable" in every line. She'd torn out the page and pasted it into her copy of *Fritz Kocher's Essays* on the back of Karl's drawing "In the Rain," which depicted a man walking across a mountain meadow in a downpour. The illustration appears near the end of "A Painter," the story in which Robert had somewhat sentimentally memorialized Karl and Flora's love affair, and depicts the moment when the protagonist realizes that art is his only mistress.[24]

The bitterness and embarrassment Ackeret felt in 1916 upon reading "Marie" were still in her heart two years later when, wielding a coldly analytic gaze, she wrote down everything she could remember about the Walser family in her letter to Hesse. Mustn't these two young artists—true artists, both of them, as had become clear—secretly have felt contempt for her intellect all along? But back in 1905, she was still devoted to these curious young Walsers who had touched her life in such different ways.

If Robert thought Biel was somewhere he could withdraw to and write, he was mistaken. Ackeret was lonely and wanted his company—all the more so now that he was a properly published author whom she could show off to her friends. She constantly tried to coax him downstairs, where the conversation inevitably irritated him. She spoke to him as one author to another, one who—as his elder—could offer guidance. His father, still working out of financial necessity, was showing his age, and Robert would have liked to provide for him, as he could have done if he'd stayed at the bank. Biel felt limiting, claustrophobic, guilt-inducing, and infantilizing. All his siblings, even Fanny, now studying dental technology in Bern, were pursuing their own professional goals. Only Robert remained uncertain in his path, though not his aspirations. In any case, Biel wasn't the place to pursue them.

In Berlin, the air was colder. How curious that it was so difficult for the city to shake off winter so far from any mountaintop. But the Prussian north and dreary frozen cobblestones of Kaiser-Friedrich-Strasse, where Karl was now living, released an icy cold. It was an elegant street, though this was a less prosperous block. Almost as chilling as the slush and icy stones was the letter that arrived from Insel on March 30, shortly after Robert's arrival, informing him that the publishing house was currently unable to accept any of his manuscripts, including the books he'd discussed with Poellnitz the previous spring. They were terribly backed up, the letter said, and invited him to get back in touch the following year.[25]

Robert was furious and frustrated. Karl listened with vicarious indignation as he railed, then took him out drinking. It was easy for Karl to talk—doors opened magically everywhere he went, women swooned, and the professional elite hastened to welcome him. What did he have that Robert lacked? Karl encouraged him to persist. He was still submitting work to magazines. The April 1 issue of the Basel-based weekly *Der Samstag*, containing his essay "A Theatrical Production," provided some consolation. Weren't publishers scoundrels, profiting off the work of authors, whom they cheerfully relegated to poverty? Remembering that the contract he'd signed with Poellnitz stipulated that once the publisher's costs from the first edition of *Fritz Kocher's Essays* had been recouped, Robert was to receive an additional 100 marks (by now badly needed), he fired off a registered letter to Insel's editorial offices. The company's dry response informed him that only forty-seven of thirteen hundred printed copies of the book had sold.

This unpleasant letter ("so we must unfortunately ask your continued patience") had been mailed on Robert's twenty-seventh birthday, and the same day's post brought the April 15 copy of *Der Samstag* containing his essay "Gloves," printed alongside a piece by . . . Flora Ackeret, with the title "Gypsies." He had probably encouraged her to submit her piece for publication, but now seeing their work side by side, as though they were equals, felt like an affront. He pulled himself together, knowing she would be awaiting his response, and with Karl at his side wrote her a playful, cheerful little note praising her text in terms certain to please her: "A beautifully painted porcelain plate could not be more lovely. Write, travel, paint, vagabond about!" He adds: "Soon I'll write so much that Hesse & Co. will be terrified."[26]

The additional reviews of *Fritz Kocher's Essays* that trickled in that spring (e.g., Franz Deibel in *Die Freistatt* and Albert Geiger in *Das Literarische Echo*) were some consolation. It cheered Robert to learn that at least some reviewers had understood his project and saw the poet's hand in the book's playful conceit.[27] But other writers new on the scene were enjoying much warmer receptions. Thomas Mann's 1901 debut, the fat family saga *Buddenbrooks,* about four generations of a Hanseatic clan, became a runaway best seller in 1903. And Hermann Hesse's first novel, *Peter Camenzind* (1904), brought its author instant renown. It was clearly possible for a young writer to be well-received. It probably helped if he was German.

Karl was well-received too. In spring 1904, audiences applauded his stage sets for Reinhardt's production of the Nestroy play before a single actor set foot onstage, and the reviews were mostly rapturous.[28] He soon found himself engaged for additional productions. He designed the costumes for Reinhardt's *A Midsummer Night's Dream* that opened on January 1, 1905, while also working on an even larger project for Reinhardt: sets for a production of Kleist's *Kate of Heilbronn* to mark the reopening of Deutsches Theater Berlin that October. The S. Fischer publishing house also commissioned him to illustrate a bibliophile edition of the play. He was still illustrating Insel books, and many of the theatrical stars he worked with, such as Gertrud Eysoldt and Tilla Durieux, were now his friends.

Robert returned to Zurich in June. From there, he wrote to Fanny that Karl was toiling around the clock and had become "a success through and through." He describes Karl's "velvet-black cat" and Czech housekeeper, both of whom "have the same eyes and the same treacherous manners." He describes reading all day long in a red-upholstered armchair with the cat on his lap and eating meals the housekeeper cooked. "I grew accustomed," he wrote, "to hackney cabs, waiters, and elegant ladies." Karl dressed him in a tasteful frock coat, no doubt hoping that his little brother with the thick Swiss accent—Karl had managed to make his own accent sound intriguing—wouldn't appear too much the bumpkin. Robert's ensemble included "a silver-blue vest, trousers that didn't fit well, a tall hat, and a pair of gloves crumpled up in my hands. I looked fantastic [. . .]. But I resolved to remain an honest individual and cast off this finery. I packed my miserable cabinetmaker's valise and set sail."[29]

Was his return to Switzerland a retreat? His letter to his sister is full of advice and moralizing ("Just cast off all pride. Pride, dear sister, makes one unhappy. Be modest yet at the same time proud.")[30] Perhaps the earful he kept getting from Karl on how to succeed in Berlin's art world and peculiar cultural ecosystem had worn his nerves raw, and he was trying to scrape together what remained of his self-esteem by offering guidance to the one younger sibling he had. Fanny was four years his junior, and he liked to act the big brother with her. A year earlier, he'd teased her about a temporary infatuation with Russian boys.[31] Now he was concerned all over again because she appeared to be seriously in love with that infinitely annoying Mühlestein, a poetaster who considered himself a bard of the first order. That was the sort of writer running around Switzerland.

So why did he return? For one thing, he needed privacy and calm to collect himself after weeks of Karl's frenetic lifestyle. He needed a moment's respite from the brotherly advice that, for all its good intentions, still displayed a lack of comprehension. Robert had grown up admiring and emulating his brother, and Karl didn't grasp how different they were from one another. Robert would never be able to sail through a crowded room as Karl did, distributing friendly nods, warmly pressing the right hands and never the wrong ones. Karl had no idea what it was like *not* to be in charge of his own career—or life, for that matter. He moved through the streets of Berlin like a charmed prince, never faltering or stalled by self-doubt. He commanded what he felt was his due, and the world agreed. How long it seemed since the two of them had shared a single room, just a few years ago, shivering through the cold months together to save on heat.

Robert pondered this from the room on Neumarkt he'd retreated to for the moment—four other walls he'd shared with his brother fewer than eight years earlier. Hadn't they been equals then, each striving to find his way in an art he was just beginning to master? Karl had arrived, Robert was still learning. He had to work more, write more, publish more. Gazing out the window, he watched the happy, lightly clad Zurichers strolling up and down Neumarkt, on their way to the theater on a summer-bright evening or enjoying a glass of beer or Fendant at one of the restaurants with outdoor tables. He mailed his stories to more magazines, to *Die Schweiz,* and even to the newspaper *Neue Zürcher Zeitung* that he liked to read at the café. It was lovely to spend a summer in Zurich. But this didn't feel like his life any longer. He was waiting for something more.

SEVEN

A Berliner and a Novelist

1905–1906

BEFORE THE SUMMER WAS OUT, Robert was once again a guest in his brother's Charlottenburg apartment. Karl was in the middle of a series of frescoes for Samuel Fischer's villa under construction in the leafy suburb Grunewald. The fabulously wealthy publisher was a self-made man who'd worked his way up from bookstore apprentice and now was printing some of the top names in German-language literature. Along with contemporary greats like Gerhart Hauptmann, Arthur Schnitzler, and Hugo von Hofmannsthal, he published the highly successful debut novels by both Thomas Mann and Hermann Hesse—hence the new house with new art to fill it. Karl painted a series of oval vignettes directly upon the plaster parlor walls. His romanticized silhouettes depicted a poet as a child, a youth, a young man, a scorned lover, a writer in his garret, and a graybeard.

The Berlin art scene was infatuated with Karl, the tall, handsome Swiss artist with red-gold hair who "looked like a sunflower."[1] When he finished the frescoes, *Kunst und Künstler* sent a photographer to document the series for its November 1905 issue. At Karl's suggestion, the journal commissioned Robert to write the accompanying text. This became Robert's debut in a Berlin-based journal, and it brought his work once more to the attention of the magazine's publisher, Bruno Cassirer.

"Life of a Poet" ("Leben eines Dichters") opens as an essay about Karl's paintings, then relates the story reflected in them. It was a challenging assignment, as the earnest-looking images don't quite add up. Karl's young poet sets out into the world in an old-fashioned carriage and then, one panel later, approaches a village on foot like a serenading bard of yore. Robert's narrator comments tersely on the figures' fanciful garb—"The

costume is that of 1830"—before embarking on a poetic reverie. The boy
in the panel "The Swan," he writes, "childishly ponders" the waters of the
pond behind his parents' country estate that "with its green and black
coloration gives an impression of fathomlessness." He goes on to spin an
anguished tale of unrequited love and unpublished work, with the poet
achieving fame only after death. The story ends with the comical suggestion that someone try beating the poet's overcoat like a rug to see whether
any manuscripts fall out, a jarring counterpoint to Karl's final image, showing a toga-clad poet being led by a muse to his own monument or grave.[2]

The *Kunst und Künstler* assignment was certainly encouraging, but
Robert knew better than to assume he'd be able to support himself—at
least for now—on what he might earn as a writer. As in Switzerland, he'd
need other income streams. But who was hiring copyists in Berlin, and
who in this northern German city would employ a Switzerland-trained
bank clerk? There were factories galore in and around Berlin, but a factory
job was the last thing he wanted.

An utterly delicious idea came to him, a most excellent prank—one
guaranteed to scandalize Karl's fancy new friends and maybe even embarrass Karl himself a little. Walking down Wilhelmstrasse near Potsdamer
Platz, Robert had noticed a sign with the words "Butler School." It was
one of several in Berlin training staff to serve in elegant households both
locally and abroad. The idea of learning how to serve the wealthy both
amused and intrigued him. Max Reinhardt was preparing to open Berlin's
first acting school in his villa behind the Reichstag, and the city's would-
be thespians were all signing up for it.[3] Was acting so different from being
a servant? Robert hadn't minded working briefly in that Zurich lady's
household, and he'd been only half-joking when he suggested Heymel
hire him as a domestic. And he'd run plenty of errands for Frau Dubler as
her husband's clerk in Wädenswil.

Five different butler schools are listed in the 1905 *Berliner Adressbuch,* three of them on Wilhelmstrasse. One of these, the school run by
Mr. G. Manthei, recommended itself in particular because its director (or
principal, as he called himself) had also published a textbook for aspiring
butlers that was already in its third edition by 1903. The book claims to be
designed for self-study, but it's mostly an advertisement for Manthei's "institute," as he called it. It opens with a list of topics covered in the school's
curriculum, including waiting at table, cleaning, carving roasts, keeping

the household accounts, napkin folding, handling "nervous persons," and massage. One reads how to position one's feet while serving soup, concoct floor wax, help ladies in and out of coaches, and fold napkins into forty-two different shapes, including "palm leaf," "bridal shoe," "four-leaf clover," and "Iron Cross." As a pendant to the school, Manthei ran a placement service for graduates. A reporter who visited the school in 1901 observed students acting out various scenarios to help prepare them for their professional lives: packing a suitcase; going on a journey with an officer, a honeymooning couple, a nervous elderly lady; announcing visitors, running errands, bowing, and opening doors.[4]

Though we don't know for sure that Robert chose this school when he enrolled for a one-month course of study in September 1905, textual evidence supports this assumption. Its traces can be detected in the description of the butler school "Institute Benjamenta" portrayed in Walser's 1909 novel *Jakob von Gunten,* though it is there so radically transformed that only its basic structure remains: Jakob notes that the institute's curriculum covers both the "practical" and "theoretical," which corresponds to Manthei's own terminology. In any case, beyond the school's later fictional representation, we know little about how Robert experienced it.

Robert's decision to "shock the bourgeois" was an implicit reproach to Karl, whose success relied on his appeal to wealthy patrons. Had he compromised his ideals? Robert wanted his art to be financially successful too but had questions about how compatible art-making was with the comfortable life of the affluent. Becoming a butler was a sort of social experiment, an intentional relinquishing of power. In a long story Walser wrote a decade later about working as a servant ("Tobold," 1917), the narrator compares his "servant idea" to the idea of knighthood pursued by Don Quixote.[5]

Having completed the course of study, Robert had a photograph taken in the elegant Wertheim department store that shows him looking grave, expectant, and anything but rebellious; the school's rigors had left their mark. Even for a person of his intelligence, there was a lot to remember, and given his physical awkwardness, it cost him effort to keep his body in check. He had always felt most at ease on open country roads where he could unleash his naturally long stride; confining himself to small, controlled gestures required vigilance. But he enjoyed learning these new skills, which amounted to a cloak of invisibility. In the photograph, his mouth is slightly ajar; the photographer had forgotten to ask him to close it, and he hadn't realized that the resulting expression would look as if he'd been caught mid-sentence. Perhaps letting his mouth hang open a little was a habitual gesture; Carl Seelig would remark on this decades later, and in *The Tanners*, Simon Tanner's sister Hedwig teases him for the same thing.[6]

Robert acquitted himself well as a student butler and, unlike many of his German classmates, he spoke French with ease, so a suitable post was soon found for him—not in Berlin but in Upper Silesia hundreds of miles to the east. Karl promptly announced this development in a postcard to Fanny, instructing her to use this bit of news to "make Hermi [Hermann] faint."[7]

The castle where "Monsieur Robert" was hired to serve as an assistant butler from the beginning of October until late December 1905 stands atop a gentle hill at the edge of a small rural town called Dąbrowa Niemodlińska. On the train line between Opole and Wrocław, Dąbrowa has belonged to Poland since 1945 but at the time was still part of the German Empire and known as Dambrau. Like most of Eastern Europe before World War II, its population was a multilingual mix of ethnicities. As many Poles as Germans lived in Upper Silesia, and roughly a quarter of the population was Czech.

When Robert arrived in Dambrau, he may have been met at the station—like the character Tobold in the story he later wrote about this episode—by a fellow servant with a horse-drawn cart; or perhaps he carried his suitcase up the hill, a modest distance even on foot. He soon caught his first glimpse of the castle's decorative belfry among the treetops. Then the chapel came into view, topped with a small belfry of its own, followed by a graceful sweep of lawn leading up to the castle itself, which looked more like an exceptionally large manor house than a fairytale castle. Behind it were parklike grounds crisscrossed by well-tended, tree-lined paths. The castle was built on a square floor plan with a large enclosed courtyard and a five-story tower at center front straddling an arched entryway wide enough to admit a carriage. In the courtyard Robert was greeted by intricate half-timbering, stairwells shaped like miniature turrets, and elegant decorative arches over the windows. A single round turret topped with an onion globe had recently been added in one corner.

Robert's month of professional training helped him anticipate the rigors that awaited. He would be in constant danger of incurring the displeasure of either his new employer—Count Konrad von Hochberg, Baron of Fürstenstein, scion of one of the wealthiest aristocratic families in Europe—or the head butler and housekeeper to whom he reported. He was inexperienced, and was he not in some sense an imposter? There was something inherently theatrical about his servanthood, and part of his job lay in persuading his fellow servants that he belonged among them. He was concerned about being exposed as a published author. In his renewed correspondence with Insel—he'd written to Carl Ernst Poeschel in September to ask whether Insel might now consider printing a volume of his stories and fairy tales, or at least a slim book of poems—he insisted Poeschel use only plain, unmarked envelopes to correspond with him.[8] He'd brought enough manuscripts to assemble a bundle of thirty-four poems (all older ones by now), which he smuggled to the post office. He then had to hide his disappointment when they were rejected by return mail because Poeschel didn't think he could sell enough copies to cover printing costs. Meanwhile, a postcard arrived from Karl, who was spending the month painting and visiting museums in Florence, Rome, Siena, and Venice. At least one of the brothers was still able to devote his life to his art.

A key requirement for any butler is discretion. So whether out of a sense of loyalty to his employers, an unwillingness to tarnish the reputation of the school that trained him, or professional responsibility, Robert refrained from consigning his experiences in the castle to print after returning to Berlin just in time to celebrate New Year's. He did entertain his friends with stories of castle life, though. Franz Blei, whom he visited soon thereafter, notes that instead of a beautiful lady whose train Robert might have carried page boy–style, he'd found only a flatfooted matron of forty who spent her days writing pamphlets for religious charities.[9] In any case, Blei reports, Robert wasn't expected to wait on the lady in person; he merely tended the large tile heating stoves, a task that could be accomplished without actually entering the rooms, thanks to trap doors installed in the corridors.

Robert let a full decade elapse before writing "Tobold," the story based on his Silesian adventures, and even then he remained discreet, referring to his employer only as "Count K" and never specifying the location. Did it make him nervous, all those years later, to imagine that someone from that era of his life might read the story and decide he had betrayed some trust? The tale's equally anonymous castle visitors include the elegant "Baroness H." ("who appeared constructed and constituted

entirely of fresh milk") and "Princess M." It's known that Baroness Elisabeth von Heyking, author of a bestselling novel published anonymously
in 1903, visited briefly during Robert's time in the castle, and the story
mentions her book. The narrator also remarks on spotting the name Van-
derbilt in the guest book, which he indiscreetly perused.[10]

The story contains little account of Tobold's dealings with his employers, concentrating instead on the servants' back-stairs interactions.
Tobold's direct superior is the Polish castellan or caretaker, a blustering,
fuming man who shouts at Tobold and orders him about. When this caretaker enters Tobold's room uninvited and threatens to strike him, Tobold
immediately reports the incident to the count's secretary, a suave Dane
who chastises the caretaker so severely even Tobold is taken aback. On
another occasion, one of the count's huntsmen encounters Tobold out for
a walk on the castle grounds and, mistaking him for a nobleman, greets
him "reverentially, that is, far too politely, thus committing an error that
seemed to give him grounds to hold a grudge against [Tobold] for a long
time afterward." Tobold clearly takes pride in performing his job well,
becoming a virtuoso of inconspicuousness. Each evening he tiptoes
through the corridors of the castle, taking light to every chamber "like
Aladdin [. . .] with his magic or miraculous lamp." He also reports enjoying the "natural spectacle" of "openly displayed, beautifully exposed, soft
white female breasts." At one point he commits the gaffe of dropping mustard upon one such splendid décolleté. On another occasion he wins a
nod of appreciation from the count after discretely removing a small worm
from beside a lady's plate at dinner.[11]

Returning to Berlin when his tour of duty in the castle ended, Robert
found Karl on the brink of euphoric exhaustion. While Robert discreetly
proffered his salvers and cigars, Karl had designed the sets for no fewer
than three operas that opened in late November and early December. One
of these, a production of Jacques Offenbach's *The Tales of Hoffmann* directed by Maximilian Moris, had marked the opening of the new opera
house Komische Oper. After some scuffling with Moris, who deemed
Karl's burgundy-hued opening set "too dark," his design had been greeted
with thunderous applause when the curtain rose, drowning out the opening notes of the overture. Berlin's most respected and feared theater critic,
Alfred Kerr, titled his review of the production "*The Tales of Hoffmann:
A Walser Dream.*"[12]

A Christmas postcard addressed to both brothers by Flora Ackeret reported that she'd have liked to send them a nearby forest as a gift but didn't want them to have to pay duty on it. The card was also signed by their father, Fanny, and Henri—but not by Lisa, who had accepted a teaching post that fall in Livorno, Italy. An irritating postscript by Hans Mühlestein, who to Robert's disgust was still in Fanny's good graces, informed the brothers that their father, "merry indeed," was dancing up a storm at that very moment. "I don't know you," the young wretch adds, "but I love you. Heartiest greetings!" Insufferable. Especially as Mühlestein, another of Widmann's "discoveries," had been writing reviews for *Der Bund* and *Neue Zürcher Zeitung.* What did Widmann see in his clichéd, sloppy rhymes? Not even Fanny seemed to know better; she asked Karl to illustrate Mühlestein's poems to help get them published as a book. Karl refused, but Mühlestein found a publisher in Bern, and the book appeared in 1906 with a dedication to Fanny—that is, one *section* was dedicated to her; another bore another woman's name. Was Fanny, like Lisa, to be unhappy in love?[13]

Robert had been having amorous adventures himself—or at least flirtations, cautious approaches that left stronger traces in his later fiction than in his archived correspondence. Indeed, some of these recorded encounters may have been entirely fictional. One character mentioned in passing in "Tobold" also makes an appearance in Walser's 1925 novel *The Robber* (*Der Räuber*): "An Englishman, captain in the British Army and apparently a close and trusted friend of the count." Tobold declares this Englishman "a quite charming person, a perfectly tolerable individual" with an "intelligent face" that "expressed benevolence, energy, and learning"—and little more is said of him.[14] In *The Robber,* on the other hand, the narrator reports that the protagonist once "allowed an English captain to pinch him on the leg" in a castle corridor: "The Robber was busy lighting lamps and stood, to this end, upon a chair, clad in a tailcoat, for he was a butler, if admittedly only an assistant butler. Whereupon this Englishman stole up behind him with furtive step and allowed himself the bit of friendliness mentioned above, and later the same day the two of them had a quick tête-à-tête in the Robber's ground-floor chamber [. . . and] the Englishman asked the Robber something tender." The tender question turns out to be, "Do you visit the ladies?" And when the protagonist says no, the captain asks, "'Then how do you take pleasure in your existence?' Instead of describing how he amused himself or managed to do without amusements, the Robber bent his head to the English-man's hand and kissed it."[15]

Walser's work contains several references to flirtations with men, though there's no concrete evidence of any serious real-life involvements. In a 1925 essay he wrote about Walther Rathenau—a text scandalous enough to be withheld from a 1980s German edition of Walser's works—he describes Rathenau as having a "melancholy temperament" along with a penchant for donning lace underpants. He also reports that this fabulously wealthy industrialist's son (who later became foreign minister of Germany) once declared him "heartless." Did young Rathenau—who was active in cultural circles at the time and served on the board of Reinhardt's new act-ing school—attempt to seduce or even fall in love with young Robert?[16]

In *The Robber,* the narrator makes this "confession":

> Rathenau and the Robber were personally acquainted. Their acquaintance dated from the time when the future minister had not yet become a current one. It was at a country estate in the Mark Brandenburg that our so easily infatuated little Robber paid a visit to the rich industrialist's son. They had met quite accidentally, you see, at Potsdamer Platz in Berlin amidst a ceaseless stream of pedestrians and vehicles. The prominent individual had invited the one scarcely worth mentioning to call on him, and the invitation was acted upon.

The description of this visit reveals only that the two men drank tea served by a tactful butler ("soundless as a shadow, as though [. . .] he consisted exclusively of a correct assessment of circumstances") in a tapestry-lined parlor. They also took a walk on the grounds of the estate, where they chat-ted about "islands, poets, and so on."[17] Walser's memories of Rathenau as-sumed greater poignancy after the foreign minister's assassination in 1922.

Did Robert's visit to Rathenau's estate predate or postdate his months at Castle Dambrau? Now a servant, now a gentleman being served by one; now strolling somewhat illicitly about castle grounds, now an hon-ored guest at a country manor: the roles of server and served intertwined both on the page and, perhaps, in real life. Robert had been living a double life for a while now, both as the subject of lived experience and as a witness storing up observations he would later put to literary use.

Berlin was a good place for exploring the complexities of one's own sexual makeup. Homosexuality at least—unlike in Switzerland at the time—was cautiously acknowledged and, in certain contexts, even celebrated in Berlin despite the rest of Europe's deeply rooted homophobia. A sodomy law was in force in Germany (the notorious Paragraph 175 that wasn't repealed until 1994), but there was already a robust and publicly visible gay and lesbian subculture in Berlin by the time Robert arrived. There was even a nonderogatory word for "gay"—*schwul*—used by members of that community to self-identify. And starting in 1885, when Bernhard von Richthofen (rumored to be *schwul* himself) was named Berlin's chief of police, bars and cafés catering to a gay clientele were no longer subject to raids by officers of the law. Drinking and dancing with other gay people had never been illegal, and under Richthofen, much of the police surveillance of the gay social scene was directed to eliminating the unsavory cottage industry of blackmailing gay men, a lucrative entrapment and evidence-gathering practice that threatened victims with denunciation, and jail time, under Paragraph 175.[18]

A survey of sexual practices conducted by sexologist Magnus Hirschfeld in 1903 and 1904 concluded that slightly more than 2 percent of German men reported having sex only with other men. Physician Paul Näcke's 1904 account, "A Visit with the Homosexuals of Berlin," described gay advocacy groups, bars, and even weekly balls with up to seven hundred in attendance. Max Liebermann and Walter Leistikow, founders of the Berlin Secession, had signed the anti–Paragraph 175 petition Hirschfeld circulated in 1898, as did Gerhart Hauptmann and Frank Wedekind.[19]

Wedekind's *Spring Awakening*, with its frank talk about the sexuality of young people—and sets designed by Karl Walser—premiered in November 1906. It was produced by Max Reinhardt and presented in the Deutsches Theater's Kammerspiele. This was only one month after Robert Musil had published his own account of teenage sexual angst in *The Confusions of Young Törless*. The feuilletons were full of theories about sexuality based on, or responding to, those proposed by Hirschfeld; and, in Vienna, Sigmund Freud, who'd just published his *Three Essays on the Theory of Sexuality*, was paving the way to a more mainstream acceptance of sexuality as a complex and ubiquitous life force.

Meanwhile, Robert was reckoning with his own apparently multivalent sexuality. For years he'd observed the way his brother walked around unhesitatingly making conquests. Women had always thrown themselves at Karl, who knew just how to respond. With Robert, things were different. And was a love life like Karl's even what he wanted? In any case, seeing the freedom that men who loved other men enjoyed in this city made an impression on him. Whatever his own sexual identity, he kept encountering gay men who wanted to claim him as one of their own.

When Robert returned to Karl's Berlin apartment at the end of 1905, he had money in his pocket from his three months in Silesia and felt the moment had come to attempt a novel. Still following that old instruction to write something that "came from within," he produced a story about a group of siblings much resembling his own, all freshly grown to adulthood and struggling to find their way in the world. Protagonist Simon Tanner is a sometime clerk, sometime vagabond who cannot stand any job for long. ("Tanner" in German derives from "Tanne" or "fir tree" and is unrelated to the English-language occupational surname.) Constitutionally incapable, it seems, of enduring any loss of freedom, Simon simultaneously takes an almost concupiscent pleasure in relinquishing his free will. After he accepts a job as a man-of-all-work in the household of a wealthy lady with a sickly son, an extended scene is devoted to the power struggle that ensues when the factotum sees his mistress drop and break a beautiful platter. She redirects her anger and frustration toward him, ordering him to pick up the pieces, and he torments her by intentionally prolonging the moments he spends kneeling at her feet with the hem of her skirt brushing his cheek, plucking each shard from the floor as slowly as possible. It's a masterful, surreptitiously erotic scene.[20]

The Tanners is transparently autobiographical in large part, presenting episodes from Robert's own life along with the lives of his siblings, though Simon has fewer siblings than Robert. Simon, the youngest, has a sister, Hedwig, who's a teacher, and three brothers: the seductive painter Kaspar, currently in Paris; the scholar Klaus, a portrait of Hermann; and an unfortunate brother named Emil, who suffers the same fate as Ernst in real life. In fact, the novel so nakedly depicts the story of Ernst's decline and institutionalization that it's hard to imagine Robert's other siblings reading it with anything less than indignation. Indeed, recalling the novel in conversation decades later, Walser remarked that he'd gone too far in exposing family secrets along with his own. In the novel, Emil's story is related by two strangers Simon overhears talking in a pub. One of them turns out to have been a close friend of Emil's. Simon interrupts their conversation in a rage when this friend concludes his story by remarking, "perhaps madness just ran in the family." Simon challenges the storyteller to look at him and say whether he beholds any trace of mental illness.[21]

In another episode, Simon sits on a park bench beside a male nurse from Naples who befriends and soon appears to fall in love with him. When Heinrich, his new friend, invites him home for dinner and then confesses he's growing fond of Simon and would like to kiss him, Simon jumps up from his chair, "finding the air in the room oppressively close": "He guessed what sort of man it was who was looking at him with such odd tenderness. But what harm could it do. 'I'll go along with it,' he thought. 'I see no reason to be uncivil to this Heinrich, who is otherwise so nice, over such a small thing!' And he yielded up his mouth and let himself be kissed." Even after this, Simon continues to spend a lot of mental energy trying not to worry about Heinrich's "strange affection" for him: he finds himself "incapable of dashing the man's hopes, even though these hopes happened to be unworthy ones." And he continues to seek out the man's company. They spend time drinking and walking around outdoors together, and Simon continues to accept his friend's displays of affection while simultaneously distancing himself from them ("Actually this is ugly," he thinks as Heinrich gazes "deeply and with desire" into his eyes before throwing an arm around his neck as they walk side-by-side). When they flop down together in the woods after an arduous uphill hike, Heinrich tries to initiate sex, but Simon forces him to stop.[22] The passage dramatizes a powerful ambivalence, with Simon enjoying his friend's companionship—and desire—while at the same time denying any reciprocity. Flirtation, a sustained desire constantly put in question, takes the place of consummation.

Walser portrays Heinrich as always impeccably correct in his behavior, stating his intentions clearly; their interactions buzz with the electricity of confessed desire. Simon's tergiversation—for he doesn't appear to know his own mind—gives him the upper hand in this relationship, erotic power that recalls the thrill he gets kneeling at his employer's feet while gathering up porcelain shards. This economy of desire and power gives the book a peculiar energy that locates it squarely in the new era that was beginning to think hard about sex and its complexities. Eros was publicly on the march, from Vienna to Berlin, and infused the air Simon and his siblings breathed. Walser's depiction of gay desire may have alarmed the writer himself. In "The Tanners" ("Geschwister Tanner"), an essay he wrote in 1914 about the novel's composition, he takes pains to report that while writing the book he paid occasional visits to girls of easy virtue at a bar where they liked to gather; perhaps this was true.[23]

The Tanners contains another love story, one clearly inspired by the Karl-Flora romance. Robert had tried out a version of this material in 1903 with "Simon: A Love Story" in which young Simon, who aspires to become a page boy, serenades a lady, Klara, who invites him into her villa and describes fantasies attuned to his: "You shall leap about me like a roe, and my hand shall stroke it, this small, graceful, innocent roe. I'll sit upon your brown body when I'm tired." Klara is married to a fearsome huntsman named Aggapaia, who suffers psychic paralysis when he imagines himself cuckolded by the aspiring page. The Simon-Klara-Aggapaia constellation recurs in *The Tanners,* but the triangle's legs have shifted: the object of this Klara's adulterous affections is now Simon's brother Kaspar, the painter. In the novel, Simon meets Klara when he comes to see a room for rent in her villa. It proves too expensive, but Klara begs him to live there for free along with his brother, with whom she immediately falls in love. In this version of the love triangle, the household falls apart not because of adultery, but because Agappaia (spelled differently here) gambles away all his money, in an echo of Carl Tobler's misguided business ventures, and joins a "group of Asian explorers" on an expedition "to discover a sunken Greek city somewhere in India."[24]

Klara moves away, and the novel loses track of her for many chapters before she reappears as a version of Robert's old Zurich acquaintance Louisa Schweizer. Klara has been seduced and abandoned by a Turkish student whose child she is raising. The owner of the photography shop where she works treats her with kindness and she assumes the role of "Queen of the Poor," offering support and guidance to the less educated inhabitants of her new neighborhood.

Walser composed *The Tanners* with astonishing speed. He began in early January 1906 and on February 21 sent a postcard to Insel asking whether the editors would like to see his "novel of approximately 400 book pages." The lukewarm response was full of caveats, so he didn't send it. And shouldn't he try to find a Berlin-based publisher? Samuel Fischer, for whom Karl had been illustrating both living-room walls and books, was one option; another was Bruno Cassirer, who had once encouraged Robert to try his hand at a novel. Cassirer, to whom he showed the manuscript, wasn't particularly taken with it, however. The book struck him as too casual, too meandering. Fortunately, Cassirer editor Christian Morgenstern, to whom Cassirer showed the manuscript before rejecting it, persuaded the publisher that Robert was a literary diamond in the rough, a young voice worth cultivating.[25]

Best known for his satirical verses, Morgenstern had just published the highly successful *Gallows Songs* with a striking cover illustration by Karl. Now he wrote to Cassirer that he considered *The Tanners* "almost more a Russian than a German book," containing "passages of genuine holiness along with a sort of profoundly natural, folk quality that I hope might be capable of infusing new youth into our literature." He compared it favorably with Hesse's *Peter Camenzind,* saying he considered Walser the more important author.[26]

Morgenstern's vision of Robert as not just an emerging talent but one who had the potential to become a key voice of the age made an impression on Cassirer, who had been hoping to discover a writer who would do for his publishing house what Mann and Hesse had done for Fischer. With its cheerful informality and loose structure, *The Tanners* didn't seem an obvious candidate; the flighty, distraction-prone narration had nothing monumental or magisterial about it, none of the gravitas that marked *Buddenbrooks* as an Important Book. But with Morgenstern's coaxing, Cassirer came to admire Walser's uncanny powers of observation on every page—a fresh, ever-surprising way of distilling the world and its inhabitants. All the essayistic skills Robert had been honing in his short prose were on display, and it seemed he could sketch characters as sharply as landscapes.

Morgenstern set about teaching Robert the basics of editing, from the proofreader's symbols used to instruct typesetters to the niceties of style. In particular he decried Robert's "needless prolixity, sloppy sentence construction, triviality-producing complacency, shaky grammar, and poorly chosen or executed images," particularly noticeable in the opening pages.[27] Robert wasn't unreceptive—it was the first time anyone had put so much effort into helping him improve the quality of his prose—though in the end not all the corrections Morgenstern suggested appeared in the published book. Robert was afraid that ironing out his style too much could destroy what was idiosyncratic and valuable about his work. His *Tanners* characters did tend to be long-winded, but even when he was writing dialogue, half the point was that each of them was painfully, irrevocably alone, with every conversation a set of interlinked monologues.

Some of the novel did wind up on the cutting-room floor, such as an episode in which Simon discovers a manuscript, written by a clerk, stuck into a stove for kindling. Editing the novel only compounded Morgenstern's admiration, and by October he was praising its "somnambulistic" quality and referring to its author as a budding genius. In his diary, he noted, "when he's grown to maturity, [. . .] he will be one of the most powerful voices calling us to freedom."[28]

When *The Tanners* was published, Robert sent a copy to Ackeret, who inscribed in the margins the names of a number of the people on whom this roman à clef was based, including Louisa Schweizer, whom of course she knew. She also glossed the figures based on Karl, Ernst, and Hermann. Beside the name Agappaia, she wrote "Agapalian"; perhaps this was someone they knew in Biel, or perhaps the name was borrowed from Simon Agapalian, a Turkish math student in Zurich whom Robert may have met there. Perhaps this Agapalian was even the model for the Turkish "student at the polytechnical university" in the novel who seduces Klara and leaves her with a child when he returns "to his native land, to Armenia." On the page of the novel recounting this seduction, Ackeret annotated: "Died in hospital giving birth to her second child (stillborn) at age 28, in 1902." Her note suggests that this part of Klara's story was based on the life of a domestic servant who died in Biel that year, while other parts, including the photographer episode, were borrowed from Schweizer's life.[29]

Robert was developing his technique of creating characters and stories by splicing together the experiences of various people he knew or had heard about through his circle of acquaintances. Thus numerous people may have noticed similarities to their own histories. Lisa probably wasn't happy to read Simon's reveries during his visit to his schoolteacher sister Hedwig in an episode clearly based on Robert's stay in the Täuffelen schoolhouse: he imagines her being abducted by a man with "a shaggy beard of the sort robbers are in the habit of wearing." In the margin beside this description, Ackeret inscribed the name "Hans Moser": Robert had written into his story the man who'd broken Lisa's heart in real life. Later in the book, a dream sequence shows Hedwig lying dead because "life caused her too much pain." Did everyone close to Robert have to suffer for his art? Even Muschi, the sleek black cat who kept Robert company while he was writing the novel (as he reports in the essay "The Tanners"), makes a cameo appearance.[30]

A book about ordinary people, many of whose stories begin and/or end on the margins of society, Walser's debut novel introduces a central theme of his mature work: an affectionate fascination with and radical veneration of the small, inconspicuous, and local. Kaspar—based on Karl, just back from Italy—inveighs against Klaus's suggestion that he ought to travel through Italy to foster his development as a painter: "Can it possibly be more beautiful there than here, where I live and work, where I behold a thousand beautiful things that will endure long after I myself have rotted away?" Simon lyrically praises the beautiful simplicity of a lunch of bread and honey, a "golden meal" he orders out of thrift at a restaurant for the poor. The book reflects who Robert was and how he sounded when he spoke; one of Karl's friends who read *The Tanners,* sculptor Georg Kolbe, said Robert was "just like the book," which he found "full of the most agreeable joie de vivre."[31]

The Tanners went on sale in time for Christmas 1906 (the official publication date was January 1907). By April it was selling so well that Cassirer put a notice in the publishers' trade journal *Börsenblatt* asking booksellers with surplus copies to return them so he could redistribute them to booksellers having trouble keeping up with demand. In July, Cassirer started preparing the second edition, which appeared that October. Morgenstern worried that Karl's cover illustration, which he'd initially praised, was hurting sales, especially in Switzerland: the green-ink image, of a man and woman standing on a villa balcony overlooking a park lush with trees, faded quickly in sunny bookstore windows. The same cover was nonetheless used for the second edition, which didn't sell as well as the first. About two thousand copies of *The Tanners* were sold, a respectable if unremarkable number for a first novel.[32]

Critics received the book enthusiastically overall. A dozen reviews appeared within six months of its publication and another half-dozen before the year was out. Most were positive, though some reviewers declared the book formless and its monologue-prone characters garrulous and difficult to distinguish. This latter observation was certainly accurate; just as we can recognize the dreamer in all the figures of a dream, *The Tanners*' characters appear to be a company of Roberts. A harsh review by Felix Salten in the Viennese journal *Die Zeit* prompted Robert's old champion Widmann—who'd already published an encomium to the book in January—to print a rebuttal lamenting the mutual incomprehension of Swiss authors and Austrian critics. But most who reviewed the book were charmed by its fresh, promising voice.[33]

Several reviewers compared *The Tanners* to Joseph von Eichendorff's 1826 novella *Memoirs of a Good-for-Nothing*—a classic of German romanticism—about a solitary perambulator of slender ambitions and means; to others, it recalled Gottfried Keller's classic Bildungsroman *Green Henry*. The atmosphere or mood of Walser's novel was particularly singled out for praise, along with the author's light hand with structure and departure from the strictures of nineteenth-century realism that still dominated, making literature a more reactionary field overall than painting. The book was widely seen as a "modern" work with a social-critical stance and an emphasis on youthful energies and pleasures. The lyricism of the prose was praised as well—especially gratifying after the scolding from Morgenstern—and soon thereafter many of the newspapers and magazines that had reviewed the book proved eager to publish short prose works by its author. It seemed the young novelist had, finally, arrived.

EIGHT

The Balloon Ride

1907–1908

BEING THE AUTHOR OF A WELL-RECEIVED novel changed what it felt like to move around Berlin with Karl and his high-achieving friends. Robert had proved himself. He wasn't even losing sleep over whether he'd be able to produce a second novel: he'd already drafted one the previous fall while *The Tanners* was still in production. This new book was more fanciful, less autobiographical. Its protagonist travels to Asia, "attaching himself," Robert explained to Christian Morgenstern, "to a mad scholar, 'the devil in a summer coat,' as an assistant. A scientific expedition!" *The Assistant* was the continuation of the theme introduced in *The Tanners* when Agappaia "throw[s] in his lot with a group of Asian explorers" and sets off for India.[1]

Robert had been thinking about voyages, influenced by all the talk of foreign travel he'd been hearing—above all from Karl, who'd been putting his wanderlust into action. Since his trip to Italy in 1905, Karl had visited Holland, Spain, Paris, and Naples. Robert had been toying with the notion of journeying somewhere seriously distant—not just a few hours' travel by train, as Silesia had been, but literally overseas. True, he'd had Simon Tanner proclaim himself vehemently opposed to travel ("Does nature go abroad? Do trees wander off to procure for themselves greener leaves in other places so they can come home and flaunt their new splendor?"). But lately he'd started dropping hints to deep-pocketed friends that he would not, in fact, be averse to acquiring his own greener leaves abroad. He sent words to this effect to Morgenstern in the fall of 1906: "I've been harboring this idea for years now, but never got around to acting on it, much as with a lover who never quite manages to speak the crucial words and take the necessary step. But to be sure, London would certainly 'do' for the time being."[2]

Bruno Cassirer offered to pay for Robert to travel to India for several months. According to a story later recounted by Karl, Robert carried the check around in his pocket for a while, then returned it to Cassirer uncashed. Walther Rathenau apparently proposed arranging a sinecure on Samoa that would have left him plenty of time to write; and Morgenstern offered him an introduction to Bernhard Dernburg, head of the Imperial Colonial Office that administered the overseas territories under German control. Even Samuel Fischer chimed in with an offer: he proposed sending Robert to Poland to write a book about his experiences there, and when Robert declined the invitation, Fischer suggested Turkey. In the end, Robert chose not to follow up on any of these leads and offers. It seems his desire for travel just wasn't strong enough to overcome whatever misgivings he had about the enterprise. And after all, in Berlin he was already "abroad." His response to Fischer, at least as he recalled it decades later, was, "No, merci! One can behave like a Turk in other places too, perhaps even more so than in Turkey. I wish to go absolutely nowhere. Why should writers travel as long as they have their imaginations?"[3]

To Morgenstern, too, he wrote that he meant to "give up all thought of going to the colonies, it would cost too much money and, more importantly, too much time": "You can't just run off to distant climes, otherwise you're at risk of losing touch with everything that is still riveting in art and artistic life. [. . .] [N]o, going to Africa is something I currently have no desire to do, nor am I free to. I would consider it a more profound experience to go to prison, but of course these are perhaps foolish words." He did say, though, that he was contemplating leaving Berlin soon, probably for Zurich, which had always been a good spot for him to collect his thoughts and rekindle the fire of inspiration. He was thinking of a new story for a novel that would feature "a refined hypochondriac, a woman with a daughter, not much landscape, not too many pretty words, possibly good ones." In short, his interest in exotic travel appears to have deserted him for good by the end of 1906.[4]

Robert's passing reference to the Asia expedition undertaken by a mad scholar in his novel *The Assistant* is now all that remains of that book. We know that he submitted the manuscript to Cassirer and that Morgenstern read it and praised the book elaborately in a letter to Cassirer in November 1906, declaring it far superior to *The Tanners* and a proof of its author's future promise. Robert was on his way, he said, to becoming "extraordinary." The book's cast of characters included a protagonist named Christian (Morgenstern described him as a slightly older version of Simon Tanner), a Mrs. Fischer, Elise, the Professor, and "the sister."[5] But this novel never appeared in print.

Cassirer took a long time deliberating whether to publish the manuscript (despite repeated queries from Morgenstern), perhaps waiting for reviews of *The Tanners* to come in. Meanwhile, Robert was back in touch with Insel's editors, who'd written after *The Tanners* was published expressing disappointment that he hadn't sent them his novel for consideration (even though they hadn't particularly encouraged him to). Now they offered to publish a "Walser edition": one volume of poems and verse dramas and another of short prose. According to internal correspondence, Insel's editors didn't think much of Robert's poems and were offering to publish them only to have a chance to print more of his prose. Heymel lavished praise on *The Tanners* in a letter to managing editor Anton Kippenberg (calling it "a work of the highest order" and Robert "perhaps the finest stylist *Die Insel* has produced") but he also complained that Robert was "very Difficult and awkward and extraordinarily touchy."[6]

Some of the material Insel now contemplated printing was no longer available. Robert wrote to Heymel that his manuscripts that had gone unpublished in 1901 were "in part lost, in part destroyed." In other words, he'd destroyed some of them after they were rejected. The manuscript of his new novel seems to have met a similar fate. Cassirer finally made up his mind to publish the book in summer 1907. In September, when Morgenstern finished editing the manuscript, he asked Robert to meet him in Zurich to discuss it. We don't know whether Robert made this trip, but in any case something went badly wrong in his negotiations with Morgenstern, who lamented soon thereafter in a letter to a friend, "These days it seems that Robert Walser is determined to disappoint me most astonishingly." Did Morgenstern's critique make Robert lose faith in the book's value? Or was he so put off by Morgenstern's tone and manner that he destroyed it out of spite? Morgenstern had been as convinced as ever of the manuscript's quality when he wrote to Cassirer's managing editor that July, urging him to "publish the book this autumn without fail, as it's highly unlikely that the publishing house is going to have any better book written for it."[7]

If nothing else, Robert was thinking hard about artistic standards and holding himself to them. In a letter to Morgenstern, he'd remarked not long before that if he were doomed to become just "a magazine supplier," he'd rather join the army. "The hair on my head is long," he wrote, "but I'm not going to have it cut until I've finished writing a story. If I could, I'd give up shaving until I've managed at least a halfway true-to-life love scene. The most banal things are and will always be the most difficult for a writer to portray. I've got to try to show off less."[8]

He'd also been thinking about Kleist again, perhaps rereading his letters too, and had written a story that spring that emphasized the passion and self-destructiveness with which this most exacting, critical, and self-critical of writers approached his art: "Weeks pass, Kleist has destroyed one work, two, three works. He wants the highest mastery, good, good. What's that? Not sure? Tear it up. Something new, wilder, more beautiful."[9] Thinking once more about Kleist's rigor and the unrelentingly high standards to which he held his own artistic production may have chastened Robert and caused him to look with less satisfaction upon the book he'd just completed.

The story "Kleist in Thun"—now generally agreed to be one of Walser's finest shorter works—is modeled on Georg Büchner's celebrated novella *Lenz*, based on an episode in the life of eighteenth-century playwright Jakob Michael Reinhold Lenz involving a psychotic breakdown. Following Büchner's example by presenting Kleist as a fictional character under psychological duress, Walser's story imagines the details of Kleist's state of mind during a period when he has plunged himself into his work with such intensity that it triggers a collapse. The story, which appeared in *Die Schaubühne* (The Stage) in June 1907, was a departure from the more essayistic texts Robert had been writing and now regularly publishing in Berlin-based magazines like *Die Schaubühne* and *Die Neue Rundschau*. This time, he'd tried his hand at a proper story with a protagonist, structure, and plot development—aspects of the writer's craft that hadn't previously been his strong suit, even in *The Tanners*. "Kleist in Thun," on the other hand, is beautifully crafted and rich in descriptions of the glorious landscapes in and around Thun.

A second story he wrote that spring—also a departure from his previous work—engaged with Kleist in a different way. "The Battle of Sempach" ("Die Schlacht bei Sempach") gives narrative form to a bit of historical material that Kleist himself (as mentioned in Chapter 4) considered making the subject of a play—a fact referenced in passing in "Kleist in Thun." Walser's story tells of a band of Swiss peasants who heroically put down an attempt to subdue them into serfdom by well-armed Austrian knights in the year 1386. Their military triumph is made possible by the self-sacrifice of one of their own number—Swiss folk hero Arnold von Winkelried—who, with only his bare hands, neutralizes enough lance-armed knights to let his countrymen prevail. The story is written in a solemn, heroic mode that celebrates Winkelried's sacrifice and then—as a denouement—shows everyday life resuming as the valiant peasants return to their workaday lives without fanfare. Kleist had planned to dramatize the story of Duke Leopold III of Austria, whose life ended on the battlefield in Sempach that day. Walser's story, focusing on the farmers, mentions the duke only in passing. Robert submitted the story to the journal *Die Zukunft* (The Future) in spring 1907. It was accepted at once and published the following January.[10]

Both "Kleist in Thun" and "The Battle of Sempach" show Walser trying out a more classical mode of storytelling clearly influenced by nineteenth-century writers. He may have been reading Kleist's short fiction as well as his plays; Kleist's stories "The Earthquake in Chile" and "The Betrothal in San Domingo" make similar use of historical material. Certainly this was a way to counteract accusations that Robert's work was childlike or light. The historical material lends both these stories weight. "The Battle of Sempach" also had a more recent model: Hugo von Hofmannsthal's "A Tale of the Cavalry," detailing two skirmishes in the Austrian bid to suppress an uprising by Italian nationalist revolutionaries in 1848. While Hofmannsthal's story eventually zeroes in on an aging sergeant who experiences a psychological breakdown after an uncanny encounter in occupied Milan, the story begins and ends (like Walser's Sempach tale) with prose narrated in a mock-documentary style, making the story seem to arise organically out of, and then melt back into, history. Hofmannsthal was revered, and Robert wanted to show those who doubted his own seriousness as a writer that he could, when he wanted, produce work of comparable depth.

Various associates had been urging Robert to pay more attention to formal matters in his writing. Cassirer in particular suggested he look to the great nineteenth-century Swiss novelist Gottfried Keller as a model of narrative structure.[11] Keller's work would come to mean a great deal to Walser, particularly his magnum opus, the novel *Green Henry*. Robert had also been gripped by the Dostoevsky fever currently raging in literary Berlin. Cassirer had been republishing one Dostoevsky novel after another (in translations by August Scholz), including *The Idiot,* whose cover Karl illustrated in spring 1906.

Studying the work of these masterful storytellers inspired Robert to think about structure in new ways—which may be one reason why his "devil in a summer coat" vanished without a trace. Perhaps he'd written *The Assistant* in as meandering a mode as *The Tanners,* and, when confronted by Morgenstern with its structural weakness, had been too frustrated to rework the manuscript. He had never been one for revision. But he felt he was capable of writing a novel with as sound a narrative structure as his recent stories.

He soon had occasion to do so: he received an invitation to submit a manuscript to Scherl, one of Germany's largest publishers, responsible among other things for the large-circulation illustrated weekly *Die Woche* (The Week). He immediately set to work and, in just a month and a half, wrote a new novel. Like its predecessor, this book bore the title *The Assistant;* it was based, however, not on an imagined trip to Asia, but on the months Robert had spent in Wädenswil in 1903. Robert had initially incorporated some of this material into *The Tanners*—in the form of a letter to Dubler written by Simon Tanner—but the fifteen pages in question had been cut during the editing process. The new novel begins with protagonist Joseph Marti's excited arrival in the only slightly fictionalized town of Bärenswil. One crisis follows another as the business of inventor Carl Tobler, Joseph's employer, begins to fail, and the book ends with the impending collapse of both home and enterprise, precipitating Joseph's departure. Robert submitted the manuscript accompanied with a request for an 8,000-mark advance (more than $54,000 in today's dollars), in accordance with his estimation both of Scherl's resources and of the book's commercial potential.[12]

The manuscript was rejected by return mail. Indignant, Robert visited the publisher's offices (at least by his own account decades later) to demand an explanation. The editor he spoke with calmly pointed out that his monetary request was ridiculous. The incensed author—did these supposed capitalists not understand that a novel could be a valuable commodity?—called the editor a "camel" (i.e., blockhead) and stormed out.

Shortly thereafter, Cassirer accepted the novel. Morgenstern reported to Cassirer that he found this manuscript even stronger than the two prior ones ("An astonishing discipline and maturity elevates it artistically far above its predecessors"). The book, he noted in his diary, showed the influence of Dostoevsky, particularly in its portrayal of the Tobler children. We don't know whether Robert also showed the manuscript to Insel, but once the novel was known to be forthcoming from Cassirer, Robert received a note from Kippenberg saying he was unable to publish a collection of Robert's shorter works after all. Cassirer commissioned a cover illustration from Karl, who drew a man with suitcase and umbrella standing at the gate of a villa surrounded by trees.[13]

The Assistant is a study in overlapping personal and professional realms as Walser sketches with impressive psychological acuity the decline of the family and enterprise into which young Joseph Marti is introduced. Engineer Tobler is a braggart and bully who demands absolute loyalty while often behaving abusively toward his employee. Tobler's wife reminisces about a former suitor being mercilessly thrashed by her enraged husband. She displaces her unhappiness onto her purportedly charmless younger daughter, Silvi, while lavishing adoration on Silvi's sister, Dora. Tobler bullies his wife, who bullies the children, and when Joseph reproaches the mother for her treatment of Silvi, it is a rehearsal for his attempt to finally stand up to his employer and defend his own interests.

The Assistant appeared in early May 1908 and was well-received, outselling *The Tanners;* Cassirer printed a second edition only six months later, and a third edition one year after that. Most of the reviews were enthusiastic although, as with the two previous books, many were also colored with condescension for this author of "naive" prose. One reviewer used the word "primitive," while another speculated that the author "might even be an autodidact." Comparisons with Keller abounded, and Wilhelm Schäfer, editor of the journal *Die Rheinlande* (The Rhineland), invoked a second Swiss nineteenth-century author, Conrad Ferdinand Meyer, as a point of reference. Cassirer must have been pleased, even though *Neue Zürcher Zeitung* and the Berlin newspaper *National-Zeitung* panned the novel.[14]

Widmann, on the other hand—to whom Robert sent a copy as soon as the book was out—came through with a hugely positive review that was so long it had to be published in two installments. He proclaimed *The Assistant* "a true Swiss novel through and through," waxing rhapsodic as he described Walser's artistry and vision as well as praising the book's tighter structure vis-à-vis *The Tanners,* its well-drawn characters, and psychological complexity. It was everything Robert could have wished for in a review, except that he was trying to be a German writer, a Berlin writer, and Widmann was emphatically claiming him for Switzerland, even describing his use of German marks as the currency in the novel as "an unnecessary concession" to the book's German publisher.[15] But no one in Berlin read *Der Bund,* and if it helped the book sell better in Switzerland than *The Tanners* had, all the better.

The book was even reviewed in the *Times Literary Supplement* in London along with Arthur Schnitzler's *The Road to the Open.* The anonymous reviewer (Fanny Johnson) described Walser as a promising younger writer—in contrast to Schnitzler, the established master. She praised his morality of vision, which seemed to her "sounder and of more hopeful augury" than Schnitzler's, as well as his "emotional equipment" that she found "in some respects richer."[16]

In the end, the novel received dozens of reviews and sold out its first two printings—but of course these printings of one thousand copies were modest compared with those of Fischer's blockbuster authors. Like *The Tanners, The Assistant* represented a critical success but not a commercial breakthrough, even though it might well have appealed to a wider audience. Perhaps Robert had simply chosen the wrong publisher. Cassirer's contemporary publishing program was minimal; did that doom his authors to minimal success?

Robert had meanwhile been making a name for himself as an author of the feuilleton texts that were a regular feature in newspapers across Europe, offering a few moments of literary entertainment among the news reports. A feuilleton might relate a humorous anecdote, sketch a street scene, describe a hat, review a book or a musical or theatrical performance, or pass on gossip. In many newspapers, this cultural section was divided from the rest of the newspaper's content by a thick horizontal line two-thirds or three-quarters of the way down the front page. The feuilleton section might also include poems or installments of novels as well as short stories. Literary journals published pieces of this sort too. Well-known

feuilletonists of the age included Siegfried Jacobsohn, Alfred Kerr, Alfred
Polgar, Arthur Schnitzler, and Stefan Zweig—and in later years Siegfried
Kracauer, Walter Benjamin, Kurt Tucholsky, and Joseph Roth. They were
widely read, including by Robert and Karl. A Walser text from the 1930s
describes a postcard showing "an attractive young person lying in bed
reading Peter Altenberg"—referring perhaps to a photograph of bare-
chested Karl in just such a pose.[17] Even Robert's beloved Kleist wrote
feuilleton texts, and founded a newspaper, *Berliner Abendblätter,* to publish them.

Robert had been writing texts of this sort since the very beginning of
his prose career ("Lake Greifen"). Most of the short prose he published in
literary journals was of the feuilleton genre, integrating essayistic and fictional techniques into the storytelling and often including the observing
"I," and sometimes a "you," as a character. Because many of these hybrid
texts did not fall easily into the categories "essay" or "story," Walser often
just called them "prose pieces" (*Prosastücke*), sometimes using—affectionately and/or ironically—the Swiss diminutive *Prosastückli,* and he called
the activity of writing them "the little prose piece business" (*Prosastück-
ligeschäft*).

Walser's prose pieces covered all sorts of topics: the morning streets,
a park, a farmer's market, Friedrichstrasse, riding the streetcar, a lion at the
zoo, visits to the theater, a department store, and bars with variety shows.
In "Aschinger" (published December 1907 in *Die Neue Rundschau*) he
wrote a tribute to a popular local chain of fast-food restaurants where one
drank one's beer standing at a table and could soak it up with open-face
sandwiches or a sausage. In "Cat Theater," published in *Die Schaubühne*
in May 1907, he makes Karl's cat Muschi the star of a melodrama in which
a kidnapped child becomes a dancer and then the wife of a government
minister while her nanny grows old searching for her. One piece he published anonymously in *Die Schaubühne* that April, "Theater News," is a
collection of brief fictional news reports claiming, among other things, that
the great actors Gertrud Eysoldt and Friedrich Kayssler (both belonging
to Max Reinhardt's ensemble) were abandoning the theater to open a cor-
set shop and bar, and that Reinhardt had decided to drape his stage with
white bedsheets instead of painted sets. (To sign his name to the piece
would have been indelicate, as Karl and Reinhardt were taking a little
break from one another.)[18]

The number of newspapers, magazines, and literary journals in which Robert published had been steadily increasing and now included *Die Freistatt* (Sanctuary) in Munich and *Der Samstag* (Saturday) in Basel as well as the Berlin publications *Die Schaubühne* and *Die Neue Rundschau*. After *The Tanners* came out, he made a point of writing to magazines where the novel had been reviewed (such as *Neue Freie Presse* [New Free Press] in Vienna) and offering them his work for publication. In November 1907, Hugo von Hofmannsthal invited him to submit to the journal *Morgen* (Morning), where Hofmannsthal was a contributing editor. This resulted in another two published pieces the following spring, "Drawing Lesson" ("Zeichenstunde") and "She Writes" ("Sie schreibt"). In 1907 Robert published his first pieces in *Simplicissimus,* where Wedekind was an editor, and in *Die Zukunft* in 1908.

It's perhaps no coincidence that Walser never wrote proper reviews. When he writes about an art show or performance, critical activity invariably gives way to flights of fancy or personal ruminations. "Mountain Halls" ("Gebirgshallen"), for example—which appeared in the February 1908 issue of *Die Schaubühne* under the title "Advertisement" ("Reklame")—ostensibly sets out to introduce readers to a variety theater called Mountain Hall (Gebirgs-Halle) near Friedrichstrasse but soon detours into philosophical reflection: "Wherever Nature is found," he writes, "there is meaning."[19]

His description of the establishment toggles unsettlingly between sublime natural landscape and tawdry commercial venue with the apostrophized "you" going "into the mountains" and then approaching "the glacier, which is the stage: a geological, geographical, and architectural curiosity." The performances that might form the centerpiece of this ostensible review remain in the background. The narrator does drily remark, apropos of a dancer, "Kleist too waited many years for recognition," but most of the description in the piece foregrounds instead the female employees urging their guest to purchase round after round of drinks, to the detriment of his wallet.[20]

These narrative swerves between high (upper-class culture, sublime nature) and low (base commercial interests, moral and artistic tawdriness) caught the eye of a young Prague lawyer named Franz Kafka, who'd recently made his literary debut in the inaugural number of Franz Blei's journal *Hyperion* in January 1908. Max Brod described how Kafka, who'd introduced him to Walser's work, often read one of his pieces aloud to him, some more than once. One of these was "Mountain Halls," which Kafka read "with enormous mirth and delight [. . .] as if before an audience of hundreds [. . .] savor[ing] a particular turn of phrase, taking pleasure in repeating it." By the end, Kafka's suppressed laughter explosively erupted. Brod saw a strong Walser influence in Kafka's prose—for example, noting an echo of the last line of "Mountain Halls" ("I quench my thirst, melodies rock me to sleep, I dream") in the ending of Kafka's "Up in the Gallery." Robert knew nothing of this response at the time.[21]

The prose pieces Robert was publishing ever more frequently brought in much-needed cash, but not enough to keep him from leaping at the invitation in spring 1907 to fill the post of secretary to the Berlin Secession. Max Liebermann, now quite friendly with Karl, had suggested Robert for the position, and Paul Cassirer agreed. Robert would be in charge of an office in the Secession's grand new building on Kurfürstendamm, a sort of palazzo containing eight spacious galleries arrayed around a central atrium, with an outdoor stage area in back for speeches and lectures during the warmer months. The exhibition period he was engaged for ran from April 20 to August 1.[22] Robert's main secretarial tasks involved handling Paul Cassirer's correspondence and showing visitors around the gallery. His clerking experience, the time he'd spent as inventor Carl Dubler's amanuensis, and his exemplary penmanship all qualified him perfectly for the position.

Robert's private office, just off the entry hall, contained an elegant desk, Secession letterhead, and a rubber stamp ("Office of the Secession") to place above his signature or initials. Several letters he wrote as secretary survive, most of them brief and utilitarian. He corresponded with Vincent van Gogh's sister-in-law about an offer to buy one of the late painter's works and circulated catalogues and tickets for the Secession show put on during his tenure. One rather flirtatious business letter addressed to Walther Rathenau asks him to stop by and keep his promise to buy a painting by E. R. Weiss, noting that "the profit has already been used up (drunk)."[23] Robert's stint in the Secession's office ended after that initial one-season appointment—had his performance left something to be desired?—but he continued to be a regular at Cassirer's parties. "The Secretary" ("Der Sekretär"), a prose piece he wrote a decade later, parodies his experience during this brief period of employment, noting that as secretary he excelled at riding around in hackney cabs and chatting up artists' wives. His boss, he writes, mostly talked poetry with him and consoled him after his dismissal by taking him out for a meal. "Frau Bähni," another story reminiscing about this period, sketches a less flattering portrait of Paul Cassirer, including a scene in which a powerful man forces his young acquaintance, or assistant, to accompany him on a visit to a woman whose husband is professionally dependent on his goodwill. The "potentate" threatens to destroy her husband unless she submits to his desires. This story may have been inspired by Cassirer's relationship with actress Tilla Durieux, who was married to painter Eugen Spiro before she left him for Cassirer—though Robert was not present at their first meeting. In her memoirs, Durieux would describe her first encounter with the brilliant and seductive Cassirer as "rattlesnake meets rabbit."[24]

Robert and Karl had dissolved their shared apartment in the summer of 1907. Why they decided to part ways remains unclear. Fega Frisch—translator of Goncharov, Turgenev, and other Russian greats and married to writer and editor Efraim Frisch—reports that Robert once dropped in on her and her husband with a badly scratched face that he identified as the handiwork of the cat Muschi. But Frisch had the impression that the brothers sometimes got into fistfights. Robert moved to a fifth-floor walkup in a back courtyard building just around the corner, taking Muschi with him. His new home—as one visitor described it—was far from homey, "as if the person who lived here took no interest in what sort of furniture he had." A suit was draped over the back of a chair (Robert had just sewn on a button) and an old copy of Goethe's novel *Wilhelm Meister's Apprenticeship* lay open on a table (Robert was studying the book's formal properties).[25]

The two Walser brothers now saw each other only once a week, as Karl reported to Fanny that December, saying that Robert was "completely immersed in his work and resists all attempts at seduction. For this, I envy and admire him." Karl had been suffering from a stomach ailment for weeks—reduced to a diet of thin porridge—and suddenly seemed to be running low on cash. His spirits, too, were low, and he was contemplating returning permanently to Switzerland the following spring. He'd been temporarily abandoned by his Czech girlfriend (and former housekeeper), Molli—now off in Vienna trying to launch her career as a dancer. Karl had paid for her training, but no one would hire her. Karl was looking after her handsome borzoi, long a fixture in the brothers' shared apartment. Robert wrote an encouraging little essay, "To an Aspiring Dancer," that was published in *Die Schaubühne* that December.[26]

The connections Robert had made through Karl continued to help him find his way among Berlin's cultural elite. At Fischer's house he met editor Moritz Heimann, who invited Robert to drop in on the Thursday-evening salons he hosted at a Kurfürstendamm café. There Robert met Oskar Loerke and other S. Fischer authors. It's now hard to understand why Robert didn't decide to join their number. The possibility must have come up even after he declined Fischer's offer of sponsored travel. A piece Walser wrote in the 1920s refers in passing to a letter received from his "apparently absolutely honest publisher" announcing that he "cannot condone the competition's taking an interest in you." Whether or not Bruno Cassirer ever wrote such a letter, it's likely he felt threatened at the prospect of losing his promising young author to Fischer, the empire builder. Perhaps this is why Cassirer began to pay Robert a monthly allowance, reminding him where his allegiances lay.[27] Robert's sense of indebtedness must have been strong.

Fischer regularly invited Robert—along with Karl, who was still illustrating books for him—to his parties even though Robert was often a difficult guest who drank too much and sometimes got out of hand. Fega Frisch reports that one evening at Fischer's house Robert flew into an inebriated rage and smashed the Caruso records lying on the gramophone table. And while in conversation with fellow guest Hugo von Hofmannsthal, a writer he admired who must have struck a tone Robert found snooty, he asked, "Can't you forget for a bit that you're famous?"[28]

Sometimes, Frisch attests, Robert could act "rather gruff and strange." He would later recall trying to persuade Frisch to let him put on her shoes for her one day when she'd asked him to tea. He also reported that Paul Cassirer liked to say that Robert and the painter Heinrich Nauen were "the two characters with the largest appetites in all Germany, and the least inclination to entertain women properly." Cassirer used to tell Karl to bring Robert along when he invited the painter for dinner, "but only on condition he's not too terribly hungry."[29]

From Robert's point of view, these wealthy, elegant Berliners were just as bourgeois as the society they loved to despise. "At the premiere not long ago," he wrote to Morgenstern—referring presumably to the recent opening of *Spring Awakening*—"how shabbily and coldly each face recognizes the other. Nothing chillingly or warmingly unfamiliar."[30] Wasn't it his duty to make a few waves and rescue these Berliners from their inborn complacency?

Durieux relates the story of a "tragicomic Christmas party" in 1907 involving both Walser brothers, who by this time were well-known in Berlin for drinking heavily and getting up to mischief. First, Karl challenged Wedekind to a round of "Hoselupfe" wrestling. Coming to his aid, Durieux and Paul Cassirer stuffed both tipsy Walsers into a cab, but they kept popping out the other side, grinning. Finally rid of the troublemakers, Wedekind and his hosts headed to Café Austria on Potsdamerstrasse for a nightcap—only to espy the brothers Walser sitting down at the next table. When Wedekind tried to escape, Robert "rose to his feet and with a friendly grin exclaimed: 'Muttonhead!' This prompted Wedekind to storm out of the café so violently that the revolving door brought him right back inside to the Walsers' table. Now the painter stood up, looking friendly and calm, smiling: 'Muttonhead!' This time Wedekind succeeded in escaping. But the two Walsers remained in his bad graces forever. They hadn't meant anything by it though, for they too revered Wedekind."[31] The antics of these unruly Walsers only heightened their prestige in this community of artists and patrons trying to enjoy both bourgeois privilege (the Cassirers' money) and avant-garde sensibility (the anguished licentiousness of *Spring Awakening*). These young Swiss wild men were interesting and, as long as they continued producing high-quality artistic work, in no danger of eviction from these circles. Indeed, Robert's brashness seems to have endeared him to Paul Cassirer in particular.

Paul was the diametrical opposite of his cousin Bruno: impulsive where Bruno was staid; fiery and brilliant where Bruno was reticent and retiring. No wonder the two hadn't gotten along as business partners. Whispered stories were also circulating about Bruno—still married to Paul's sister—falling in love with Paul's estranged wife. Certainly both cousins loved art. Robert had seen all the Cézannes, Monets, and Manets in Bruno's apartment—Bruno had even prevailed on Karl to suggest a complementary color scheme for the walls (canary yellow, forget-me-not blue). And Paul had wanted to be a writer himself as a young man consorting with Wedekind and company in Munich. In any case, Paul was more fun to spend time with than Bruno. While Bruno's passion was racehorses, Paul preferred to go in search of adventure.³²

Robert accompanied Paul on various outings. In spring 1907 they rode a steamboat down the Havel River west of Berlin to see the blossoming fruit trees of Werder, eating and drinking beneath spreading canopies of blooms. And a thrilling invitation arrived in summer 1908, when Paul asked Robert to join him for a balloon ride from Berlin to Königsberg. The balloon was steered by Paul's cousin Alfred, owner of a pilot's license. The passengers signed a paper agreeing to obey all the pilot's commands while holding the balloon rental company blameless in the event of bodily injury.³³

A balloon ride wasn't exactly a trip abroad, but it was a trip aloft, and it presented a view of things—landscapes, cities, houses, people—from an entirely new perspective. Walser later recalled ascending at dusk from a field in Bitterfeld (on the train line to Leipzig) in a basket "well supplied with cold cutlets and beverages." The trio "swam peacefully through the night over the slumberous earth, and landed the next day on the Baltic coast." Königsberg—the city now known as Kaliningrad, Russia—would be the farthest Robert would ever venture from his native Switzerland. In a letter to Fanny that July, he boasted, "We only barely avoided flying right into the Baltic Sea, where things wouldn't have gone so well for us. Everyone here is saying I slept through the whole trip. It's unnerving what gossips people here are." Back in Berlin, Robert wrote "Balloon Journey," a description of his adventure, with a changed cast of characters, that he published in *Die Neue Rundschau*.³⁴ Experiencing something like this was a magical part of his new life; and part of the magic was writing about it.

NINE

The Fall

1908–1913

THAT BALLOON RIDE MARKED the high point of Robert Walser's public career. When Paul Cassirer took him aloft, Robert was still basking in the success of his second published novel and was thinking about his next one. A thirty-year-old writer without family wealth to buttress his aspirations, Robert had made a name for himself solely on the basis of his talent and work. His dream of establishing himself in Berlin, capital of the German-language literary world, had come to fruition.

But unhappy circumstances had also played a role in placing him at Paul Cassirer's side that day, on an excursion for which Cassirer might otherwise have chosen Karl to be his companion. Karl was in Japan, sent there by Cassirer to get him out of Berlin. Karl's girlfriend Molli, the aspiring dancer, had returned from Vienna that spring to learn that in her absence the insatiable Karl had risen from his sickbed and taken a new lover. Hedwig Agnes ("Trude") Czarnetzki was a bookkeeper and seamstress from West Prussia who'd followed her sister to Berlin, where she stopped on the street one day to say hello to a borzoi on a leash. Karl and Trude fell in love, and when Molli discovered she'd been replaced in Karl's affections, she killed herself.[1]

Karl was devastated. Robert remarked somewhat callously to Fega Frisch how "regal" he found Molli's "grand exit": "She might, after all, have pointed the gun at my brother instead."[2] When the news broke, Cassirer opened his wallet and sent Karl on a five-month journey. As his traveling companion, Cassirer selected Bernhard Kellermann, a twenty-nine-year-old S. Fischer author. The two were to travel to Japan via Moscow, where they would catch the Trans-Siberian Railway, then return by boat to Genua. They were under strict orders to collaborate on some

work or other that Cassirer could publish upon their return. It had been
seven years since Paul and Bruno Cassirer had parted ways in 1901, and,
according to the terms of their settlement, Paul could now publish books
again.

In Karl's absence, Robert moved into his top-floor apartment on
Schöneberger Ufer overlooking the Landwehr Canal, in a building that
also housed the Austro-Hungarian General Consulate. Things were qui-
eter away from the writer-infested cafés of Berlin's "New West," though
the area around Potsdamer Brücke had cafés of its own. Electric streetcars
crossed paths there with hansom cabs, and the lovely canal was framed
with a tree-lined promenade on either side. Robert's four-legged charges
were not thriving, though. Lola the borzoi fell ill and had to be put on a
special diet, and Muschi stopped doing her business outdoors. Robert
reluctantly found her another home, joking to Fanny in a letter that he
hoped she hadn't become snake fodder for the Zoological Garden. Fanny,
at least, still hadn't married Hans Mühlestein, now working as a private
tutor in Dresden.[3]

Since Robert had a novel-in-progress Bruno Cassirer was eager to
publish—and eager to see Samuel Fischer *not* publish—it seemed an op-
portune moment to suggest a book of poems. Cassirer soon agreed to publish the very same book Insel had rejected, a collection consisting
primarily, if not exclusively, of work written in or before 1900. In 1907,
Robert had published a handful of poems in Franz Blei's journal *Die
Opale* that closely resembled his early work—so closely it was hard to
know whether they were indeed more recently written. If so, it meant that
Robert's poetic style had remained unchanged even as he'd grown as a
prose author.

Cannily, Cassirer decided to publish Robert's poems as an art book.
Karl had already begun a series of etchings to accompany the poems back
when it looked like Insel would publish the edition. Now the sixteen finished etchings—along with the book's forty poems—were part of a unified
design. Despite the book's steep price tag of 45 marks (roughly $300 in
today's dollars), the signed edition of three hundred copies sold well. Reviews invariably focused on the illustrations, an attractive plus for buyers:
it was a relatively economical way to acquire a collection of small works by
a respected artist. Karl's book design framed the poems elegantly in beautiful wide margins underneath a wordless blue cardboard cover with gold,

yellow, and red ornaments and a big yellow lyre surrounded by stars. The title page depicted the author as a slender young man seated on a bench atop a grassy cliff. Each copy was numbered and signed—by Karl, who also forged Robert's signature for the occasion.[4]

The story of Robert Walser's life, as has been noted earlier in these pages, is full of gaps. This is particularly true of his Berlin years, partly because many relevant documents (such as correspondence, manuscripts, and publishers' archives) were destroyed during World War II. Walser also seems not to have made a practice of saving letters sent to him, much as he loved to write and, presumably, to receive them. The record of his life in Berlin thins out in 1908 and remains thin until his departure in 1913. Thus, many of the stories recounted here about his experiences during his last half-decade in Berlin have been reconstructed with the help of his later accounts of the period in his literary texts—which, as has already been established, cannot be relied on to fulfill a documentary function. Fortunately, it was in Berlin where Walser had the most, and most prominent, friends and associates, several of whose lives are independently documented, providing some record of his personal interactions during these years. In later periods of his life, his footsteps will be fainter and farther apart, more difficult to track.

Little is known about the composition of Walser's third published novel, *Jakob von Gunten: A Diary* (*Jakob von Gunten: Ein Tagebuch*), which Bruno Cassirer brought out in spring 1909 with a minimalist cover by Karl. It was presumably written in late 1908 after Robert moved from Karl's apartment to an avenue at the city's western edge that had opened to vehicles less than two years earlier. It was close to Grunewald—not just the fancy suburb where Samuel Fischer lived but also the forest it was named for, popular with Berliners for its woodland trails.

Arguably the finest of Walser's novels, *Jakob von Gunten* was his own favorite among his longer works. The book departs significantly from the narrative mode of *The Tanners* and *The Assistant*. While those two are largely realistic and rely heavily on the author's personal experiences, *Jakob von Gunten* is often fantastical, expressionist, and subject to surreal flights. The novel is set in a school for servants (Institute Benjamenta) clearly inspired by the butler academy Robert himself attended, but very little of the workaday reality of his schooling finds its way into the book.

The institute's teachers "are asleep, or they are dead, or seemingly dead, or they are fossilized, no matter, in any case we get nothing from them." The institute's primary textbook is titled *What Is the Aim of Benjamenta's Boys' School?*, the sole lesson, reviewed over and over, "How Should a Boy Behave?" The school's staff consists only of principal Herr Benjamenta and his sister, Lisa Benjamenta, who is in charge of all instruction. One pedagogical exercise involves scrubbing the classroom, dormitory, and stairs. The facility also contains the Benjamentas's private apartment, which Jakob refers to as the "inner chambers"—a secret, magical realm that occasions his most fanciful speculations.[5]

Like *Fritz Kocher's Essays, Jakob von Gunten* is written in short sections from a first-person perspective—ostensibly entries in the protagonist's diary. Long on atmosphere and short on plot, the book resembles *The Assistant* in structure, beginning with the young protagonist's arrival and ending with the closing of the school. As in the earlier novel, the institution at the center of the story is headed by a charismatic but tyrannical older man who becomes an object of the protagonist's fascination, even love. The climactic scene is a visit to the mysterious "inner chambers" with Lisa Benjamenta as guide. Jakob's narrative voice is breathy, excitable, and (in typical Walserian style) distraction-prone as he lovingly sketches the portraits of the school's half-dozen pupils, whose ages remain strangely indeterminate. They are referred to throughout the novel as "boys," but they come across as young men, producing a cognitive dissonance that accentuates the mood of shimmering unreality.

Unlike Simon Tanner and Joseph Marti, Jakob von Gunten is a young aristocrat, the son of a *Grossrat* (member of the Bernese cantonal legislature) who has run away from home out of fear "of being suffocated by [his father's] excellence." Enrolling in butler school, he is not rising but slumming. His aspiration to become "a charming, utterly spherical zero" disavows his birthright (a Kleistian move).[6] But Jakob has more in common with Walser's overtly autobiographical protagonists than it might at first appear. Robert, too, had enjoyed relative prosperity in early childhood; and the Robert who enrolled in butler school at age twenty-seven was already a published author with literary ambitions, not someone for whom butlering represented a step up the career ladder. Jakob never fully succeeds in casting off his high-born sensibilities, which causes friction with his comrade Kraus, who aspires to become a butler because he is convinced this is the highest station life will make available to him. In this school, Jakob is a visitor from a higher realm of class privilege—more so than even the Benjamentas—and the remnants of his disavowed status are perhaps, the book slyly suggests, what inspires his teacher's untoward admiration. Even as the novel plays with power relations and their mutability, it also tells a story about the permanence of privilege.

For the first time in a book-length work, Robert tried on a narrative persona, experimenting with a first-person point of view. Jakob's quirky voice dips more deeply into lyricism than the third-person narrators of Walser's two earlier novels, serving—along with the book's partly fantastical content—to create a sense of mystery. Perhaps this was a way of parrying accusations in the reviews of these earlier books that he was a "naive" writer, "innocent," just a scribe recording his own experiences. Now Robert was throwing his hat in the ring with Frank Wedekind and Robert Musil, both authors of celebrated works set in a schoolboy milieu—*Spring Awakening* and *The Confusions of Young Törless,* which plumbed the inner lives of teenagers, exploring the jagged edges of nascent sexuality and the havoc it can wreak on the young psyche. *Jakob von Gunten* is a gentler book, with more sighing and quiet longing than aggression, though it does include a scene in which an older student, Tremala, a former merchant mariner, approaches Jakob from behind and makes a grab for his crotch. Horrified, Jakob fights him off, explaining how "disgusting" and "loathsome" he finds this "depraved person" and his "vile tendencies." Compared with Simon Tanner, who was content to let himself be kissed by his friend Heinrich, Jakob takes far greater pains to distance himself from any notion of homoerotic attraction, responding with indignation when Herr Benjamenta confesses, "I have to contain myself [. . .] I shall kiss you if I'm not careful, you splendid boy."[7]

Jakob's relationship with the principal becomes increasingly sexualized as the novel progresses, escalating from Jakob's observation that the principal is faintly trembling as they converse to an encounter in which the principal tries to strangle him. The balance of power between the two oscillates wildly, often in a single conversation. Eventually Benjamenta proposes to Jakob that the two of them go off together to seek their fortunes in the world. While Jakob expresses displeasure ("Are you mad?"), he soon has a dream in which he follows Benjamenta into the desert "as if we had both escaped forever, or at least for a very long time, from what people call European culture." The two ride camels, with Benjamenta looking "like an Arab." Soon after, "the Indians" make him a prince, and he and Jakob "organiz[e] a revolution in India."[8] Awaking from this dream, Jakob declares himself prepared to throw in his lot with Benjamenta. Perhaps these are threads left over from Walser's ill-fated second novel, that first manuscript titled *The Assistant.*

Despite *Jakob von Gunten*'s apparent distance from Robert's life, two of his siblings play starring roles in it. Lisa Benjamenta—the beautiful, strangely sad teacher clearly inspired by Robert's older sister whose name she bears—eventually dies of heartbreak after telling Jakob, "Someone thought he would love me one day, thought he wanted to have me, but he hesitated, left me waiting, and I hesitated too." This, then, was the second novel in which Robert thematized (in changed form this time) his sister's jilting. Lisa herself was still off in Italy; she returned to Switzerland later that year to take up a teaching position in Bern. And Karl was clearly the model for Jakob's older brother Johann, living the high life in Berlin society. Early in the book, Jakob expresses skepticism about seeing his brother again, fearing Johann is now too grand a person to want anything to do with him. But the two are delighted to reunite after a chance encounter on the street. When Jakob visits his brother's tastefully furnished apartment, both Muschi and Lola enjoy cameos. Other bit players include several teachers from the Biel *Progymnasium* who had previously appeared in Walser's prose piece "Diary of a Pupil," published in *Die Zukunft* that December. Someone from Biel annotated a copy with their real names.[9]

Jakob von Gunten appeared on April 17, 1909, two days after Robert's thirty-first birthday. Within a fortnight a dream review appeared in *Der Tag* (The Day), the newspaper published by Scherl, whose offices he'd purportedly been laughed out of two years earlier. Right there on the front page, Hermann Hesse—the golden boy whose debut novel *Peter Camenzind* had sold out three dozen printings for Fischer—sang Robert's praises. The review appeared in the evening issue on April 28—an evening Robert spent at Neues Opern-Theater in the company of Paul Cassirer. Did they pick up a copy from a newsboy on their way to a nightcap?

Hesse didn't just rave about *Jakob von Gunten*. The review starts at the beginning of Walser's career, with *Fritz Kocher's Essays,* and goes on to devote an admiring paragraph to each book, pronouncing each more engaging and accomplished than the previous one—with the exception of

Walser's poems, which Hesse dismisses. While admiring Walser's "charming stylistic surefootedness," Hesse found that his ability to lovingly capture the individuality of each person and landscape he describes made him "an important writer." After observing a continuity among Walser's books ("Jakob is Kocher, is Tanner, is the assistant Marti, is Robert Walser"), Hesse pronounces *Jakob von Gunten* more mature than the others, with "everything that in the earlier books sounded prettier and sweeter [now] deeper and more bitter," the characters "distorted and yet uncannily realistic, as in photographs taken from too close up." Walser's "repetition and almost furtive circling of the dark spots within his own nature" reminds Hesse of Knut Hamsun. He declares Robert a significant modern author who has been wrongly overlooked.[10]

During this fertile, exciting spring, Robert had also been writing and publishing a great deal of new short prose. *Die Schaubühne,* for example— the theater weekly founded by hotheaded young critic Siegfried Jacobsohn—published "Wenzel," the story of a would-be actor (see Chapter 2). The story displays the pleasure Robert had been taking in giving his characters maddeningly extended lines of dialogue, page-long disquisitions that elevate material like a father-son power struggle over the son's future into lofty declarations about art. Twenty years later, Walser would remark that Jacobsohn had been hugely influential in his development, "drawing my attention, as it were, to the demands a new age justifiably makes on a writer."[11]

Jacobsohn published twenty-six Walser pieces before the end of 1907, including "Kleist in Thun" and the anonymous "Theater News" discussed in Chapter 8. Roughly every second issue of *Die Schaubühne* featured something by him, published alongside some of the most respected writers and critics of the age: Alfred Polgar, Julius Bab, Peter Altenberg, Lion Feuchtwanger, and Ferdinand Hardekopf. Some of Walser's saucier pieces appeared under the pseudonym "Kutsch," such as "What's Happening with My Play?" in which a director's failure to respond to a play submitted twelve years earlier prompts a risibly melodramatic riposte: "You behold me, sir, purple with rage, but I urgently implore you: kindly find my outbursts ridiculous. Have me thrown downstairs. Slap my face and rinse your hands, soiled by this blow, in my blood. Should you command it, I'll slit my own throat."[12] While we don't know how these pieces came to appear under a pseudonym, Walser clearly enjoyed the freedom that this anonymity (even if transparent) gave him to indulge his taste for satire.

He signed his own name to an unflattering description of Friedrich Kayssler's performance in Kleist's *Prince Friedrich of Homburg* (which Robert hadn't gone to see) and "The Writer," which informs us, "Never does a writer born to write lose courage; he trusts practically uninterruptedly in the world and the thousand new possibilities it offers him each morning." Robert also tried his hand at current events for Samuel Fischer's quarterly *Die Neue Rundschau*, assuming the point of view of Abdul Hamid II, sultan of the Ottoman Empire, whose dethroning in 1909 was much covered in the German press. "Farewell" shows Robert trying to bring an imaginative approach to contemporary history much as he had with "The Battle of Sempach." Perhaps unsurprisingly, the piece relies heavily on orientalist tropes.[13]

Another point-of-view piece he wrote for Fischer's journal that summer was outrageous in other ways: "The Little Berliner" ("Die kleine Berlinerin") is narrated by a twelve-year-old girl transparently recognizable as Paul Cassirer's daughter, Suzanne Aimée. In this purported excerpt from the girl's diary, she chatters on about her privileged Berlin life: about strolls with her governess through Tiergarten, visits with her mother to Venice, and—scandalously—her father's temper, which is occasionally unleashed on her. "Papa boxed my ears today," she begins—words that sound rougher in German, which doesn't distinguish between boxed ears and a slapped face. Many more opinions follow: "Parents who don't consider it necessary to withhold their personal storms from their children degrade them to slaves in no time. A father should overcome his bad moods in private—but how difficult that is!"[14] Writing this story was a little act of rebellion on Robert's part against the hand that had so often fed him. It's unknown whether his insubordination had consequences.

Meanwhile, something peculiar was happening with *Jakob von Gunten*—or rather not happening. Sales should have soared after Hesse's accolades, and other critics should have chimed in with further encomiums. But instead of a flood of ecstatic reviews, lukewarm assessments trickled in. Fritz Marti, feuilleton editor of *Neue Zürcher Zeitung*, praised the book's atmosphere but complained that it lacked even the skeleton of a coherent plot, much less clarity and vision. He called it a "mere mosaic," its protagonist a cipher. The *Frankfurter Zeitung* and *Die Zeit* critics declared the book slight as well, and Josef Hofmiller trashed it outright in *Süddeutsche Monatshefte* (while praising the book of poems).[15]

Widmann lauded the book but was put off by what he saw as the vulgarity of the Tremala episode. Additional reviews that arrived over the following months continued to praise the book's haunting atmosphere and lovely writing but declared it devoid of plot, substance, and significance. One belated review in *Berliner Börsen-Courier* the following summer was the most insulting of all, describing the book as a new Bible for the cult of Walser, a new idol that prophet Bruno Cassirer wanted German audiences to pray to.[16]

Sales remained weak. Disheartened by how few copies had sold, Cassirer released a faux second printing two months later, slapping the words "second printing" on a new title page (he'd bound only half the first printing) in the hope of making the book appear more popular than it was. Efraim Frisch—now employed by Cassirer as an editor—wrote to Morgenstern that he blamed Cassirer's lack of marketing savvy for the fact that Robert's novel wasn't selling: "things would be looking very different now if Fischer were his publisher."[17]

By remaining faithful to Cassirer, Robert had effectively doomed his own career. He had finally written a novel that proved him worthy of standing beside Thomas Mann, Hermann Hesse, and Robert Musil as one of the important new voices of twentieth-century German literature, and what did he have to show for it? A book marketed to artists. Berlin was full of potential readers who would never learn of his book's existence. He was at the height of his powers, thirty-one years old, and his star had stopped rising. Was it too late to ask Fischer to take him on? Every one of his novels had failed to sell, and he was hardly a young author any longer.

An additional problem with *Jakob von Gunten*'s poor showing was that it made Robert less attractive to magazine and newspaper editors. There was less excitement about his work now than just a year or two earlier, and it was becoming increasingly difficult for him to summon the discipline and energy he needed to write material he was no longer confident he could place. The newspaper *Berliner Tageblatt,* which had published a pair of pieces by him in 1907 and again in 1908, published nothing of his in 1909. *Die Schaubühne,* once his best outlet, publishing fifteen of his pieces in 1907, accepted only three that year. In December 1909, the

Düsseldorf-based journal *Die Rheinlande* (whose founding editor Wilhelm Schäfer had sprung to the defense of *The Assistant* in an earlier review) accepted "Food for Thought," perhaps the gloomiest piece of writing Robert had ever produced: "How uncertain, how difficult people make one another's lives! How they belittle each other and are at pains to suspect and dishonor. [. . .] What efforts people make to disguise themselves with the intention of causing harm."[18]

Robert gave up yet another apartment in early 1910. It was a shame, because he'd finally made up his mind to pay for a listing in the 1910 *Berliner Adressbuch* (as Karl had been doing since 1905). But Karl had invited Robert to stay in his spacious, new, and temporarily vacant apartment—the artist was on his honeymoon in Switzerland. In January, Karl had married Trude, the woman he'd met while walking Molli's borzoi in 1908. Robert continued living with the newlyweds throughout that spring. Writing remained difficult, as did publishing. At least one story Robert sent to *Die Schaubühne* that season was rejected: "The Playwright's Wife," a persona piece à la "The Little Berliner," though much shorter. *Die Schaubühne* published him only four times that year, including one piece, "An Actor," that describes a powerful lion who looks out with "princely strength" and "the gaze of a god" from a tiny cage in Berlin's Zoological Garden.[19]

   Trude ultimately grew tired of watching Robert mope around. According to biographer Robert Mächler, he made Karl nervous by standing behind him (while he painted?) for half an hour at a time. He wasn't in a mood to socialize. He may have begun one or more novels during this period. In a prose piece Walser published in 1925, "Concerning a Sort of Duel," the narrator claims to have written six novels in Berlin, "three of which I saw fit to tear up." Asked decades later about the "rumor" that he'd burned three of his manuscripts in Berlin, Walser gave a hedging confirmation ("That's quite possible"), adding, "In those days I was hellbent on writing novels. But I came to understand that my heart was set on a form that was too expansive for my talents. So I withdrew into the snail shell of short stories and feuilletons." In "A Homecoming in the Snow," an essay about this period from 1917, he writes that he "was forced to realize that many things could not be as swiftly accomplished as I would have liked to imagine. [. . .] Exertions carried out in vain rendered me effectively ill. I destroyed much that I had created with great effort." The pressure was overwhelming.[20]

And so he did what he had done back in Zurich years before when he wanted to retreat to a place of anonymity and safety: in the summer of 1910 he moved to the outskirts of town, so far out, in fact, that he was no longer technically in Berlin. The building was so close to the Westend S-bahn station that he could watch the trains arriving and departing from his building's east-facing windows. The tracks cut a deep gash in the landscape, a sort of industrial apocalyptic urban wasteland that was becoming ubiquitous throughout Europe's metropolises. From there, he could walk, if he wished, the three miles to the colony of pretty villas in Grunewald where Fischer lived. It was like crossing over into an alien realm. At least it was spring now, and the woods nearby were filled with flowers, as was the little cemetery Luisenkirchhof II just around the corner.

In 1915, Walser wrote "Frau Wilke," one of several stories published between 1914 and 1916 that appear to be based on his experiences during his last years in Berlin. He used the real name of his landlady, Jenny Wilke, a retired teacher, and describes withdrawing from the social life he'd previously enjoyed, becoming a loner once again, and writing far less than before. For a while, in fact, he didn't write at all. Every time he sat down to try, his thoughts would freeze up and his hand would clench, making it painful to grip his pen. Dipping pen into ink summoned up a harsh inner critic. No one wanted to read what he wrote, so why was he wasting his time?

He'd experienced writer's cramp before while sprinting through the composition of each of his novels. This was different. Even the very thought of writing made his hand hurt. It was as though his muscles were patiently but persistently instructing him to give up. In a 1927 letter, he described this period of his life as "a time when [the writer of these lines] frightfully hated his pen, I can't begin to tell you how sick of it he was; he became an outright idiot the moment he made the least use of it."[21] For the rest of 1910 and 1911 he struggled with paralyzing self-loathing, writing little, writing nothing. He hardly recognized his own handwriting—it looked crabbed, shaky, and stiff, displaying the herculean effort it took to force out each word, while every idea seemed worthless. He took long walks through the surrounding neighborhoods and woods. Winter in Westend smelled of the coal that people dragged upstairs in buckets to feed their heating stoves. He lugged many a bucket for Frau Wilke.

Small flashes of light, hope, and pleasure sometimes arrived. Robert made at least one trip to the Baltic coast, the German Riviera. The first was probably in 1911, when Karl was summering in Wustrow on the Fischland peninsula outside Ribnitz, one of the seaside towns whose "moods immemorial" and "slender churches and aristocratic institutes for young ladies" Walser mentions in passing in *The Robber,* referring to the convent there. He also visited the island of Rügen, "the length and breadth of which" the protagonist of *The Robber* "paced out on foot." How strange and beautiful the sea was. He'd read about it as a boy in landlocked, mountainous Switzerland, and now here it lay before him with its waves, salty scents, ever-changing reflections of sunlight on water, and mysterious depths. The sea, he recalled in a feuilleton text written not long afterward, was "deep-blue, with cheerful brown sailboats on the beautiful water." He was remembering the *Zeesenboote,* the traditional, flat-bottomed, brown-sailed boats developed for use in the shallow waters of the lagoon on the peninsula's inland edge. It was lovely to spend a few days there with Karl that summer, sleeping late, breakfasting, and playing cards in the garden behind the hotel.[22]

In March 1911, Efraim Frisch published a review essay in *Die Neue Rundschau* that praised Walser's work in general and *Jakob von Gunten* in particular, describing the experience of reading it as "dreaming a wonderful dream." In October, Paul Cassirer printed a double portrait of Robert—sketch by Karl, essay by Max Brod—in *Pan,* a weekly that Cassirer had cofounded with Alfred Kerr. Brod, introduced to Robert's short prose by Kafka, received a copy of *Jakob von Gunten* as a birthday present from him in 1910. That same year Brod sent Robert his new book of poems, *Diary in Verses,* inscribing it to him "with deepest admiration." The substantial "Commentary" he wrote for *Pan* paints an astonishing portrait of Walser's prose, describing it as more complex than that of Dickens and Hamsun, in each of whom Brod detects "two layers" (e.g., when Dickens writes something humorous, a somber truth is barely concealed below). Brod identifies Walser as the first writer whose work has three layers: beneath the apparent naiveté, Brod writes, lies a layer of "irony, artfulness, delicacy of feeling," and beneath that he detects a further layer where Walser can be seen to be "genuinely naïve, powerful, and Swiss-German." Brod analyzes the artistry of Walser's prose in admiring detail, from sentence rhythms and melody to his use of syntax and neologisms to unsettle the reader's expectations. In short, Brod believed Walser to be truly one of the age's greatest authors.[23]

Brod and Walser never met, though Brod made several trips from Prague to Berlin in the early nineteen-teens. Did he try and fail to see Walser? Sociable, well-connected, and gossipy, Brod apparently heard enough scuttlebutt to feel justified in informing his Prague colleague Egon Erwin Kisch—just planning a trip to Berlin himself in 1913—that Robert was a drinker.[24]

Out in Westend, Robert lived in relative isolation. He occasionally managed to write something and submit to one of the journals that used to publish him back when he was still someone. *Die Schaubühne* didn't accept anything at all by him in 1911 but took a short essay titled "Drama" for the January 1912 issue. Perhaps Jacobsohn felt worried about Robert and wanted to help; this was neither the sort of work *Die Schaubühne* usually printed nor did it concern the stage. "Drama" is a three-hundred-word manifesto of moroseness. It's as if Walser was so traumatized by the reproach of slightness that he took pains to write with the utmost solemnity. The result is glum: "Oftentimes a marriage is a tomb, and gaiety is transformed into dismal, muttering, bleached-out indifference," he intones. He ends this belabored screed of *ressentiment* with a dreary Q&A: "Why are we mutually unedifying? Because we are uncourteous and uncouth." He published an almost equally gloomy (though more ironic) piece, "What Became of Me," that February in *Pan*. He was, at least according to the narrator of "Frau Wilke," "in a bad way," his mind "as if broken in fragments before my grieving eyes."[25]

Sometimes in his desperation to write something—anything—he would pick up a pencil. The implement felt so different in his hand that it tricked his fingers into writing despite themselves while offering relief from a painful cramp "both physical and mental" along with the sense of being hopelessly stuck. When he wrote in pencil, it didn't seem so serious an undertaking. It was a low-impact way of experimentally setting down his thoughts, including ideas for future texts. He would occasionally write something short and copy it over in pen—which somehow wasn't as hard as grasping the pen while he was thinking or write-thinking. In the blank space at the top of "The Playwright's Wife," a manuscript Jacobsohn returned to him, he sketched out a few lines that might become part of some other text: "I just imagine it, so firmly. Admittedly, admittedly, beguilements do exist. This is all too possible. Perhaps I am mistaken."[26] He wrote eight lines before crossing them out such that they were both there and not there. Did he even own an eraser?

He also managed to write some pieces that sounded more like him. In March, *Die Schaubühne* published his satirical tribute to nineteenth-century playwright Charlotte Birch-Pfeiffer, in which he writes more about her body (rudely: "a nimble hectoliter barrel") than her work. This was soon followed by an offhanded review of Mozart's *Don Giovanni,* and then, in April, by a piece that showed him in top form again: "Lenz," a micro-drama comprising eight brief scenes from the playwright's life. Walser's Lenz behaves improperly, sneaking into one lady's room to kiss her stockings and then throwing himself at the feet of another who wants nothing to do with him. He finds himself ejected from court with the approval of an imperious and self-satisfied Goethe. It's perhaps understandable that Robert—given his current artistic semi-isolation—would have been thinking again about writers who were denied artistic recognition because of their inability to fit in socially. First snubbed for his odd behavior, Lenz is eventually undone by mental illness.[27] Ironically, the dark vein Robert mined in this piece was what Bruno Cassirer had been disappointed not to find in his previous work—but hadn't it been there all along?

A few months later, Robert published several more new pieces: one about Büchner, another about popular nineteenth-century playwright August von Kotzebue, and a third about being forced as a child by his little sister Fanny to tell stories. For better or worse, he was back on track as a writer of short prose, producing pieces that sounded more like his earlier work. Was he now donning his erstwhile lightheartedness as a mask? Of all the personas a writer may adopt, perhaps the most difficult is one's own. Jacobsohn had accepted ten of Robert's pieces for *Die Schaubühne* by year's end, an encouraging development. Robert went out, saw people, wrote more. He viewed the van Gogh paintings Paul Cassirer was exhibiting and wrote an essay about one—*L'Arlésienne,* which Cassirer eventually bought to display in his own apartment—that appeared in *Kunst und Künstler* in June 1912. "In front of this picture," Robert wrote, "one has all kinds of thoughts, and to someone absorbed in it many questions occur, questions at once so simple and so strange and so disconcerting that they may seem unanswerable."[28]

Brod and Kafka must have been talking up Walser to other writers in Prague, because in May 1912 their associate Otto Pick lavished praise on *Jakob von Gunten* in an article on modern German writing in the journal *Novina*. Brod had another chance to show his admiration for Robert's work that winter when he invited him to contribute to a new literary almanac Brod was editing for publisher Ernst Rowohlt in Leipzig. Robert sent him a poem and a pair of short prose pieces. The last piece Robert published in *Die Schaubühne* that year—in October 1912—was "Ovation," yet another Walser piece that may have inspired Kafka's "Up in the Gallery," among other works. Walser's sketch (beginning "Just imagine . . .") portrays a scene in which an "actress, singer, or dancer" has inspired her audience to thunderous applause that is described spatially as layers of strangely overlapping images (hail, a drizzle of flowers, a cloud, a divine mist) before our attention is directed to the artist's "tiny, exquisite feet." An enthralled baron offers the girl money and is rebuffed, leaving the story to return to its ecstatic description of the sounds and sensations of the all-encompassing applause. Didn't Robert, too, deserve applause? In any case, Kafka was still thinking about his work in October 1917 when he wrote in his diary that Walser reminded him of Dickens in his "blurring employment of abstract metaphors."[29]

Building owner Anna Scheer became Robert's new landlady after Jenny Wilke's death. He would write stories about her too. Scheer proved just as lonely an old woman as Wilke had been. Unlike Wilke, though, Scheer was rich. She had successfully speculated in real estate and owned several buildings. Robert's abode was a hotel turned rooming house. Fega Frisch, attempting to pay Robert a surprise visit there one day, discovered a series of "petit-bourgeois rooms," each door labeled with a card announcing the occupant's name. In Walser's stories about this period in his life, his fellow tenants are elided, making his protagonists the only source of companionship for their elderly landladies. In reality, Robert had neighbors. One was painter Erich Eltze, whom Robert might have met through Karl. Other tenants included seamstresses, a butler, carters, a factory worker, a bartender, several office employees, and a potter whose wife was in the job-placement business. In Walser's "Frau Scheer" (1915), Scheer allows her lodger to live rent-free in exchange for his help running errands, deal-ing with tenants and contractors, and picking up sums of money from the bank on her instructions; she often cooks for him as well. If this was also true of Robert, he was an assistant all over again, working for his room and board, much as he had in Wädenswil. In an unpublished piece from 1919, the narrator reports being offered so many good things to eat that he starts to limit his intake out of fear of getting fat.[30]

Robert was writing again, but only short pieces, not the novel it would take to reinvigorate his career. In "The New Novel" (1916), Walser describes an author who can no longer show himself in public because he's made the mistake of insinuating that he's working on a new book. Everyone he runs into asks about it—including his publisher, who be-comes increasingly disgruntled when the promised manuscript fails to materialize, eventually refusing to receive the disappointing author until he produces something.[31] At some point while Robert was living out in Westend, Bruno Cassirer withdrew his patronage, declaring himself un-willing to pay a monthly stipend to an author not seriously engaged in writing a book Cassirer could publish.

Recalling such a moment of crisis in *The Robber,* Walser relates: "One day my benefactor drew my attention to the inappropriateness which seemed to him to slumber in the possibility of his further financial support. This announcement made me nearly dumb with astonishment. [. . .] My landlady found me weeping." The loss of Cassirer's patronage was certainly a dramatic development, though in several texts written years later, Walser reports that he had begun to use the money to pursue various entertainments instead of working, becoming "more something of an adventurer than a productive author." While avoiding his desk, Robert became a regular (by his own perhaps fictionalized account) at the "Cow-shed," a bar and variety show on Invalidenstrasse in Berlin's proletarian north, where "ear-rending" music was on offer and the entire staff was constantly thirsty. He wrote something about the place for *Die Schaubühne* that Jacobsohn accepted and paid for but never printed.[32] Disappointment went down easier with a glass of beer.

In autumn 1912, Robert started thinking about publishing a book that wasn't a novel. He wrote to Paul Cassirer asking whether he might be in-terested in publishing a volume of his essays for 300 marks (roughly

$1,800 in today's dollars). The answer was no. Years later Walser remained indignant at this refusal, recalling how badly he'd needed the money and how Cassirer had coldly given him the news through an emissary.[33] Returning to Bruno Cassirer was out of the question—he'd made it clear that the only thing that would interest him was a publishable novel.

Fortunately Robert still knew writers who might help him. Frisch had just moved to Munich to become a full-time editor at the Georg Müller publishing house, and Brod retained his Rowohlt affiliation. Hints that Robert needed a new publisher quickly resulted in a pair of invitations to submit proposals. In lieu of a novel, Robert pitched the book of essays to Rowohlt and one collection each of stories and verse dramas to Müller, requesting 300 marks for each of these three manuscripts.

To his surprise, both publishers accepted. Müller sent him an advance of 300 marks, and Robert mailed him the stories; and he signed a contract for his book of essays with Rowohlt in October. Robert could hardly believe this sudden turn of fortune. For once he had good news to share with Karl, who agreed to provide illustrations for at least the book of stories, all of which had previously appeared in literary journals. Most dated from Robert's first few years in Berlin, and some even earlier— including stories from *Die Insel* and "Lake Greifen," his first published prose piece from 1899—and most had been included in the collection he'd offered Insel in 1907. The only recent piece was "Paganini: Variation," which he'd published in the journal *Die Rheinlande* earlier that year. There was a single story from 1909 and nothing at all from 1910 or 1911; he'd written and published a modest number of feuilleton texts, but nothing he wanted to call a "story." Those meager years made the 300 marks in his pocket and the pledge of an additional 600 seem all the more precious.

Rowohlt's payment arrived less than a month later. Negotiations with Müller, however, proved complicated. Robert had been using the more obviously appealing story collection—for which Karl had drawn four sample illustrations—as part of a package deal to ensure publication of the less marketable verse plays Müller was now having second thoughts about. After weeks of correspondence, Robert offered the stories and plays to Rowohlt, who quickly accepted them. He agreed to refund the honorarium paid by Müller and to pay Karl a princely 1,500 marks for twenty-five illustrations including drawings for the book of stories and covers for both books. Rowohlt even showed unexpected enthusiasm for the plays, scouring back issues of *Die Insel* in search of additional pieces to include. With another publisher now interested, Müller tried to backpedal, offering to throw in a contract for a future novel, but Robert didn't bite. Insulted by Müller's previous reluctance, he refused to bargain, and so he became a Rowohlt author, just like Brod's friend Kafka, whose first book of stories, *Contemplation* (*Betrachtung*), had come out that December.[34]

A dramatic change occurred in Robert's living situation while these negotiations were under way: Frau Scheer went into the hospital for an operation and while there suffered a fatal stroke on October 28, 1912. Robert was shocked and deeply saddened. This hardly maternal woman had in the end mothered him quite a lot, and now he was alone again. Did he have other friendships during this period? The narrator of the story "Frau Scheer" reports having a girlfriend, "delightful Auguste"—but he advises her to leave him, since he is not only poor but is "steeling [him]self for even more poverty," and applauds her sound judgment when she does so.[35] Whether Auguste had a real-life counterpart is unknown.

Robert was obliged to vacate the apartment as a result of Scheer's death, so he moved back in with Karl and Trude in mid-January 1913, remaining their guest for several weeks.[36] He pondered and discussed his situation with Karl. The advances he'd received were a great help, far more than what he'd been earning from magazine publications, which didn't add up to a livelihood. He needed to write another novel. But it had been four years since he'd last written one he was happy with, and he was no longer sure he could. He felt defeated—and even he understood that he was drinking too much. Was there any point to his staying in Germany?[37] If he left, perhaps he could shore up his energies and then return to writing novels. In Berlin, he would constantly be confronted with the debacle his career as a novelist had become. With no new work to show, there was no professional advantage to remaining in the proximity of all the writers and artists he used to consort with. He packed up his battered pride and boarded a train back to Switzerland.

TEN

The Return to Switzerland

1913–1914

THE LAST STORY WALSER published before leaving Germany, "The Hermitage," appeared in *Die Rheinlande* in January 1913 and is set "somewhere in Switzerland, in a mountainous region." After nostalgically invoking a peaceful remote landscape and a life of solitary tranquility, it concludes, "How I'd love to be the hermit and live there in the hermitage."[1] Robert was in fact already planning his retreat to a place and situation that fit this description well. He would not be alone there, however; he was retreating into the arms of the closest person he had left to a mother—Lisa, who had recently accepted a new post in the tiny village of Bellelay high up in the Jura Mountains above Biel.

Cradled in a mountain valley at 3,068 feet, Bellelay is reached via two trains and a post bus that ascend past stone cliff faces and tree-covered slopes. Besides its large Premonstratensian monastery, the village boasts a small post office, one inn, and a dairy where the nutty semihard cheese called Tête de Moine (monk's head) is produced. Bellelay Abbey was converted into a psychiatric hospital at the end of the nineteenth century to serve mainly "incurable" patients.

Lisa was hired in 1912 to teach the asylum staff's children. After her return from Livorno in 1909, she'd moved to Bern to complete her certification for "secondary school" (corresponding roughly to junior high school in the United States). She briefly taught at a Bern orphanage but began looking for another post after clashing with the headmistress over questions of pedagogy.[2] In Bellelay she oversaw a one-room schoolhouse for both primary and secondary pupils. As in Täuffelen a decade earlier, she lived upstairs from her classroom—in a small apartment with a kitchen niche—and took most of her meals in the hospital's dining hall.

Lisa's walls were covered with pictures, including Karl's portrait of
Robert in robber's garb from their teenage years. The living room held a
sofa, a large table with an embroidered cloth, a piano, and a packed book-
shelf. Her only companion in this modest residence was a small dog—at
least until Robert's arrival. He would later say it was "pure luck" he'd
found his way into Lisa's care—especially after all the heavy drinking and
"impossible" behavior he'd indulged in during his last few years in Berlin,
giving him "such a reputation" that he didn't dare return to Zurich.[3]

In a series of brief texts published a year after his return to Switzerland, Walser reminisced—perhaps with some fictional touches—about his
arrival in Bellelay: the journey into the mountains (the last leg of which, a
path through the forest, he covered on foot) and his arrival well after dark
at the schoolhouse. A light was burning upstairs, and his knock set the dog
to barking. A time of recovery ensued, with Lisa providing for his needs
while he assisted her in small ways, lugging wood upstairs for the heating
stove, making tea, washing plates and cups; they were playing house as
they'd done in Täuffelen a decade before. Except now they were both fully
adults—he thirty-five, she approaching forty—old enough for their single-
hood to possibly be permanent. Robert later wrote about the beautiful
walks he took among the tall fir trees for which the region is known. He
ascended the peaks of the Montoz and Moron and, when spring arrived,
rambled through meadows filled with Jacob's-ladder and daffodils.[4]

According to Lisa's closest friend at the time, Frieda Mermet, she had
eagerly awaited Robert's arrival but was also apprehensive; would there be
room in her small apartment for both him and his disappointment? She
knew from his letters that he was in a bad way. Karl had said so too. Would
he drink too much in Bellelay's one little pub and embarrass her? He'd
written about her in his books, exposing her most private pain to public
scrutiny. But he was still her beloved younger brother. She'd spent many
an evening discussing him with Mermet, who ran the asylum's laundry.[5]

For Robert—who would remain in Bellelay for the rest of that
spring—these were months spent in isolation from the world but also in
isolation from loneliness, since he had Lisa's companionship. It felt like a
reprieve, a time for him to gather himself, to recover. He spent long after-
noons reading his way through the classics in her library and thinking over
what he could do to get back on track. He had three books forthcoming,
and even if he never wrote another novel, he could certainly produce more

stories and essays that he should be able to publish. His career was by no means over, though it would perhaps not blossom in the grand style he'd imagined.

In Bellelay, Robert rested. He wrote, but not much. He took long walks with Lisa, sometimes joined by Mermet on weekends, and often walked about on his own while Lisa was at school. He amused himself in her absence and later enjoyed her company, often sharing communal meals in the dining hall with Mermet, the hospital's bookkeeper, the head nurse, and, occasionally, the head doctor. As one of Lisa's pupils later recalled, Robert kept his distance from the Bellelay schoolchildren: "He never had a proper conversation with any of us wild boys, but always replied graciously when we said hello to him, giving a friendly, knowing smile." Mermet's son, Louis—nine or ten years old when Robert arrived in Bellelay—also reported that his teacher's brother "didn't speak much with children, though he would sometimes chat with me briefly."[6]

Sometimes when Lisa was working, Robert would write at the table in her living room. He knew that "Meta"—relating a drunken Berlin encounter with a prostitute—would displease her. Next, he wrote a brief walk story describing a ramble through a nocturnal landscape, ending in a comfortable bed in an inn.[7] These stories were mailed to Wilhelm Schäfer, who printed them in the journal *Deutsche Monatshefte,* an offshoot of *Die Rheinlande.* Neither was Robert's best work, but still, he was writing stories and getting them published.

Advance copies of his book *Essays (Aufsätze)*—his first since 1909— arrived later that spring. Karl's cover featured a simple drawing of an apple, a pear, and two cherries arranged atop a book. Robert's book, in other words, was adorned with an image of a book's adornment. The handsome, beautifully printed volume bore Kurt Wolff's name instead of Rowohlt's, as Rowohlt had been bought out of the publishing house he'd founded. Shortly afterward, Max Brod's *Arcadia: An Almanac for Poetry (Arkadia: Ein Jahrbuch für Dichtkunst)* arrived—also published by Wolff. It contained four pieces by Robert as well as work by Franz Blei, Kurt Tucholsky, and Kafka (a new story, "The Judgment"). Brod also sent along a new volume of his own essays, *On the Beauty of Ugly Pictures,* which included Brod's essay on Walser from *Pan.*[8]

Robert proudly showed his new publications to Lisa and her friends. He was especially pleased to show them to Mermet, who was making an

ever greater impression on him. One year Robert's senior, she was originally from Germany but had moved to France with her coachman husband—whom she subsequently left. A single mother, she managed the
laundry that supplied clean linens to the entire hospital, supervising a staff
made up largely of patients. In the absence of washing machines—new
technology that hadn't yet made its way to Bellelay—all the hospital's
sheets and towels were hand-scrubbed in huge wooden tubs. After washing, the linens were hung up to dry and then taken to the ironing room,
where Mermet's oversight was crucial. "We always worked with around ten
patients," she later explained. "For the most part, these women were quiet
patients who liked coming to the laundry and were industrious workers."[9]

As for Robert, she found him "very reserved": "He was polite, and
could be very nice, but only when the people were to his liking. [. . .] He
always talked a great deal, but not so much about Nature and the things
we were seeing, he often spoke about books and acquaintances. He was
very well-read and knew a great deal, he was knowledgeable about many
different subjects, and he always had his own personal opinion about
things."[10] Mermet was clearly one of the people Robert found "to his liking." She was a tall, strong, decisive woman who hadn't had an easy life
and therefore knew a thing or two. Lisa respected her and cherished her
friendship. Robert found her admirable as well and possibly attractive too.
She wasn't as pretty as Lisa, but there was an air of knowingness about her,
a dignity she'd preserved despite her difficult life.

In Bellelay, Robert found relief from the feeling that had plagued him
near the end of his Berlin years of having run out of things to write about
or "grazed up all the motifs like a cow its meadow." Now ideas were arriving in his head once more. He submitted more stories to *Deutsche
Monatshefte,* including one that appeared in the April 1913 issue, "The
Kiss." One of the most nightmarish texts Walser ever published, this gruesome piece describes a dream in which an enormous disembodied kiss
descends from great heights to the sleeper's lips, terrifying him.[11]

On Lisa's shelves, Robert found all the books and journals he and
Karl had sent her over the years. He flipped through her copy of *Kunst
und Künstler* from July 1904 and wrote an ekphrastic piece based on Karl's
painting *At the Window.* Then he found Karl's painting *The Dream* in a
Berlin Secession catalogue from 1903. He sent "Two Pictures by My
Brother" to the journal *Schweizerland* in Chur, which accepted them.[12]

Reviews of *Essays* started to come in. The April 1913 edition of *Die Neue Rundschau* ran a review by Brod that pronounced the book a "masterpiece." In the same article, Brod reviewed Kafka's first book of stories, *Contemplation,* declaring Walser and Kafka comparable in their emphasis on language over subject matter. Brod describes how Kafka, at work on "The Stoker," didn't want to study up on America, since he was writing "the America of his heart and mind"—for example, giving the Statue of Liberty a sword to hold instead of a torch because it "fits better in the sentence." "Walser," Brod muses, "would have done the same." Kurt Tucholsky, writing under his pseudonym Peter Panter in the April 24 issue of *Die Schaubühne,* reprised Brod's notion of the "three-layer writer" as he recommended *Essays,* praising Walser for breathing life into old clichés and "transfigur[ing] things long overlooked on every page of his novels."[13]

Once Robert was writing regularly again, it seemed time to strike out on his own. He decided to come back down the mountain in June—but to go where? His misgivings about returning to Berlin aside, Lisa made no secret of the fact that she was concerned about him. He considered Zurich but then thought better of it, finding it—as he would later report— "advisable to behave as inconspicuously as possible," having "really nothing to crow over." Lisa advocated for a solution that would reassure her as to his well-being: a temperance hotel in Biel.[14]

Hotel Blaues Kreuz was housed in a six-story building overlooking the canal just off Biel's busy main square Zentralplatz. Run by members of the Blue Cross temperance organization, it served no alcohol in its restaurant. Even with book manuscript money in his pocket, Robert couldn't have afforded to be a hotel guest there for long, but a room was for rent on the building's attic floor where the chambermaids lived, and room and board for this garret room cost only 90 francs per month. Arriving home after an outing, Robert would walk up the elegantly carpeted main stairs like all the other guests, then continue to ascend flight after flight until the final bend in the staircase brought him to the long hallway of staff quarters. From his room at the southwest corner of the building, he could look out over the rooftops to Lake Biel and the Jura foothills that flanked the city's western edge. The building's flat roof held a viewing platform often enjoyed by the hotel's guests as well as its resident writer. He took his meals down in the dining room, where he could, if he wished, be simultaneously in company and alone. The hotel's guests, he later reported in a nostalgic essay, included "actors, journalists, watchmakers, and traveling salesmen." He found this all perfectly satisfactory.[15]

Ernst Hubacher, a childhood acquaintance now serving as a pastor in nearby Grenchen, stopped by to visit and found Robert's room spartan, furnished only with a bed, table, and chair. A map of Europe was thumbtacked to the wall. In a piece titled "Poets" published in early 1917, Walser facetiously explained how writers like to live: "It is a fact that they prefer to live, often, in attics, high up, with views all around, because from there they enjoy the broadest and freest outlook upon the world. They also like, as is well known, to be independent and unconstrained." On the question of comfort, he reports that "poets, lyrical as well as epic and dramatic, very seldom heat their mathematical or philosophical rooms. 'If you sweat all summer, you can freeze a bit for a change all winter,' they say, and so they adjust, in a very talented manner, to both heat and cold." Robert himself economized by wearing an overcoat in his room in winter instead of paying for heat, his feet ensconced in slippers he sewed out of rags. In summer, the sun baking down upon the roof tiles directly overhead made his quarters stifling. In July 1913, Robert wrote to Brod that he'd been going swimming in Lake Biel, rain or shine, from his "palace garret." From the Blaues Kreuz one could walk along the canal all the way to the lakefront.[16]

Robert was now the only Walser sibling in Biel. Fanny, working as a dental technician, was in Bern, as was Hermann, professor of human geography at the University of Bern. Oscar had married and was working at a bank in Locarno. Ernst was still an in-patient at the Waldau clinic, and Karl was in Berlin. The only other family member left in Biel was their father, now lodging with an elderly couple in a rundown building at the edge of Biel's Old Town.

Everything we know of Adolf Walser's life during this period comes via his son's literary reminiscences. In January 1914, *Deutsche Monatshefte* published Robert's "Letter from a Father to His Son," in which the father recalls various indignities inflicted on his young son (such as forcing him to do chores while his companions are playing) as beneficial to his character or at least a source of satisfaction to the stress-plagued father. Old resentments, it seemed, were surfacing. The following month, the same journal published Robert's "Father," an affectionate portrait of an old man who has become eccentric with age, "the declared and faithful friend of certain strict, odd, [. . .] dear, good, deeply ingrained habits." The two are uncomfortable around each other, the essay reports, but the son sometimes visits his father nonetheless, especially after supper, to "chat about the town and its inhabitants."[17]

Between the appearance of these two pieces, Adolf Walser died. Eighty-one years old, he succumbed on January 28 after a brief illness. Robert wrote to Mermet, "Papa's death came so quickly, but if it hadn't come now, it would have come soon." Despite his business failures and poverty, Adolf had enjoyed a long life and good health, remaining vital enough to join his children for walks even during his final year. Two years after his death, Robert published "Portrait of Father," in which each of seven siblings pays tribute to their recently departed father, noting in particular their regret at having felt more respect for their mother than for him, valuing her struggles over his nonchalance. In this story from 1916, seven siblings speak; Adolf Walser's death notice, however, listed only six mourners—all the siblings except Ernst.[18]

Robert soon fell into a routine of working at the small table in his room in the mornings, then going out into the city for lunch or a walk or both. Spring in Biel was beautiful, with flowers in all the front gardens. These were the streets he had once walked to go to school, then to the bank for his apprenticeship. Now his commute to work was a few steps, from bed to writing table. But after work, the city was his to roam, as was the surrounding countryside. He published more pieces in *Die Zukunft* and the leftist journal *März*, whose new editor was Theodor Heuss, future president of the Federal Republic of Germany. Hermann Hesse had been one of *März*'s founders and often wrote for it. Robert's first contribution to the journal, "Helbling's Story" ("Helblings Geschichte"), published in August 1913, is a nihilistic persona tale related in a strange, fragmented mode, with the narrator frequently contradicting himself or modifying what he has just said as he describes his precarious life as a bank clerk and his engagement to a girl who finds him dull: "Perhaps I have taken the wrong profession, and yet I confidently believe that in any profession I would be the same, do the same, and fail in the same way. I enjoy, as a result of my supposed slothfulness, little respect. People call me a dreamer and a lazybones. Oh, what a talent people have for giving the wrong labels! Of course, it is true: I do not particularly like work." This narrative strategy of second-guessing or even repudiating each successive statement results in a strangely stuttering narrative that feels unmoored, giving the story an odd, vaguely nervous energy. The mode of telling suggests a psychological pathology behind the narrator's report. By the end of "Helbling's Story," the narrator is asking himself, "Could it really be that I am ill? So much is wrong; I am deficient, actually, in everything. Could it be that I am an unlucky person? Could it be that I have unusual tendencies? Could it be a sort of sickness to concern oneself always, as I do, with such questions?" The story ends with a vision of him "naked on a high rock" in a world from which everything has been subtracted.[19]

"Helbling's Story" set the stage for what was to be a whole subcategory of Walser's fiction in the mid-nineteen-teens, in which an ever more frantic fugal repetition dominates the narrative, drowning out every other storytelling principle. "Nervous" (1916) is perhaps the quintessential story in this style, its title naming the particular drama it relates.[20]

Robert went on writing for *Deutsche Monatshefte,* regularly sending manuscripts north to Düsseldorf. One, "The Boy," is about the son of a lion tamer who adopts his father's profession, stepping into the circus ring the day after the father is fatally mauled by his lion in front of the crowd. When the boy enters the lion's cage, the beast miraculously obeys him. Another, "The Idol," tells of a man who visits the ethnological museum and finds himself seized by a compulsion to prostrate himself before an ancient wooden figure on display there. Both of these stories—like "The Kiss"—were more troubling, difficult, and darker pieces than Robert had previously written—a far cry from the entertaining feuilletons he'd sent to *Die Schaubühne* just two years earlier. Between these stories and the manically repetitive ones, he was expanding on his short-prose craft and experimenting with work in a minor key.[21]

Being back in Biel also put him in a nostalgic mood, making him revisit scenes of his youth and early manhood. He began to take literary stock of his recent and distant past for the first time since departing for Berlin and wrote a number of the autobiographical sketches already mentioned in these pages, such as "Johanna" (about his fellow lodger in postman Senn's apartment in Zurich) and "Apollo and Diana" (featuring his landlady in Thun). Some of the events on which these tales were based had taken place in the previous century. Perhaps he wouldn't have become so stuck in his writing in Berlin if he'd worried less about inventing all-new material to write about and drawn more on the huge store of experiences he had at his disposal just waiting to be given literary form.

Brod kept getting in touch every time he planned a trip to Berlin. He didn't realize Robert was back in Switzerland for good. (Maybe Robert didn't realize it either.) From Brod, Robert learned that Franz Blei had helped found yet another new journal, *Die Weissen Blätter* (The White Pages). Robert submitted work with a cocky cover letter predicting that the enclosed pieces would be accepted, and Blei did in fact accept the little sheaf of essayistic sketches, publishing them in February 1914 under the title "Seven Pieces." This idea of publishing short feuilleton-like texts in clusters (as Kafka had with "Contemplation") was appealing. Robert repeated the procedure with *März, Deutsche Monatshefte, Die Neue Rundschau,* and *Der Neue Merkur.* He was back in business, his earnings sufficient to cover his modest lifestyle.

Now and then Robert would take the train to Bellelay to visit Lisa; now and then she would come down the mountain for a visit herself. He would stay with her for a night or two, taking long walks with her and Mermet (and sometimes little Louis as well). With these two women, he was always the center of attention; he enjoyed entertaining them with stories from his memory and imagination. In return, they fed him, washed his clothes, and were rapt listeners. And they had tales of their own—modest local stories that pleased him—about the children and patients they worked with every day.

Visiting Lisa in the shadow of the psychiatric clinic reminded Robert of Ernst's confinement at Waldau. How strange to think he'd been there for fifteen years. Perhaps these thoughts of Ernst and the Bellelay patients inspired the nightmare of being locked away in an institution that Robert included among the texts he sent to *Deutsche Monatshefte* for publication in February 1914. In "The Dream," the narrator finds himself held against his will, a patient and prisoner insisting to "officials" that he doesn't understand "all this"; these "incomprehensible individuals," busy with various tasks or staring into space, ignore him.[22]

At the same time, the beauty of the monastery/institution nestled amid the Jura Mountains impressed itself upon Robert as the very picture of peace. Bellelay was a refuge from the pressures of the world. He was now also ready to acknowledge his romantic interest in Mermet. On December 13,

1913, he initiated a correspondence that would span three decades. He wrote to her flirtatiously, closing with the lines: "Last Sunday I sat nicely at home, leading a proper parlor life, every bit the husband. You can see from this little letter that I've been thinking of you. It's a pleasure for me to think of you. With amicable greetings, Robert Walser." Soon he heard from Lisa that Mermet would be going to Biel to do her Christmas shopping, and he arranged to spend the day accompanying her on her errands.[23]

That was their first date. Afterward, he wrote her a letter describing the mountain walks he would have liked to take her on in Leubringen and Magglingen instead of running errands—walks he'd taken by himself following her departure. She'd made him a present of some schnapps that he admitted to drinking "straight out of the bottle," which is perhaps what emboldened him to add: "It is a delight to think of your dear eyes, your dear face, and your dear slender figure. May I devote my most heartfelt thoughts to you, dear, admired Frau Mermet?"[24] But if he hoped to win her heart, it was perhaps a tactical error to emphasize the leisureliness of his existence (time for long walks on workdays, time for drinking) to a woman whose work was challenging and physically strenuous and who had to devote most of her leisure hours to caring for her son.

Still, she was intrigued by this brilliant and talented man with his published books and entertaining stories. And, since Christmas was approaching, she sent him a present: a pair of socks. Having now received two gifts, he wrote to thank her. "Sometime, I would like to sit close beside you and gaze into your eyes for a very long while. Surely that would be most entertaining," he wrote, making her a gift of these pretty words.[25] This exchange set a pattern they repeated for years to come: in return for packages of food and articles of clothing, he offered—with several notable exceptions—only gratitude. Mermet must have been painfully aware from the start how unlikely it would be for a man like this to ever be able to provide for a family. Much as she liked Robert, she had to consider the financial precariousness of his existence. She already had another mouth to feed.

Mermet nonetheless enjoyed Robert's flattering attentions, which even included an element of intrigue: to avoid local gossip, the two exchanged their letters covertly through Lisa, who passed on Robert's letters to Mermet and tucked Mermet's responses into her own letters to her brother. The missives flew back and forth, and soon Robert's flirting had given way to explicit confessions of desire. He wrote to Mermet about her lips, which he says would comfortably accommodate "a small, warm, friendly kiss"; her feet (he fantasized about kissing them in a pair of delicate little slippers he'd seen in a shop window); and the enticing glimpse of her legs he'd caught the previous summer when she raised her skirt to walk through the tall grass of a meadow.[26]

Mermet wrote to him about how she often felt that being a good mother to Louis was all she'd been placed on earth to do. She wanted to put the brakes on Robert's impetuous pursuit: he was rushing her, and possibly also himself. She asked him (in person) to slow down, noting (as he reported their conversation) that it "isn't so easy to speak about tender, profound things so quickly." Certainly her concern made sense. Even if Robert was in love with her, how could he propose, given his circumstances? If she entered into a relationship with him, would it prove a casual liaison and possibly damage her reputation? Meanwhile he continued to send her assurances of his affection. At the end of an evening spent at Adolf's home, where Lisa and Mermet cooked together, Robert helped Mermet with the dishes, an intimately domestic moment. The greetings he sent her next were "as heartfelt as any human being has ever sent to another whom he was fond of." In the heat of his emotion, he purchased an expensive gift for her: a gold coin of the sort presented at baptisms, instructing her either to use it to buy something for Louis, without saying where the money had come from, or to place it discreetly in the child's piggy bank.[27]

Robert's newest book appeared later that winter. *Stories* (*Geschichten*) featured thirty drawings by Karl and a cover illustration depicting a writer at his desk. It was published simultaneously in three editions: paperback, hardcover, and a numbered edition of one hundred with hand-colored drawings. (The "luxury edition" of *Essays* had numbered only twenty-five copies.) Decades later, publisher Kurt Wolff remarked that he'd published the stories on the assumption that they would reach "fewer than a hundred readers," but he wanted to publish them "for these one hundred readers," finding the stories "not as simple as they might seem on first reading." He began production on his next collection of Walser prose, *Little Fictions* (*Kleine Dichtungen*), even before *Stories* came out.[28]

Robert Musil reviewed *Stories* side by side with Kafka's *Contemplation* in the spring 1914 issue of *Die Neue Rundschau*. Like Tucholsky and Brod before him, he emphasized the complexity of Walser's work:

An atmosphere of marionettes, romantic irony; but also something in this joke that reminds one faintly of Morgenstern's poems, where the gravity of real circumstances suddenly begins to slide along a train of verbal associations; only with Walser the association is never purely verbal, but always one of meaning as well, so that the emotional tack he happens to be on at the moment suddenly appears to be about to take a great leap, veers, and then goes on contentedly swaying in the direction of a new enticement.[29]

Walser's "very human kind of playfulness" and his "uncommon command of language"—"one could fall in love" with it, Musil said—were why he deemed Walser a more consequential writer than Kafka, whom he dismissed as derivative, "a special case of the Walser type." (This was, to be sure, before Kafka had published or even written most of the work for which he is now revered.) Musil found Walser sui generis, inimitable, his work "not a suitable foundation for a literary genre." Critic Joachim Benn, who'd trashed Mann's *Death in Venice* in the same journal the year before, sang another hymn to Walser in the April 1914 issue of *Die Rheinlande*. Benn pronounced Walser "one of the few new creative voices of the age," a definitive writer of his time, as Goethe was of the Sturm und Drang era.[30]

Robert's thoughts were again returning to the novel form. He wrote to Schäfer that he would be taking a sabbatical from writing short prose: "All my strivings must now be concentrated on once more achieving a great rounded whole," for a writer "must from time to time stick his head all the way into darkness, into mystery." To Paul Fechter, feuilleton editor at *Vossische Zeitung* in Berlin, he confided that the novels division of the Ullstein Newspaper Publishing Company (now the publisher of *Vossische Zeitung*) had invited him to submit a longer work for serialization. A work serialized in a major newspaper would reach far more readers than he'd ever experienced—and also pay better.[31]

Schäfer, who'd been publishing Robert's work for several years, decided to nominate him for the annual prize awarded by the Women's League to Honor Writers of the Rhineland. Schäfer and Hesse had cofounded the association in 1909. Its thousand-plus members contributed to a fund used to honor a writer chosen from a shortlist determined by the two men and a third colleague. In addition to the award, the winning author's manuscript was printed in a special edition distributed to all the association's members. In 1914, Schäfer persuaded Hesse to recommend *Little Fictions,* which was chosen that July. This was the first literary prize of any sort Robert had ever received. (It would also be the last.) The prize came with a purse of 2,000 marks—around $12,000 in today's dollars—far exceeding the 300-mark advances he'd received for each of his books with Kurt Wolff.[32]

Buoyed up by this general atmosphere of promise and appreciation, Robert began to take more liberties in his correspondence with Mermet, allowing himself explicitly sexual content. In one letter sent in spring 1914, he thanks her for permitting him to imagine himself giving her little boy a piggyback ride, then adds:

> Today in a shop window on Nidaugasse, I saw an enchanting set of pink ladies' knit underwear and also a snow-white set, and it occurred to me that a garment of this sort would look charming on you, dear Frau Mermet, and warm your dear, delicate body. I would like to see you some time in such dear soft underthings, what a sweet, angelic sight that would be. You must be sure to dress warmly, dear Frau Mermet, and put on nice warm underpants in this harsh weather. You are surely angry with me now and indignant that I have made so bold as to speak of your underpants, which are always kept so delicately and carefully hidden from view. I would like to see your dear underpants, dear Frau Mermet, and kiss them, for they are surely darling.[33]

He was testing her and also himself. Would she allow him to go on addressing her in so clearly improper a manner? This letter was probably not delivered via Lisa but mailed directly, suggesting that Mermet was willing to let their correspondence be public knowledge. His cheekiness didn't cause her to cut off contact. On the contrary, she visited him in Biel shortly after receiving this letter, walked with him between errands, and even accompanied him to his room, where he lifted her up in his arms so she could peer out the little skylight and he could enjoy the pleasure of holding her. The experience was so memorable that he described it in two separate letters to her.[34]

Their conversation did not seem to flow particularly well, however. "We weren't able to say very much to each other," he wrote to her afterward, "but this is something one doesn't manage so quickly, and often one likes to hesitate for a long time with the beautiful things one might have to say."[35] He was courting her by mail—perhaps forcing a sense of intimacy by exceeding the bounds of propriety—only to find himself awkward and tongue-tied in her presence. Feeling socially ill at ease was so natural to him that the emotional tumult of desire mixed with an ever-growing real affection must have been discombobulating. It's unclear whether Mermet shared details of this budding romance with Lisa, who was suddenly a third wheel.

Despite Robert's odd manner and communications, he wasn't making a bad impression on Mermet. She later reported that he wasn't drinking much during these years. More than his oddities or improprieties, she mostly recalled his intelligence, wittiness, pride (he could be touchy, she said), and pleasing appearance. She described all the Walser siblings as attractive, remarking that Lisa had been considered the prettiest girl in Biel when she was young, with beautiful eyes, and that Robert's eyes, too, were striking. She remembered him as "tall and slim but not scrawny; he was good-looking."[36]

Everything changed dramatically that summer. In the aftermath of Archduke Franz Ferdinand's assassination in June, Germany declared war on Russia on August 1, and, two days later, on France. Europe was suddenly mired in a complex and confusing web of alliances and preemptive mobilizations, and Switzerland was surrounded by warring countries. The French border was a mere twenty miles from Biel, and fewer than four miles from Bellelay.

Switzerland was well-prepared for self-defense. On August 1, the Military Department of the Swiss Federal Council announced that general mobilization would begin on Monday, August 3. Robert's unit, Landwehr Battalion 134, Third Division, First Platoon, belonging to the Forty-first Infantry Regiment, was instructed to report for duty on August 5. Every able-bodied Swiss man was required to serve, either among the First Line troops (for men up to age thirty-two), Landwehr (up to forty), or Landsturm (up to forty-eight); the 425,000 troops mobilized that first week accounted for more than 10 percent of the country's population.[37]

The day after Switzerland called up its troops, Germany invaded Belgium, which like Switzerland offered a logistically tempting shortcut to France. As General Ulrich Wille of the Swiss Army reported to the National Assembly at the close of the war, the purpose of this military action had been to "protect our country against having our neutrality disregarded by one or the other of the armies of our warring neighbors and to answer every violation of our neutrality with the force of arms."[38] With France and Germany at war, it was clear that Swiss neutrality would have to be vigorously defended, as had happened in 1871 during the Franco-Prussian war, when an army of eighty-seven thousand French soldiers, routed by the Germans, crossed the border into Switzerland, where they were quickly captured and disarmed.

Robert's unit of fusiliers, each armed with a 7-mm standard-issue army rifle, assembled in Bern and bunked down for the night in the municipal *Gymnasium*—the school where Hermann had taught geography for fifteen years. The next morning they assembled to swear their fealty to the Swiss Confederation. Then the battalion—878 soldiers, 19 officers, and 44 horses—set out on a sweaty nine-mile march west to Mühleberg. It was a hot August day, their uniform jackets a burden as they trudged, weighed down with rifles and supplies.[39] For Robert, this four-hour march was perhaps less onerous than for many of his companions. His legs were strong from running up the mountain to Bellelay and his other long hikes. The next day's report indicated that the pace had been set too fast, resulting in chaos as exhausted men broke ranks to rest.

After a night in Mühleberg, the regiment marched for another day, their destination the town of Erlach, at the southwestern edge of Lake Biel, where they were to be stationed for a month. The morning of August 9, they gathered on a nearby meadow for Sunday prayers: "God is our refuge and strength, a very present help in trouble. Therefore will not we fear, though the earth be removed, and though the mountains be carried into the midst of the sea. . . ."

The fusiliers devoted many hours to target practice—excellent marksmanship being a particular strength in a country where men of military age were required to pass yearly shooting tests. Exercise strengthened their discipline as well as their physiques, and they took turns standing watch at night. Their activity in this region also included construction of the all-important Murten fortification line. Switzerland had

long been building defensive fortifications—in particular around St. Gott-
hard and St. Maurice—to prepare for future military conflicts. These net-
works of obstacles and fortified lines of defense were designed to protect
Switzerland's key cities, Bern above all, from armed attack. Given the relatively small size of the Swiss Army compared with the military forces of
neighboring countries, strategic planning that used the country's rugged
geography to good advantage was crucial.[40]

Work on the fortifications involved, above all, a great deal of
digging—strenuous labor that caused widespread disgruntlement among
the troops thus employed. Obstacles were erected as well as concrete shel-
ters to shield the soldiers operating newfangled machine guns. Watch had
to be posted round the clock. The area was restricted to minimize public
knowledge of the fortifications' specifics. The troops' positions were secret, too, not to be revealed in letters. It was exhausting, tedious work. All
were instructed to watch the skies for French or German planes invading
Swiss airspace; foreign aircraft were to be shot at.[41]

On Sunday, August 30, a rare day off, Robert hurried up the mountain to visit Mermet and Lisa. On his way back the next morning, he scribbled and mailed off a letter to Mermet while changing trains in Biel. The
two of them had played a game of Tiddlywinks—marketed in Switzerland
as the Flea Game because of how the little chips, or "winks," flew through
the air. They'd also drunk enough red wine to make Robert oversleep the
next morning and have to race down the mountain to Dachsfelden to catch
his train.[42]

On September 2, Robert's battalion marched to Bern to participate in
a military procession. Hundreds of soldiers paraded past General Wille,
bayonets flashing, while a military band played. The usually reserved Bernese came out to cheer, perhaps with Fanny and Hermann among them.
Colonel Heusser addressed the assembled troops, congratulating them on
completing their service. "But do not forget," he added, "that you are soldiers, and remain at the ready so that you can quickly answer your country's
call when it comes again." The morning of September 4, Robert was free.[43]

Even for Swiss civilians, there was little respite from news of the hostilities that continued to roil Europe. The war had upturned so many lives.
For Robert, among other things, it derailed his plan to write a novel. The
general uncertainty was unnerving, and knowing he might be called up on
short notice at any time, interrupting work on a longer project, made it

difficult to start one. He'd written each of his previous novels in an intense burst of concentrated activity. Robert wrote to Mermet that going about his life with the expectation of being called up and "los[ing] all freedom" once more was "not at all nice."[44] Wouldn't any brilliant ideas he might have soon be pounded out of him by weeks of military exercises?

Nor was it at all certain that the German journals he'd been publishing in would still want to print stories and essays from Switzerland with a war on. The journal *Die Rheinlande,* for example—originally devoted to promoting literature from up and down the Rhine, from Switzerland to the North Sea—immediately struck a more patriotic note in its offerings, reflecting the "Spirit of 1914"; and the Women's League associated with the journal renamed itself Women's League to Honor German Writers.[45]

The single Walser story *Die Rheinlande* published that fall, "Two Women," was probably written after Robert's return from his month in Erlach. The first of the two unhappy women described in this piece wastes her youth pining after a selfish man with a "theatrical robber-baron beard." The second is courted by a man who becomes an oppressive tyrant once they're married, an attribute explicitly linked in the story to his being "ein echt deutscher Mann," a genuine German man.[46] These were strange words indeed to read in a German literary magazine in October 1914. Had Robert submitted the story as a provocation, a response to the blatantly war-glorifying articles printed in that journal (and others)? He published nothing else in any German magazine for the rest of that year.

Robert's fear that he wouldn't be able to enjoy civilian life for long proved justified; he was called up again a mere two and a half weeks later. He managed a visit to Bellelay in the interim, though, taking advantage of the early fall weather to make the trip on foot, arriving ravenous. Mermet's son later recalled gaping in astonishment at the vast quantities of food their visitor put away and being reprimanded by him: "What are you staring at? It's incredibly rude to gawk at other people's plates like that."[47] The Bellelay kitchen served vegetables fresh from the garden and meat from neighboring farms, certainly appreciated by the hungry hiker after a month of canteen fare.

Robert set out for his second round of service on September 21, this time heading to St. Maurice, a tiny town perched high in the mountains overlooking the Rhône. The roads leading to Italy via the Alpine passes of

Valais run through St. Maurice, making the town, its twelfth-century bridge, and its nineteenth-century defense tower strategically important. Robert's company posted watch and performed exercises amid magnificent panoramas he must have found exhilaratingly different from the green Jura landscapes he knew from home. He didn't write about the Alps, however; doing so during the war might have revealed the troops' location and therefore been treasonous. Instead, when he was back in Biel after this tour of duty, he wrote about the soldier's life in general terms. "The soldier," he wrote, "is calm, honest, obedient, modest. Grumbling and quarreling are not permitted him."[48]

He sent "The Soldier" not to a German magazine but to the widely circulated Zurich newspaper *Neue Zürcher Zeitung,* which published it in December 1914. In November, the paper had published a short essay of his—"Remember This"—exhorting the reader to keep all the lovely things of this world in mind despite its darkness. He'd gone years without submitting work to *Neue Zürcher Zeitung* after feuilleton editor Fritz Marti panned both *The Assistant* and *Jakob von Gunten.* But Marti died in August 1914, and his successor, art and theater critic Hans Trog, was happy to publish Walser pieces. And when Trog was succeeded that winter by critic Eduard Korrodi, long a Walser fan, Walser prose began to appear regularly in the paper's feuilleton section. In January 1915 alone, Korrodi published a trio of reflective little essays and the story about visiting Robert's aunt described in Chapter 4.[49] Korrodi made Robert something he'd never been before: a Swiss author with a regular Swiss readership.

Back in Biel, Robert wrote to Mermet, signing his letter with a heartfelt "kiss" he scratched out before the word was complete (*Ku[ss]*), replacing it with an anodyne "greeting" (*Gruss*). Flirting on paper was so much easier than in person. He also sent her a present he'd picked up in Bern: fancy lebkuchen with the city's mascot bear drawn on top in icing. When she wrote that she'd be coming down to Biel again for some shopping, he asked whether he could accompany her and proposed another round of Tiddlywinks, with the winner to be rewarded with kisses.[50]

Besides love, he was thinking of business again too, specifically his book *Little Fictions* that Wolff was supposed to be printing for the Women's League. He'd queried Wolff shortly before the outbreak of hostilities and never heard back. It turned out Wolff had been called up for military service in July and since early August had been serving as adjutant in a

German field artillery regiment stationed in France. In September, he was awarded the Iron Cross.[51] No wonder Robert's book hadn't been foremost in his mind. Wolff's deputy, Georg Heinrich Meyer, sent Robert his overdue 300-mark honorarium.

Robert was expected to sign all the copies of *Little Fictions* that would be distributed to the league's 1,048 members. He'd hoped Wolff's staff could just send him a stack of title pages to sign before the book was bound, but that proved impossible, so he caught a train to Leipzig in early January 1915 to sign books. He continued on to Berlin afterward for a quick visit with Karl, who was ill again and in low spirits. There was a lot to discuss—they hadn't seen each other for nearly a year. Robert was glad to be back in Berlin's familiar streets again, though they now seemed loud and chaotic. The smell of coal hung in the air, and the snow in the streets was soiled. Reminders of the war were everywhere. The morning edition of *Berliner Tageblatt* printed a map of the Carpathians showing the latest fighting, south and east of Krakow—not so close to Dambrau but not so far away either, and fewer than four hundred miles from Berlin.[52] Compared with these actual battles, Robert's military exercises seemed like child's play. Did he remember writing to Morgenstern early in his Berlin years that if he were doomed to become just "a magazine supplier," he'd prefer to join the army?[53] Back in Switzerland, he'd done both. Robert didn't know it, but this quick trip north on business would be the last time he would ever set foot in Berlin, or venture beyond the borders of his native land.

ELEVEN

A Walk in Wartime

1915–1917

ONE WAY TO FEEL YOU BELONG to a country is to fight for it or at least work to defend it from attack. During the war years, Robert's ambivalence about where he belonged gave way to feelings of national pride. While before the war he'd occasionally suggested that he might eventually return to Berlin, now he seemed content where he was, and publishing in Switzerland, rather than Germany, became an affirmative preference and not just a choice made of necessity. As a Swiss author in Switzerland, he found himself celebrated. And while being called up for military service disrupted his writing life, fusilier Robert Walser managed to continue his professional correspondence even in the field. He got along well with his fellow riflemen, though he was occasionally chastised for laziness by a commanding officer.[1] And the work was not without its appeal. The soldier's trade, like that of the butler, combined subservience with skill. There was new equipment to master, new skills to learn, and almost all the work took place outdoors.

Robert's regiment was called up twice in 1915.[2] The first of these deployments—in Cudrefin on Lake Neuchâtel, where he spent April and half of May practicing his marksmanship and building fortifications while quartered in a schoolhouse—was, as Robert remarked in a letter to Frieda Mermet, "perfectly agreeable."[3] The second stint was far more challenging. In early October, his unit was sent to work on the Hauenstein fortifications at Hägendorf, southeast of Basel. This was a strategically sensitive location, and the soldiers were under instructions to camouflage all work materials that might be visible from the air and to take cover when enemy planes were spotted. There was a lot of uphill marching and lugging of equipment, surprise maneuvers with other companies simulating attacks, and uncomfortable, chilly nights spent bivouacking in the woods.[4]

Robert's battalion was composed of men who were thirty-three to forty years old, and some of them were no longer so hardy. Even Robert, accustomed to Spartan living, would have been grateful for a proper bed to sleep in and a proper meal in a dining room. His regiment was frequently uprooted, packing their gear and relocating to new quarters several times during this deployment. He appreciated the reminders of the outside world that arrived in the form of care packages from Mermet. She sent him a warm undershirt, a bag of the fritters known as *Schenkeli* ("little haunches")—pointy at both ends and deep-fried—and some cheese: real food from the real world of civilian life, tasting of peacetime. Writing to thank her, he reported—disclosing his location, and not for the first time— that his unit was quartered in a dancehall in the small Catholic village of Wisen, where they'd been performing military exercises, drills, and shifts on watch.

The following week they returned to work on the fortifications—this time on the slopes of the Wisenberg—an activity that would occupy them for most of the next month. The work was tedious, strenuous, and repetitive, producing sore muscles and blistered palms. Even the officers were disgruntled. One of the divisions had twice dug out an extremely long trench, and the engineers still hadn't decided what kind of pipe to lay in it. Would they have to dig it out a third time? They were still up in the mountains when the first snowfall arrived, and Mermet sent Robert some wool socks, more undershirts, cheese that he snacked on between trench-digging shifts, and, best of all, a bottle of gentian schnapps. Squeezed in among his fellow soldiers in the cramped dayroom that smelled of labor and exhaustion, he wrote her hurried thank-you notes.

Military service was a great equalizer. All these men from different walks of life now found themselves subject to the same discomfort, indignities, and plodding, endless labor. They were gears in the defense machine successfully keeping the worst of war-torn Europe's suffering outside Switzerland's borders. While Belgium had been trampled from the very beginning of the war, Switzerland's sovereignty was intact, its citizens spared the brutal injuries being inflicted to the north, where soldiers cowering in trenches were having their lungs torn apart by poison gas, their limbs shattered by exploding shells. Avoiding this trauma was clearly worth the sacrifice of time and freedom required for the country's defense, yet morale was low among Swiss troops as the war dragged on, with many soldiers applying to be released from service early, on health and other grounds. Before Robert's regiment was dismissed at the end of its scheduled deployment on December 4, the commanding officer of each battalion issued a forceful request for volunteers—soldiers willing to continue work on the fortifications that would be essential if the war crossed their borders.[5] Some signed up, Robert did not.

Having experienced wartime Germany at the beginning of the year, Robert valued the relative sense of normalcy Switzerland provided as the war dragged on. And while the large numbers of men called up to serve each month certainly had its impact, those not on duty were going about their lives more or less as usual without the fear and deprivation he'd glimpsed in Leipzig and Berlin, where it seemed everyone knew someone at the front. To have a son, husband, or brother in the Swiss military was far less worrisome. Even cultural life continued much as before. The ongoing hostilities across the border were certainly on people's minds, but they were not their only, or even their primary, concern.

En route to Germany that past January to sign copies of *Little Fictions* for the Women's League, Robert had stopped in Zurich to meet Hans Bodmer, organizer of the Literary Club of the Hottingen Readers' Circle, which was planning an evening lecture by *Neue Zürcher Zeitung*'s Hans Trog on the work of both Walser brothers. Bodmer had agreed to make their meeting an ambulatory one, and they ascended Robert's beloved Zürichberg high above the city to walk as they spoke. At Bodmer's request, Robert had collected samples of Karl's work from his studio in Berlin to drop off during his trip home and also sent Bodmer clippings of reviews of his own books to incorporate into the presentation. Trog's lecture took place on January 25, 1915, at Zurich's Tonhalle (concert hall) without either Walser present. It was enthusiastically reviewed by Korrodi in *Neue Zürcher Zeitung* and published in the August/September issue of *Schweizerland*.[6] Even with a war on, the Walser brothers counted for something in Switzerland.

Thanks to the war, it was another half-year before *Little Fictions* arrived in bookstores. Unlike Robert's previous two collections, *Essays* and *Sto-*

ries—compilations of his Berlin and pre-Berlin writings—*Little Fictions* consisted of work written after his return to Switzerland. Most of the pieces in *Little Fictions*—eighty-seven in all—are "little" indeed, written specifically with magazine or newspaper publication in mind. The book's dominant mode is the walk story: lyrical meditations on landscapes or other rural spaces, with the narrator strolling through these environments as the story unfolds, a gambit Robert had used in his very first published work of fiction, "Lake Greifen," more than fifteen years earlier. That particular piece remained emblematic of his work, and Trog read it aloud to conclude his lecture on the Walser brothers.[7]

Many other stories in *Little Fictions* are nostalgia pieces, vignettes recalling earlier epochs of Robert's life. "The Pole" describes a young stable-hand in Dambrau who gets drunk at the pub and starts dancing "in the Polish style," displaying unsuspected grace (*Grazie*)—a word whose emphatic repetition places this vignette in dialogue with Kleist's famous essay "On the Marionette Theater."[8] Observations on metropolitan society and cityscapes are strikingly absent from *Little Fictions,* except those briefly sketched as backdrops for reminiscences. The book's heavy emphasis on landscape and rural locales make it emphatically Swiss. As an epigraph, Robert used a few lines he'd inscribed more than a decade before in a copy of *Fritz Kocher's Essays* for Richard Dehmel and his wife.

> I wandered on and wander still,
> My walking though was not the same.
> Now gaiety lit up my face
> Now—as the sky itself can change—
> My pleasure quickly disappeared
> Into an endless day of pain.[9]

All these years later, Walser's little poem still captured something about the experience of the world as seen from a perspective in motion—with change the only constant. It seemed the proper accompaniment to these little pieces that were all about their own smallness, staking a claim for the importance and validity of subtle minor observations amid the era's jangling militaristic bombast.

Karl's attractive cover illustration for the first printing of *Little Fictions* showed a man reclining on a bench under a tree. The Women's

League had picked his book for peacetime. Were readers interested in such stories now? Wartime production delays gave the league's leadership time to second-guess their choice, and they decided to distribute a second book along with Robert's: a patriotic German play recalling a historic battle. This too was a Kurt Wolff book, though it's unclear whether the decision to publish it had been made by Wolff or his deputy. Not until March 1915, after Robert asked Wolff's deputy to intercede on his behalf, did the league disburse his 2,000-mark prize. Although he'd asked to have the prize money—roughly $12,000 in today's dollars—sent to him in Biel, it was instead deposited into an account for him at the Dürener Bank in North Rhine–Westphalia. He was never able to access these funds—at first because money was impossible to transfer during wartime, and later because they lost all value during Germany's postwar hyperinflation. Wolff's publishing house issued the second printing of *Little Fictions,* for the general market, in summer 1915. It was praised in *Der Bund* and—by another Wolff author, Kurt Pinthus—in *Zeitschrift für Bücherfreunde* (Book Lovers' Journal), but its overall reception was modest and its few reviews mostly mixed.[10]

The year 1915 proved surprisingly productive for Robert as a writer. Freed by his soldierly obligations from feeling he should be working on a longer project, he dove into short prose with renewed zeal and sent out many submissions and query letters. Even with the war on, and despite his initial misgivings, Germany's magazines remained important outlets for his work. Enthusiasm for the war was starting to tarnish in German intellectual circles. The newspapers were full of bloodshed. The Kaiser sent zeppelins to bomb England while German and French soldiers pummeled each other in Alsace, just across the Swiss border. And some journals happily printed the work of this self-styled "fantastical dreamer."[11]

Robert submitted a piece titled "Imaginings," which he "hoped he might suppose [might bear] some relationship to current events," to the Munich journal *Zeit-Echo: Kriegs-Tagebuch der Künstler* (Echo of the Time: Artists' War Diary). "Imaginings" is an abstract little tale about a place where happy, kind people support one another in every endeavor. "The most important law there is love; friendship the most important rule. Poor and rich do not exist. In this place where healthy mankind is at home, there have never been kings or a Kaiser." The piece ends with the words,

"I do of course realize that this is all a fantasy."[12] What better response to "current events" than envisioning a place of harmony and peace?

Some of his imaginings were retrospective. Walser's wartime writings include several pieces already discussed in these pages ("Frau Wilke," "Frau Bähni," "Würzburg") because they describe previous eras in their author's life. "From the Life of Tobold," a nostalgic account of his experiences as a butler in Dambrau, was one of the thirteen Walser texts *Neue Zürcher Zeitung* published in 1915. These included new essays about the soldier's life, too. "Something about the Soldier" and "In the Army" both speak with amused detachment about the vicissitudes of army life (constant cleaning, mindlessly repeated exercises and tasks, bad air in the barracks, the pleasure of receiving mail). "What does a soldier think about all the live-long day?," asks the narrator of "In the Army." "Well, in order for the thing known as militarism to function, he should think nothing at all, or intentionally as little as possible." At the same time, these pieces belie an affection for all the "beauties and freedoms" of military service that "cannot be bought for money." Something appealed to Robert about being part of this huge organized-disorganized project of national defense and submitting to the compulsion to subordinate himself to something larger. Writing these pieces allowed him to link the intellectual labor of writing and the mind-emptying drudgery of army life.[13]

In between tours of duty, Robert continued to seek out Mermet's company. Released from service in December 1914, he hurried up to Bellelay the very next day. Soon after, she came to Biel to buy Louis a new jacket and accepted Robert's invitation to take a walk down the rustic footpath of Taubenloch Gorge just outside town. The torrent of water rushing through the narrow gorge was a fine correlative for all the pent-up feelings he could never manage to put into words when he was with her, though she chattered away, apparently enjoying his company even as he felt paralyzed with awkwardness. This year she would finally be divorced after nearly a decade's separation from her husband, and she told Robert she might consider marrying again, if only for Louis's sake. These words made his heart pound, and he wrote to her afterward about what a powerful impression they made on him. She had sent Louis (now twelve years old) off to Bern for secondary school, making this a plausible moment for her friendship with Robert to develop into a proper romance. He made it clear to her that he wanted them to marry.[14] But she kept hesitating, perhaps because he also said and wrote things that made him sound oblivious to her needs, feelings, and fears.

Once he regaled her with a story about a fellow resident at the Hotel Blaues Kreuz, an editor named Gustav Adolf Frey, who'd made a fool of himself by falling in love with one of the chambermaids—as if it would never occur to her to wonder how much difference Robert saw between a chambermaid and a laundress. For all his poverty, he was a writer—an intellectual—and her first husband had been a coachman. Robert didn't mean to insult her; it just never occurred to him that his words might cause her pain. Did he only see in her someone who could take good care of him? She helped Lisa mend the holes in the heap of socks he'd sent.[15] Maybe he did need taking care of. Or, no, it wasn't that exactly; he appeared content to spend his life utterly neglected by everyone in the world.

He liked to write to her about undergarments. In the same letter in which he sought to reassure her about sending Louis off to school, he extemporized at length about a pair of leg warmers he'd glimpsed in a shop window that he imagined sliding up beneath her skirt as a service to her. How could she not wonder: Would he ever help her with anything she actually needed help with? Could he be a father or role model to Louis? He did seem to feel affection for the boy, but affection of an odd sort. In one letter, he asked Mermet to send him a pair of Louis's outgrown trousers as a memento, saying he wanted to "love them and venerate them and gaze at them adoringly."[16] Whatever in God's name did he mean? When he wrote to her of the war and how fortunate they were that it had remained outside Switzerland's borders, this observation immediately reminded him of a motion picture he'd seen with an actress dressed in tight-fitting white jodhpurs and knee-high boots, a sight that prompted him to imagine hoisting Mermet up into the saddle and afterward holding the saddle to his lips to kiss the spot where she had sat. Which in turn reminded him of his desire to own a pair of Louis's pants. Such trains of thought unnerved her.

In the end, she did send him a pair of short trousers Louis had outgrown, and Robert, thanking her, wrote that they reminded him of ladies' underpants, such as the ones he would like to see soon "on a dear individual who has a perky little nose and is as slender as a pretty young fir tree."[17] He'd offered these compliments (cute nose, slender figure) many

Elisa Walser-Marti,
ca. 1871, with sons
Adolf and Hermann;
photograph taken at
Atelier Louis Roulet, Biel.

Robert Walser as a baby, 1878 or 1879,
photographed by Johann Deppeler.

Robert Walser the year of his confirmation, 1893.

In 1894, Karl Walser painted his brother Robert dressed as Karl Moor,
the protagonist of Friedrich Schiller's play *The Robbers*.
Watercolor on paper, 36.5 × 25 cm.

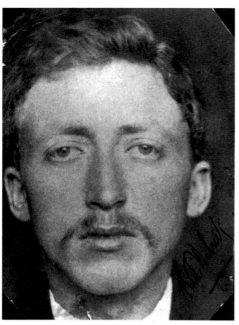

Karl Walser around 1899.

Robert Walser, photographed in 1899
by his childhood friend Paul Renfer
at his photography studio in Biel.

Karl Walser, *The Dream,* 1903. Oil on cardboard, 73 × 45.5 cm.
(Kunstsammlungen Chemnitz–Museum Gunzenhauser)

Lisa Walser around 1900; photograph
taken at Atelier Schricker, Biel.

Robert Walser in 1905 after completing
butler school; photograph taken at
Globus Atelier, Wertheim department
store, Berlin.

Robert Walser in 1907.

Robert Walser in 1909.

Karl Walser and Hedwig ("Trude") Czarnetzki-Walser around 1912.

Frieda Mermet and her son Louis in 1909;
photograph taken at Atelier Schricker, Biel.

Robert Walser photographed by journalist Walter Kern on April 3,
1928, in his furnished room at Luisenstrasse 14, Bern.

Microscript 116,
December 1928, actual size, written on a
"compliments of the author" card sent
on behalf of Max Brod.

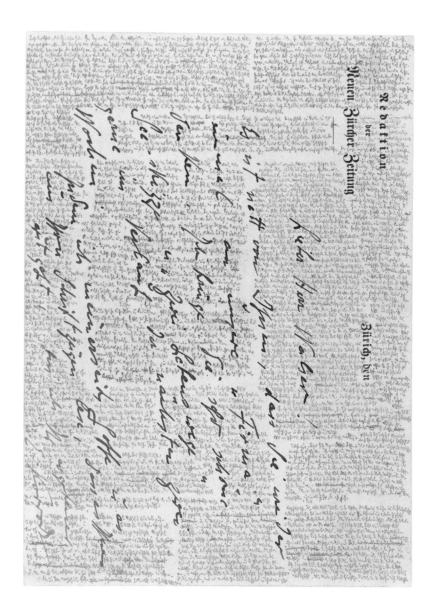

Microscript 9,
June or July 1932, actual size, written on
an acceptance letter from Eduard Korrodi.

Robert Walser photographed by Carl Seelig on
an outing, 1941 or 1942.

Robert Walser photographed in
April 1949 at the Cantonal Asylum
Appenzell-Ausserrhoden, Herisau.

Robert Walser lying dead in the snow, photographed on December 25, 1956, by examining magistrate Kurt Giezendanner, Herisau.

times before. But was saying he found her attractive the right way to persuade her to join her life with his?

He knew how his racy letters might sound to others. Fanny had come to see him that past February, and the siblings took a walk up the mountainside to Leubringen, where they stopped for some refreshment at an inn Robert had patronized with Mermet not long before. It turned out that on this prior visit Mermet had left behind her notebook, which the proprietress now handed over to Robert "with a very probing glance, as if she found me very interesting."[18] One of his letters was tucked inside.

Eventually, though, his desire to see her came to seem inversely proportional to her proximity. He'd so missed her when he was digging trenches for hours on end, but when he was free to run up the mountain any time he felt like it, their meetings no longer seemed so urgent. The following winter, his letters were filled with excuses and promises to visit her again once the snow melted. Desiring to give her a real gift but uncertain what that should be, he recalled her saying that Louis's trousers were threadbare. He put 25 francs in an envelope and mailed it to her with a note asking her to use the money to buy something for Louis for Christmas. He also offered to pay for a new suit of clothes for the boy to replace the jacket and trousers that were wearing out. She accepted the gift with thanks. As a present for Robert, she picked out a nice umbrella.[19]

Even as the ardor in his letters to her gradually cooled, giving way to a tone of calmer affection, he still occasionally threw in the odd flirtatious remark: he wanted to kneel at her feet and tie her shoes, to be the handkerchief with which she blew her sweet little nose, and to lift her in his arms the next time they went for a hike together and came to a wall that required clambering over. But it wasn't the same as a year ago. Now he was content to daydream about her for weeks without needing to see her. "Our correspondence gives me great pleasure," he wrote. "Writing each other letters is like gently, carefully touching."[20]

Bachelorhood also had its advantages. The regularity of life at Blaues Kreuz helped Robert concentrate on his work. Each day resembled the next, with minor fluctuations in routine like changes in the weather. Every day he went downstairs at the appointed time and sat with the same dining companions, a taciturn engineer and the editor whose infatuation had made him a hotel laughingstock. A female guest noticed Robert's torn jacket and insisted he let her repair it. Women served him meals and cleaned his room. "I love uniformity very much," he wrote to Mermet, "and that is healthy. Besides, I've long outgrown the feverishness of youth."[21] Doing as he pleased facilitated his writing, too. And he'd certainly been productive.

As he began to draw more heavily upon his memories for material, his stories grew more expansive. Where before he might have wrapped up his thoughts on a topic after just a couple of pages, now he dug deep into his personal history and drew forth fistfuls of stories he was eager to relate, places he was hungry to revisit if only in thought—locales now made distant not merely by miles, but by the war as well. Sometimes he wrote to the point of exhaustion, until his head spun. These days, he rarely sent a story to an editor without mentioning the "industriousness" with which he'd written it.

"Hans," one of Robert's longest stories to date—more than thirty pages—was composed during March 1916. He sent it to the editor of the journal *Schweiz* with a cover letter remarking that he had "sought to imbue the piece with a political standpoint that will surely be found acceptable." After several pages of walking and wandering, the title character is called up to serve in the army and finds himself inspired by a sense of patriotism. The story ends with the line, "He took a train to Bern and reported for duty."[22] The piece was accepted, and Robert took out a subscription.

He was now well-enough known as a Swiss short-prose author that magazine editors were eager to print his work. When Emil Wiedmer started planning a new journal, for example, he solicited Robert's work in advance and dropped his name in the circular advertising subscriptions. The same was starting to be true for Swiss book publishers as well; two of them queried him before the summer was out. The Swiss publishing house Huber was planning a novella series called Swiss Storytellers in separately bound small-format, eighty-page volumes priced at less than 1 franc each. The editor, Walter Lohmeyer, hoped to include a Walser volume. He offered a healthy fee of 250 francs—around $2,000 in today's dollars.[23] (Robert had been asking journals for 50 francs for a story—a sum that seemed high to some of the editors who published him.)

Robert first sent back a noncommittal note. But the invitation turned into an itch that needed scratching, so he wrote something long enough to fulfill the series' requirements—a work that, though not a novel, had the heft, variety, subject matter, and movement of a serious extended work.

This time he drew not on the past but on his present: the city of Biel and the many walks he took there crisscrossing its streets and especially the big square called Zentralplatz just steps from the front door of the Blaues Kreuz.

"I have to report," he wrote, "that one fine morning, I do not know any more for sure what time it was, as the desire to take a walk came over me, I put my hat on my head, left my writing room, or room of phantoms, and ran down the stairs to hurry out into the street." The novella "The Walk" ("Der Spaziergang") would prove a linchpin in Robert Walser's oeuvre—it is his single best-known piece of writing. Its narrator flees his "room of phantoms"—all the thoughts and stories from the past swirling around his head?—and sets out on a perambulation lasting dozens of pages, a narrative structured as a series of encounters. Most of these episodes are comically entertaining. He visits a bookstore, where he plays a prank on the bookseller; a bank, where he is informed that a large sum has just been deposited into his account by "some noble and kind benefactresses"; the post office; the tax-revenue office; and a tailor shop, where the tailor's slipshod workmanship horrifies him.[24]

He also has run-ins with two monstrous individuals: the giant Tomzack, a figure of intense loneliness and social rejection, who suddenly appears in the road before him, provoking terror; and Frau Aebi, an older woman who invites him to lunch and soon reveals herself to be a ghoul of hospitality who forcefully commands him to cram more and more food down his gullet until he's terrified yet again. Even a comrade "from the 134/III Landwehr battalion" makes a cameo appearance.[25] The narrator meticulously describes the effect each encounter has on him. Only at the end of the novella does he divulge the nature of the pain from which he's been fleeing for so many pages.

"The Walk" contains lines, spoken to a tax official from whom the narrator requests lenience, generally understood to represent Walser's defense of his mode of living:

> Walk I must [. . .] to invigorate myself and to maintain contact with the living world, without perceiving which I could not write the half of one more single word, or produce the tiniest poem in verse or prose. Without walking, I would be dead, and my profession, which I love passionately, would be destroyed.

Also, without walking and gathering reports, I would not be
able to render one single further report, or the tiniest of essays,
let alone a real, long story.[26]

This impassioned defense of walking as a literary, and thus professional
activity comes from a narrator perhaps not identical to Walser himself in
all his particularities—but the two are certainly in agreement on this score.
The speech suggests how Walser regarded a way of living that from the
outside must have looked much like a life of leisure. While the staff and
fellow denizens of the Blaues Kreuz may have seen a tenant who often
failed to emerge from his room until lunchtime and after lunch went out
for a stroll, Robert saw his life as one of labor, with every element of his
existence optimized for maximal productivity. Rising from bed, he flung
himself into his work, and only after its completion would he engage with
the world's distractions. Then he would wander about, collecting impressions to be used in his work. He had developed a mode of existence that
worked well for him while avoiding the messy intimacies that inevitably
arose when lodging in private apartments, as he'd experienced in Berlin.
As a hotel boarder, he enjoyed a certain degree of privacy along with his
meals and maid service. He was perfectly capable of making his own bed,
but what objections could be made to a chambermaid performing this task
while he was at lunch, relaxing after his own professional exertions?

Just a few weeks after the query from Huber in August 1916, another invitation to submit a work of two to four signatures in length (thirty-two to
sixty-four printed pages) arrived from another Swiss publishing house,
Rascher, which had recently taken over the journal *Die Weissen Blätter,*
where Robert had continued to publish. On October 10, less than a month
after completing "The Walk," Robert submitted his new manuscript, *Prose
Pieces* (*Prosastücke*), to Rascher. Its eighteen mostly quite short texts were
just enough to fill four signatures if printed with each piece starting on a
new page. Only one had been previously published.[27]
    For some of the texts in *Prose Pieces,* Robert dug into his past for
material: "The Brothers" (discussed in Chapter 2) relates Karl and Robert's youthful adventures in Stuttgart in a solemnly nostalgic style, while
"Koffermann and Zimmermann" parodies the fashion among Berlin publishers of sending their authors abroad. In "The Wicked Woman," Robert

presented a highly unflattering portrait of Flora Ackeret as an aging harpy
so filled with bitterness that she torments the young women of her acquaintance and is universally reviled. Recognizing herself in the portrait—
and in two others Robert had recently published in *Neue Zürcher
Zeitung*—Ackeret was deeply offended.[28] That was apparently a bridge he
was prepared to burn.

Some of the pieces in the book reflect the haste of their composition:
Robert knew he soon might have to button himself back into his military
uniform. "Lake Piece," which opens the volume, is an idyllic tribute to Biel's
waterfront: "This piece is very simple, it describes a lovely summer evening
and all the many people who promenaded back and forth on the shore of
the lake." In "Toothache," the narrator seeks medical help and, for economy's sake, lets himself be practiced upon by a dental student. When he admits to being a writer, the student's supervisor notes that a writer seeking
cut-rate dental care can't be much of a success. Like several other works in
the collection, this one introduces a theme, develops it for a little while, and
then ends with a brief closing gesture (in this case the narrator's assertion
that lack of success can't dampen his good spirits).[29] One gets the impression that Robert was hell-bent on filling enough pages for the four signatures he'd been allotted, even on days when he perhaps didn't particularly
feel like writing. It was his job, and he was doing it. But something else was
happening at the same time: in a few stories, the strategy of repetition he
pursued in the service of rapid composition developed a life of its own.

The narrator of "The Sausage," for example, is distraught because
he no longer has the sausage he already ate. In grotesque detail he describes the sausage, his consumption of it, and all the regrets he harbors
now that he can no longer devour the tasty item. The reader's growing
certainty that this ever more frantic-sounding narrator is completely unhinged lends the story considerable drama. This narrative formula of cen-
tering the story's tension in the repetitions themselves became a hallmark
of Walser's middle-period prose.[30]

Walser plays with another sort of repetition in the collection's final
two pieces, "Schwendimann" and "I Have Nothing." In each story, the
protagonist walks from place to place, searching for something while asking identical questions over and over, until the journey ends in either
death or resignation. This, too, is a recognizable Walserian mode of combining elements borrowed from fairy tales (the journey, the repetitive

quest, a lighthearted tone) with dark subject matter, each protagonist a cipher. What makes these two stories remarkable is the way the incessant repetitions in the storytelling take precedence over the subject matter, putting in question the necessity of having subject matter at all.

Rascher accepted Robert's manuscript by return post, and galley proofs arrived before the month was out. Robert tried to add one final story to the book, but by ignoring his requests to include a table of contents and begin each text on a new page, the publisher had managed to squeeze the manuscript into three signatures, reducing the compensation to 150 francs from the 200 Robert expected. Rascher inquired about the possibility of getting cover art from Karl. As it turned out, Karl had just arrived for a sojourn on St. Peter's Island in the middle of Lake Biel, so it was easy enough for Robert to put in the request. Though Karl, too, was unhappy with Rascher's remuneration, he provided a drawing of a man sitting on a wooden chest beside a window, head sunk as if in thought.[31] *Prose Pieces* was published in time for Christmas 1916. Rascher bought an ad in the German publishing industry's trade journal reminding the reading public that only books published in neutral countries could be sent as gifts to prisoners of war.[32] The newspaper *Zürcher Post* reprinted "I Have Nothing" in its December 16 issue along with an early review of the book. It was the first Walser book to appear in more than two years, and the first to appear in Switzerland.

The Walk still hadn't been published yet because of production delays. But Huber had meanwhile acquired a Leipzig distributor, ensuring it would be available in Germany as well as Switzerland. Lohmeyer made it clear that Huber was eager to publish additional books by Robert, so he now had two Swiss publishers actively interested in his work. He took advantage of the occasion to negotiate a better price from Huber—70 francs per signature rather than 50.[33]

And then two presses became three: Bern publisher Alexander Francke also asked for a book. Robert sent a proposal and soon had a third volume forthcoming. This new collection, three times the length of *Prose Pieces,* bore the title *Little Prose (Kleine Prosa)*. Its twenty-one stories, most of which were recent, included longer works such as "Tobold," the account of Robert's adventures as a butler described in Chapter 7.[34]

A number of the stories in *Little Prose* featured his new repetitive style. "Nothing at All," "So! I've Got You," and "The End of the World" combine this technique with a fairy-tale-like storytelling mode to solemn effect. The narrator of "Fritz," speaking humorously, wonders after every assertion whether it wouldn't have been better had the opposite been the case. The apotheosis of this new style came in "Basta," "Helbling," and "Fräulein Knuchel," in which frenetic repetition simulates a nervous tic, manic and alarming. "Lovely hair, lovely eyes, dainty hands, pretty little feet, a nice figure, and delicate white skin had Fräulein Knuchel, but she didn't have a husband, not Fräulein Knuchel," the narrator of Walser's eponymous story reports, then goes on to reiterate this list of attributes over and over in the course of assuring us of this Fräulein's definitive spouselessness while endlessly enumerating the reasons for it.[35] This style of storytelling rejects every remaining trace of the nineteenth-century sensibility Robert had once aspired to. At the same time, an element of psychological realism remains in these narratives that stutteringly portray a frantic state of mind.

Little Prose appeared in early April 1917, and Robert promptly sent a copy to Hermann Hesse. One day later, feeling nervous that Hesse might misinterpret the gift as a demand for a review, he followed up with a postcard assuring Hesse that his sending the book was meant as a courtesy and nothing more.[36] If Hesse thought him paranoid, that was better than appearing presumptuous. On the other hand, why shouldn't this book be reviewed by all the best writers? Hesse didn't review the book, but Hans Trog did, positively and promptly, in Neue Zürcher Zeitung. By June, reviewers were singing its praises in the newspapers Strassburger Post, Der Bund, and National-Zeitung (Basel), along with Emil Wiedmer in the journal Das Buch: Blätter für Kritik (The Book: A Critical Gazette).

Robert liked discussing typeface options with his publishers. For all the modernity of his writing, his tastes in type were old-fashioned and generally ran to the heavy German Gothic typefaces then falling into disuse in the publishing industry in favor of lighter, more modern roman types. Little Prose, like most of Robert's books, was set in a nineteenth-century-style black-letter type. As Robert explained to Huber, he preferred "a plain, time-honored, respectable Fraktur reminiscent of school primers: simple, honest, and unreformed, traditional through and through, warm, and above all: round." He wanted his books, he said, to resemble "first editions of classic authors like Schiller, Lessing, Goethe, etc." and to have

a "breezy, soft" layout with the lines of text well-spaced and no superfluous ornamentation. He rejected one typeface Huber suggested as "too
spiky and pointy."[37]

Typesetting, as it turns out, was one of the factors delaying the production of *The Walk*. According to Lohmeyer, the lines of text in Robert's
manuscript were spaced so closely together that the typesetter couldn't
read the manuscript easily enough to use a typesetting machine and had
to revert to a more laborious manual process. An additional issue was
Karl. Huber had commissioned a cover for the book from him, but Karl
remained incommunicado for months, and even Robert had to admit he
wasn't sure of his brother's whereabouts.[38]

Meanwhile, Robert received a query from one Herr Schwarz at the
Kurt Wolff publishing house asking for his help locating a painting Karl
had done of Robert that they were hoping to use to illustrate a pair of
Robert's texts in an anthology. Based on Renfer's photograph of Robert
from 1899, this portrait had been reproduced in 1914 in *Kunst und
Künstler* as part of a long article about Karl's work. The painting translates
the photograph into an outdoor scene, with Robert seated on a mossy rock
beneath a tree on a wooded hillside. Robert had recently described Karl's
picture in "Life of a Poet," published in 1916 in *Die Neue Rundschau*. But
he told Schwarz he was unable to recall who owned it and referred him to
Bruno Cassirer. Something had happened to this painting: decades later,
Robert remarked to Carl Seelig that Karl had sold it to Heinrich Simon,
former owner of *Frankfurter Zeitung*. But Seelig had heard from Oscar
Walser's wife, Fridolina, that according to Lisa, Robert had destroyed the
picture. Confronted with this story, Robert didn't deny it.[39] Had he felt the
portrait to be his rightful property and not his brother's to sell?

Robert had been negotiating with Huber on following *The Walk* with an
omnibus collection, *Studies and Stories* (*Studien und Novellen*), to include
his entire literary output of the prior three years. After initially agreeing,
Lohmeyer balked upon receiving the enormous manuscript—a fat stack of
handwritten texts, galley proofs, and newspaper clippings—some of which
he found weak. In his correspondence, Lohmeyer tiptoed around his disappointment with the work. He was handling Robert as one handles
someone deemed "difficult," perhaps because earlier that year during negotiations concerning *The Walk*, Robert had misconstrued a clause in the

proposed contract and demanded his manuscript's return. He was being difficult this time, too. Before their negotiations were over, Robert accused Lohmeyer of being "girlishly trepidatious" and offered the volume to another house (Orell Füssli, which rejected it).[40]

They ultimately settled on a different plan. Robert looked through his collected wartime writings again and extracted all the stories and sketches having to do with poetry and poets. He reread each, and rewrote most of them, attending both to their form and to the elegance of their sentences. He then offered Lohmeyer a new book, *Poet's Life* (*Poetenleben*), to be published later that year. Lohmeyer agreed. Behind the scenes, publisher Rudolf Huber was somewhat less enthusiastic, writing to Lohmeyer that he found the book's first few pieces filled with "monotonous landscape and toilette descriptions" but agreeing they should accept the manuscript as it was, since the author would surely react poorly to requests for further revision.[41] A contract was sent, and Robert signed. He would be paid 500 francs for this volume (roughly $3,500 in today's dollars), to be published in the fall of 1917.

When Lohmeyer tired of not hearing back from Karl about the cover for *The Walk,* Huber commissioned Otto Baumberger, a noted graphic artist based in Zurich. The book's first copies appeared in late June 1917 with an errata slip pasted inside, as the volumes had already been sewn together with a title page crediting the cover to "Karl Walser, Berlin." And the book sold like crazy. The first printing of thirty-six hundred copies went so fast that Huber printed another three thousand that September and five thousand more the following spring. The reviews were good, too. Korrodi in *Neue Zürcher Zeitung* declared the book a "cheerful little masterpiece" and one of Walser's best shorter works. *Thurgauer Zeitung* called it "masterful."[42] *The Walk* was Robert's first book to be transparently set where he was living at the time he wrote it. And it established him definitively—if belatedly—as one of Switzerland's leading authors.

The Aftermath of War

1917–1920

DURING THE WAR, Robert lost a brother. The deceased was not a war casualty, unless you count the inner war he'd been fighting for years. Ernst Walser, who'd entered Waldau Asylum in 1898, died there on November 17, 1916, at the age of forty-three. The news of his death arrived in the middle of Robert's work frenzy that fall, and while he left his desk long enough to gather with his siblings to remember their departed brother, he soon returned to his "writing room, or room of phantoms."[1] Much as Ernst's life and death were on his mind, he didn't use them as material. Somehow Karl's early indiscretions and Lisa's heartbreak seemed fairer game than the fate of this unhappy brother whose mind had come apart at the seams. Robert's siblings had been horrified when he described Ernst's institutionalization in *The Tanners* nearly a decade before. Now he left the story alone.

For Robert, Ernst's death marked the beginning of a protracted season of loss that would persist throughout the war years and beyond. This would prove to be a decisive period in his life, his last best chance to resurrect his career even as Europe was descending ever deeper into chaos. He understood all too well that merely continuing to publish stories and essays in magazines and newspapers was no longer enough to keep him financially afloat nor to raise his profile as a writer. More than ever, he needed book publications—which might mean a collection of his shorter writings but *should,* as he saw it, mean a novel, his first since *Jakob von Gunten.* If in Berlin he had felt himself crumbling under the expectation that he produce another novel, now he was discovering it was just as hard to write a book when no one was pressuring him at all.

For all his recent industry, Robert's income remained low while his expenses, especially for food, were rapidly mounting. Even in neutral Switzerland, inflation was now at 16 percent and rising, and the war was causing significant supply-chain interruptions. Before the war, 85 percent of the grain baked into Switzerland's bread had been imported, along with most of the fodder for the cows producing the country's all-important milk supply. Now bread prices soared, nearly doubling over the course of the war, and meat was rising even higher. Milk grew scarce in 1916 follow- ing a weak hay harvest and frigid spring, making cheese scarce as well. Rationing began in 1917 for key food items, with shortages developing in cities especially. Robert was less and less reticent about sending Frieda Mermet explicit requests for tea, sugar, cheese, and other items. Wood and coal were running low by winter 1917, with the Hotel Blaues Kreuz in danger of running out.[2]

On July 16, 1917, Robert was deployed again, this time to the mountainous Italian border in Switzerland's Ticino region, whose climate was mild enough for palm trees and magnolias to grow amid an Alpine landscape of enormous scale and grandeur. From their base in Bellinzona, Robert and his fellow soldiers clambered high into these mountains to take turns standing watch—though often, he wrote to Mermet, their watch-keeping involved "more lying and lazing about than standing." It was pleasantly warm when the sun was out, though nights were cold.[3]

Between watch shifts the soldiers practiced marching and shooting and shored up the fortifications. In the Alps, trenches were made not by digging but by erecting stone walls—hard work of a different sort. They were reminded that the mountains were dangerous as well as beautiful when a soldier slipped and fell to his death. The entire battalion assem- bled for his funeral. Forced to spend long hours without writing or read- ing, Robert found himself thinking of Mermet again, though she'd increasingly slipped from his thoughts in recent months. He sent her a postcard of Castle Mesocco, remarking on the beautiful walk he'd taken through the mountain valley with two of his comrades.[4]

Now that he was a soldier again, it felt right to have a woman back home to write to. He shamelessly hinted there was little cheese to be had up in the mountains, and Mermet promptly sent a care package.[5] The Swiss national holiday on August 1 was celebrated amid the peaks with speeches and the battalion's band playing in the fresh Alpine air. One morning Robert's company stood guard at a rail station while a train filled with wounded Austrian soldiers heading home from Italy passed through— a grim reminder of the horrors soldiers of neighboring countries were grappling with while their Swiss counterparts idled on mountaintops.

Robert had hoped to read his *Poet's Life* proofs before he was called up again, but they weren't ready in time. And so, for several days in Ticino he stayed up half the night reading galleys beside the oil lamp in the day-room while his fellow soldiers slept. A second installment of proofs reached him only after his company had relocated to All'Acqua, where their quarters were tighter. Fortunately, one of the sergeants took pity on him and offered his private room as a study.[6] Robert finished his proof-reading at forty-six-hundred feet.

High up in the narrow Bedretto mountain valley, All'Acqua lay at a strategic crossroads. From the Airolo station, the company ascended the pass on foot and then, surrounded by breathtaking Alpine landscapes, spent ten days working on the fortifications that protected it. Writing to Mermet, Robert praised the clear air, the "snow-white torrents plunging down from the heights into the valley," and the red wine. To Fanny, he wrote of beautiful walks taken to "Santa Maria, high up on a splendid mountain (the place is crawling with mountains) and to Lake Cama, which was enchantingly wild and romantic."[7] He remained at high altitude until September 5.

Robert's next tour of duty, five months later, was in the Jura Mountains on Switzerland's northern border. An air of urgency he hadn't felt before accompanied this call to arms; Battalion 143 assembled in Bern the morning of February 18, 1918, piled into a northbound train, and arrived in Delémont, deep in the wooded hills near the French border, at 1:15 a.m. Quartered in an old dancehall in nearby Courroux, Robert's unit spent a week practicing marksmanship. While this was certainly more pleasant than construction work, it was impossible to forget how close they were to the border. Should French troops enter Swiss territory, their battalion would be on the front line. A "telephone patrol" ran cables between each company's position; this was a modern war.

Though they were only about fifteen miles from Bellelay, the soldiers were instructed not to stray beyond nearby Glovelier during their Sundays off. So instead of visiting Mermet, Robert took a walk and then wrote her a letter about it. Requesting more cheese, he flirtatiously suggested he might drop by in uniform to see her, breaking protocol by informing her that his battalion was soon being sent to the border proper. In the end they stayed where they were, fighting mock battles against other units and performing training exercises. During a single day, they might be drilled in fielding surprise fire, offensive tactics, and the use of hand grenades, bayonets, and gas masks.[8]

The battalion woke at 5:30 a.m. on the morning of March 9 to news that the enemy was approaching from Porrentruy to the north. Instantly awake, the men flung on their uniforms. Robert's company was assigned to lead the battalion to Develier and then steeply uphill toward Bourrignon, about one mile from the border. Pressing as quickly as they could up a road jagged with switchbacks, they ascended higher and deeper into the hills, then scrambled into the woods to occupy defensive positions flanking the road, prepared to engage the enemy. It had warmed up since they'd arrived in the Jura weeks earlier; even here in the higher elevations, the snowbanks were melting in the sunshine, making it easier to hide. They crouched and waited. In the end, this turned out to be just another exercise, a maneuver, and they received orders to march back down the hill. "A really rough day," is all Robert had to say about it afterward when he wrote to Mermet.[9] On March 16, he was home again.

Though Walser never wrote much in his letters and literary works about the experience of doing military service, it went without saying for him that these were duties to be performed without grumbling, part of the shared work of upholding the Swiss commonweal he truly valued. It wasn't satire when he wrote, in the story "Hans" published in August 1916, "and now it is time to do my duty as an honest soldier [. . .] to serve the land among whose sons I count myself." Even as a Berliner writing about "assistant" Joseph Marti's having to serve a brief prison term for missing a compulsory military training, Walser has Marti, confronted with a fellow prisoner who speaks derisively about his "glorious little fatherland," respond first with indignation and then with a dream in which his beloved homeland appears spread out before him like a gorgeous tapestry.[10]

While Robert was keeping watch on his Ticino mountaintop, Emil Wiedmer published a glowing review of *Little Prose* in *März,* then sent a letter saying he intended to feature Robert in a monograph on Swiss literature he was writing for Rascher. As soon as Robert returned to Biel, he had his publishers send Wiedmer copies of his books. Wiedmer visited him in Biel on October 2, 1917, and afterward Robert wrote an autobiographical statement at Wiedmer's request, his first that we know of. This statement is extraordinary in at least two ways. First, he makes an explicit claim for the documentary status of some of his stories, identifying several of them—and one novel—as autobiographical ("Wenzel," "The Brothers," "Dr. Franz Blei," "Tobold," and *The Tanners*).[11] Second, he appears highly nostalgic for the early years of his writing career, when he worked as a clerk in Zurich:

> Half a poet's, half a mercantile existence. In other words, a double life that was accordingly full of charm, life, lessons. When Trog writes in his essay that Walser cannot have been a good clerk, this is a fundamental error. The poet can furnish proof that he was highly esteemed in the office for his industry and punctuality. Walser gives himself out in his books to be a substantially more frivolous figure than he ever was. He does this to achieve a certain roundness and totality. The artistic principle. The time when he was a clerk in Zurich and elsewhere was—for his soul, imagination, and heart—the most beautiful and happiest period of his life. He was very happy as a clerk.[12]

Perhaps Robert's current sense of financial instability in Biel fueled this nostalgia for steady paychecks; he seems to have forgotten how frequently he quit these jobs.

In this note written for the man poised to become his first biographer, Robert emphasized his seriousness as a literary figure. Writing of his return from Berlin to Biel, he quotes a line by the great nineteenth-century poet Friedrich Hölderlin: "thus do I hasten along the archway of life, returning from whence I came."[13] In thrall to the poet's powerful use of language as well as moved by his fate—Hölderlin had been undone by mental illness much like Ernst—Robert had published a piece about Hölderlin in *Vossische Zeitung* in 1915.

Poet's Life came out in November 1917 with a slipcase and a belly band featuring Max Brod's remarks about "two-layer" and "three-layer" writ-

ers.[14] Robert sent autographed copies to Trog, Korrodi, Wiedmer, Lohmeyer, Brod, and Hesse, who quickly reciprocated with a volume of
paintings and etchings by Alfred Welti for which he'd written the introduction.[15] In a tipsy letter dated November 15, Robert responded to
Hesse's suggestion that it was the duty of writers to press for peace:

> It may be wrong to sit, as I do, for example, in an expensive
> overcoat, inside an old Venetian palace, allowing oneself to be
> waited upon by seven hundred nimble servants. [. . .] Word is
> going around that Robert Walser is leading the noble life of a
> dreamer, idler, and petit bourgeois, instead of "fighting." [. . .
> But] what great or good aims can be achieved by articles in
> newspapers and magazines? [. . .] I believe that you understand
> better than anyone why I like to live a quiet and thoughtful life.[16]

Hesse had been working for the Prisoner-of-War Welfare Division of the
German embassy in Bern, where his duties included selecting reading material to be sent to German prisoners of war abroad. He clearly saw Robert
as like-minded and praised *Poet's Life* warmly in *Neue Zürcher Zeitung* that
same month, comparing the book to one that he described as "one of the
few small perfect works of world literature"—Joseph von Eichendorff's
classic romantic novella *Memoirs of a Good-for-Nothing*. "This Robert
Walser," Hesse writes, "who has already played a good deal of delicate
chamber music, strikes even purer, sweeter, more buoyant notes in this new
little book than in the earlier ones. If writers like Walser were among the
'leading minds,' there would be no war. If he had one hundred thousand
readers, the world would be better." In a postcard thanking Hesse for his
review, Robert affirmed his love of Eichendorff, regretting only that contemporary readers might be put off by his choice of a "foolish young fellow" as
a protagonist and the straightforward storytelling, "with nothing horrific,
Strindbergian, sickly, askew, shifty, dastardly, or blood-curdling about it."[17]

Other critics sang the book's praises as well. The 114 promotional
copies Huber had distributed generated a bounty of reviews. By the end
of 1917, eighteen articles proclaimed Walser "a masterful sovereign of elegance," a "true poet," and "the Swiss Jean Paul," among other accolades.
The book sold well, too—nearly eleven hundred copies (half the print
run) in the first two years alone.[18]

Meanwhile, Robert was busy revising the six longer stories he wanted to include in his next collection. He hadn't done much revision during his Zurich and early Berlin years, but once he'd gotten into the habit of drafting his texts in pencil and then making changes while copying these drafts, editing and revising his work increasingly became part of his practice. He'd combed through the manuscript of *Poet's Life,* reworking sentence after sentence of pieces previously published in newspapers and magazines. He revised for rhythm, timing, and style rather than content, though his changes sometimes involved shifts in narrative strategy. The version of "Frau Wilke" published in *Neue Zürcher Zeitung* in 1915, for example, began with the lines, "How they carried the poor, old woman away. What made me think of this just now? And the way I came to stay with Frau Wilke. Frau Wilke was her name." He revised the story to start with what had originally been its sixth sentence ("One day, when I was looking for a suitable room, I entered a curious house"), subtracting some of its meandering self-reflexiveness.[19] Now he aimed to focus the reader's attention on the story he was telling and the character being described. Was he thinking more about the nineteenth-century novelists he admired, perhaps in preparation for a return to novel-writing?

In a letter to Huber that November, he wrote that he was

> striving more and more to offer entertainment, i.e. insofar as possible to just tell stories and construct proper tales. I've, for example, let myself hold Dickens in such high esteem because he is the absolute and ingenious provider of perfectly good, rich entertainment. In this, even Keller seems to me less great. It's true that one cannot offer the reader nothing but linguistic artistry. The extraordinary thing about Dickens, it seems to me, is that, like Shakespeare, he always manages to be entertaining and at the same time a great artist.[20]

Keeping these principles in mind, Robert revised every sentence of his novella *The Walk,* tightening phrases, cutting back on chatter.[21] He wanted it to be clear by the end of the story that the point of the narrator's frenetic activity was to stay a few steps ahead of his painful memories. Distracting the reader with superfluous commentary wouldn't achieve that goal.

On February 1, 1918, just before reporting for military service in the Jura Mountains, Robert sent his new collection to Lohmeyer. The title, *Lake Country* (*Seeland*), refers to the region surrounding Lake Biel, Lake Neuchâtel, and Lake Morat—though in German the word *Seeland,* as Robert pointed out in his accompanying letter, also has "something magical" about it—perhaps because *See* can mean "sea" as well as "lake." In accordance with his recent habit when corresponding with publishers, Robert praised the submitted work, emphasizing both his intense labor and its merits as "a book that while not without errors is surely also not unimportant." "I feel myself justified," he adds, "in finding it a by all means good, serious, and valuable contribution." He asked Lohmeyer to publish the book by Pentecost and pay him 800 francs (roughly $4,000 in today's dollars) in acknowledgment of his six weeks of intense revising.[22]

Lohmeyer disappointed him. The price of paper had gone up along with everything else, and he didn't feel he could commit to the project. Fortunately, Max Rascher was feeling more sanguine. In 1917, with financial backing from Paul Cassirer, he had started a new publishing venture, Max Rascher Verlag, dedicated to publishing pacifist literature. He now declared himself willing to pay 800 francs for *Lake Country,* though he made the acceptance conditional on Karl's agreeing to illustrate the book.[23]

Karl—now sojourning in Twann, on the shore of Lake Biel—agreed to provide five etchings for the book for a 1,000-franc fee. This wasn't a project he was undertaking out of filial loyalty. In addition to whatever other tensions had recently arisen between the brothers, Robert explained that Karl didn't necessarily like everything Robert wrote very much, or even at all. "As similar as the two of us may be in one or the other respect," Robert wrote, "with regard to our views on life, our habits, character, and circumstances, there is, it seems to me, a significant difference between the brothers, and this *Lake Country* is assuredly not at all to his taste."[24]

Once he'd sent off the *Lake Country* manuscript, Robert turned his attention to other literary housekeeping. He still had some two dozen mostly shorter pieces he'd originally planned to include in the larger collection *Studies and Stories.* Rather than submit this manuscript to Rascher, he wrote to Kurt Wolff, proposing a collection to be titled *Chamber Music* (*Kammermusik*), a metaphor borrowed from Hesse's *Poet's Life* review. He also queried Insel about collecting the dramatic sketches he'd published in its journal sixteen years earlier. But Insel, it turned out, was out of paper. "Out of paper" was also what he heard from the Kurt Wolff offices. A wartime paper shortage was impacting publishers all across Germany.[25] But Bruno Cassirer proved willing to take on the project despite the uncertainties of paper availability. It seemed these plays, written in 1902 at a time of youthful optimism, would become a book at last.

In August 1918, Robert—who prided himself on his robust health—fell seriously ill. "I was fairly sick and therefore went on vacation for a few days," he laconically remarked in a business letter; but really it was a matter of weeks rather than days. He spent this "vacation" in Bellelay, though it's unclear whether Lisa took him into her own little apartment or found him a sickbed elsewhere. He spent time confined to bed, and when he started feeling better, he joined Lisa and Mermet for meals again in the asylum's dining room.[26]

This was no head cold; Robert was among the 50 percent of the Swiss population to be infected with influenza as it swept through the country in the summer and fall of 1918. This deadly pandemic that spread throughout Europe and around the world took more lives among the combatant nations of the Great War than the fighting itself. Egon Schiele, Max Weber, Guillaume Apollinaire, and Sigmund Freud's daughter Sophie all died of it. In Switzerland, some twenty-two thousand lives were lost to the disease in 1918 alone. Unlike other influenzas, this one proved particularly virulent among healthy men between twenty and forty years of age, making it swiftly lethal in the close quarters of soldiers' barracks, where infection raged before spreading to the general population. Those who fell ill were instructed to avoid contact with others; many communities even issued enforceable regulations to this effect, and many schools, including in Biel, were closed and transformed into field hospitals. Thankfully, forty-year-old Robert soon recovered his health.[27]

The Swiss victims of the pandemic included some eighteen hundred active-duty soldiers, half of whom were infected not while defending the country's borders against military invasion but in its cities, defending the interests of the state against striking Swiss workers. The strikes were motivated by anger over rising food costs and revelations about how highly profitable the war had become for a small number of Swiss industries—profits that had not been shared with workers. While Swiss factories manufactured much of the ammunition used in the war, many Swiss citizens had been unable to heat their homes during the winter of 1917–1918. The price of coal quintupled because of the shortages, yet there was somehow always enough to power the profitable factories.[28]

Across Switzerland's northern border, meanwhile, a revolution was in progress. Beginning on October 29, 1918, striking sailors and workers had effectively overthrown the German monarchy with a series of escalating protests that resulted in the proclamation of a republic on November 9 and the abdication of Kaiser Wilhelm II. Even after the armistice was signed on November 11, effectively ending the war, Germany continued to be rocked by battles between rival factions seeking control, and Switzerland was also shaken by a series of strikes. One launched by Zurich bank employees on September 30 culminated in a nationwide general strike on November 12 during which an estimated 250,000 workers walked off the job. The organizers' demands included proportional representation in government, a forty-eight-hour work week, old-age pensions, disability insurance, and women's suffrage. The military was called up in response to these protests—ninety-five thousand armed troops, including twenty thousand in Zurich alone, where the cavalry cordoned off Paradeplatz, Robert's former workplace. Protests and street fights occurred in Biel as well, and on November 14 three protesters were shot to death by soldiers in the nearby town of Grenchen. Other casualties included the hundreds of soldiers and protesters who contracted influenza in the crowd. In early December, Robert reported to Mermet the daily occurrence of seeing the coffins of influenza-felled soldiers being carried to the Biel train station.[29]

Watching strikers protest on Zentralplatz from his garret window, Robert was unimpressed. To him, the general strike was "disastrous, and not particularly well thought-out," the strikers riffraff who didn't know their place. He'd been mildly amused the previous June upon seeing a group of young municipal workers protest food shortages with piano accompaniment, songs, speeches, and "terrifying red flags reminiscent of Russia and Russian affairs." But when the Swiss Army was called in to establish order, he found the demonstrations decidedly less entertaining.[30]

On November 15, he wrote to Mermet: "In any case, it's better for all of us for things in our country to be orderly and peaceful, as you'll no doubt willingly agree. And the workers should go on working for the time being instead of trying to run the government, which couldn't turn out well, since these people haven't yet been schooled and are not cultivated, as is necessary if one is to take charge of important matters." His erstwhile passion for socialism lay far behind him. That younger Robert might have been among the bank clerks joining the strike. Now he was older and more traditional in his outlook, and even though he himself had enjoyed only an eighth-grade education, he deemed the working-class protesters unqualified to hold positions of responsibility, a deference to authority seemingly at odds with the analyses of power structures in his own writings. To be sure, he also criticized those in power in equally vehement terms: "Nothing but blockheads, muttonheads everywhere you look. Idiots racing into the factories to manufacture ammunition, and other idiots and cretins without end. [. . .] Children, dear Frau Mermet, little children, foolish little boys with their little heads full of mischief, would govern and rule the world better than today's wretched national and world leaders, or else women—women like you or many another—should be queens and regents, that much is perfectly clear to me."

Robert's feelings toward Mermet, no longer fueled by the urgency of desire, had modulated over the past year into something less romantic and more fraternal. Writing to her was like keeping a diary, a request to bear witness to his life. "If it were feasible," he wrote in one letter, "I would be your dutiful, always courteous, thrifty, reliable, faithful husband first thing tomorrow morning—assuming, of course, that you wished to have me." But his next sentence began, "Aside from such joking. . . ." He still showed no compunction about requesting favors and care packages from her, even during periods when he was remiss in visiting, for instance asking her to mail him the summer suit he'd previously given her to wash, iron, and mend. He praised her method of packing the victuals she sent him in repurposed cardboard boxes.[31]

Yet he still flirted with her epistolarily, as if to justify his claims upon her attention and material support. And he still floated the occasional explicitly erotic remark, such as suggesting that he'd like to eat a bonbon she'd previously chewed. He no longer wrote as an aspiring lover, but rather as someone just keeping his hand in, as it were. She seemed unruffled by this but would also remind him that her primary responsibility was to her son, who was preparing to leave school to begin an apprenticeship. Robert, secure in the knowledge that further flirtation would beget no consequences, carried on with this enjoyable pastime. In a letter beginning with the words "Dear Mama," he asks, "Would it give you pleasure, dear Frau Mermet, to possess me from head to foot, approximately the way a master possesses a dog?," before offering an additional fantasy:

> Do you know what I would like, dear Frau Mermet? I wish you were a genteel, beautiful madam and I would be your maid and have on a maid's apron and would serve you, and when you were dissatisfied with me, when I had somehow provoked your displeasure, you would box my ears, yes?, and I would burst out laughing at these sweet slaps on my face. That would be a more appealing life for me than a writer's existence, which admittedly isn't bad either.[32]

Nor was he bashful about regaling her with stories of his attraction to other women. Two weeks after returning from his convalescence in Bellelay, he wrote her about his fascination with the Fräulein Gouvernante (general manager) of the Hotel Blaues Kreuz, a woman with a good figure, tall and slender like Mermet, and also with something "decisive" in her character, a certain "down-to-earthness." He also mentions a young girl, an acquaintance of Lisa's, who sent him two pots of honey as a present and began a correspondence with him. Was he trying to make Mermet jealous? When she wrote in response that she wished she were young and pretty, he replied, "Certainly there may be younger limbs and prettier faces than yours, dear Frau Mermet, please forgive how openly I'm speaking. But after all you are not ugly, nor are you old yet, and you have a very sweet, agreeable nature. Beauty plays a major role, but even more important is the inclination a woman can inspire." These remarks by a "misogynist, cannibal, and bachelor"—as he called himself in another letter—did not keep her from sending another care package of bread, butter, and pork chops. She even mailed him ration coupons for bread and butter. He would continue to flirt with her off and on—for example, writing suggestively in May 1919 that "raw woman-flesh" was his favorite sort of meat—but there would never again be any serious courtship between them.[33]

Courtship *was* on Robert's mind, however, his lack of financial security notwithstanding. With his fortieth birthday behind him, it was urgent for him to marry if he wanted to escape eternal bachelorhood. A wife would take care of him and serve as a bulwark against loneliness. Mermet was out of the question; she'd withdrawn even at the height of their initial infatuation. Decades later, Mermet confessed to Carl Seelig that she might well have married Robert if she'd been in a more financially stable position herself. "I lacked the courage," she wrote, "to enter without money into this family that was thin-skinned and touched by a tragic fate." Lisa told Seelig that Robert had "tortured" Mermet with his endless indecision. Perhaps if he had approached her with a firm intention and decisive suit, rather than endlessly sounding her out, things might have gone differently.[34]

As other women continued to catch his eye, one in particular was coming to mean something to him. He'd known the pretty schoolteacher Marguerite Chavannes for decades as Fanny's classmate and, later, Lisa's friend. Chavannes, who liked to boast that she was born in Paris, was single despite her impish good looks and girlish manner. She lived in the same apartment building as her married sister and would always arrange to have her young niece with her when Robert came to call, as receiving him alone would have been improper. One excuse he had to visit was that Chavannes, as a favor to Lisa, was storing furniture left over from their parents' household, and sometimes the Walser siblings would gather in her apartment to socialize. Chavannes later reminisced about the stories Robert told when he returned from one of his long walks. Once, she said, he kissed her on the shoulder, then begged her pardon, embarrassed. Another time, he made her "a proper, romantic marriage proposal"; she said this must have been in 1919 or 1920, though she was recalling the incident at nearly a quarter of a century's remove. In any case, he began visiting her by December 1918 at the latest. But his friendship with Chavannes did not prove consequential enough to leave any further trace in his work or surviving correspondence.[35]

On May 1, 1919, the Walser family suffered a bitter and unforeseen loss: Hermann Walser, professor of geography at the University of Bern, took his own life. An obituary published in the journal of the Halleriana Bernensis, an academic club he'd belonged to as a student, described him as an introvert who always "struggled against a certain shyness and diffidence" and held himself to painfully rigid standards. Stymied by his childhood poverty, the author explains, Hermann felt "profoundly oppressed" by the misfortunes that plagued his family and was tormented by ever greater "psychological and physical sufferings." In his suicide note, Hermann bids farewell first to "Röbi and Kari, *Oski*" (underlining Oscar's nick-name), then to a short list of other friends and colleagues, oddly not nam-ing Lisa or even Fanny, the sibling he'd seen the most over the previous years. He was forty-eight years old and unmarried. Like his brother Ernst, he was buried in Schosshalden Cemetery in Bern.[36]

Hermann's death left Robert shaken. As familiar as he was with Her-mann's often gloomy disposition (hadn't he and Karl once enjoyed mak-ing fun of it?), Hermann's life had appeared the epitome of stability. Hermann had enjoyed professional success and esteem and financial se-curity but still chose not to live. It was sobering.

Robert was becoming closer again to his younger sister, Fanny, whom he now often visited. She was the Walser sibling most affected by Hermann's death, distraught enough that Lisa brought her to stay in Bel-lelay for a while after the funeral. Robert's closeness to Fanny perhaps provided some consolation for his rift with Karl, which widened when Karl realized that "Life of a Painter" was to be reprinted as part of *Lake Country,* which he'd been contracted to illustrate. This fanciful portrait wasn't one of the Karl-as-homewrecker stories Robert had written in Ber-lin, but it did highlight the fascination Karl exerted on women. Conscious of his reputation and less tolerant than formerly of being instrumentalized in his brother's work, Karl asked to have the piece removed from the col-lection, but the pages were already back from the printer. Creating the etchings for the book, Karl skipped that story.[37]

The Karl-Robert rift—culminating in the complete cessation of con-tact during the 1920s—has been the object of much speculation. Seelig surmised that the two parted ways mainly because Karl's wife, Trude, dis-approved of his eternally down-at-heels brother. Mermet said she believed it was due to an argument over book illustrations, and because Robert's ego had become so fragile during his years of diminished professional success that he was easy to offend. Margrit Kistler, whose sister met Karl in Zurich a few years after the brothers' falling out, reported that they quarreled because Robert had fallen in love with Trude and made a pass at her.[38]

Fifty years after the fact, Trude herself (who outlived both brothers by three decades) would tell a different story, one she shared only when pressed. She said that when she and Karl returned from Berlin to Switzer-land during the war, Robert and Lisa came to visit them in Twann. The

two siblings shared the guest room of the house Karl and Trude were renting, and in the morning Lisa, very upset, complained to Trude that Robert
had beleaguered her all night and kept trying to get into bed with her. It
isn't clear to what extent this report from someone who long harbored a
dislike of Robert can be taken at face value, but if an incident of this sort
did occur, it would also explain the apparent cooling in the relationship
between Robert and Lisa that lasted well into the 1920s. In 1929, Lisa
herself would tell a doctor that Robert had "behaved indecently toward
her" when visiting in the past.[39]

The summer after Hermann's death, a badly needed new friend arrived in
Robert's life. Emil Schibli, thirteen years his junior, had just started teaching in Lengnau, a short train ride from Biel. Schibli had previously worked
in the Rascher and Francke bookstores in Zurich and Bern, where—as he
later recalled with indignation—he never once had a customer ask him
for a book by Robert Walser.[40] He'd just published his first collection of
poems, with aspirations for more. One summer evening he showed up at
the Blaues Kreuz and asked the waitress who took his order which diner
was Walser. When Robert finished eating, Schibli introduced himself
and asked whether Robert might join him for a walk. At first, they strolled
in awkward silence, but as they continued along the shore of Lake
Biel, Robert started to open up to his new companion. Shortly before
9:00 p.m.—departure time for the last train to Lengnau—Schibli made
Robert a proposal: to accompany him back to Lengnau on foot and then
spend the night as a guest in the Schiblis' home. Robert agreed.

Like Robert, Schibli had a difficult boyhood. As a child, he'd been
indentured to a farmer and worked to earn his keep. His wife, the published poet Frieda Schibli-Furrer, had given up writing in deference to her
husband. Unable to find an apartment they could afford in the aftermath
of the war, the Schiblis were living as guests at the Lengnau parsonage.
When they did find an apartment of their own in April 1920, Robert
showed up to help carry boxes. He continued to meet Schibli for walks
and visit the couple in Lengnau on occasion, though he had mixed feelings about the literary merit of Schibli's work.[41]

Schibli, on the other hand, was in awe of Robert and somewhat
intimidated by him. In a 1927 essay, he marvels over the contrast
between Robert's narrative persona and his in-the-flesh appearance.

While Walser's books, he wrote, were inhabited by something "light, graceful, whispering, and fundamentally joyous," he found the writer himself "ungainly, taciturn, and rough-hewn, resembling a workman, metalsmith, or mechanic," and prophesied that this writer who was "secretly a king" would be honored by posterity even though he was now "clad in vagrant's garb" and suffering from isolation and poverty. Schibli's wife, Frieda, described Robert as "closed-off and despite his modesty so unapproachable that it wasn't easy to engage him in conversation. He was very friendly and polite. When he spoke, it was slowly, in a low voice, and deliberately, looking directly at you all the while."[42]

Others also found Robert increasingly unapproachable during these years. Emil Wiedmer was walking with friends on the woodland trails of the Verena Gorge Hermitage, outside Solothurn, when a tall figure startled them: "I involuntarily drew back before the robust stranger who, in a strangely sinister manner, without giving us a single glance, thrust his way wordlessly through our ranks, the broad, heavy, tall figure somewhat stooped, his jacket over one arm, the inevitable hat in his hand, the back of his neck and face bright red, and the heavy military shoes thick with dust—in short, the very picture of a walker who must have been on the move for hours, indeed from early morning."[43] This glimpse of Robert as a loner so deeply absorbed in his own thoughts as to take no heed of anyone else was similar to what Claire Zahler, a childhood friend of Lisa's, experienced. A teacher in Biel during Robert's years at the Blaues Kreuz, she reported that despite their having been friendly in their youth, with Robert often dropping by to see her while visiting from Zurich, he now avoided all contact: "He walked the streets looking so unapproachable and withdrawn that I didn't dare speak to him." Even Robert's pastor friend Ernst Hubacher witnessed his touchiness when he invited him to dinner and, finding him ill at ease, attempted to lighten the mood by teasing him with "an ironic remark about his oddness." Robert "instantly flushed bright red, his eyes blazing, and hissed at me with ill-concealed fury: 'Do you take me for some sort of clown?' " Hubacher was rescued by the arrival of his five-year-old twins; Robert immediately grabbed a picture-book Bible off the table and started telling stories that soon enchanted his two young listeners and their parents.[44]

People in whose company Robert felt utterly at ease included Gertrud Stettler and Klara Wolf, whom he met through Schibli. This lively pair of young schoolteachers—friends and roommates in their mid-twenties—lived in Meinisberg, between Biel and Lengnau. The pair took a liking to the older writer, who accepted invitations to visit them on more than one occasion. Once they invited him to dinner and, knowing he would be arriving on foot from Biel, asked him to pick up Klara's sister Lydia in Safnern on the way. Lydia found him "unusually gallant" and remarked on both his bowler hat and his courtly ways: when her shoelace came undone, he insisted on kneeling on the ground before her to tie it. But she also noticed his shabby appearance—his worn, poorly repaired suit.[45]

This circumstance did not dissuade her sister Klara from flirting with Robert and leading him down to the banks of the Old Aare. Once he let her wear the bowler hat, which he'd inherited from Hermann. As she wrote decades later to Seelig: "I was still so giddy in those days that I think if he'd asked me to marry him, I would have accepted out of pity for his material poverty. I'd always had such maternal feelings for those in desperate straits." But he didn't ask. Provoking their neighbors' disapproval, Klara and Gertrud let Robert stay with them for several days as a sort of holiday. Robert continued his correspondence with Klara for more than a year, to Mermet's apparent displeasure (of course he told her about it), but in October 1921 he informed her that he'd stopped writing to Klara, "if only for your sake."[46]

The poverty so obvious to Klara's sister Lydia was beginning to dominate Robert's life ever more cruelly. Schibli too had noticed the writer's trousers, adorned with large knee patches he'd clumsily sewn on himself—the entire suit was threadbare. Robert wasn't earning enough from his stories and articles to sustain his lifestyle, modest as it was. Room and board at the Blaues Kreuz cost 90 francs per month, he later reported to Seelig (around $450 in today's dollars), and to save money he would go without heat, instead wrapping himself in his army coat and warming his feet in slippers he made out of rags. Because of the restrictive exchange rates that continued even after the war, he was not only unable to transfer the prize money from the Women's League to Honor Writers of the Rhineland; he also could not receive payments from German magazines and newspapers. He asked at least one journal from which money was due to delay payment for this reason.[47]

Under these circumstances, it did nothing to improve his financial situation when Bruno Cassirer published his plays in 1919. But *Comedy* (*Komödie*) was a lovely little volume with a cover illustration (a cherub holding a mask) by the same Emil Rudolph Weiss whose work Robert had once tried to sell Walther Rathenau in his Berlin Secession days. The book contained Robert's four early plays from *Die Insel* (*The Lads, Poets, Cinderella,* and *Snow White*) prefaced with a note recalling the advice he was given in 1899 to write something that "came from within." Cassirer simultaneously reissued the book of Robert's poems he'd published in 1908 as a modest hardcover edition. But during this age of postwar poverty and revolution, plays and poems alike found few readers and no German reviewers. The one Swiss reviewer who wrote about the poems—Otto von Greyerz in *Der Bund*—trashed the book so viciously that Robert's Blaues Kreuz neighbors "turned pale when they told me how I'd been savaged," he later reported.[48]

Robert had continued to propose additional collections of short prose, querying Rascher after all about *Chamber Music* as well as a new book, *Little Mouse* (*Mäuschen*), and pitching three possible volumes to the Hermann Meister publishing house in Heidelberg, *Little Painting* (*Kleine Malerei*), *Flower Bouquet* (*Blumenstrauss*), and *Dear Little Swallow* (*Liebe kleine Schwalbe*). But even though he kept reducing his payment requests—such as suggesting in December 1919 that Hermann Meister pay him only 50 marks for each book manuscript, while the value of the mark was quickly dropping—publishers were struggling in the postwar economy, and none of these collections ever saw print.[49]

When a Kurt Wolff editor turned down *Chamber Music* in 1918 for want of paper, he closed his note with an admonition to "give up this 'pocket change' writing and think about writing a novel again." Robert himself was perfectly aware that if he wanted to change his fortunes as a writer, it could only be with a novel. Ideas had indeed been percolating in his head, and one in particular had risen to the surface. With plenty of time to muse when he was ill, his thoughts traveled back to his early years in Zurich, his employment as a clerk, and an intoxicating, long-gone feeling that life might have a great deal more to offer him.[50] That fall he set to work, unloosing a deluge of memories upon the page. A novel began to take shape about a young man, a clerk and poet, filled with ambition and optimism.

Robert completed a first draft by December 12, 1918, and offered Rascher the novel *Tobold* for consideration. He was copying it over, he wrote, and could submit the manuscript by the end of January. It's notable, given his tendency to hector publishers to print his books quickly, that he anticipated spending six weeks copying out what he characterized as a short, tightly structured work. His previous three novels had been submitted more or less in their first drafts, with all revisions made directly upon the original manuscript. With *Tobold*, things were different. It is the first book we know him to have composed entirely in pencil. The novelty of this new method excited him enough to be mentioned in his correspondence. A pencil also features in the short prose piece "Freiburg," written around this same time for an anthology Hesse was editing. "I'm in excellent spirits," the narrator reports, "first because instead of writing with a sharp steel pen I'm just using a pencil, and second, because I am recalling having slipped away from Bern one Sunday in the company of a young lady for an outing to Freiburg. Here I sharpen my pencil."[51]

In late 1926, Walser would explain the genesis of his "pencil method" in a prose piece: "one day I found that it made me nervous to start right in with the pen," his narrator explains, adding, "it occurred to me always first to commit my prose to paper in pencil before inking it into definitiveness." This method "involved a detour and increased labor," but "I felt it would make me healthy. [. . .] Among other things, it seemed to me the pencil let me work more dreamily, peacefully, cozily, contemplatively; I believed that the process [. . .] would blossom into a peculiar form of happiness."[52]

In a letter to editor Max Rychner in 1927, Walser wrote that he'd been drafting all his texts in pencil for approximately a decade, a practice that slowed down his writing process and "taught [him] patience." He began to write in pencil, he explains, because

> (this all began in Berlin) I suffered a real breakdown in my hand on account of the pen, a sort of cramp from whose clutches I slowly, laboriously freed myself by means of the pencil. A swoon, a cramp, a stupor—these are always both physical and mental. So I experienced a period of disruption that was mirrored, as it were, in my handwriting and its disintegration, and when I copied out the texts from this pencil assignment, I learned again, like a little boy, to write.

Drafting his work in pencil relieved him of the writer's cramp he'd come to associate with the feeling of having run out of ideas—having "grazed up all the motifs like a cow its meadow"—that he experienced first in Berlin and eventually also in Biel.[53]

Robert was pleased with the draft of *Tobold,* his first novel since *Jakob von Gunten,* for combining a turn-of-the-century setting with, as he wrote to Rascher, "a great deal that is contemporary and current." The novel was constructed around the eponymous protagonist's encounters and relationship with another young person. The name Tobold had already appeared several times in Walser's work. In "The Strange Fellow" (1912), he wrote that this name "came to him between sleeping and waking." Robert suggested that if Rascher wanted to publish the book, it could even precede *Lake Country*—still awaiting Karl's etchings. Robert requested a fee of 1,000 francs (roughly $5,000 in today's dollars)—five times what he'd proposed for *Chamber Music.*[54]

Copying and revising *Tobold* took longer than expected, particularly as Robert had to interrupt this work several times to read galleys and page proofs for *Lake Country.* He finally submitted the manuscript in late March 1919. It was 129 pages long, consisting of thirty-five chapters. Each chapter, he wrote in his cover letter, "constitutes a solid, precise painting in its own right," while the book itself "differs from my earlier novels in its concision." He had finally managed the feat he'd been preparing himself for all these years. And so he was devastated when Rascher rejected *Tobold* two weeks after receiving the manuscript—for economic reasons.[55]

The German *Papiermark* or "paper mark"—the country's official currency since the start of the war—had begun the precipitous collapse that would result in hyperinflation by 1923. The mark lost 80 percent of its value in 1919, the year Germany signed the Treaty of Versailles, obliging it to pay 33 billion US dollars in war indemnity. By April of that year, when Rascher turned down Robert's novel, it was already clear that it would be all but impossible for a book printed in Switzerland to earn a profit in Germany. Paper shortages were still an issue, too. When Rascher returned the manuscript, he expressed hope that the economic situation would improve soon and invited Robert to resubmit *Tobold* then.[56]

There was also another problem: once again, a manuscript of Robert's had been judged difficult to read. Rascher asked that when resubmitting the book, he do so "as a typescript, if at all possible." Even in his fair-copy manuscripts, Robert's cramped handwriting was now regularly giving his publishers trouble. Huber had first remarked, with regard to

The Walk, that the lines of text were spaced too closely together for a type-setter to read without effort. And in April 1918, Otto Flake rejected a piece Robert submitted to *Deutsche Allgemeine Zeitung* partly because the handwriting was too small. *Prose Pieces* had been written compactly too: eighteen texts on just eighteen manuscript pages. And in December, Rascher wrote that he'd had the *Lake Country* manuscript transcribed "to make the typesetter's job easier."[57] Robert hadn't necessarily been writing smaller on purpose. Paper was scarce, though, and becoming ever more expensive. Why leave blank space on a page?

The German inflation that prevented Rascher from offering Robert a contract for his novel also meant that any money being held for him in Germany was swiftly losing value, including payments German magazines sent to his account in Düren.[58] There was no point moving these funds to Switzerland because of the exchange rate. The Düren account was like a mirage: sums that once might have sustained his existence for many months were becoming nearly worthless, and it was uncertain when and whether he would be able to see any meaningful income from Germany again.

By late spring 1919, Robert's financial situation was dire, even after a surprise windfall the previous year. A subvention from the Swiss Schiller Foundation, overseen by Hans Bodmer, provided him with 500-franc grants for both 1918 and 1919. The award felt like a miracle, but it wasn't enough. After receiving the first half of the subvention in spring 1918, Robert asked Bodmer in December whether he could receive the second installment early, as he desperately needed it. He also talked Rascher into disbursing the first 400 francs for *Lake Country* before the book was typeset. Even with these cash infusions, Robert was "in bitter financial straits" by May 1919, as he wrote to Rascher, requesting the remainder of his *Lake Country* advance.[59]

Even more desperate in July, he requested a loan of 1,000 francs from the Swiss Finance Department against the 1,700-mark balance in his Düren account. He was referred to the Relief and Creditors' Association for Russia—an organization that made loans to Swiss citizens who'd fled Russia during the war, leaving their bank accounts behind—and then was rejected, as he didn't qualify. But Bodmer arranged a supplementary 200-franc award from the Swiss Schiller Foundation that September, followed by another 100 francs a year later.[60]

Discouraged by the apparent impossibility of making a living by publishing articles and books, Robert started to consider alternatives. "If I can just manage to sustain my writer's existence for the rest of this year," he wrote to Rascher, "I will count myself happy, feel resentment toward no one, and after this I will make my exit, i.e. take some job and disappear into the masses." He repeated this sentiment to Bodmer. He had an idea, he said, for one more proper book, after which he intended to "slip into some nice little office post." To Mermet he remarked that he wanted to finish a new book and "put his writerly affairs in order," after which he could "become an attendant in Bellelay or the emperor of who knows what empire, or take an office job, or go to work in a factory."[61]

A bit of relief arrived approximately around this time—the exact date isn't known—in the form of a distribution from Hermann's legacy. This inheritance of nearly 5,000 francs (roughly $24,000 in today's dollars) must have seemed a royal sum to Robert. But given the expense of sustaining even a modest lifestyle in his increasingly expensive homeland—where inflation surpassed 25 percent in 1919—he knew the reprieve was temporary.[62]

In 1920, Schibli proposed that the Hottingen Readers' Circle, the Zurich literary club led by Hans Bodmer that had presented Hans Trog's lecture on the Brothers Walser in 1915, book Robert as part of a public event. Robert had been queried several times in 1918 about reading in Zurich (sans honorarium) and had begged off. But this time he would be paid. Robert was to read his poetry and prose in the chamber-music room of Zurich's Tonhalle on November 8, the main attraction on a program that would also include a tribute to poet Karl Stamm, who'd died of influenza the previous year. Robert was pleased about the invitation, though also embarrassed that it emerged from Schibli's appeal to Korrodi and Bodmer for ways to help him; he scolded Schibli before accepting.[63]

Bodmer invited Robert to be a guest in his home for the occasion. Rather than take the train, Robert made the trip from Biel to Zurich on foot—a three-day trek—arriving dusty and exhausted the day before the reading. He brought along a copy of *Poet's Life* to inscribe to Bodmer, who proposed a private trial run of the presentation. But after Robert had read for only a few minutes, Bodmer interrupted, exclaiming, "Why, you can't read at all!" Robert was dumbstruck and furious—he'd come all this way for a sorely needed honorarium. Bodmer quickly assured him that the honorarium would be paid in any case and proposed a substitute reader. So it was that Hans Trog appeared before the audience the following evening to announce that Robert Walser was ill and unable to attend. Trog read while Robert sat in the front row of the auditorium. Bodmer and Trog had counted on no one recognizing him, and their assumption proved correct. Trog read his work well, and Robert, sitting among these elegantly dressed Zurichers in their fancy concert hall, enjoyed and applauded the performance. He reported to Mermet only that the evening had gone "really very well." Soon afterward, the Swiss Schiller Foundation selected *The Tanners* to distribute to its members as a Christmas gift, and Robert carefully signed his name on each of the one hundred labels Bodmer sent him to be pasted into the books.[64]

Robert later wrote two conflicting accounts of the Hottingen Readers' Circle episode. The first—a prose piece titled "The Literary Evening," published in 1921—devoted five and a half pages to the foot journey from Biel to Zurich and only a few lines to an encounter with an old acquaintance who proposed that the narrator let him read in his place, relieving him of a role that "wasn't well-suited to him." The second, an unpublished manuscript likely written in 1926, contains a reprise of the conversation with Bodmer: the interlocutor accuses the narrator of "stuttering" and "being unable to speak German."[65] In this latter version, though, Robert stands up for himself and insists that any awkwardness in his presentation would not prevent its being lively and inspired.

After more than three years of delays, and with the date 1919 printed on its copyright page, *Lake Country* finally appeared in December 1920, to very little notice. It received only a handful of reviews, including friendly appreciations by Trog in *Neue Zürcher Zeitung* and Wiedmer in *Solothurner Zeitung,* and was reviewed only in Switzerland. Though only six hundred copies had been printed—a luxury edition priced at 350 francs and signed by Karl as well as 20-franc paperbacks—a decade later only half the print run had been sold.[66] It was a discouraging end to a project that had been shepherded into print with so much care and effort.

In 1920, perhaps inspired by Cassirer's publication of *Comedy,* Robert returned to writing verse dramas, though much shorter ones than *Cinderella* and *Snow White,* his work of twenty years before. He wrote a *Sleeping Beauty* that resembles the two earlier fairy-tale plays in style and tone. The enchanted castle's inhabitants express annoyance at being roused from their dreams, and the princess is disappointed by her unexceptional rescuer but resolves to accept him anyhow. The longest of these new plays, *The Lovers*, is a strange sort of walk story in which the protagonist, Oskar, introduces a young woman to the art of walking, leading her from landscape to landscape, admiring each change of scene, until he becomes a sort of hermit who shuts himself away with his books. In *The Christ Child*, Joseph and Mary are astonished to learn from the visitors crowding their tiny stable that their infant is special, with one of the foreign kings revealing that the child will eventually suffer. The last of this new batch of playlets was a tribute to the Eichendorff novella to which Hesse had compared Walser's work. *The Good-for-Nothing* is a literary remix involving a great deal of boasting on the protagonist's part. Robert placed three of his new verse dramas in *Der Neue Merkur, Pro Helvetia,* and *Die Neue Rundschau* that fall and winter and the following winter published his Eichendorff tribute in *Pro Helvetia*.[67]

The next book of Robert's to make its way into the public sphere should have been his novel *Tobold,* but something had gone wrong. After Rascher's rejection, Robert offered the book to Huber, but then he started having doubts about the book's quality. He kept discovering parts of it that didn't hold together. He'd become so used to writing short prose that long narrative threads no longer came as naturally to him as they once had. What if the novel wasn't any good after all?

He'd submitted excerpts and outtakes from *Tobold* to *Der Neue Merkur* and *Saturn,* a journal published by Hermann Meister. But then he thought better of the excerpt he'd sent to *Der Neue Merkur* and wrote to Efraim Frisch asking him not to print it. No excerpt from the novel appeared in *Saturn* either. Had he given up on it? He usually sent a book to publisher after publisher until he found a home for it. In August 1920, he sent nine passages from *Tobold* to Bodmer, who'd asked to read the novel and offered to help place excerpts. There's no record of what Bodmer thought of the book, but Robert's Zurich reading four months later included parts of *The Walk* and "Kleist in Thun" and nothing at all from *Tobold*.[68] Perhaps this manuscript, too, became a casualty, destroyed by its author once Robert felt defeated by the book's imperfections. Not a page of it survives.

The failure of *Tobold* made Robert think more seriously about looking for a steady, reliable office job to support himself. In 1919, he hadn't been prepared to start job-hunting yet, but in November 1920, he once more brought up the possibility of finding work in Bellelay. Lisa, he wrote to Mermet, believed he might get hired as an attendant. She thought it was time he faced facts about the state of his writing career and looked for alternate sources of income. He wondered whether Mermet might welcome sharing a workplace with him or would prefer he seek a post elsewhere. She confessed that she was more comfortable with him finding some other job. As for Lisa, things were strained between them. He recalled that in the weeks leading up to Christmas 1919, Mermet had recommended he not visit his sister over Christmas because of her exhaustion. Would his constant presence in Bellelay be even more of a burden on her?[69]

In the end, it wasn't Lisa but Fanny who helped Robert find work. She heard about a temporary position he could apply for at the State Archive of the Canton of Bern. On December 28, 1920, Robert accepted head archivist Gottlieb Kurz's offer of employment as assistant archivist. He was to take up his new post in Bern on January 3, 1921.[70] And so his years in Biel ended not with the triumph of a successful novel but with a defeat arguably as decisive as the one that caused him to flee Berlin in 1913. Leaving Biel, he was withdrawing not only from a city but from a lifestyle that allowed him to go out for a walk at any hour he pleased. He would surrender his freedom once more.

The Secret Novel

1921–1925

WHEN HE LEFT BIEL, Robert abandoned not just the childhood memories lingering in its long-familiar streets, and the proximity of Lisa and Frieda Mermet, but also the town's comfortable provinciality. Bern, three times larger, was Switzerland's more worldly seat of government. "Under the influence of that powerful, vital city," Robert later told Carl Seelig, "I began to write less like a shepherd boy; my writing became more manly and international."[1] In Bern he truly came into his own and developed the stylistic and narrative approaches that would define his legacy as a writer. But this artistic growth took place during a period of increasing isolation and unease.

Tucked into a bend of the Aare River, the government buildings of Bern's historical center rise high above the bright green water. Beautiful old towers punctuate the city's central axis, and covered stone walkways framed with arches line its streets on either side. Robert's job at the State Archive—which he owed to council member Alfred Rudolf, who'd been friendly with Hermann—was a temporary post: three months of cataloguing historical documents. But a quarter-year of salaried work was nothing to sneeze at, nor was the pay: 350 francs a month (around $2,000 in today's dollars).[2] The archive was housed in the cellar of the old Rathaus, seat of both the city and cantonal governments, a grand fifteenth-century edifice renovated during the nineteenth century in neo-Gothic style with two tree-lined covered staircases leading up to an elegant arched entryway.[3] In a letter to Mermet, Robert described his work as "leafing through old documents"—a description he expanded on in a prose piece, published soon after, reporting on his first six weeks in Bern: "I leaf through all sorts of old files, letters, reports, ordinances, decrees, I draw up indexes and make an effort to do so in a businesslike manner."[4] As the first office job he'd held in fourteen years (since leaving the Berlin Secession), this position tested Robert's ability to subordinate himself to the strictures of office life.

Accounts describing the conclusion of Robert's tenure at the archive conflict. Decades later, Robert told Seelig he was fired from his position upon "falling out with the director after an impertinent remark." Mermet recalled him "having difficulties with his supervisor." But the archive's employment records indicate that Robert served out the entire quarter year for which he'd been hired and was kept on for an additional month.[5] Did he quarrel with Kurz during his final weeks of employment? In "Elfenau," published in *Leipziger Tageblatt* in June 1921, he reports:

> My supervisor was incredibly courteous the other day, he declared me incapable of doing anything. Was that something I could take lying down?
>
> "Rubbish," I replied, "I can do all sorts of things, for example I can give notice. Would that please you? Do let me know what you think."
>
> He had no choice but to agree. And so I abandoned my labors, bid him adieu, and took my leave.[6]

Was he relating an actual incident (real or inflated) or just a rebellious fantasy?

Robert still spoke favorably of his experience at the archive as late as April 18, when he wrote to Mermet that it proved he was still capable of performing work other than writing with good results. He listed his profession as "office clerk" in the *Address Book of the City of Bern* for two years thereafter, changing it to "writer" only in 1924. A fictional portrait of Kurz appears in Walser's 1925 novel *The Robber*, noting that the senior and assistant archivists often conversed on philosophical topics and that the protagonist's boss "did his best to soothe him, giving voice to the conviction that there existed just as many considerate, sympathetic persons as greedy ones incapable of contributing to the public good."[7] The position at the archive was the last office job Robert would ever hold.

On the outskirts of town, beyond the last tram stop, Robert sublet an attic room from the Stättler-Walker family, which included two sisters,

Anna and Franziska, who were friends of Fanny. The city was newly expanding into these southern districts, and new buildings, including many
villas, were going up everywhere. It was a scant half-hour's walk into town.
Robert often spent his lunch break strolling about in the center. After
work, he would go in search of food—or a glass or two of beer at Restaurant Fédéral across from the Swiss Parliament. He saw no point trying to
write after spending all day at the office. On days off, he sometimes met
Fanny at Gfeller's for a plate of *Rösti* or cake.[8]

It was mid-February before he addressed a letter to Mermet (who'd
sent him new socks). "He who works experiences very little," he wrote,
adding that one of his teeth, "a splendid, serviceable incisor," had fallen
out of his mouth, leaving a prominent gap. (Perhaps Fanny, now working
as a dental technician, helped get it replaced.) His missing tooth features
in "The Latest News" ("Neueste Nachricht"), published in *Die Weltbühne*
in March 1921, in which he also reports: "I'm somewhat better dressed
now than before, I wear an extremely elegant hat and behave accordingly,
I pay my bills on time, and lodge with a lady with two daughters who used
to pal around with two doctors of philosophy."[9] Unkindly gossiping, he
adds that both daughters were dropped by their suitors.

Robert later wrote a good deal about the Stättler-Walker sisters and
their widowed mother—satirically, for the most part. In *The Robber,* he describes "a family named Stalder consisting of a mother and two daughters
who liked to squabble with [their tenant], for they found squabbling, it
seemed, a worthwhile activity in its own right." Both of these fictionalized
young women are in hot romantic pursuit of the protagonist, whom they
constantly criticize, calling him by turns "a skinflint" and "a spendthrift,"
"cheeky" and "timid." They insist he spend his evenings in their company,
which he is loathe to do, finding their middle-class sensibilities tiresome.
Eventually the women resort to extreme measures: "One of them displayed
to him her bare shoulders, while the other went so far as to offer him a
glimpse, though admittedly only a skimpy, paltry one, into the fairy tale realm
of her *dessous,* by standing on a table."[10] It's unclear how much (if any) of this
was based on fact. Robert remained the Stättler-Walkers' tenant for more
than a year, even accompanying them when they moved in November 1921.

On Saturdays, Robert explored the countryside surrounding Bern. He
might walk a few miles, or many, perhaps to the village of Laupen (twelve

and a half miles to the west) or Hofwil (seven to the north), moving so rapidly that his striding legs and swift, leaping thoughts became inseparable. One of these trips took him deep into the Emmental, the landscape of his mother's childhood that he'd visited more than twenty years earlier when he lived in Thun. He published a piece about this new journey, noting that he ate at Hotel Bären in Sumiswald, where a scene in Gotthelf's *The Black Spider* is set. He wrote a similar piece about a thirty-six-mile foot journey to Thun and back, reporting, "How it delighted me to set foot in a city where I'd once been a clerk." He visited the town hall and castle, finding everything just as he remembered, and then strolled by Kleist's old house before trekking back to Bern.[11]

After his archive job ended, he added Biel to his list of destinations. He paid occasional visits to Lisa and Mermet and showed up for his obligatory military inspections, walking twenty miles each way. Other outings included a visit to the Schützenmatte park and sporting grounds outside Basel, where he rode a horse at the hippodrome (greatly enjoying the experience, as he wrote to Mermet) and tried out the newfangled "moving sidewalk" on display there—falling on his face, but without serious consequence.[12]

The essays Robert wrote and published during his first months in Bern resembled those he'd been writing in Biel. These short feuilletonistic pieces—describing walks he'd taken, places he'd seen, conversations he'd had or imagined—were all narrated in a realistic, somewhat chatty mode. A tram ride—how stimulating! A stroll through Elfenau Park—how invigorating! He was excited to have so much new scenery to write about. He later told Seelig that by the end of his time in Biel, he'd felt as though the "motifs and details that I drew from Biel and its surroundings were gradually beginning to run dry." Now he had new material, lots of it, and was finding new places to publish, such as the newspaper *Leipziger Tageblatt*. He continued to place work in *Die Weltbühne, Das Tage-Buch* (published by Rowohlt), and *Neue Zürcher Zeitung*.[13]

A new 1,000-franc subvention (around $5,500 in today's dollars) from the Swiss Schiller Foundation arrived in May 1921, a fine piece of encouragement for a writer freshly lacking a day job. Robert was now free and eager to devote himself once more to longer work. Rather than return to the *Tobold* manuscript (if it even still existed), he began work on something new.

Robert's new manuscript—*Theodor, a Small Novel* (*Theodor, ein kleiner Roman*)—was set in Berlin, the title character a sort of secretary to a Paul Cassirer–like figure named Reinhold. Robert spliced into this story a second one resembling the Agappaia episode in *The Tanners:* Theodor falls in love with the married Frau Steiner and boldly pursues her friendship under her husband's nose—but this time both young suitor and cuckold possess Cassirer-like self-assurance. Their battle of wills culminates in a showdown (each having prophylactically acquired a pistol), with Steiner trying to force Theodor to board a train that will take him out of their lives forever. Appreciating each other's determination, they bond.

Robert completed the manuscript in fall 1921 and set about looking for a publisher. Unfortunately, the publishing industry was no better off than it had been two years earlier, when he'd tried to place *Tobold.* In fact, Germany's inflation had gotten even worse, making book publishing more difficult than ever. In November, Swiss Writers' Association president Robert Faesi encouraged Robert to join the association and apply for a loan through its new subvention program, which gave writers advances on the strength of their manuscripts, to be repaid after the books were published.[14]

Robert was granted a 2,500-franc loan (roughly $14,000 in today's dollars), with the first installment (1,500 francs) paid out on December 19, 1921. When he sought advice about potential publishers for his novel, Faesi confirmed that Rascher, Huber, and Franke were out of the question under the current economic circumstances and suggested Rheinverlag (now run by Walter Lohmeyer) and Grethlein.[15] Lohmeyer quickly declined the novel, but Grethlein—with offices in Leipzig and Zurich—was interested. Its director, former diplomat Curt Hauschild, wanted to develop a list of leading Swiss writers and was purchasing the rights to their older works as well as contracting for new ones. In Robert's case, that meant acquiring his three early novels from Bruno Cassirer and buying the unsold copies. But Grethlein was unwilling to pay the 3,000-franc advance Robert requested—2,500 of which would have been claimed by the Swiss Writers' Association in repayment of its loan.

Attempting to persuade Robert to accept less, Hauschild visited him in 1922 and suggested specific wording for a letter to Cassirer, as Robert later reported to the association. The fragmentary draft of such a missive (written in tiny pencil script) was found on the back of a letter Robert sent to Mermet. But he never wrote to Cassirer; it would have been shameful to ask him to relinquish his financial interest in Robert's novels as a personal favor. Hauschild himself complained to the association in 1924: "Mr. Walser does not respond to positive suggestions as others do. To be completely frank: he is an eccentric gentleman, a bohemian, a crackpot." Robert had apparently told him he was contemplating taking a job at a shipping firm.[16]

Hauschild had an additional reason to consider Robert eccentric. As recounted in Mächler's 1966 biography, the letter Hauschild received inviting him to visit was signed "Caesar, Mr. Walser's valet." When Hauschild arrived at the appointed hour, the garret door was opened by a man in his shirtsleeves who announced that his master, Mr. Walser, would be with him in a moment and then withdrew, shutting the door. When it reopened shortly afterward, the same man stepped out, now wearing a jacket, and introduced himself as Walser. Hauschild was not amused by this clowning. A similar encounter is described in *The Robber* (with a fictional servant named Julius). Assuming the story took place as described, it certainly bears witness to Robert's frustration at being asked to make financial concessions to an obviously well-to-do publisher. Writing to the association in fall 1922 to ask for the subvention's second installment despite lacking a contract, Robert lamented having no current income from his writing at all.[17]

Following a further unsuccessful bid at placing the novel with the Hugo Schmidt publishing house in Munich, it occurred to Robert to try Rowohlt in Berlin. This was a new house founded after the war by the same Ernst Rowohlt who—a decade earlier—had accepted Robert's collection *Stories* before Kurt Wolff bought him out. He now agreed to read Robert's new novel, and in his office the manuscript languished. In 1928, Robert wrote to the Swiss Writers' Association that Rowohlt had been sitting on the manuscript for four years, and later still he told Seelig he had no idea what became of it. But it seems he too had quickly lost faith in his own book: in an unpublished piece titled "Diary" from 1926, he described the novel as containing "numerous errors with respect to reality," and he referred to it in a letter to another editor in 1927 as "flawed."[18]

All that survives today of the *Theodor* manuscript is a twenty-five-page extract published in the December 15, 1923, issue of the journal *Wissen und Leben*.[19] Stylistically, these scenes resemble Walser's first two novels, *The Tanners* and *The Assistant*. As in *Jakob von Gunten*, the first-person narrative is presented in diary form, and the protagonist is a familiar denizen of the Walserian universe. Approaching Reinhold to ask for a job, young Theodor fidgets just like Joseph Marti and awkwardly grabs a fistful of cigarettes when invited to smoke in hopes of demonstrating more self-assurance than he feels, though his cheekiness is already as conspicuous as his insecurity. He displays unfeigned delight on learning that Frau Steiner harbors feelings for him. Yet *Theodor* displays a layer of self-reflexive complexity not seen in Walser's early novels. Introducing himself to the Steiners, Theodor informs the lady of the house that he is under orders from a publisher to produce a novel (later he'll call it a "diary"), to which end he needs to rack up experiences by making new acquaintances, above all, women.[20] This structural sleight-of-hand (positioning the novel's protagonist simultaneously as its author) foreshadows Walser's later novel *The Robber*.

According to a reader's report the Swiss Writers' Association commissioned from author Lisa Wenger, *Theodor* was "a singular work" whose author "has different ideas from anyone else." She describes a scene in which Theodor falls on his knees and pours out his heart to his beloved despite her husband sitting right beside them. Other passages Wenger singles out for praise feature a hermit living in the woods among wild animals (a motif Robert had explored in his short play *The Lovers*) and a scene in which a young girl, longing to start a family, offers Theodor her love. "No one does this," Wenger remarks. "But after you've read the scene, you wish they did." She strongly recommends the novel receive a subvention even though she finds it "clumsy" and "a bit thin" in parts. To her, the book demonstrates that "the author has a great deal to say" and deserves the association's support.[21]

Faesi invited Robert to present *Theodor* at a meeting of the Literary Club of the Hottingen Readers' Circle. The reading took place on March 8, 1922, at the elegant Zunfthaus zur Waag on Zurich's Fraumünsterplatz. Painter Ernst Morgenthaler later described the scene: "I came into a small, brightly lit room with serious-looking gentlemen seated around a massive table. These were all important literary figures, truly the cultural elite of Zurich. At the head of the table sat a red-haired man in a rough gray jacket. With his flaming head and his red hands, he seemed entirely out of place in this assembly. It was Robert Walser, who then opened a manuscript and began to read."[22] Eduard Korrodi, reporting on the event in *Neue Zürcher Zeitung*, described Robert's manner of reading as "very idiosyncratic, certainly not

orthodox, handling some parts oddly, others excellently." Korrodi praises the
novel's "quiet magic," noting how it begins with the protagonist laying aside
a book because he wants to "encounter beauty in life, too." Eternally cheerful, Theodor declares that when he happens to be well-dressed, it wouldn't
surprise him to receive a few banknotes as a gift, for he looks like a fellow with
something in his wallet. The evening ended, Korrodi writes, with "the warmest applause," a formulation Robert borrowed when he described the event
to Mermet, adding only that he had read from his manuscript for around
three-quarters of an hour, stopping frequently to sip red wine.[23]

The Literary Club newsletter reports: "With the same freshness,
naturalness, and delicacy as in his debut *The Tanners*, he has his hero
Theodor in this new work, written in diary form, narrate his manifold
experiences in the deliciously naïve and warm manner of which Walser is
a master." Another view was less positive: writer Cécile Lauber and her
husband read the manuscript, and Werner Lauber later told Seelig both
of them had found the book "unharmonious" and of lesser quality than
Walser's three previous novels. In Lauber's opinion, the excerpts that
editor Max Rychner had chosen for *Wissen und Leben*—ten sections from
different parts of the novel—were the best parts of the book.[24]

Robert was to have spent the night after the reading as a guest of Ernst
Hubacher's brother Hermann, a sculptor. But Hermann was ill, and his
wife persuaded their friend Ernst Morgenthaler—a long-time Walser fan—
to host Robert instead. Exhausted after staying out all night for carnival,
Morgenthaler struggled to stay awake during the reading. He'd hoped to
go straight home to bed afterward, but Robert insisted on having a drink
at an old haunt of his in the shadow of the cathedral. Sitting across from
Morgenthaler, he praised the Literary Club members so effusively his
companion couldn't tell whether he was being ironic. "Extremely talkative, as one often sees with people who live in isolation and then turn
loquacious in company and under the influence of alcohol," Morgenthaler
later reported. Robert droned on, oblivious to his host's weariness, and
refused to leave until closing time. As they were finally walking home,
Morgenthaler happened to mention that his brother-in-law lived in a
building they were passing, and Robert insisted they ring the bell, since a
"real live brother-in-law" would surely be eager to offer his hospitality.
The brother-in-law, roused from sleep, invited them in and spent the rest

of the night drinking with Robert while Morgenthaler dozed in an armchair. At five in the morning, they set off again for Morgenthaler's home
in Wollishofen on the bank of Lake Zurich. "Robert Walser must have
liked it at our house," Morgenthaler concluded dryly, "because he stayed
fourteen days."[25]

Writing of these fourteen days in a letter to Mermet dated March 22,
1922, Robert noted that he'd been "very well looked after" and had "once
more made the acquaintance of all sorts of people from artistic circles"—
something he'd been missing in Biel and Bern. In Zurich he attended a
writers' gathering and came back talking about Hermann Hiltbrunner's
report on his visit to Knut Hamsun, pronouncing it *"very* interesting"
(again, Morgenthaler wasn't sure how ironically this was meant). He also
went to the movies, saw a production of Beethoven's *Fidelio* at the Stadt-
theater, and was delighted by a performance of Mozart's *The Magic Flute*
("one of the most beautiful works ever composed"). But Robert was so
disappointed by a production of *The Merchant of Venice* that he walked
out—apparently without alerting Robert Faesi, his companion for the
evening. He also told Mermet he'd been spending time "with young people, it was all very lovely, and the weather was so lovely too."[26]

Morgenthaler had more to say about the "young people" Robert spent
time with. To look after their two sons, he and his wife (artist Sasha Morgenthaler) employed an au pair—a native of Biel named Hedwig Schneider to
whom Robert took an instant liking. He was soon utterly smitten with this
unworldly girl, half a child herself at age seventeen, with two long braids
down her back. According to Morgenthaler, forty-three-year-old Robert

> would sit with her in the kitchen, follow her up to the attic, fol-
> low her down to the cellar, and anytime there was anything he
> could help out with, he would chivalrously place his services at
> her disposal. He gave the girl his books and wrote dedications
> in them as if to a marquise. Later she received letters from him
> written in his beautiful handwriting that looked like copperplate.
> In complicated phrases, the poet gave voice to the great rever-
> ence, to all the high esteem in which he held the female sex.[27]

It was perhaps because of this infatuation that Robert reported to Mermet
his being in uncharacteristically high spirits upon returning to Bern: "In

Zurich everyone said I was looking younger than ever, and there's no doubt some truth to this, I think so too, and I even fancy that I've begun to feel young again on the inside without any particular intention on my part. Recently life has seemed to me very, very beautiful." His affections, however, were not reciprocated; their object appeared puzzled, even unnerved by them. "She didn't understand," writes Morgenthaler, and she was "if anything a bit frightened by this red-haired man and this onslaught of feelings that cannot entirely have escaped the child, inexperienced as she was." Robert sent her a postcard from Nidau, her birthplace. He sent her a copy of *Fritz Kocher's Essays*—perhaps thinking it his most suitable book for a reader of tender age?—and received at least one letter from her. Nothing ever came of his attachment to young Hedwig, but he never forgot her; years later, he reminisced to Seelig about this girl he fell in love with that spring in Zurich.[28]

Extended stays in the homes of friends were becoming a regular part of Robert's lifestyle. The year before he visited the Morgenthalers, he spent a week with their mutual friend sculptor Hermann Hubacher. Hubacher was the grandson of the art teacher with whom both Robert and Karl had studied drawing in school; he had been so strict he once punished young Karl for spoiling a watercolor he was painting by commanding him to drink the glass of water he'd been dipping his brush into.[29] Hubacher must have invited Robert to drop by the family's summer home in Faulensee on the shores of Lake Thun because he showed up unannounced one summer evening, having walked twenty-five miles from Bern.

Hubacher was out, but his wife, Anna, welcomed the sweat-drenched visitor and fed him supper. Robert stayed for a week, picking berries with his hostess and playing with their children in the garden. Anna recalled that he told the "strangest stories" that she "would have loved to listen to" but was afraid of displeasing him—the stories were meant for the children. She fondly recalled the philosophical conversations he would have with her "from bush to bush" while berry-picking: "His views were never banal or dictated by public opinion. With him, you never knew what was coming next. It was always something original, the product of his own heart and mind."[30]

Robert also spent hours watching Hermann sculpt. The Hubachers had a young servant whose "delicate beauty made quite an impression on him"—though he did not develop the sort of infatuation with her he would with Hedwig Schneider the following spring. Anna tricked Robert into going to a shop where she could buy him a pair of shirts, as he'd arrived without a change of clothes and his shoulders were too broad for Hermann's. At week's end, Hermann rowed Robert across the lake to Merlingen, from where he walked home.[31] He returned for another visit the following year.

Robert was increasingly relying on the kindness and hospitality of others. Having no proper home of his own, he found it a reprieve to be a visitor in someone else's home, particularly in pastoral surrounds. And all his stories made him an interesting guest. He was also at times noticeably odd in his behavior and affect. Social niceties, the little conventions that ward off awkwardness, meant little to him. This also applied to his interactions with families he rented rooms from. When he moved out of the Stättler-Walker apartment, Robert reported to Mermet that one of the sisters "bid me farewell with all sorts of reproaches, saying I was a cad and a dog [and] chased after music hall ladies." "The only true part of it," he defended himself, "is that I extended certain courtesies to a lady from Geneva who sings at a music hall. Anni W. got mad when I told her about it."[32]

These tensions extended to his own sisters, and he complained to Mermet that they were not "behaving in an honest and open way" with him. Returning from a visit to her in Bellelay, he discovered that Fanny and Lisa had visited his landladies in his absence—that is, entered his home without his foreknowledge—even bringing with them a friend from Biel whom Fanny knew Robert abhorred. Robert was furious with Fanny for this betrayal, which he described in a letter to Mermet, peppering the margins with "bullheaded!!!" and "suffragette!!!!" He asked Mermet to keep his displeasure to herself and continue to "be nice to" Lisa, as the entire matter was "ridiculous," but he also asked her to agree that his sisters were "*provoking*" him.[33]

At the end of January 1922, Robert rented a new room in the home of one Karl Schaffner, just down the block from the first apartment he'd shared with the Stättler-Walkers. He lasted here only two months before moving to lodgings in the heart of the historical center, with a view of the cathedral out the back. In a letter to Mermet he mused, in French, "I'm a real vagabond, aren't I, to be changing pensions so quickly?"[34]

His new landlady, Emma Lenz-Gräub, appears in several of his literary texts. A widow twelve years his senior, she is generally portrayed as the victim of an unhappy marriage who saw her tenant as a romantic prospect. She owned a milliner's shop and was often overworked, but—at least according to one literary portrait—she refused her tenant's offers of assistance.

Some of what Walser wrote about her has erotic undertones. "The Green Spider" from 1924–1925 gives her flashing green eyes and attractively freckled skin. In another portrait, the narrator gets a thrill from nibbling her leftovers in the kitchen, and he is delighted to barge in on her once just as she is about to wash her feet.[35] Whatever Robert's actual interactions with this widow, she certainly gave his imagination plenty to dwell on for the two years he spent as her tenant.

Robert had a stroke of good fortune later in 1922: he received an inheritance from his father's youngest brother, architect Friedrich Walser-Hindermann of Basel. Walser-Hindermann, who died on May 14 at the age of eighty-two, left Robert 1,500 francs (around $9,800 in today's dollars).[36] This modest windfall was well-timed; Robert had been worried about what would happen when Hermann's legacy ran out, and just half a year earlier he had written to Faesi that he was considering seeking salaried employment again.[37] Life was more expensive in Bern than in Biel. While his room at the Blaues Kreuz had cost 20 francs per month (90 with full board), a room in Bern could cost 40 (around $260 in today's dollars).[38] That September, he also pressed (successfully) to have the second installment of the subvention for *Theodor* paid out early.

The historical record around this inheritance is somewhat murky. Lisa wrote to Seelig in 1937 that each Walser sibling was left 10,000 francs by an uncle in 1920 and that this money had allowed Robert to "be more carefree." Her statement was assumed to refer to Walser-Hindermann's estate, but his testament indicates that he left only 1,500 each to Robert and Karl and 3,000 each to Fanny, Lisa, and Oscar. Could part of the inheritance have been provided "off the books" to avoid taxes? In any case, "Uncle Fritz" was well aware that his artist nephews Karl and Robert—to whom he left a smaller amount, at least officially—were less well-off than their siblings; when Robert first moved to Berlin, their uncle is reported to have remarked, "Now we have two starvelings in Berlin." As far as we know, Walser had no other uncles from whom this inheritance might have derived; Elisa Walser-Marti's brother and brother-in-law both died young, and Walser-Hindermann was his father's last surviving brother.[39]

Between 1922 and 1926, Robert lived at thirteen different addresses, reprising the rapid shift of living quarters he'd practiced toward the end of his Zurich years (and experienced in childhood). "I enjoy this way of living," he wrote to Mermet in 1925, though "lodgings that are both appealing and inexpensive" were difficult to find. Several of his texts from this period describe the benefits of life as an urban nomad. In "Diary" he declares it a way of "invigorating myself, seeking to add variety, which I hope can be at least to some extent comprehended and therefore found acceptable." The narrator of "Erich" remarks, "In order to keep himself entertained, he frequently changed his room." And "Am I Demanding?" ("Bin ich anspruchsvoll?") reports: "I like looking for a room [. . .]. You can look into houses which you would otherwise not look into."[40]

The professions of the people Robert lodged with include electrician, greengrocer, book printer, office worker, warehouse supervisor, and laundry owner. While some of his Bernese landladies show up as characters in his work, no landlord does. He also never spent long in any household headed by a man. Did he enjoy imagining himself the man of the house? Given how many hours he inevitably spent each day in these spaces where he slept and wrote, his rented rooms provided much of the backdrop for his life. And if he ever came to feel ill at ease in one of them, what reason was there to stay? Swiftly moving from room to room was like a slow-motion real-estate version of walking. But he later told Seelig that his frequent moves also had another explanation: he believed that some of these rooms were haunted. "One would be wrong to think that Bern is always so cozy. On the contrary. There are spooks and ghosts all over. That is why I moved so often. Many rooms had something uncanny about them." It would later become apparent—as discussed in Chapters 14 and 15—that Robert began to suffer from (mostly auditory) hallucinations during the course of the 1920s. Perhaps what he experienced as ghostly activity in his rented rooms were the first signs of that affliction.[41]

Robert was fortunate to be admired by Eduard Korrodi—*Neue Zürcher Zeitung*'s feuilleton editor since 1915 and a literary kingmaker in Switzerland. He was the sort of critic who could afford to enrage Hesse by challenging him in print to deny he was the novelist behind the pseudonym Emil Sinclair (author of *Demian*). When *Lake Country* came out in 1920, Korrodi purchased a copy of the 200-franc half-vellum edition and sent it to Robert, affectionately inscribed, as a Christmas present. More than any other editor, he had continued to publish Robert's short prose throughout the war years and their aftermath, as well as singling him out for praise in his 1924 book *Contemporary Swiss Writing,* which dismisses many of Walser's contemporaries as Gottfried Keller epigones.[42]

Other of Robert's professional relationships were more difficult or marked by distrust. When *Der Bund* appointed a new feuilleton editor, Hugo Marti, in 1922, Robert sent Marti a note saying he hoped to meet him and would be sitting in the café of the Loeb department store between four and five o'clock. Marti didn't show up. When they did finally meet— by appointment, in Marti's office—Robert announced that he expected 100 francs for two short pieces he was submitting. Marti pronounced this impossible, prompting Robert to send an angry letter saying that because of Marti's refusal he would no longer be inclined "to visit you in friend-ship," adding by way of signature, "What a shame that your incompetence caused you to be impolite to—Robert Walser."[43] Eventually he calmed down and submitted more work that *Der Bund* published.

Robert also felt slighted when, in June 1921, Efraim Frisch rejected a piece he'd submitted to *Der Neue Merkur* by saying it was too much like others they'd already published and asking him to send something else instead. Outraged, Robert wrote a vitriolic screed of a letter criticizing the journal and vowing to return unopened any future issues mailed to him. Half a year later, he sent Frisch another essay with the tersest of notes; it was not accepted or at any rate never appeared.[44]

Another argument, in 1924, led to Robert's resignation from the Swiss Writers' Association. This time the offender was writer Alfred Fankhauser—editor of the Social-Democrat daily *Berner Tagwacht,* an as-sociation board member, and a friend of Emil Schibli, who'd introduced them. Fankhauser didn't realize Robert was a dozen years older and not his peer. On their "fateful evening," he reports, he was sitting in the train station café when Robert joined him and started talking about the walks he'd taken that day, including to the village Ortschwaben, where he stopped at the inn. Delighted by the coincidence, Fankhauser exclaimed that his sister worked there and must have waited on him. Robert retorted, "Are you trying to marry me off to your sister?" "God preserve my sister from you!," Fankhauser countered, seeing a healthy dose of irony in both sides of the exchange.

But Robert continued to look annoyed even after other friends ar-rived (Felix Loeffel, a sculptor named Kunz and his wife, a book printer named Lierow), and he started complaining about the restaurant Du Thé-atre, where he'd been refused service. The people there, he vulgarly ex-claimed in dialect, never stop "eye-fucking." Fankhauser escorted Robert to the establishment in question, where he made the mistake of telling him that reading some of Robert's poetry quoted in a review had convinced him that Robert was the only German-language poet capable of translating Verlaine. "This was apparently a massive insult," Fankhauser reports, "be-cause R.W. immediately jumped up and shouted at me: 'You think I should be translating that old goat Verlaine? Why should I have to carry his bags?' " Fankhauser thought Robert was joking until Robert pointedly avoided him on the street the next day. A month later, Fankhauser heard that Robert had resigned his Swiss Writers' Association membership be-cause of their encounter. (The membership might also have been an un-pleasant reminder that he had never repaid the loan he'd received for his novel *Theodor* in 1921.)[45]

Robert had always been a great reader, but his peripatetic lifestyle was hardly conducive to amassing a personal library. When he received copies of the journals in which his work appeared, he generally sent them to Lisa or Mermet, retrieving them when he wanted to assemble a collection. He told Seelig he kept on hand a stack of Reclam volumes—cheap pocket-sized editions of the classics. And he frequently borrowed books, some-times returning them by mail. In 1924, for example, he asked Mermet to send him books from his sister's library: Jeremias Gotthelf's novel *Money and Spirit* and Stendhal's *Italian Chronicles.* He requested the former after a newspaper reprinted Gotthelf's story "The Observations of Journeyman Jakob." Reading it, he wrote to Mermet, was "like eating crispy roast meat"; it struck him as authentic in an age when so many authors were just "dem-onstrating that they can 'write.' " He also was reading Jean Paul, the influ-ence of whose "singularly beautiful sentences" he identified in Gotthelf, confessing he'd read Jean Paul's novella *Life of the Cheerful Little School-master Maria Wutz* as many as twenty times. In another letter to Mermet, he praises Proust, who, he says, "never seems to run out of breath." In Bern, where he no longer heard French spoken around him as often as in Biel, he also took to reading books in that language, for practice.[46]

Feeling nostalgic during his first year in Bern, he wrote to Mermet: "I'll never regret having spent so long in Biel. For one thing, it was a splendid place to live and secondly it was a station in my professional and human development." Several years later, the narrator of "The Ruin" ("Die Ruine") reminisces: "For eight years, I found the lake beautiful on a daily basis. [. . .] Every day I walked up the selfsame, certainly quite nice, dear, good, obliging mountain." Walser also, in that text, inflates the romantic prospects he'd enjoyed in Biel, boasting that "at least half a dozen" of the chambermaids living beside him in the attic fell in love with him, as did the hotel's general manager, "but without having any hope of gaining my affections, of course." (Robert, we remember, had described his own romantic interest in the manager to Mermet.) The narrator even claims he bored a hole in the wall to spy on the girls next door.[47]

In fact, Robert's years in Biel had been quiet ones. Living in a temperance hotel gave him stability and community—people he saw every day who shared news and gossip. In Bern, his life was radically different. Instead of taking his meals in a dining room, he usually went out, often staying out all evening. Bern had a lively cabaret scene, and Robert got to know it well. He began to write frequently about inebriation. Though he regularly spoke of wanting to marry and settle down, the longer he lived this undomesticated existence, the less marriageable he became. Living off what remained of his inheritances and the Writers' Association funds, he was ever conscious of the need to economize; renting a proper apartment such as a wife might share would soon have exhausted his savings. At the same time, he appeared to retain an optimistic view of his own eligibility. His infatuation with the Morgenthalers' au pair was just one example. Upon arriving home from that visit, he wrote to Ernst Morgenthaler that reading *The Brothers Karamazov* (which he'd borrowed from Schibli) had persuaded him it was time to hurry up and find a wife of his own, marrying being "no easy experiment, but surely also not an all too difficult and impossible one."[48]

Having a wife to look after him might certainly have been helpful in early 1923 when he suffered a sciatica attack severe enough to require hospitalization. He reported to Mermet that in the aftermath, he began keeping a careful watch on his body, diligently avoiding drafts, making sure to get regular gentle exercise, and keeping his room nice and warm "as if looking after a spoiled prince"—a dramatic departure from his earlier practice of skimping on heat to save money. His sciatica was treated with saline injections, heating pads, aspirin, and ultraviolet light. He nonetheless went on using his feet for transportation, as when walking the ninety miles from Bern to Geneva the following autumn—in a mere thirty hours, as he boasted to Mermet.[49]

Perhaps in conjunction with his frustration over *Theodor*, Robert's production grew sluggish in 1922 and 1923, when he published fewer short texts than in any year since 1907. With his novels *Tobold* and *Theodor* both stillbirths, he had tried to follow his old formula of assembling shorter pieces into book manuscripts, but none of the publishers he queried would take on such a project. Robert also unsuccessfully attempted to publish a second collection of plays, a companion piece to *Comedy*. Insel turned the project down in the winter of 1921–1922, and he'd presumably queried Cassirer beforehand.[50]

The publishing industry was still struggling in the war's inflationary aftermath, while Robert's work was starting to look less and less marketable. In early 1925, when Efraim Frisch inquired whether Deutsche Verlags-Anstalt in Munich might be interested in publishing a volume of Robert's sketches, he was told it would be "impossible to find a wider readership for this sort of book" and that the editor considered it "highly unlikely that Walser will ever again complete any other major work." It was a mistake not to have let Grethlein publish *Theodor* under whatever terms the house wanted; investing in the earlier Cassirer novels would have given Hauschild a powerful incentive to advance Robert's reputation. As late as 1924, Hauschild was still lamenting in a letter that Robert had been unwilling to negotiate with him. Publishers had inevitably become risk-averse, and an author whose works hadn't sold well in the past was a gamble.[51]

By 1924, however, Robert's productivity slump had ended. In July, he remarked jokingly to Mermet that he'd recently written more than one hundred pieces ("green and blue and red things") over the previous six weeks—so many that he needed an assistant, "a sweet attentive girl to put them in shape and copy them over"; she needn't, he added, "be wearing much."[52] As he turned out texts using his pencil draft technique, the revision and copying process became a production bottleneck; occasionally, a text would be left uncopied. At the same time, his work was changing.

In 1922 Robert wrote a lot of short descriptive essays full of the feuilletonistic observations newspaper editors liked. "Five o'clock tea," one piece begins, "is truly entertaining. One listens to music, sips coffee, and tries to comport oneself in an agreeable manner. [. . .] That smoking is not permitted appeals perhaps above all to the smoker: he can display his adaptability." Robert was now well-practiced at achieving detached irony, allowing the narrator to inhabit the character described while simultaneously analyzing his behavior from across the room. And there was no shortage of subjects for these texts. "We don't need to see anything out of the ordinary," he'd written in 1914, "we already see so much." But this kind of writing had already proved an aesthetic dead end, and he'd spent most of his career trying to get away from it, pushing himself in the direction of stories with plots, forward motion, and character development. These things didn't come naturally to him, though. Could that have been why *Theodor* and *Tobold* had failed? What if he stopped trying to produce nineteenth-century fiction?[53]

Beginning in 1923, his work changed tack. In "Napoleon and Countess Walewska," describing a movie scene in which Napoleon eats cherries as he waits for the countess to succumb to his charms, Robert wrote a sentence that in English reads, "As the Emperor chewed cherries, he gazed down contritely." In German, the word for "contritely" (*zerknirscht*) sounds enough like the word for cherry (*Kirsch*) to create a humorous crossing of linguistic signals in a sentence thick with alliteration and interior rhyme ("Indem der Kaiser Kirschen kaute, schaute er zerknirscht"). Korrodi published the piece in *Neue Zürcher Zeitung*, perhaps inspiring irate readers to threaten to cancel their subscriptions "if the nonsense didn't stop," as Korrodi later told Schibli happened every time he printed something by Walser.[54]

In "Coats," the narrator describes returning coats to their owners after a concert, remarking, "An obligingness urge took hold of me." Compounds structured like "obligingness urge" (*Zuvorkommenheitsbedürfnis*) are not uncommon in German. It's routine, for example, to refer to a seat as a *Sitzgelegenheit* ("seating opportunity"). But the neologism "obligingness urge" is different. There's something quietly radical about asking these words to cohabit. Obligingness indicates kindness to others; Walser's word exposes it as kindness to oneself. "Prose writers adore the poetical" ("Prosaisten lieben Poesie") he asserts in the very next sentence, adding by way of illustration: "Becoated, girls go to see Mozart's *Magic Flute*" ("Bemäntelt besuchen Mädchen Mozarts 'Zauberflöte' "), a dense but melodious line whose playfulness lies in the fact that the words are obviously combined as much for sound as sense.[55] It's provocative to point out that women on their way to the opera might have on *coats*—a maddeningly obvious and irrelevant detail—while at the same time the sentence's nicely knitted-together sounds signify, well, *significance,* which is wittily withheld.

The signature move of Walser's mid-to-late-1920s prose is exploiting the sound qualities of words at the expense of semantic content, or deploying them in ways that appear to run counter, or at least slantwise, to their literal sense. In one piece, for example, he has a customer enter a grocery shop asking whether an item is *bekömmlich*; the word means "easily digestible," but Walser uses it as if it meant "available" (via the verb *bekommen*, "to receive")—which it does not.[56] Forcing the reader to process words as conflicting semantic pairs creates multiple simultaneous readings all relating to the topic under discussion in various ways. This new multidimensional form of reading was certainly based on the principle of punning. But these puns are so skillfully deployed that to say Walser's work began to contain more puns is saying far too little. He'd been using puns in his work since the beginning, after all. (Recall the line from *Fritz Kocher's Essays:* "When everything's so white, we write our lessons so much better," with "white" and "write" based on a German homonym.)

His sentences expanded and sprouted tendrils, growing fractally more complex with a profusion of clauses, each addition complicating an already complex thought with new ideas and associations. This way of writing suggested the state of mind of a highly distractible person entertaining several thoughts at once, as in this passage describing a pair of lovers in "Ophelia," published in December 1924 in *Wissen und Leben:*

> If they now sat united upon a chopped-down tree trunk at the edge of the woods lost in the extensive pleasure gardens of their thoughts, if here after a spell of gazing down before her the lady began to weep with the utmost sweetness and also great bitterness and this weeping appeared to be pouring itself into an unceasingness while no sound passed her lips, as though any word would have been superfluous, and if I myself, describing all of this to you, am unable to tear myself free from an unseemly softness and am having the greatest difficulty remaining mentally in a state of vital superiority and continuing

to hold my head high as I write, and if the lad, with all the lack
of self-restraint being offered him by his lady, who under these
circumstances can be considered poor, was forced to see his
own self-restraint smashed to bits, as namely his triumph over
sentiment grew to become a veritable flood of pity, I would
nonetheless like to append to this melodrama that an institution for epileptics stood nearby that still stands there to this
day for the benefit of those thus afflicted.[57]

In this experiment with structure, the story takes place in the conditional
("if" . . .) clauses preceding the grammatical main clause ("I would like
to append"), which itself contains what appears an irrelevant aside.
References to the writing's present tense inform both the main clause and
one of the four conditional clauses ("as I write"), confounding the relationship between the telling and the told by obscuring the sentence's focal
point.

   This maximalist prose of exaggerated expression is rich in abstract
nouns—such as "unceasingness" (*Unaufhörlichkeit*)—forced into service
as concrete nouns, often to humorous effect. "Corridoricity" (*Korri-
dorlichkeit*), for example, signifies behavior that takes place in corridors,
such as abruptly slipping away while someone is talking to you. Adjectives
blossom into metaphors: "Robert, a finger-thin, spider-web-delicate modesty plant," begins another tale, with "modesty plant" its own compound
neologism (*Bescheidenheitspflanze*), suggesting both "outgrowth of modesty" and "plant epitomizing modesty."[58] This overwrought linguistic ornamentation went far beyond what Robert had earlier taken pains to
subtract from his work, as when he trimmed away verbiage from his novella *The Walk* to make the narrative sleeker and more emotionally on
point. That story's ornaments—the interspersed "I have to recall" or "I
might add"—played verbosity for humor without increasing narrative
complexity. Now, however, he was using style to intervene decisively in the
storytelling itself, foregrounding linguistic detail over denotation in a way
that challenged every conventional notion of what it meant to signify.[59]

An unexpected benefactor appeared in Robert's life in 1923. Walser had
met writer Franz Hessel years earlier in Berlin, where both attended Samuel Fischer's 1907 Christmas party. Hessel was now co-editing *Vers und*

Prosa, a new journal Rowohlt was publishing and to which Robert was invited to submit. The journal published eleven of his pieces, some of which became Walser classics: "Dostoevsky's Idiot," "The Monkey," "Parisian Newspapers," and "Letter to Edith." Hessel was also a trusted Rowohlt advisor on book projects: the lucrative forty-four-volume mass-market Balzac edition he edited rescued the house from the devastation of postwar inflation. In 1924, Hessel persuaded Rowohlt to commission a book of Walser stories—*The Rose (Die Rose),* which appeared in February 1925 with a cover by Karl. Unlike most of Robert's earlier collections, this one did not merely assemble previously published work. The only reprints among its forty-two essays, stories, and hybrid prose works were pieces Hessel had published in *Vers und Prosa* the year before. *The Rose* was the first book Robert had published since 1920; it was also the last published during his lifetime that he himself oversaw.[60]

The collection reflects his new aesthetic direction if not his most radical writing of this period. While much of *The Rose* harks back to motifs and strategies of his earlier prose—it includes several walk stories and feuilleton-style essays—it also features a new genre he'd been experimenting with: the penny-dreadful recap. These stories recount the plots of cheap novelettes of the sort sold at train-station kiosks; he'd recently developed a taste for these entertaining quick reads that also provided him with new material. Some of these retellings are straightforward plot recaps, while others contain some of the most elaborate writing *The Rose* has to offer. "The Uncle" presents a man who courts his niece with kindness and gifts, prompting the girl to perch upon the lap of her "virtually-trembling-with-life-happiness-despite-having-attained-a-certain-number-of-years" uncle, whose eyes pop open "like five-franc coins" at his own "unexpected successlet with the little birdie." "He who formerly modestied now monarched," Walser writes in "Teacher and Porter," taking advantage of German's ability to turn anything into a verb, even the nouns "modesty" and "monarch." In "A Slap in the Face et cetera," he coins the portmanteau verb *spazifizotteln,* composed of *spazieren* (to walk) and *zotteln* (to dawdle) by way of *spezifizieren* (to specify). And an inebriated narrator gives linguistic form to his own drunkenness in "Letter to Edith": "I swayed now into a pastry shop café, and reeling, if I may, put some cognac away. To please me, Grieg was played by two musicians, but the proprietor brought out his munitions."[61]

The Rose seems to offer self-portraits while simultaneously suggesting one not place too much faith in them. In "A Lump of Sugar," the narrator reports, "I found a dumpling with mustard delicious, which won't keep me from noting the possibility of a first-person book's 'I' being modestly metaphorical, not authorial." That piece follows "The Child," which flirts with autofiction in sentences like "Once the child was a man who walked about very man-of-the-worldishly"; "The child was now a good forty years old or actually in fact a bit more" (Robert himself was forty-six); "Earlier on the child had written nice fat books"; and "Since he failed to produce a novel, he was accused of sloth."[62]

But as if to duck the danger of self-exposure, Walser later in "The Child" adds a line that has become proverbial regarding his relationship to autobiographical writing: "No one is entitled to behave towards me as if he knew me."[63] It's as if his desire to bare his soul were wrestling with self-preservation, especially as he would go on in this same text to write quite sensational things in the first person, inviting readers to indeed feel they knew him and to shake their heads disapprovingly or in pity. But was it really himself he was describing? It was precisely his point that we would never know and to some extent, perhaps, neither would he. Was self-knowledge desirable, or even possible?

Having created a smokescreen of uncertainty, the narrator of "The Child" reports: "I've never been kissed by a girl. Recently I saw a boy whom I immediately felt I wished to serve as friend or teacher, so greatly did his face please me. He resembled my ladylove, and I couldn't take my eyes off him. It surprises and pleases me that I have a sweetheart; I find that quite clever of me. Isn't a sweetheart a splendid excuse for all sorts of things?"[64] This gender, and generational, confusion is striking. *The Rose* marks Robert's first publication to include subject matter of this sort. The narrator of "A Lump of Sugar" uses a willow switch as a jump rope, remarking, "Perhaps I'll soon enroll in a finishing school for girls." In the dialogue "Weakness and Strength," the narrator describes his first visit to a bordello, where he discovers that the woman he selects to have sex with arouses his respect but—despite her skill—not his manhood; "nothing in me," he writes, "desired anything of her." Begging her forgiveness, he explains: "I didn't know myself and thought that by visiting you I could gain self-insight. I understand you, but don't yet understand myself." A doctor writes him a prescription, but the fact remains that he wants nothing from the bordello staff, as he is "already satisfied" and "without need." It was a daring confession to deliver in the first person, even in an ostensibly fictional text.[65]

In late 1924, with *The Rose* forthcoming, Robert made another push to publish more work from his backlog of manuscripts (and also to find pre-print opportunities for some of the stories from the collection). He submitted thirty pages of short prose to Basel's *National-Zeitung* in November and shortly afterward approached Orell Füssli about publishing a collection of twenty-seven texts under the title *Watercolors (Aquarell)*. The book was rejected, and *National-Zeitung* printed only two pieces. Perhaps this was the spirit of discouragement and financial worry that prompted him to write to Mermet requesting she preorder a copy of *The Rose* directly from him for 20 francs—more than three times the official price. He later asked her to offer copies to two acquaintances in Bellelay for 15 francs each.[66]

The Rose arrived with a splash. Rowohlt bought several full-page advertisements in major magazines and top billing in the monthly publishers' advertising circular. Dozens of reviews soon followed. While some—like Franz Blei's—praised the writing's delicate artfulness, others dismissed the book as slight. Hesse weighed in with a backhanded compliment, describing the stories as charming tidbits ("sweet flirtations [. . .] naive little foolishnesses [. . .] lovely ethereal miniature poems") that made him wish the author would write another of his "most beautiful prose books" like *The Assistant* or *The Tanners*. And despite Rowohlt's publicity investment and the flurry of attention following the book's appearance, it didn't sell.[67]

It had now been more than fifteen years since Robert had last published a novel. It seemed that despite the artistic strides he had made as an author of short prose, the absence of a major longer work meant that the sort of recognition that might also have drawn readers to his stories and essays would now continue to elude him, particularly given how challenging much of this short work now was. He was stuck, and each attempt he'd made in recent years to write his way out of this dead end had led to failure. Perhaps this is why, when he did write another novel in the summer of 1925, he kept it to himself.

Walser's secret novel was very different from the books Hesse had described as his "most beautiful." *The Robber* is strange, difficult, and profoundly experimental. So rich in digressions that detours seem to be its primary narrative mode, it is also thick with metaphors sprawling so out of control they seem to offer their own alternate realities. While the story is told in the third person, a first-person narrator gradually emerges to speak ever more persistently about the storytelling process. Narrator and protagonist are eventually revealed to be one and the same—a notion buttressed by the narrator's categorically denying it. Like Robert play-acting his own manservant, the book's main character lends his role dignity by describing himself through the fictional eyes of his own invention—even as he himself is the author's invention. The novel culminates in a great scene of reckoning, with the Robber publicly justifying his conduct in a church filled with women.

Robbery serves as a metaphor for writing in the novel: to write about someone is to steal from them. The story proceeds by a strategy of constant deferment. Prospective topics are frequently announced and dropped, with promises to return to them often renewed but only occasionally fulfilled. The opening sentences—"Edith loves him. More on this later"—set the stage for a game of narrative hide-and-seek that continues throughout the novel. The reader is constantly being told what's coming up next (often it isn't) and asked to be patient.

The Robber is also a love story with multiple objects of desire. Edith, the waitress described as the protagonist's beloved, appears under the same name in several stories in *The Rose*. Wanda, the daughter of wealthy parents, appears too young to be appropriately courted; the first time the Robber approaches her, she responds, "Go away [. . .] it's very nice that you love me, but for heaven's sake where is Mama?" He also cultivates a relationship with a woman described as a vagabond and social outcast, whom he meets in the woods for walks and conversation. The oldest woman among these love objects is the protagonist's landlady, a widow named Selma with whom he flirts outrageously even as he falls behind on his rent; in one scene, her used coffee spoon serves as an erotic fetish. A thick thread of homoerotic tension runs through the novel as well, including episodes discussed in Chapter 7 featuring the flirtatious Englishman and Walther Rathenau (who was murdered by members of a right-wing terrorist organization in 1922). The Robber also spends an afternoon following a little boy—"an international lad"—asking whether he might be the boy's "servant girl" and at one point even contriving to kiss his knees.[68]

The protagonist's anxiety about his sexuality is a prominent leitmotif. Finding it worrisome that he lacks all desire to sleep with women, the Robber visits a professor who lectures him on the importance of a fulfilling sex life, and memories of this visit pop up throughout the book. The theme of fluid gender identity, already introduced in *The Rose,* surfaces here more explicitly and emphatically. The narrator reports that the Robber has been transformed into a maidservant and enjoys running around in a skirt, adding that this novel is "concerned with the possibility that, at times, the Robber might really have become a girl, a sweet young thing."[69]

The Robber even visits a doctor out of concern that something is fundamentally wrong with him. Explaining that he sometimes suspects himself of being a girl, he also confesses to being aroused by fantasies of servitude, regardless of the gender of the person to whom he subordinates himself, while at the same time experiencing no sensuality at all in his feelings for the woman with whom he is "purely, soulfully in love." The doctor issues him a clean bill of health and instructs him to go on living as before. By novel's end, the Robber and Edith settle into an ambiguous semi-relationship that centers around eternally postponing the fulfillment of desire in keeping with the book's main narrative principle, and the Robber makes peace with his own complexities, asserting his erotic drive to serve and be subjugated as a norm. As a document of the erotics of subjugation, *The Robber* belongs on a shelf beside Leopold von Sacher-Masoch, whose works Walser knew and was perhaps inspired by when he wrote this novel. "Perhaps I should never have read him," muses the narrator of "Sacher-Masoch"—prepublished in *Prager Tagblatt* before it appeared in *The Rose*—"but I willingly confess that I did."[70]

The Robber is rich in the extravagant coinages familiar from *The Rose. Töchterchenhaftigkeiten* (littledaughterlinesses), for example, stands in for "daughters." The book also showcases Walser's new method of layering sentences with a thick sediment of relativizing adverbs, as when the narrator considers taking on the role of romantic emissary: "Generally speaking, I am at present in, admittedly, a doubtless almost somewhat too diplomatic mood to take on such a mission lightly."[71] Adverbs proliferate endlessly—so to speak, as it were, virtually, nearly, in a certain sense, perhaps, possibly, probably, thus, naturally, of course—eating away at the stability of each assertion. And sprawling metaphors make the narrator seem incapable of a trustworthy description.

Consider this sketch of Edith in the church: "She sat right in front and was dressed all in snow-white, and her cheeks, down these cheeks plunged a red like a dauntless knight plunging over a cliff into an abyss in order to break the spell over the countryside with his sacrifice."[72] The runaway simile ("like a dauntless knight . . .") carries us off into an apparently unrelated scenario. One blush, and we find ourselves astray in a fairy tale where spells are cast on countrysides and knights in shining armor come charging down hillsides to rescue—whom? Blushing maidens? Whose daydream is this headlong metaphor?

The Robber—longer than *Jakob von Gunten* though only two-thirds the length of *The Assistant*—survives only in the original pencil draft written on twenty-four octavo-size sheets of art-print paper Robert had acquired somehow. He was able to fit so much text on so few pages because his handwriting in these drafts had shrunk radically over the years. By 1924, the date of the earliest pencil draft that survives today, his writing was a diminutive two millimeters high. Composed in the old-fashioned German script he favored—heavy on vertical strokes—and often executed with a none-too-sharp pencil, these manuscripts were now virtually illegible to anyone but him, their individual letters and words more gestured at than articulated. It isn't clear whether he himself could easily read a draft no longer fresh in his mind. Today, these tiny manuscripts are referred to as "microscripts" (*Mikrogramme*)—a term Walser never used.[73]

Copying over a draft, he would insert diagonal slashes marking the start of each new page of the fair copy. The absence of marks in the pencil draft of *The Robber* suggests he never prepared a copy to send to potential publishers. Why didn't he offer the novel to Rowohlt? Wouldn't Hessel have been eager to read it (even if Rowohlt was treating him dismissively because of *The Rose*'s commercial failure, as he complained in a letter)?[74] Maybe he feared the book was flawed and didn't want to go through the misery of finding this out during the laborious copying process. He had written another novel, proving to himself that he could. And perhaps there was a quiet, rebellious satisfaction to having done the thing everyone kept asking him to do all these years and *not telling them about it*. The feeling that the world owed him more respect had grown strong in him. And there was always the fear that publishers and readers would find this wild tangle of a novel unpalatable. Or was it just a self-destructive choice, unconsciously-intentionally derailing what remained of his career?

Of course, if he wanted to marry, writing about getting down on the ground to kiss a little boy's knees wasn't the wisest move. Perhaps it was better to set the novel and all its stories aside. He would write to Max Brod in 1927, "Every book that has been printed is, after all, a grave for its author, isn't it?"[75] Writing this novel in such a way that no one else could read it (a landlady snooping in these pages would be unable to decipher them) kept his fears at bay. Unread, the book preserved his secrets, a sort of infinite reprieve. He must have spent weeks writing this novel, yet it is mentioned nowhere in his surviving letters, and so we know as little about its origins as we do about his plans for it. This is the point in Robert Walser's life where the mysteries begin to deepen.

The Unraveling

1925–1929

ROBERT WALSER REACHED THE PINNACLE of his artistic development around 1925, at age forty-seven. *The Robber*'s lush prose ushered in a several-year period when he produced the best of the magnificent strange tales that comprise his so-called late work. It was a time of intense focus but also one of intermittent distress, marked by financial worries, heavy drinking, and, increasingly, psychological instability.

The approach to writing that dominates in the literally hundreds of short works Walser wrote between 1925 and 1929 understands language as not just descriptive but constitutive in constructing a literary reality. Rather than trying to make language function as a transparent medium for complex messages, Walser's texts acknowledge the inherent artificiality of telling stories with words. Letting go of plot and every conventional notion of narration, he delved deep into the interior of his sentences, finding worlds there for exploration.

In the absence of a manifesto, we are left to extrapolate Walser's artistic principles from his work. The closest he ever comes to a declaration of intent is his unpublished essay "My Efforts," from 1928 or 1929, in which he writes of "experimenting in the linguistic field in the hope that there exist[s] in language an unknown vivacity that it is a pleasure to awaken."[1] Rather than enlisting words in the service of representation, he made the words themselves the story, unleashing their secret force. This project is more akin to the branch of modernism associated with Gertrude Stein and James Joyce than to any of the German-language modernists (such as Kafka and Musil) whom Walser may have read. But as far as we know, Walser was unaware of both these English-language writers.[2] He'd always preferred classic authors from the nineteenth century and earlier; nowhere do his letters and literary texts display much appetite for literary innovators of his own generation.

Aside from *The Rose,* Walser's late work appeared only in periodicals, and critics who'd formed their opinions of his oeuvre years before tended to stick to them, cementing the notion of Walser as a naive creator of wide-eyed dreamers, a sort of eternal journeyman rambling happy-go-lucky through the world. Even some colleagues who considered themselves his champions pigeonholed his work, like Hesse, who extolled the "pure, sweet, and ethereal" pages of *Poet's Life* as "delicate chamber music" and found *The Rose* charming but slight. And Thomas Mann, all of three years Walser's senior, sent him a fan letter after reading *The Rose,* praising him—at least in Robert's paraphrase of this no-longer-extant missive—as a "very, very refined, noble, well-behaved, and naughty child."[3]

Neither understood that when Walser used words like "lovely," "nice," "sweet," or "good"—especially late in his career—he was always also mocking the sensibility that finds these qualities appealing. And the figure of the child was deployed as a commentary on how society assigns value to human beings. Occasionally, Robert tried to correct his public image. In 1926, for example, he asked professional reciter Hans Bänninger, who'd requested permission to perform several short works on the radio, to omit "I Have Nothing" from the program, this being one of his more naive-sounding texts. Bänninger included the piece nonetheless.[4]

Since most of Walser's works were short, it was easy to take him for a minimalist. But he wasn't a minimalist; he was a miniaturist, and within the small scope of his pieces—often modest both in length and in subject matter—he practiced maximalism, seeing how much he could pack into how little. This maximal miniaturism justifies the epithet "clairvoyant of the small" coined for him by writer W. G. Sebald, who counted Walser among his main inspirations. When Walser wrote, "We don't need to see anything out of the ordinary. We already see so much," his point wasn't that one should get drunk on nature, in a state of eternal rapture; it was that literature didn't always have to be about travel to far-off lands or "important" topics like wars and revolution—pace Kleist, pace Schiller. Great literature could also reflect and refract ordinary experiences—such as taking a walk. Walser later told Carl Seelig: "I am immediately wary of writers who excel at plot and claim practically the whole world for their characters. Everyday things are beautiful and rich enough that we can coax poetic sparks from them."[5]

"A Sort of Cleopatra," written in 1928 or 1929 and unpublished during Walser's lifetime, represents the apotheosis of his late maximalist style. Its opening sentence—introducing a modern woman in her living room—sprawls:

> Not having learned all too much with regard to herself in the course of her not particularly numerous experiences, she proceeded to acquire, on the basis of an income piling up as if playfully or jestingly, a household which featured silver and gold forks, knives and soup spoons and also leafy plants and a number of sofa pillows, and then from here it was a mere trifle for her imagination—beginning suddenly to awaken or grow active after having slept or reposed perhaps for days or even weeks—to instill in her the peacock-feather-fluttering illusion, gliding gently past as if upon a river in a boat bedecked with garlands, that she was a sort of Cleopatra longing for viper bites.

The passage's jittery distractedness and final swerve to a subversive metaphorical reality set the scene for the story of a woman dismayed at the paucity of authentic experience in her life, the absence of genuine sentiment, vivid sensation. When she imagines herself "a sort of Cleopatra" in this Shakespeare-inspired orientalist fantasy, it is with the notion—as is explored later in the text—that the historical Cleopatra lived during a simpler, more straightforward, and more authentically felt time. The speeded-up hubbub of modern life—represented here by aggressively intricate syntax—is portrayed as a dilution or diminution of experience. The story's key line is the only one that displays no syntactic fireworks: "Often she wished to wish for nothing at all." Robert clearly sympathized.[6]

Writing of this challenging complexity came with risks for a writer financially dependent on the patronage of newspaper editors and by extension the reading public. No one could have accused him of pandering to his audience. His savings were dwindling, but still—despite occasional statements to the contrary in his letters—he seemed to find tightening his belt preferable to seeking a return to financial security through another office job. Would he even have been able to find one now with his fiftieth birthday rapidly approaching?

Instead, he kept looking for ways to earn more with his writing, such as by publishing another collection of short prose. After *Watercolors* was rejected by Orell Füssli in 1925, Robert wrote to Blei asking his opinion of a new "hodgepodge book" compiling poems, dramatic sketches, and stories. Hatching yet another book plan in spring 1926, he asked Mermet to send him all the recent newspaper clippings she'd saved, scolding when the pack of clippings she sent proved incomplete. None of these projects came to anything. Even *New Poems* (*Neue Gedichte*), a volume of Walser poetry announced by Rowohlt that was to include a cycle of sonnets Robert had published in *Prager Presse* in 1925, remained unpublished. And many of his pencil drafts—poems and prose alike—remained uncopied, having been judged by their author unlikely to find a home in print.[7]

Among the uncopied texts left behind in the "pencil territory" (as Robert referred to these drafts in a June 20, 1927, letter to Max Rychner) was a sequence of twenty-four brief dramatic sketches featuring a young protagonist named Felix, whose life resembles Walser's own early boyhood (for which reason these "Felix Scenes" are quoted from several times in Chapters 1 and 2).[8] These nostalgic and often humorous sketches—the last of which abandons the play format for third-person narrative prose—were written just before *The Robber*. As far as we know, he never attempted to publish any of them.

Robert was so frustrated with editors and publishers by 1926 that when Walter Muschg wrote to solicit work for his new journal, *Annalen,* Robert complained that editors often used "tricks" to "provoke" him, such as "accepting one or several pieces of mine and then never publishing them, giving the author to understand that patience was a good exercise." He was particularly inclined to be suspicious of Muschg, also an editor at Orell Füssli, which was now rumored to be charging poets to publish their books. In 1927, Robert made one final attempt to place a collection of poems with Max Brod as intermediary. The Paul Zsolnay publishing house in Vienna had just printed Brod's new novel. But even as

Robert accepted Brod's offer of help, he piled scorn and sarcasm on Zsolnay, calling him "a scoundrel [. . .] who runs like a rabbit before the outrageous suggestion that he might [. . .] publish poems," as well as a "sorry bastard," "snot-faced publisher," and "cur." The query came to nothing. The Berlin publisher Spiegel also invited Robert to submit work that year but went bankrupt shortly thereafter.[9]

Robert wasn't the only writer having difficulty placing books with publishers. The market was narrowing even for novels—in part because of the availability of movies and the radio, new forms of entertainment that Robert also enjoyed and occasionally wrote about. This shift in the public's consumption patterns was much discussed. Samuel Fischer weighed in with an essay in the 1926 S. Fischer almanac: "It's very telling," he writes, "that at present the book is counted among the most dispensable objects of daily life. We exercise, dance, spend our evenings in front of the radio or at the movies, our hours not spent at work are entirely accounted for, and we cannot find the time to read a book." Kurt Wolff published an open letter in *Frankfurter Zeitung* in November 1927 deploring the "undeniable fact" that "for some time now too few books are being purchased, and these few sales are limited primarily to new releases."[10]

Newspapers were a big business, and Robert might still have made a living as a writer for newspapers and magazines if he published enough. *Neue Zürcher Zeitung,* for example, appeared seven days a week and at least three times a day except for Sundays (twice a day). That meant a lot of pages to fill, so editors were constantly in search of material. But there were frequently hitches now, such as a magazine printing a text of his without payment or an editor requesting work and then not getting back to him. "Publishing houses are just a bunch of big desk drawers," he remarked to Mermet. This sustained precarity put him in the company of writers he admired who—in various ways—subtracted themselves from the cultural economy. Hölderlin, Kleist, Büchner, Walser: this was a line of succession he could feel proud to belong to. He knew he was a great writer. He knew he was a failure. These two thoughts could coexist. He joked to Mermet that even during a period of relative unproductivity he remained "the ninth-greatest Swiss writer."[11]

Financially, the most important newspapers printing Robert's work in the second half of the 1920s were *Berliner Tageblatt* (publishing sixty-eight pieces between 1925 and 1933) and *Prager Presse* (with 204 between

1925 and 1937). *Berliner Tageblatt* was a major German newspaper with a massive circulation (160,000 copies in 1919), affording him far more readers than anywhere else he'd ever published. It also paid better: for example, between 1926 and 1928 it paid 75 marks (roughly $300 in today's dollars) for a piece of prose. Robert told Mermet he received more from *Berliner Tageblatt* for eight texts than Rowohlt paid him for *The Rose*.[12]

Although founded as a German-language Czechoslovak government organ, *Prager Presse* was respected for its feuilleton section overseen by Otto Pick, an associate of Kafka and Brod who'd reviewed *Jakob von Gunten* in 1912. Walser had been published in Czech as early as 1913, when the journal *Rovzoj* printed "Cinema" and "A Genius" in translations by Arne Laurin. "Comedy Evening" had appeared in 1915 in the journal *Novina* in a translation by Jaroslav Dohnal. On the recommendation of Franz Blei, *Prager Presse* started publishing Walser texts beginning in 1925. Robert had already been appearing in the larger-circulation *Prager Tagblatt*, where Brod took over as feuilleton editor in 1924. Robert joked about the prominence the Czech capital had assumed in his life, calling himself a "Czechoslovakian attaché" and suggesting to Brod he could imagine relocating to Prague if a position ("perhaps at a Prague theater") were found for him. Particularly for his poems—which, as he later remarked to Seelig, always "flew back to me like boomerangs" from German and Swiss publications—these two Czech papers were crucial outlets. *Prager Presse* printed some eighty of his poems, and *Prager Tagblatt* around thirty.[13]

The Anthroposophist organ *Individualität,* edited by Rudolf Steiner's former secretary, Willy Storrer, published nine Walser pieces between 1926 and 1930. Uninterested in the journal's spiritual emphasis, Robert submitted essays disparaging Steiner's successor as president of the Anthroposophical Society, but his critiques were too subtle to draw notice. Unfortunately, the journal paid a paltry 20 francs per text, far less than others; for example, the German magazine *Simplicissimus,* where Robert published several pieces between 1925 and 1928, paid three times as much.[14]

Publishing only two or three pieces in *Berliner Tageblatt* each month would have provided enough income for Robert to subsist on; but after an initial flurry in late 1925, editor Fred Hildenbrandt fell into a rhythm of publishing a Walser text only every three weeks or so. *Prager Presse* published him more often but paid less. Robert later lamented this low pay to

Seelig, though he also emphasized how much it meant to him that *Prager Presse* would publish virtually anything he sent Otto Pick's way. His Swiss newspaper editors were much more critical of his submissions (as was Hildenbrandt on occasion). Robert sometimes couldn't resist letting Eduard Korrodi at *Neue Zürcher Zeitung* know that a piece he'd rejected had been well-received in Prague.[15]

Korrodi—once a key supporter—had recently grown critical of Walser's work, even in print, describing his prose as "emotional bric-a-brac" and "overly ornate." In 1926, after a dust-up over unflattering words Robert had written about him in a letter to another Zurich editor, who'd shared these lines with their subject, Korrodi stopped publishing Walser altogether. Relating the incident to Mermet, Robert was unabashed, referring to Korrodi as Krokus (crocus) and Krokodilödeli (a portmanteau of "crocodile" and "tedious"). Korrodi circled back in spring 1927, but Robert chose not to submit work to him.[16]

Arguably Walser's most important editor during the mid-1920s was Max Rychner—two decades Robert's junior and a protégé of Korrodi's—who became an important conversation partner for him despite a rocky start to their acquaintance. When Rychner first wrote to solicit work for *Wissen und Leben* in 1923, Robert asked for an in-person meeting. But when Rychner traveled to Bern on the agreed-upon date, Robert didn't answer his knock. Apologizing in a letter in which he enclosed a signed copy of *Comedy,* Robert explained he'd been "at Café du Theatre, picking up a lady's dropped glove, browsing through magazines, and eating meringues." Rychner later told his daughter he'd heard footsteps in Robert's room as he stood there in the hall, concluding that the writer was "at home, but not for me." For whatever reason, Robert had found himself unprepared to open the door to a stranger that day. Rychner nonetheless published excerpts from *Theodor* later that year.[17]

In early 1924, Rychner asked Robert to send him a proper short story rather than more feuilleton essays. The result was "Ophelia," the last of Walser's plot-based short narrative works, published in the journal's Christmas issue. Having requested a princely fee of 300 francs (roughly $1,800 in today's dollars), Robert accepted half that sum with elaborate resignation ("in your persuasively composed letter, your lines of reasoning tower up huge as Alpine kings and enemies of the nation before my honorarium-hungry story-submitting soul"). He parodied Rychner in *The*

Rose, making reference in "Kurt" to "a review where only the married are allowed to appear" after Rychner inveighed in an article against the literature of solitary masculinity. But Robert also sent him his lengthy reminiscence of Biel, "The Ruin" (see Chapter 13), which appeared in March 1926.[18]

With Rychner, Robert engaged in his most substantial literary conversations that survive in written form, taking pains to explain his positions when the two disagreed. Robert took issue, for example, with certain pieces Rychner published, such as an excerpt from Paul Valéry's *Monsieur Teste.* Declaring Valéry's "worldwide fame" unmerited, Robert predicted he would soon be replaced by some other "international monarch." In particular, Robert questioned whether one could write a poem by intellectual force of will alone (as Valéry insisted).[19] For Robert, by contrast, writing poetry required the poet to set aside the intellect to allow a force beyond or outside logic to take over:

> In my opinion, a beautiful poem must be a beautiful body that blossoms forth from well-measured words that have been casually—almost without idea—set down on paper. The words form the skin that is tightly stretched about the content, i.e. the body. Art consists not of saying words but of shaping a poem-body, i.e. seeing to it that the words are only the means by which the poem-body is created [. . .]. It's an art to act more foolish and ignorant than one truly is, a sort of cunning in which few succeed.[20]

This professed "art" of acting "foolish and ignorant" reads like a defense against critiques of Robert's work as slight or childish. Taking a stance against Valéry, who privileged intention and intellect, Walser aligned himself instead with Shakespeare, noting that Rychner had once referred to him as "a Shakespeare of the little prose piece." In another letter, he expressed the belief that writers should tactfully conceal the models who inspire their stories; he'd come a long way from the young man who wrote about one brother's pursuit of married women and another's mental illness. Why should writers restrict themselves to actual occurrences, even in essays? This was also the spirit in which he wrote to the newspaper *Frankfurter Rundschau* to respond to a letter to the editor "correcting"

Walser's depiction of a performance of Georg Büchner's comedy *Leonce and Lena* that—contrary to his essay's claim—he hadn't attended.[21]

Sometime in the mid-1920s Robert began employing a new business strategy to market his work to newspapers. Literary agencies had proliferated in Germany since before the war, and Walser's letters suggest he worked with agents affiliated with Rowohlt, the DuMont Schauberg publishing house, and Ullstein, Germany's largest media conglomerate.[22] One example of a text placed by an agency is "Table d'hôte," published first in 1926 in *Neue Zürcher Zeitung* and then in 1929 in *Königsberger Hartungsche Zeitung* in the Baltic coastal city to which Robert once traveled by balloon.[23] Agents also sold Walser's work in Karlsruhe, Saarbrücken, Erfurt, Prague, Danzig (Gdańsk), and Stettin (Szczecin). Since newspaper publications were ephemeral, there was no reason not to republish in Danzig what had already appeared in Zurich. And having an agency place his work and handle the business side of things fulfilled a longstanding desire of Robert's—as demonstrated by his correspondence with the Swiss Writers' Association asking the staff to take over the task of querying publishers about *Theodor*.

In May 1927, Robert rejoined the General Association of Writers, a Berlin-based organization whose services included protecting its members against copyright infringement and recovering fees on commission. He had subscribed to the association's newsletter and clipping service when he lived in Berlin. After renewing his long-lapsed membership, he instructed the association to collect back fees from the radio station Rundfunk Hannover, which had broadcast his work without permission. This was another aspect of the writing business that he was happy to delegate.[24]

That same spring Robert received a letter from *Berliner Tageblatt* informing him that the newspaper was going to stop publishing his work for a while. The letter, which he described as "a slap in the face," included the recommendation that he stop writing altogether for half a year. He was devastated. A decade later, looking back on this period in his life, he told Seelig that this rejection of his work had been justified: "Yes, it was true, I had written myself dry. Burned out like an oven." It was a reprise of the burnout he had experienced at the end of his Berlin years and again in Biel. But how would he live if he couldn't write? As a man who lived by his pen (pencil), he didn't have the luxury of taking a vacation from work. "I pushed myself to write, despite this warning," he told Seelig, "but I labored over foolish trifles." Still mulling over the rejection at the time, he told another correspondent, "At the moment, I'm doing rather poorly, that is: so-so, because something like a crisis seems to have taken place in my writing."[25]

A few weeks later, he was still seriously weighing the possibility that a break from writing might benefit him. He told Storrer he was considering taking as much as a year off in order "to transform, to change, possibly to improve." "My greatest wish for some time now," he adds, "has been nothing other or lovelier than to temporarily give up writing for the very sake of pen-wielding and writing." As late as 1928, he lamented to Mermet that writing about his experiences interfered with his experiencing them. "What goes unmentioned lives with the greatest vitality, since every mentioning, every reference takes something away from the person in question." (This was a point already made in *The Robber.*) He later told Seelig: "Sometimes in Bern I was like a man possessed. I chased poetic motifs like a hunter his prey."[26]

In the end, it would be only five months until *Berliner Tageblatt* published him again. *Prager Presse* never stopped, though his work appeared slightly less frequently in 1927 than during the previous year. Meanwhile, despite the "crisis in his writing," he accumulated a backlog of unpublished material. In late August 1927, he reported that business was "lousy, i.e. crappy, i.e. bad, i.e. rotten" and that he was going swimming in the Aare every day to avoid "producing too much," as "literary circumstances force me to work as slowly as possible." This trend continued in the months that followed. To Pick he wrote that he had developed the habit of "now and then [tossing] torn-up manuscripts into the wastepaper basket in the instinct that it is nice, refined, tidy, and classy to always be sacrificing something or other, and to moderate my production."[27]

In addition to at least occasionally throwing manuscripts away, Robert also reduced the number of pencil drafts he copied over. As with *The Robber* in 1925, he weighed whether it was worth the clerical labor of producing a fair manuscript copy of a given piece, and in many cases he decided it wasn't. Most of these drafts were composed on scrap paper cut into pieces proportional to the tiny gray script, often with several texts crowded onto a single small page—poems and prose interspersed. Sometimes a text would begin on one page and end on another, and sometimes while copying, he would combine more than one piece to create a composite work. He recycled every sort of paper that came his way: business card, honorarium notice, telegram, postcard, the cover of a "penny dreadful," tear-off desk calendar pages carefully bisected. His pencil script colonized the blank space between any lines of print or writing. He repurposed the "compliments of the author" card tucked inside a novel by Brod, scratching out the word "author" and replacing it with "poor little Max" before covering both sides of the card with drafts of a prose piece ("Journey to a Small Town") and several poems.[28]

The seeds of Walser's micrography were planted as far back as the 1902 letter to Fanny in which he took pains to shape his text into a tiny perfect rectangle.[29] And when the protagonist of *The Tanners* decides to write an essay, he starts by cutting his paper into strips. For Walser, writing small became particularly appealing when the thrift inspired by his fear of poverty made the conservation of resources (paper, ink) align with his desire for privacy in this instinctual gesture of self-preservation. By 1927, his pencil script shrank even further, to an average height of just one millimeter. He wrote these manuscripts by the dozens, hunching over each tiny page grateful for his still-excellent eyesight, then laboriously copied over some of them to send to editors, and left ever more of them uncopied, stored in a shoebox.

In September 1925, Robert received fan mail from a seventeen-year-old girl in Koblenz, Germany, named Therese Breitbach. She wrote to ask his advice for her older brother, Joseph, who wanted to become a writer despite their parents' disapproval. This was the beginning of an extensive correspondence, and young Therese (whom Robert never met) became something of a confidante. Even in his first letter to her, he confessed that he'd recently returned to writing poetry out of love. In his second letter, he spelled out his romantic situation in further detail: he fell in love with "a young girl who seemed already to have an inclination toward corpulence," then he met a waitress, forgot all about the first girl, wrote poems to the new one, and now wasn't sure if he still loved her. These were motifs he'd just written about in *The Robber*, but they were apparently not entirely fictional, as Robert mentioned to Seelig years later having been "in love with two waitresses in Bern."[30]

As their correspondence developed, he began to playfully name-drop in his letters to her, once claiming (a flat-out lie) that Hermann Hesse had just married a Bernese waitress, who'd impressed him by calling him a milksop, and that Robert himself had been among the wedding guests. Apparently taking the report seriously, Therese asked Robert to pass on her greetings, which he promised to do, meanwhile remarking on the lie in an essay ("Discussion") published in *Prager Presse*. When Paul Cassirer shot himself in Berlin in January 1926 rather than sign the divorce papers Tilla Durieux demanded, Robert reminisced to Breitbach about his strange friendship with the art dealer.[31]

He also wrote to her in solemn tones—mirroring lines from *The Robber*—of being concerned about his mental health. "For a time," he wrote, "people here thought I was insane, and would say aloud, in the arcades, as I was walking past: He should be in the asylum. [. . .] I have lived in rooms where all night I could not close my eyes for fear." He confessed these night terrors to others, too, for example writing in October 1927 to Brod that sometimes "at night in the silence" he was "afraid like a foolish boy—afraid of myself or of some imagined thing creeping up on me." Mermet said years later that Robert started to become unwell soon after moving to Bern, never feeling at home the way he had in Biel. A sense of agitation kept him moving rapidly from one room to the next, never finding peace. And the nightmares that beset him were sometimes of frightening intensity. The narrator of one unpublished text from winter 1928–1929 describes a terrifying nocturnal visitation: "I felt a leathery, villainous hand touching my face"—a detail so raw it doesn't seem like something invented out of whole cloth. Walser later told Seelig, "During my last years in Bern I was plagued by wild dreams—thunder, shouting, a choking in my throat, hallucinatory voices—so that I often awoke screaming."[32]

To complicate matters further, Robert's path through life was increasingly lubricated with alcohol. The frequent benders that had marked the end of his time in Berlin, prompting Lisa to shepherd him to an abstinence hotel, returned. With his evenings to himself—often spent away from home, since "home" was inevitably the same little room where he did all his writing—he often found himself occupying tables and chairs in public places where rent had to be paid in the form of food and beverage consumption. And what did a self-respecting gentleman on a tight budget consume all evening long? In 1927, he told Therese Breitbach that his usual supper was "café complet"—that is, café au lait accompanied by bread, butter, jam, and cheese—in the train station café. He was still eating this habitual light supper in late 1928, he reported to Mermet. But after that modest meal was consumed, his most likely options for the remainder of the evening were wine and beer. Just as the narrator of his story "Letter to Edith" in *The Rose* described such heavy alcohol consumption it made even his sentences reel and sway, Robert now wrote openly about his drinking bouts to Mermet and others.[33]

In a letter from late 1923 or early 1924, he reports that he spent Christmas Eve at the elegant hotel Schweizerhof, across from the train station, and "made a flirt attempt vis-à-vis a bare-armed madame" who was annoyed by his attentions—offered, he admits, while he was possibly a bit soused, but he insists his intoxication was "perfectly restrained and respectable, in other words Christmas-Eve-ish." In the same letter, he asks Mermet to send him a bottle of wine. (She sent two, which he polished off in a single day.) In late December 1925, he reported to editor Hugo Marti of *Der Bund* that he had just drunk two bottles of wine and now felt "somewhat too material" (i.e., epicurean) to write. Was he always "restrained and respectable" while drinking in public? Mermet would later remember him as a person who "very much enjoyed eating and drinking but wasn't a drinker." She did add, though, that "in Bern, he sometimes drank his fear away." Indeed, there is much to suggest he was self-medicating. Mermet herself was concerned enough to extract from him a promise (soon broken) to lay off the alcohol. Remembering this period in conversation with Seelig, Walser concluded that the "temptations of drink and a life of ease" in Bern had "a negative effect" on him and that he drank up most of the payments he received from magazines.[34]

In *The Robber,* which reprises several episodes known to be autobiographical (such as Robert's pretending to be his own valet or dangerously jumping up on the railings of a bridge 150 feet above the Aare), the protagonist's eccentricity is explicitly linked to poor mental health. The Robber, avers the narrator, "was surely ill 'in those days,' when he arrived in our city, filled with a curious disbalancement, unease. Certain inner voices, so to speak, tormented him." The book's various assertions that a character much resembling the author—for the Robber (*Räuber*) is clearly a Räubert or Robbert—was psychologically fragile, possibly even hearing voices, were perhaps part of why Walser left the novel's pencil draft uncopied. Persecution mania also features prominently in the manuscript. The Robber feels he's being hunted, and the narrator reports these fears impartially. "In what," the narrator asks, "do these persecutions consist? In attempts to wear him down, to make him irritable, nervous, agitated. In a word, people have been trying to instill morals in him." One example of a "persecution" is that people appear to be yawning at the Robber wherever he goes; at one point, he tosses his cigarette butt into one such open mouth. Robert wrote to Breitbach in May 1927, "One has the impression that in all possible directions, mouse or wolf traps have been set up, in other words groups of interested parties who cozy up to you for the sole purpose of taking revenge for something or other."[35]

It was increasingly difficult for Robert to imagine his bachelorhood ever coming to an end. With every passing year, his financial situation grew more precarious. He did assure Mermet in September 1927 that he was "in funds at the moment," but early signs of the financial crisis that would shake the world in 1929 were already apparent. In November 1927, Robert wrote to Mermet of the shrinking payments he was receiving from magazines because of the general economic decline. When the Swiss Writers' Association—which he'd resigned from in 1924—tried to collect on the loan it had disbursed in 1921 for *Theodor*, he put its representative off, as he'd learned to do so many years before at Carl Dubler's elbow.[36]

At age forty-eight, he struck a world-weary tone in his letters to Mermet, writing, for example, that he felt he was becoming "old, infirm." He wrote of his age to professional contacts too, asking Pick, for instance, to have forbearance if an almost fifty-year-old writer, too old to hope for help from a patron, had to sell work to as many different outlets as possible.[37] As his fiftieth birthday approached, he dropped hints about it to the editors who'd been publishing him regularly, Pick, Brod, and Storrer. Storrer's response was the most satisfying: he commissioned a new photograph of Robert for *Individualität* from a journalist who was also an amateur photographer.

When Walter Kern arrived on April 3, 1928, to photograph Robert at home, he found him living in a room striking only in its banality, with a hackneyed slogan rhyming "daylight" (*Licht*) with "duty" (*Pflicht*) hanging on the wall. The contrast between these surroundings and the person of the writer was glaring: "He himself is splendidly clearheaded," Kern

wrote to his editor.[38] After the photo session, Kern took him out for a spaghetti dinner and bottle of wine. In Kern's pictures, Robert's expression
is difficult to read. He looks expectant, perhaps even pleased, but at the
same time guarded.

Kern picked what he thought the best of these shots (with Robert
facing the camera) to be an *Individualität* exclusive. Unfortunately, the
editors settled on an image showing Robert in profile with his bed in the
background, emphasizing the small size of his quarters and therefore his
poverty. But the picture was accompanied by a flattering tribute written by
Hans Wilhelm Keller. When Kern asked Robert's permission to offer the
other photos from the shoot to glossies, Robert asked him to stick to Swiss
magazines, saying he didn't want to "do any sort of propaganda" in Germany.[39] Why not let the German magazines and publishers who used to
print his work learn of his birthday from their Swiss competitors?

In the *Prager Presse* offices, Pick no doubt assumed he was doing
Robert a favor by engaging Franz Blei—still a prominent literary figure—to
write about him on the occasion of this round birthday. But something had
gone wrong in that relationship. Robert complained to Brod that Blei was
holding on to his manuscripts and not responding to queries. And the
"tribute" Blei submitted was a catastrophe—a condescending rehash of
how he first discovered Robert's poems in *Der Bund* decades earlier. Blei
wrote only of Robert's juvenilia, emphasizing his youthful naiveté, ungainly
appearance, and romantic notions (such as aspiring to be a page boy), making no mention of the dozen books and hundreds of pages of short prose
and poems he'd published since. Blei even claimed Robert had stopped
writing poems as a young man. Robert had only just described Blei as his
"enemy" to Kern, who'd insisted on lending him Blei's translation of a
book by André Gide that Kern admired (and Robert did not).[40]

Blei's clichéd portrait of Robert as *puer aeternus* and naive romantic
was the last thing Robert needed in his attempts to salvage his image and
career. It was all the more unfortunate that the autobiographical poem
"Fiftieth Birthday" he'd sent *Prager Presse* to be printed that same day
devoted most of its hendecasyllabic lines to Robert's early years as a poet
in Zurich, covering his later career in a quick summary at the end. At least
the second Walser piece published in the issue was well-suited to debunk
any accusations of childish simplicity. "When Authors Are Ill" presents a
scene from Danish writer Jens Peter Jacobsen's novel *Niels Lyhne* and self-

reflexively conflates the characters with their author, who suffered from tuberculosis. Among other things, the piece gives complex narrative form to the intricately ambivalent feelings of a pair of lovers. Of a woman smitten with her children's tutor, Walser writes: "At times she would quietly, softly lose herself in reverie with irresistible lassitude. Resolutenesses within her that had something indecisive about them prompted her after a little while to emerge from the house, only here to discover that tutors can be larger than life once they have cast off all consciousness of station, while she herself might be seized by a self-disregard of startling proportions."[41] This text clearly bore no relation to the simplistic portrait Blei had painted.

Robert's relationships with his siblings Karl and Lisa remained fraught. No reconciliation with Karl ever came about, and the sense of reserve vis-à-vis Lisa persisted. Robert corresponded with her far less often than with Mermet, and when he borrowed books from Lisa's library, he often returned them by mailing them to Mermet. Sometimes he also asked her to pass on a greeting. Mermet continued to perform sisterly if not wifely offices, mending and pressing his clothes, commissioning a pair of house slippers from a Bellelay cobbler, and sending him a particular tiny-holed Jura cheese he was fond of. When Robert visited Bellelay, it's unclear whether he continued to stay in Lisa's apartment. The invitations came from Mermet, not Lisa, and we know that on at least one occasion he lodged at the Hôtel de l'Ours.[42] Around Christmas 1925, he refused an invitation because Fanny was staying with Lisa, leaving no room for him; staying with Mermet, a single woman, was never an option.

Nonetheless, Robert and Mermet started vacationing together. Robert would carry her suitcase, after admonishing her not to pack too much. In 1924 they visited Erlach, where Robert had done military service, and in September 1925 they traveled to Murten/Morat, a picturesque medieval walled town with lakeside promenades. They planned to spend several days sightseeing. Mermet had reserved rooms for them in a hotel that attracted a bourgeois clientele, with whom they were obliged to rub elbows in a dining room so crowded it was impossible to avoid overhearing others' conversations. Mermet saw Robert's mood darken one day at lunch, and then—as she later described the scene—he exploded: "Robert Walser rose to his feet, cursing in a loud voice at all the people sitting at table. Everyone was struck dumb, and it's a good thing too, because if someone had responded to his fit of rage, there might have been an unpleasant scene, but as it was Robert Walser calmed down again, no doubt horrified himself at what had occurred." Mortified, Mermet saw no choice but to check them out of the hotel early and return home. The experience convinced her, she told Seelig, that she would "no longer be able to go anywhere with R. Walser because he was no longer able to control himself." He'd always been "difficult" with people he disliked, she said, but this incident was different, "pathological," for which reason she told no one about it except Lisa, and "only to show her that Robert [. . .] was truly ill." The next time Robert wrote to Mermet, he acknowledged the incident only by noting, "No doubt you vividly remember my acting the respectable Bernese gentleman with sauerkraut and sausage"—then changed the subject in the same sentence. That 1925 incident wasn't the first of its sort in Robert's life, either; in a 1924 letter to Mermet he reported having indulged in "large-scale *Chittis*" in "several elegant restaurants," *Chitti* being a Bernese word for what is known in American English as a "shit fit."[43]

Even this very personal experience of Robert's erratic behavior did not make Mermet withdraw her friendship. He remained a welcome guest in Bellelay, and Mermet continued to issue invitations to him. Although he stayed away over Christmas 1925, he did visit the following May (staying at the hotel). In October 1926, he stayed for two weeks, returning on foot as he had often done before, this time walking along the Weissenstein ridge, then down to Solothurn and Bern, a journey of almost fifty miles. He was invited back again in June 1927, May 1928, and October 1928.[44]

He enjoyed these stays. Everyone in Bellelay knew he was a writer, that is, a person deserving of respect, and he would regularly be invited along with Lisa and Mermet to join clinic director Oskar Rothenhäusler and his wife for a meal or tea.[45] He enjoyed the beautiful historic grounds and was sorry to hear that the ruins of the early-eighteenth-century church belonging to the former monastery were to be restored. He also liked cavorting with Lisa's little dog, Jim.

Seeing the same faces during communal meals in the staff dining room was comfortably reassuring the way dinners at the Blaues Kreuz had been. Rothenhäusler's pre-1920 predecessor, Hugo Hiss, had been friendly with Lisa and her writer brother too. And Robert enjoyed spending time with friends of Mermet and Lisa such as Sister Marie, a senior nurse from the women's section of the clinic who once invited them all to share a goose breast she'd received as a gift. Mermet recalled with amusement Robert relating how one day he'd been sitting outside the schoolhouse with the former night watchman—who liked to do a little business on the side—when the man offered to sell him a watch for cheap. Robert replied, "I've got one," triumphantly pulling out the beautiful gold watch he'd inherited from his father, a prized possession.[46]

Robert had once remarked to Lisa that he could never write in Bellelay, where even the patients seemed well-cared-for, because he "had it too good" there. Agreeable as these visits were for him, Lisa would confess years later that she "often found him difficult to bear" and even "suffered a great deal under his tyrannical moods when he visited me for longer periods of time."[47] Lisa did her best to minimize Robert's contact with the clinic's "incurables." His peculiarities worried her, as did his occasional fearfulness and agitation.

Each sibling was becoming concerned about the other. In July 1927, Robert wrote to Mermet that he was struck by the change in Lisa's appearance and how often she spoke of her (literal) dreams, which made him worry about her nerves. He'd seen her at the home of her friend Rosa Schmid, a Bern piano teacher whom Robert had been friendly with since at least 1925. According to Rosa's niece, it was family lore that Robert had once proposed marriage to Rosa and she had refused him because she wanted to preserve her energies for a possible singing career. This niece, in first grade when she met Robert, found him friendly enough to venture an intimate question—whether her feet (which she displayed, removing her sandals) were clean enough for gymnastics class. He smiled and said he believed they were, though she might want to consider washing them afterward.[48]

He rarely saw other members of his family now. Fanny had married Arnold Hegi in 1926 and emigrated to Latvia, where Arnold was managing an estate. Karl was incommunicado. Robert had, however, paid a visit to Oscar and his wife, Fridolina, in Basel in summer 1924. Oscar, who'd worked his way up from bank clerk to general manager, was the sibling Robert had seen the least since leaving home, in part because Oscar disapproved of the life choices of his two younger artist brothers. When he invited Robert to visit, it was because Fridolina had begun writing poems and desired his professional opinion. Little is known about any relationships Robert had with members of his extended family, beyond the fact that in December 1928, he paid a visit to a cousin, Hans Marty, an importer of English fabrics in Burgdorf who made him the gift of a suit.[49]

Asked by Seelig years later whom he associated with in Bern, Walser replied, "With myself!" But despite spending so much time alone in the late 1920s, he did have a social circle composed of households in both Bern and other parts of Switzerland where he had (at least by his own account) open invitations to visit. He boasted to Breitbach in April 1928 of having "at least four" such invitations in Thun as well as Küsnacht (where Ernst Morgenthaler now lived). He also had drinking companions—he mentions fellow writer Hans Bloesch, for instance, in a letter to Mermet, though he says he doesn't know him well—along with the occasional friend or acquaintance who might invite him for a meal. To Seelig, he also later mentioned "the daughter of a Jewish publisher" and "waitresses."[50]

In May 1928, Robert met the family of Margrit Kistler, then a teenager. Her parents, who admired his work, invited him to dinner by sending Margrit and a sister to deliver the invitation along with a bouquet of primroses. Remembering the encounter forty-five years later, Kistler reports that Robert received the girls graciously in his attic room. He asked them to sit down on a green plush sofa while he "tenderly admired the flowers with his blue fairy-tale eyes." Margrit inadvertently provoked him to agitation by expressing her sympathy for his lack of renown, causing the "insulted poet" to "pace around the circular table, eyes flashing with rage, like a wounded lion." But he accepted the family's invitation and soon became a regular fixture in their home, sometimes showing up uninvited and "consuming gigantic quantities of spaghetti." He developed an infatuation with Margrit's mother and began to "stroke her hand gently" during a visit one day, at first surreptitiously, then more openly. The parents tolerated this behavior as fans of his work and were troubled above all by how difficult it was to get him to leave until well past midnight, for which reason these dinners were eventually replaced by invitations to Sunday afternoon coffee.[51]

Despite these tensions, the Kistler family invited Robert to spend Christmas with them that year. When a curtain was set alight by a Christmas tree candle, he remained nonplussed and just walked about "calmly stamping out the large and small sparks on the carpet with his sturdy shoes" while the father took charge of extinguishing the blaze. As a Christmas present, the family bought Robert a ticket to see the theatrical production of Humperdinck's *Hansel and Gretel*. He was disgruntled to learn that his companion for the evening was not the mother but the family's youngest daughter (they'd drawn lots). Writing to Mermet afterward, he reported having spent Christmas "with Mr. Kistler, a very educated man. His wife is very sweet and at the same time sly, for example she calls me 'My' Mr. Walser. She successfully laid claim to me with a gift of chocolate fondant. In my opinion, she is a very dangerous baby, i.e. a child."[52]

Mrs. Kistler wasn't the first woman he'd decided had designs on him. Bringing up the Murten debacle again in a letter to Mermet half a year after the incident in the hotel, he blamed his fit of rage on the behavior of a painter's wife who, as he explained in an invective-filled epistolary tirade, had tried to seduce him and, when he rejected her, "shouted out in the dining room, 'nothing will ever come of that person' " (a phrase that also figures in the opening lines of *The Robber*). Around the same time, after receiving a letter from a friend of Fanny's who wanted to meet him, Robert reported to Mermet that this Miss Häsler had written him a several-page-long letter "inquiring whether she might be suitable for going on walks and occasional necking." He traded letters with her all the same and accepted her invitation to see a performance of Richard Wagner's *Parsifal* in early April even though (as he pointed out to her) he didn't much like Wagner. He made a point of being intentionally rude to her, such as describing in a letter the alluring perfume and sexy red shoes of a woman he'd seen on the street. He told Mermet he found Häsler "a choice example of an utterly charmless spinster" but continued to see her occasionally for several months.[53]

A more intellectual consideration of sex and sexuality appears in Robert's correspondence with Pick:

> [O]ne can make sexuality an art, and so-called sadists, for example, can quite readily be masochized while at the same time the necessary sum of sadism can be awakened within masochists. [...] In contemplating these things, by the way, I have come to the conclusion that in all preeminent ruler figures, an inclination to submit, to serve can be seen; while on the other hand a quite natural urge to rule and govern can arise within the most obedient servant, for sexuality keeps spinning like the

Earth, like a globe, and these two main directions or principal components of sexual life are like its two poles.[54]

This notion of the masochist's secret sadism and the sadist's hidden masochism explicitly reflects the implicitly sexual power structures he'd considered in his work from early on, such as when servant Simon in *The Tanners* infuriates his employer with insubordinate slowness while gathering up platter shards. Sexuality was perhaps an odd topic to discuss with a professional contact he'd never met, but on-paper relationships were becoming ever more important as a way to keep loneliness at bay; and Robert was making up in his letters for the absence of suitable interlocutors in Bern.

Therese Breitbach in distant Germany was an ideal correspondent, given how little risk there was they would ever meet. He could enjoy constructing a charming self-portrait with impunity. (She did invite him to visit her in Koblenz, saying her parents would be glad to host him, an invitation he acknowledged but did not accept.) Still, he couldn't resist the occasional remark that pushed the boundaries of propriety and once even asked for a professional favor—writing to the journal *Die Literarische Welt* "as a German girl," insisting they disburse his overdue fees (it worked). But she was too young and far away to be counted among the ranks of his "mamas"—as he was beginning to refer to his female friends who showed any inclination at all to look after him, be they landladies, love interests, or friendly acquaintances. He was surrounded by "an entire stately row of mamas," he wrote to Mermet in August 1925, and his first letter to Häsler informed her that "here in Bern I have a dozen dear, kind mamas." In a microscript from around the same time he explained, "You see, for simplicity's sake I elevate all the ladies in whom I take an interest to the status of mamas by feeling myself to be a sort of child with regard to them, and now of course I must see to it that all these mamas are more or less satisfied with me or at least pretend to be."[55]

Walking to the point of physical exhaustion was coming to seem like medicine, a way to get the better of agitation. One summer night in 1926, woken by a nightmare, Robert arose, left his "room of phantoms," and walked all the way to Thun, arriving at six in the morning. By noon, he stood atop the Niesen—thirty-seven miles from Bern—where he picnicked at 7,740 feet on sardines and bread. Then he returned the way he came, passing through Thun at dusk and arriving home in Bern around mid-night. His aging body had proved itself still capable of significant discipline and exertion, still subject to his will. He wasn't as strong as he'd once been, though, and the occasional dizzy spells dating from his bout with the 1918 flu still persisted.[56] Also enervating was the thought that all his literary talents, all his dreams and strivings, had come to naught, that he had painted himself into a corner he could never escape.

The constant relocations from room to room wearied him as well. The more adept he became at making his home anywhere, the clearer it became that he'd had no real home for a long while. This was still true when, in late 1925, he found a room in the historical Elfenau ("Elf Meadow") estate, whose idyllic grounds had long been one of his favorite places to walk; in "Elfenau" from 1921, the narrator is welcomed into this magical refuge by a mysterious woman, whereupon a new "rapturously ethereal life" fills his mind with "eternally blue skies." Robert published an essay in March 1926 in *Prager Presse,* praising his new room, the good air, and the "gentle hill" below which the Aare "tranquilly glides past."[57]

As winter gave way to brightly blossoming spring in these pastoral surrounds, Robert discovered a new way to combat loneliness: befriending the children constantly running around the estate's lawns and meadows. He wrote to Mermet that he now had "a group of tiny girlfriends, proletarian children," and compared himself to the Pied Piper. Though nothing suggests his interactions with them were anything but correct, at least one mother disapproved of her daughter's association with this middle-aged man. Soon after noticing that nine-year-old Trudi looked worried one day, Robert received a note from her mother, Frieda Gall. He forwarded it to Mermet and asked her to treat it with discretion. We don't know what the note said, but one week later he moved out, telling Mermet only that he left because his landlady's son was getting too big to go on sharing a room with her.[58]

His search for a new home must have been precipitous, since the room on Junkerngasse he moved into on May 1, 1926, had been put on offer only one day earlier in the city's free advertising circular. According to the ad, the room featured simple furnishings, electricity, and a private entrance; the tenant sought was to be a "tidy worker."[59] Robert lived there only one month before moving to another room where he also stayed only a month, followed by one where his tenure was a mere two weeks.

Finally, in August 1926, he found a room into which he settled for the next two and a half years. His landladies at Luisenstrasse 14 were middle-aged spinsters: an office worker named Ida Häberlin and her sister Martha. They charged 40 francs rent for what Robert described to Mermet as a "relatively rather nice" room, dating from the 1880s, on the top floor of an elegant building in Kirchenfeld at the corner of the tree-lined avenue Thunstrasse.[60] It was a corner he knew well, having lived both directly across the street (Thunstrasse 21) and cattycorner (Thunstrasse 20) the previous year.

His odd behavior, however, was growing ever more conspicuous. Hermann Hubacher, with whom Robert had spent lovely summer days in Faulensee several years earlier, experienced a strange final encounter with him on the streets of Bern. Catching sight of Hubacher advancing toward him through the arcades, Robert spun to face a shop window, apparently trying to avoid contact. Was it because he knew that Karl and Hubacher were close? In any case, Hubacher walked right up to him, touching his arm in greeting.

His face red, he angrily turned toward me, measuring me from top to bottom like a stranger, and said only, "May I help you?" Not letting myself be deterred, I asked simply, "How are you, and how's your work going?" Ignoring the passersby who were beginning to take notice, he snapped at me, "What business is it of yours whether I'm working or not working? It's none of your business, none at all!" Pulling myself together, I calmly replied: "Listen, Walser, when I run into an artist whom I haven't seen in a while, I always start by asking about his work, and then I know all the rest as well!" "Voilà, une réponse," he said, retreating a step, doffing his famous hat, and giving a matchless bow. Some of the people around us were smirking as I took him amiably by the arm, and we went strolling down the arcades, chatting as if nothing had happened. Walser asked after my wife and our son, whom he was fond of, then in front of the Zeitglocke tower he suddenly gave me the slip in the middle of our conversation, leaping onto a tram that was just pulling out. From the footboard, he waved a farewell vaguely in my direction.[61]

Hubacher later told Seelig his brother Ernst once ran into Robert in the train station in the company of a woman holding a monkey. Robert asked Ernst where he was traveling, and when he heard it was Paris, replied: "Why not? But believe me: if I stroll from here to the bear pit, I'll have just as many adventures as you."[62]

Robert's reticence was showing itself in professional contexts as well. Invited to give a reading in Thun by Adolf Schaer-Ris in fall 1927, Robert hesitated to accept, sharing several misgivings with his would-be host: he might "read badly," he was shy, he wasn't good at socializing. When Schaer-Ris proved unable to furnish the 200-franc fee he requested, he declined the invitation. The following February, he also turned down an offer to return to the Hottingen Readers' Circle.[63]

Schaer-Ris, however, wasn't so quick to give in. After Robert turned him down, he paid him a visit. Recalling the encounter fifteen years later, he declared his first glimpse of Robert "unforgettable":

> The shabbily clothed, gaunt figure that showed itself anxiously in the crack of the door [. . .] seemed about to slam it right away and bolt it shut. [. . .] Only his large eyes—gleaming incredibly soulfully—revealed that this was an extraordinary human being. Otherwise you might have mistaken him for a common laborer. His voice sounded hesitant but also extremely warm and kind. A proper conversation didn't develop. I had the impression I was standing before a human tragedy, and the name Hölderlin shot through my head.[64]

Another visitor was artist Emil Stumpp, who came to sketch Robert's portrait for the Zurich magazine *Annalen* in summer 1928. He, too, noticed the writer's "burning, large, dark blue eyes that could take on an obstinate, dangerous expression," and his threadbare suit. Unlike with Schaer-Ris, Stumpp and Robert were soon immersed in lively conversation and took a twilight walk along the Aare to the bear pit where, as Robert informed his visitor, Lenin often stood. Two of the younger bears were just racing up the tree in their enclosure. The two humans then repaired to the Volkshaus restaurant to share a bottle of red wine before Robert escorted Stumpp to the station, toting his bag.[65]

In the year following Robert's fiftieth birthday, his psychological state deteriorated badly, culminating in a crisis in early 1929 that involved overwhelming feelings of paranoia and hallucinations. Most of what little is known today about the details of the breakdown he suffered has been pieced together from institutional records. The clinical history of Robert Walser began on Thursday, January 24, 1929, when Lisa took her brother for a consultation with psychiatrist Walter Morgenthaler.

Lisa sought Morgenthaler's help because he'd been their brother Ernst's doctor at Waldau Asylum. She pressed for an immediate appointment, having hurried from Bellelay to Bern after being contacted by Robert's landladies saying it was an emergency, that Robert had gone mad and threatened them with a knife—at least this is how Mermet (who stayed behind in Bellelay) later described the situation.[66]

The knife incident that set off this chain of events had occurred the previous evening. Perhaps the two terrified Häberlin sisters had locked themselves in a bedroom afterward before venturing out together early the next morning—neither wanting to remain alone in the apartment with Robert—to send Lisa a telegram. Lisa quickly canceled school for the day and, perhaps without telling even Mermet where she was going, rushed to the train station and arrived in Bern mid-morning.

Morgenthaler's consultation notes were entered into Robert's medical record. "Miss Walser, a teacher in Bellelay," he writes, "appeared in my office hours on Jan. 24, 1929, and indicated that for quite some time now her brother had become increasingly depressed and inhibited [*gehemmt*], that he was afraid, heard voices, and was agitated at night." His own observation of the patient: "markedly depressed and severely inhibited." He also noted that Robert understood that he was ill and "complained of being unable to work, periods of fearfulness, etc." Robert said he didn't want to be institutionalized, he wanted to "go stay with his sister in Bellelay." Morgenthaler wrote that this was "inadvisable due to external circumstances," adding that it appeared Robert was "urgently" in need of institutionalization. Perhaps these "external circumstances" included not only the small size of Lisa's apartment but also the psychic toll it would take on her to assume responsibility for Robert's care.[67]

According to statements by Lisa preserved in this record, Robert "made marriage proposals to both [Häberlin] sisters and immediately afterward asked them to stab him to death." The proposals, it was later clarified, came on successive days. But the Häberlins had been alarmed by their tenant's behavior for some time. On one occasion, the record notes, he "screamed so loudly it terrified them." They also said he suffered from hallucinations. Robert later told Seelig he attempted suicide more than once during this period but "was unable even to make a proper noose."[68]

Morgenthaler instructed Lisa to take her brother directly to Waldau, on the outskirts of Bern, and commit him. Robert understood and agreed. Hesitating outside the main entryway when they arrived, he turned to her and asked, "Are we doing the right thing?"[69] She remained silent, and they went in.

The Quiet Years

1929–1956

ENTERING WALDAU AS A PATIENT, Robert Walser embraced a new mode of existence. He relinquished aspirations he'd held for decades, surrendered control of his days, and began his apprenticeship in the art of not writing. He'd always said he could produce only in freedom, with the autonomy to organize his entire life around his work. But his psychological duress had taken such a toll on every aspect of his being that his writing suffered too. At first, he faltered only in the outward-facing parts of the profession, such as his relationships with editors. Later, fueled by a sense of futility, he turned so far inward that his writing often seemed destined for his eyes alone. An era of resignation and ultimately of silence began.

Lisa took Robert to Waldau much as she'd once delivered him to a temperance hotel when his life was in shambles. For all the tension in their relationship, she remained a fiercely loyal caretaker, even as she witnessed his self-destructiveness and the very Walserian pride he clung to in his decline. If he'd been less proud—more flexible, more forgiving of himself and others—perhaps he might have achieved the comfortable middle age she wished for him. It was painful to see his distress and hard to refuse his request to live with her, but she didn't have the strength, nor could she risk being personally endangered by him if he lost control.

Waldau's palatial main building, topped by a clock tower, sits at the end of a long tree-lined drive in the hilly countryside northeast of Bern, which at the time was surrounded by farmland and a few patches of forest. Robert knew the region from his walks and visits to nearby Schosshalden Cemetery, where Hermann and Ernst were buried. From the moment he entered this grand building, he became an object of inquiry, monitored by attendants and doctors who took a professional interest in his inner life. Starting in 1929, Robert Walser's story is narrated only by others, above all by the doctors who examined and cared for him. This twenty-eight-year period—a full third of his life—fills only a single chapter of the present book. But while these decades were less eventful than those that preceded them, their uneventfulness is an important part of this story.

Robert's intake interview at Waldau—according to an entry in his medical record—included a personal consultation with the clinic's director, Wilhelm von Speyr, who, despite the institution's size, made a practice of speaking with newly admitted patients whenever possible. Waldau housed between eight hundred and nine hundred patients, with a further hundred placed in private homes while under treatment. Robert soon came to trust von Speyr—a native of Basel seventeen years his senior—and later told Carl Seelig they "got along well."[1]

A professor of psychiatry at the University of Bern, von Speyr was a cultivated man who, like Robert, had lost his mother as a child. He'd briefly had Nietzsche as a high school teacher (for Ancient Greek) and had written a dissertation on alcoholism among the mentally ill in the Basel asylum. At Waldau, this lifelong bachelor put in long hours and made himself available for conversations with his patients, convinced of the importance of showing them respect. (He also personally read each patient's incoming and outgoing correspondence.) When he was named the director of Waldau in 1890, von Speyr put an end to the practice of routinely restraining patients with straitjackets and locking them in enclosed bathtubs. Only the most dangerous and disruptive patients were kept in isolation. He banned alcohol (even for staff) and forbade employees from using physical force against patients except in self-defense. A believer in work therapy, he bought farmland adjacent to the asylum and assigned patients agricultural tasks, never adopting the modern treatment techniques—lobotomy, electroshock, and insulin shock therapy—being developed around the time Robert arrived at Waldau.[2]

Evaluating Robert, von Speyr recorded a list of symptoms similar to those noted by Morgenthaler: "He has been incapable of working for several weeks, can no longer concentrate, suffers from insomnia; eventually admits he's been hearing voices recently. He feels depressed and has intermittently had suicidal thoughts but doesn't think this should be taken

seriously." He adds that Robert reported "living a very miserable existence" and experiencing depression in the past as well. When von Speyr
recommended that Robert immediately enter the asylum as a patient, Robert agreed but hesitated when it was time to sign the papers. He worried
(as per von Speyr's report) that he might never be released and feared his
commitment would harm his reputation as a writer. After he signed, an
attendant took him to a ward in the asylum's New Building, which held
six fourteen-bed rooms where patients could be observed overnight.[3]

Following his usual practice of gathering information from his patients' families, von Speyr then conducted a private interview with Lisa,
who told him that Robert had wanted to live in Bellelay with her, but she
couldn't look after him because of her profession. "Patient has always
been peculiar," von Speyr wrote, "especially with respect to sexuality, has
always masturbated a lot. On an earlier visit to her home, he behaved indecently toward her." Lisa also repeated the story of Robert's proposing
marriage and then offering a knife to the Häberlin sisters.[4]

Interviewed after his first night in the asylum, Robert reported not
minding the dormitory arrangement. "He didn't sleep well," the protocol
notes, "but he wasn't sleeping much at home either. Admits to hearing
voices. He has visions too; when he shuts his eyes, he sees all sorts of images without being asleep, i.e. not dreams." Robert was slow and careful
with his answers, intent on not saying something inaccurate or wrong. He
told the doctor that he "had always been nervous, sometimes more, sometimes less," and that he occasionally found himself in a bad mood for no
reason. He'd fallen ill approximately ten days earlier, suddenly beset with
"voices and paranoia. He felt people were laughing at him and was afraid
of being disliked [. . .] and that someone wanted to give him a thrashing."
He was aware, he told the doctor, that his fluctuating moods alarmed his
landladies, who'd asked his sister for help. His own opinion was that he'd
stayed too long in the Häberlins' apartment; it had been better for him to
keep changing rooms, and now the lack of change was making him nervous. Dr. Morgenthaler had advised him to go to the asylum, and he had
remained out of consideration for his sister.[5]

Von Speyr's notes on Robert's intake interview are handwritten and
fill most of the first two pages of his medical record. At some point, von
Speyr or someone else rolled the first page of the report into a typewriter
to add Robert's personal data: the month and year of his birth, his profes-

sion (writer), his marital status (single), and his sister's address, along with the registration number assigned to him, 10.428. While the date of his admission was entered in pen, the box reserved for a provisional diagnosis was left blank, and in the "definitive diagnosis" box, someone typed the word "schizophrenia."

Viewed from the twenty-first century, Robert Walser's schizophrenia diagnosis—and the long-term institutionalization that came with it—is easy to second-guess. His case was clearly very different from that of his brother Ernst, diagnosed with catatonic schizophrenia at age twenty-five after his friends and family witnessed his rapid descent into disorganized thinking. At the same time, it would be a mistake to see Walser's hospitalization as unjustified. He was certainly ill, even if a patient presenting with his symptoms today might be treated with a combination of medication and psychotherapy after a relatively short hospital stay.

Robert's illness was characterized above all by longstanding depression sometimes combined with paranoia and sudden mood swings that he himself experienced as pathological. He occasionally displayed a stiffness or flatness of affect, and he experienced auditory hallucinations that increased in frequency and severity around New Year's 1929, culminating in the psychotic episode that led to his hospitalization. Today, these symptoms would likely result in a different diagnosis, though it is difficult to speculate on the basis of a medical record recorded by psychiatric professionals using early-twentieth-century diagnostic templates. There's also a great deal we simply don't know about Walser's psychological profile. No firm evidence exists of his experiencing manic states, for instance, though his long all-night walks—and occasional night-long talking and drinking sessions—might suggest the energy of mania.

Nor is it clear from his medical record whether he was diagnosed by von Speyr, Morgenthaler, or one of the other Waldau doctors. In any case, the diagnosis was uncontroversial from an early-twentieth-century standpoint. "The most common mental illness"—as Morgenthaler described it in his 1930 textbook for psychiatric attendants—schizophrenia was a blanket diagnosis covering a wider range of disorders than it does now.[6] Morgenthaler's understanding of the disease derived from that of Emil Kraepelin, Eugen Bleuler (who coined the term "schizophrenia"), and Ernst Kretschmer. It was believed to involve not only the brain but also various glands, such as the testes, ovaries, and thyroid, and to be triggered by hormonal changes (puberty, pregnancy, the physical decline of middle age), sometimes coupled with external factors like depression, grief, or trauma. Morgenthaler saw eccentricity (introversion, shyness, social awkwardness) as a risk factor and writes that depression and other mood disorders are commonly observed in conjunction with schizophrenic illness.[7]

Morgenthaler's diagnostic schema includes stiffness of affect, eccentricity, disorganization of thought and speech, ambivalence (the tendency to think and feel in mutually contradictory terms), hallucinations, and delusions (including paranoia). Robert presented not only with depression but also (by his doctors' observation and his own self-description) four other key symptoms: stiffness of affect, eccentricity, hallucinations, and delusions.

Given the distress, worry, and depression Robert had been experiencing, it was perhaps a relief to entrust himself to a well-organized system of care. For the first time since his last stint of military service, he was spending the night in a roomful of other sleepers. He'd been assigned to Men's Dormitory II, his bed one of a long row of identical white metal bedframes with mattresses, each containing a fellow patient. After three nights, he told a doctor he still wasn't sleeping well—the voices found him even here—but he felt safe. He asked whether it was a mistake to feel this way.[8]

The doctors taking notes on Robert's condition remarked shortly after his arrival that he didn't interact much with other patients, a trend that continued as January gave way to February. He would sit off by himself, reading or at least looking at a book (one doctor observing him wasn't convinced he was actually reading) while across the room other patients listened to the radio. Robert wasn't the only bookish member of Waldau's population, but he resisted being drawn into conversations and indeed seemed intent on appearing unapproachable; the report mentions "something scornful in his expression." One doctor noted the great care with which he chose his words when he did speak, for example when describing his insomnia: "the inimical voices of my own personal being deride me and intervene disruptively in my thoughts." Robert also asked whether such voices could be caused by an ear disorder. He'd awoken that morning to a cacophony of inner voices and bells—the latter coming presumably from the Waldau chapel.[9]

At the end of January, Robert wrote to Lisa thanking her for her support and telling her he was sleeping relatively well and reading a great deal, though he had not yet gone back to writing, and that he enjoyed the radio music in the dayroom. He sent a similar note to the Häberlin sisters. Two weeks later, writing to Lisa again, he reported that his anxiety attacks had entirely disappeared in the asylum, which he thought was precisely because he hadn't been trying to write there. He now believed his breakdown was produced by a combination of writer's block ("a creative crisis") and spending too much time alone. Feeling better, he could now read the newspaper without getting worked up and was enjoying stories by Tolstoy (though he found his play *The Living Corpse* too "delicately European" rather than "splendidly Russian"). He was learning to play chess and had even ventured to address some words to fellow patients. He'd been assigned household tasks, such as helping another patient polish the parquet floors. He'd resigned himself to staying in the asylum longer than he'd initially expected, and when Martha Häberlin wrote asking for the key to his old room, he sent it to her right away.[10]

A possibly not-insignificant factor in Robert's improvement was that no alcohol was available in the clinic, though—perhaps in compensation— he found himself smoking a great deal, enough that this became a topic of discussion with Lisa. By the end of February, he was sleeping better and reported that the voices bothered him less. He had taken up billiards but still avoided interactions with other patients, preferring to play alone, practicing the steadying of eye, hand, and breath as he used the cue to maneuver each ball into its pocket. He began to think about leaving. He'd had his rest; wasn't it time to go back to writing, back into the world? It was hard to imagine writing as long as he was in confinement—though as he mentioned to one of the doctors, he worried that he might need to find an office job for the sake of financial stability, and wouldn't that be difficult with the stigma of the asylum attached to his name?[11]

He was doing even better by March—sleeping well and free of anxiety— and had gained several pounds. At his routine medical examination, he was found to be "somewhat more than medium height, stiff posture, face extremely ruddy, reddish hair, protruding eyes, teeth in very poor condition, several missing." His general health was described as good, although the doctor noticed sudden-onset tachycardia in the middle of the examination. His hands were "cold, blue, and damp."[12]

Robert's routine at the asylum included spending around three hours a day working in the garden—as patients physically capable of such exertions were expected to. He'd resented the physical labor at first but then made his peace with it and even boasted to Seelig that he once received a spontaneous round of applause from a group of female patients for his vigorous sawing. He still heard voices, but he was surrounded by fellow sufferers and a well-regimented staff whose presence assured him he was safe. In early April, he told a doctor he was developing "resistance" to the voices, not hearing them as loudly as before, though they continued to bother him at night. There were different voices, he said, some of them supportive, others unpleasant, hateful. But he was feeling more comfortable with them and with life in the asylum. Lisa had visited him, and he told the doctor he'd been able to "chat cheerfully" with her, though he remained reserved with others, particularly women; he said he'd kept women at a distance in Bern as well. He read a great deal—Molière, Rousseau, Tolstoy, Gottfried Keller, Conrad Ferdinand Meyer—and improved at both billiards and chess.[13]

Lisa visited again in April and this time sat for an interview with one of Robert's doctors, who took notes on her longstanding frustration with her brother, whom she described as "a big egotist" who was always quitting jobs, insisted that his long walks were necessary, refused to perform any other work besides writing, and "tormented" her during visits in Bellelay, doing whatever he liked. He also, she said, "tormented" Frieda Mermet, who had considered accepting his proposal of marriage before deciding he wasn't serious about it. Mermet told Lisa that Robert "didn't need a wife at all" and was sexually eccentric. Lisa's testimony was added to Robert's medical record without commentary. Mermet herself had made the trip from Bellelay to visit Robert that March.[14]

All spring, Robert worked in the garden and performed light household labor, such as tidying the dayroom or the billiards room. He enjoyed working in the garden and was unhappy when a bad cough or an outbreak of hoof-and-mouth disease at the farm prevented him from doing so. This way of life was coming to seem familiar to him, though he continued to resist interactions with fellow residents, at times reacting rudely and impatiently, at others withdrawing with a courteous smile. And despite the voices still lingering at the edges of his consciousness, he returned to writing. In June, he sent Otto Pick a new poem, giving the Häberlins' return address—a practice he continued with other professional correspondence. By late 1929 he'd sold enough work to periodicals to speak with the asylum management about using the money he'd earned to cover the costs of his hospitalization.[15]

In keeping with the asylum's distractions and schedule, he wrote shorter pieces exclusively, mainly poems. In December 1929, he told Mermet that most of this writing was done early in the morning and that he had produced "a sort of diary in the form of separate, individually unrelated poems." Some of these were eventually published—most in *Prager Presse* and *Berliner Tageblatt,* with a handful in *Prager Tagblatt, Frankfurter Zeitung, Sport im Bild,* and *Die Literarische Welt.* Many remained unpublished. Like his poems of the previous several years, these vary widely in tone, subject matter, and form. Many are rhymed and in meter, others free verse. Some are heavy with melancholy, others paint satirical portraits of real or imagined people. In the funny ones, Walser sounds like earlier versions of his writing self, as when he turns the name of comic poet Joachim Ringelnatz into the adjective "ringelnatzig" to rhyme with "patzig" (awkward, clumsy).[16] Certain poems resemble little essays on topics like traveling for pleasure, or recount strolls in the countryside, but it's hard to read them as a record of what Robert was experiencing. Rather, they reflect his changing moods on a given day, taking on diaristic character insofar as writing them became a regular reflective practice for him.

Only occasionally are overtly autobiographical threads woven in, as in the 1930 unpublished poem "Agreeableness of Lament" ("Annehmlichkeit des Klagens"):

> No one need suppose himself abandoned
> but there are many, I think, who
> imagine they are forlorn.
> I live here like a child, enraptured
> by the idea that I have been forgotten.
> Perhaps there are only a few who can
> delight in such a thought. Everywhere's a little
> sunshine, I tell myself, and wind and shade
> and moments resplendent with joy
> or sorrow, plunging eagle-like from heights

of humankind and down into the soul.
Certainly humans forget each other quickly,
and yet one must, it seems to me,
accept guilt for the circumstance
that those one has forgotten have in turn
themselves become forgetful.
Lamenting something natural
can sometimes be agreeable indeed.[17]

He goes even further in the poem "He Was Not Nice" ("Er war nicht nett," also 1930, also unpublished):

Now he may no longer as before
go walking at whim through the beautiful world,
banter with women and in the morning light
give strolling figures his fleeting attention;
now he is living in a sort of monastery.
His ruler sent him by her own volition
to where all he may do is gaze into books
so that gradually he may improve, for he was
discourteous to her of whom presently he
thinks—thinks without pause—and this she knows,
and her knowledge that things are thus and not
otherwise makes her ever more beautiful. Tormenting him
is sweet to her.[18]

These two poems—one melancholy, one accusatory, seeming to conflate Lisa with an elusive object of desire—portray a person experiencing feelings of confusion, powerlessness, and, to some extent, resentment. Robert may also have been milking moods for literary effect. Given his loose adherence to autobiographical truth throughout his career, there's no reason to assume he would begin holding up an impartial mirror to his own soul now. The poems composed in Waldau that saw print tended to be the more playful and intricately rhymed ones.

It's unclear which of the prose pieces Walser published during his Waldau years were actually written in the asylum. Pick often accepted much more writing than *Prager Presse* had immediate use for, printing pieces years, and sometimes as much as a decade, later.[19] We know, for example, that Walser's essay "Thoughts on Cezanne," published in March 1929, was written and submitted in early 1926. At least three pieces written in 1925 ("Chivalresque Romance," "You Wicked Sun," and "A Gottfried Keller Figure") appeared in 1933. While Walser's poems often came out in the paper's Sunday supplement, his prose pieces were usually published in the feuilleton section of the regular daily newspaper, where space considerations, often requiring last-minute changes, played an important role.

Although Robert resumed submitting work to Pick in June 1929, he didn't confide in him until March 1930 that he'd "been living for a year now in an asylum at the edge of town, although there isn't much wrong with me, I mean that I am otherwise, i.e. in general, in good health." Even after this confession he still used the Häberlins' address to write to Pick. The extant correspondence confirms only a small number of submissions, and only of poetry. On the other hand, we know he submitted short prose to *Neue Zürcher Zeitung* as late as June 1932, when Korrodi accepted "Two Life Paths" and "The Lake." The acceptance note Korrodi sent became a microscript palimpsest.[20]

Once Robert returned to writing and publishing, his attitude toward his surroundings changed; it no longer felt urgent to plan for a return to life outside the asylum. A doctor noted that he "put on airs somewhat" and could be quarrelsome but also that he kept to his routine, including regular work shifts, and that he would sometimes allow another patient to join him for an evening game of billiards. Robert finally felt ready to try sleeping in a private room in March 1930, but after two nights alone he asked to return to the dormitory—the voices began to haunt him right away, keeping him awake. He occasionally still experienced paranoid thoughts, for example confiding to Lisa in fall 1930 that he was no longer able to publish essays in Germany because the brother of a now deceased fellow patient, one Dr. Merz, was conspiring against him.[21]

As a Waldau resident, Robert sometimes took afternoon walks with an attendant as chaperone. On July 3, 1931, his medical record notes that he participated in the "long walk" outing with attendants and other patients and enjoyed it, and that when Lisa visited, they would stroll down the hill together and have lunch in Bern. Robert would then return on his own, reliably arriving at the agreed-upon time. He often ended his workday with a brief amble around the asylum grounds. On Sundays, rather than go out, he would remain in the dayroom, reading; he told the doctor that he spent enough time outdoors during the week.[22]

Robert's doctors persuaded him to move from the dormitory to a double room in December 1931, and it turned out that the presence of a single additional person sufficed for him to pass a quiet night. He got along well with this roommate, Mr. Anneler. Other patients, though, complained about Robert's behavior, finding him generally inconsiderate. They said he would take greedy helpings of dishes being passed around at meals and played billiards loudly even when others in the room were struggling to hear the radio. Complaints were lodged that he'd sometimes lock himself in the toilet for lengthy morning stretches while others waited. According to his doctors, these grievances didn't concern him.[23]

Robert's Waldau equilibrium was shattered when von Speyr retired in March 1933 at age eighty. The clinic's new director, Jakob Klaesi, immediately set about reorganizing the institution. His first priority was to reduce its population, which had grown to around one thousand. As Klaesi wrote in the asylum's 1933 annual report, "In order to reduce overcrowding in all the wards as quickly as possible [...] a large number of 'quiet' and improved patients no longer in urgent need of institutionalization were released, either to poorhouses, hospitals, private home care, or into the care of their own family members." Other patients were assigned to Waldau's agricultural "colonies," smaller residential units with medical staff where patients performed work that was both therapeutic and helped defray the costs of their institutionalization.[24]

Robert was an obvious candidate for transfer or release. A "quiet" patient from the start, he had resumed professional activity in the asylum, and although he remained oddly stiff in his bearing—as well as inconsiderate of, and reluctant to interact with, other patients—this didn't justify long-term institutionalization. He still heard voices but had demonstrated his ability to manage his condition and comport himself in an orderly fashion, respecting the many rules governing asylum life and reliably performing his assigned tasks. And if he couldn't be alone at night, perhaps a place could be found for him with shared accommodations.

Feeling that Robert would benefit from an institutional structure, Klaesi recommended he move to one of Waldau's colonies. But Robert refused. Rather than accept a transfer, he told Klaesi that he wanted to be released, to find a job and live independently again. An entry in his medical record from June 18, 1933, records a summary of these conversations, noting Robert's stated preference and also Klaesi's assessment that the patient was failing to take steps toward making a life on the outside possible for himself, for example, by seeking employment.[25] (There is no evidence Robert received assistance from anyone at Waldau with regard to a job search.)

Robert had been paying his way at Waldau with money from his publications, but his income plummeted in 1933 because of political developments in Germany. Adolf Hitler, appointed German chancellor in January, had suspended civil liberties in late February, plunging the German publishing industry into disarray. Bruno Cassirer, anticipating the impossibility of keeping open a Jewish-run business, made preparations to emigrate that April by transferring what rights he could to foreign publishers such as Zurich-based Rascher, who took on *The Tanners* in a contract countersigned by Robert.[26] *Berliner Tageblatt* printed only two Walser pieces in 1932 (compared with thirteen in 1931) following the departure of feuilleton editor Fred Hildenbrandt; and editor-in-chief Theodor Wolff was dismissed in March 1933, putting an end to Robert's relationship with that paper, though two final texts from the backlog appeared in June and July 1933. *Prager Presse* had continued to publish him, printing five more poems and two prose pieces from its backlog between January and May 1933, but it had always paid at a lower rate.

Lisa worried that if Robert were released, he would wind up in financial or psychological distress, or both, becoming her responsibility again. Karl and Oscar had refused to contribute to their brother's financial support after his first half-year at Waldau, arguing that he wasn't actually ill and was remaining in the asylum out of laziness; they saw his return to publishing as proof that he had recovered enough to resume responsibility for his life and earn a living either through writing or some other job. Oscar had suggested Robert sign a power of attorney granting him the ability to manage Robert's financial affairs in the interests of all the siblings. When Robert refused, Oscar reproached Lisa with indulging their brother's whims. Karl was so angry at Lisa for pressuring him to help (at one point she had a lawyer draw up a letter describing his responsibilities) that he cut off contact with her. Fanny was also unable to help—Lisa had been sending her money too—but Frieda Mermet would contribute on at least one occasion.[27]

Lisa asked the director of the Bellelay hospital for advice. He recommended sending Robert to the asylum in Herisau, in the Canton of Appenzell Ausserrhoden in eastern Switzerland, which was run by a conservative director unlikely to subject Robert to dangerous new treatment methods.[28] Appenzell Ausserrhoden was also the official canton of citizenship for the Walser siblings under Swiss law, on the basis of their paternal lineage—meaning that if Robert were ever to become a ward of the state, the canton would assume responsibility for his care. Robert was aghast at the notion that he, a lifelong city dweller, should agree to move to a part of rural Switzerland in which he had never set foot.

Robert had another reason for not wanting to be transferred to Herisau: clinic director Otto Hinrichsen was an old acquaintance from whom he'd parted on bad terms. They'd met around 1897 in Zurich where Hinrichsen, a German from the Baltic coast who was friendly with Franz Blei, was completing his medical degree. Robert never thought much of Hinrichsen or the plays and poems he published under the pseudonym Otto Hinnerk. Hinrichsen had (anonymously) published a rave review of Robert's fairy-tale play *Cinderella* in 1901, but some sort of dispute had arisen between them, resulting in Robert sending Hinrichsen some lines whose tone he now regretted: he expressed his worry to Lisa that Hinrichsen might still remember this "unkind letter" all these years later.[29]

Klaesi was adamant that Robert leave Waldau, however, and Lisa was determined to preserve her autonomy. She wrote Hinrichsen, asking him to accept Robert as a patient. When he replied that his institution lacked room for a new patient, Klaesi wrote more forcefully on Lisa's behalf and achieved the desired result. The doctor's certificate Klaesi sent Hinrichsen noted that Robert "did not attend much to his own affairs and saw it as only natural for his sister [. . .] to handle anything disagreeable for him and always take care of whatever needed doing." In the end, the choice of Herisau was Lisa's sole responsibility, with both Oscar and Karl refusing to countersign the paperwork.[30]

Robert's transfer was traumatic. Never before had he experienced such a complete suspension of personal autonomy. At Waldau, he'd grown used to an atmosphere of respect, with the staff seeing him as a writer who was ill. That cushion of benevolence went a long way toward making life in the asylum bearable. He still retained some freedoms. He could take a walk or go into town—though it was understood he would discuss these intentions in advance and return at a set time. Waldau provided equilibrium and support. It wasn't what he had hoped his life would be, but it worked.

The morning of June 19, 1933, the day of his transfer, Robert refused to get out of bed. Only after several attendants gathered at his bedside, making it clear (as noted in his medical record) "that he would have to submit to their superior force," did he cooperate. He was accompanied by a single attendant on the trip, who reported that Robert gradually cheered up, becoming "calm, talkative, and in good spirits" and finally taking leave of the attendant (at least according to the Waldau medical record) with the remark that he had "had a pleasant journey and liked it in Herisau."[31]

The administrative capital of Canton Appenzell Ausserrhoden, Herisau (population 13,500 then as now) lies nestled in a valley. In earlier centuries, the linen industry made a number of local families rich, a legacy still visible in the town's ornate eighteenth-century façades and brightly painted shutters. Like Waldau, Herisau's Cantonal Asylum was situated on the outskirts of town, on a hill to the southwest. The clinic was Switzerland's first to be built using a pavilion structure, with separate buildings—referred to by locals as "the yellow village"—serving different functions and segregating patients by gender and severity of illness. Framed with blossoming fruit trees and evergreens, the clinic is surrounded by grassy meadows full of wildflowers, beyond which a path curves up into the hills. In the distance, the peak of the majestic Säntis is visible, part of an Alpine panorama.

Robert's hope that Hinrichsen had forgotten him was dashed during their first interview. Perhaps Hinrichsen, who'd just published a new play with Rascher, had looked forward to renewing their acquaintance. But any offer of camaraderie on his part could only have looked like condescension to Robert, still in shock over his forced transfer and painfully conscious of the power differential between asylum director and patient. Hinrichsen arranged a private room—a free upgrade, as it were, since the third-class service level for which Robert was registered did not include such amenities. But Robert asked to be transferred to a group dormitory after a single night in this room; it still frightened him to sleep alone. Hinrichsen reported to Lisa on June 26, 1933, that Robert had shown no sign of pleasure when Hinrichsen suggested he use the private room for writing, "as if he no longer had any desire to do so, or as if—as he said—he no longer had any customers for his writing, since it was above all German newspapers that had still been printing him, which can scarcely be the case today."[32]

Robert was assigned quarters in the building for "quiet" men, with upstairs dormitories housing ten to twelve patients each and a dayroom on the ground floor. Herisau patients underwent "work therapy," but this was a very different sort of labor than at Waldau. Patients here performed repetitive indoor tasks such as teasing wool to prepare it for carding and gluing together paper bags. Hinrichsen's approach to work therapy was inspired by psychiatrist Hermann Simon, who theorized in an influential 1929 article that routine activity helped psychiatric patients recover, while idleness encouraged the development of psychoses.[33]

The collapse of the German publications that once printed his work gave Robert an excuse to avoid the humiliation of writing under surveillance, overseen by this lesser talent now wielding power over him. Robert was already primed to distrust Hinrichsen and seek signs of condescension without being aware of his new doctor's research specialty: the demise of literary creativity in mental illness. For Hinrichsen, a writer who falls ill loses the ability to produce artistic work; his key example was Hölderlin, whose severe mental illness ended his career. If an ailing writer continued to write, Hinrichsen believed, it demonstrated that a core of sound mental health persisted despite the disease.[34]

In a diary entry several weeks after Robert's arrival, Hinrichsen responded to the Walser essay "Mother Nature" ("Mutter Natur") published in the Sunday, July 9, 1933, edition of *Neue Zürcher Zeitung* with the note "Naiveté = weakness of mind."[35] He then muses on how a writer's non-normative perceptions may align with a predisposition to mental illness. In noting only the essay's naive tone, Hinrichsen missed the irony of describing this "Mother" in terms of violent natural disasters: volcanic eruptions, floods, and avalanches. In Robert's medical record, Hinrichsen updated the "schizophrenia" diagnosis from Waldau with more specific qualifiers: a provisional diagnosis of "hebephrenia" (disorganized schizophrenia) followed by a definitive diagnosis of "chronic catatonia." Catatonia—considered a form of schizophrenia at the time—had also been Ernst's diagnosis.[36]

Robert's dislike and distrust of Hinrichsen persisted throughout the nearly eight years during which the doctor oversaw Robert's care. Robert consistently rejected Hinrichsen's attempts to draw him into writer-to-writer literary conversations. When a Hinrichsen play was performed in St. Gallen, the doctor asked whether Robert had heard about his "triumph." He also suggested—whether joking or not isn't clear—that Robert compose a poem in honor of his upcoming seventieth birthday and gave Robert a play of his to read—which Robert ignored. Walser later described Hinrichsen to Seelig as "something like the distillate of a fawning courtier and a circus performer." His response to Hinrichsen's attempts at chumminess was silence—"restraint," as he explained to Seelig, being "the only weapon I possess." But it was a weapon that backfired. By remaining stubbornly silent when questioned by Hinrichsen, Robert offered him confirmation of his diagnosis of "catatonia," helping to create the impression he was sicker than he was. It's true he was sick. He was also sick of Hinrichsen. When one of the doctors noted in Robert's medical record on December 12, 1935, that Robert had spoken with him at length about his voices, Hinrichsen added a note in the margin: "never with me."[37]

Regarding the question of whether Robert might someday be released, his siblings—in particular Lisa—deferred to the doctor's judgment. Hinrichsen always vehemently opposed this possibility; his conviction that a mentally ill individual could not also be an artistically successful writer foretold failure in his eyes. And Robert likewise reacted with ambivalence every time the subject of his release came up; the possibility may have interested him, but he couldn't, or wouldn't, act on it. (Seelig reported Robert saying he'd been waiting for someone else to make arrangements for him to live in freedom, seemingly unaware of the contradiction this statement implied.)[38]

The auditory hallucinations he still regularly experienced were a complicating factor. By his own description, usually two or three voices—including one he often identified as female—attacked him with harsh and unpleasant words most of the time. These included both crude expressions he was unwilling to repeat as well as occasional words of praise and even jokes. In later years he reported the voices becoming less affable, though it was sometimes possible to engage with them. Robert regarded the voices as symptomatic of a physical disorder—he told a doctor in 1934 that he "suffered from a serious illness in that he heard voices, but it wasn't a mental illness." Five years later he expressed surprise that these voices coming "from outside him" knew about his childhood. They persisted over the years, falling silent only when he was in conversation with another person or when he began to write; but they would soon interrupt with critical commentary, making it impossible for him to concentrate. He was frequently heard responding aloud to them. In 1939 he told a doctor that he started hearing the voices at Waldau, but since they'd been mentioned in his initial interviews with Morgenthaler and von Speyr, he must have misremembered this. It's painful to imagine his last pre-Waldau writings being produced amid this mental background noise.[39]

Robert's medical record in Herisau also records occasional instances of paranoia, as when he suddenly became afraid of a fellow patient who criticized his twine-sorting technique in the cellar where they were processing materials for the post office; Robert said the man was "threatening his life" and asked to be taken back upstairs at once. But Hinrichsen noted later in the file that Robert was, in his estimation, "not paranoid" or at least "not classically so."[40]

Soon after Robert arrived in Herisau, Hinrichsen, deeming him incapable of managing his own finances, persuaded Lisa to have her brother declared incompetent and assigned a legal guardian. Robert objected, which Hinrichsen noted in the official medical evaluation he submitted to the bureau in charge of guardianship decisions. In his report from January 19, 1934, Hinrichsen writes that his patient is "temporally, spatially, and personally oriented, lucid, calm, friendly in his communications, but also decidedly apathetic, is content to live here in the asylum and does not press for release." Hinrichsen's conclusion: "In light of his mental illness, Mr. Robert Walser is incapable of properly seeing to his own affairs."[41] According to Swiss law, a diagnosis of mental illness was sufficient to demonstrate incompetence.

The application to have Robert declared legally incompetent had to be filed in Bern, where he'd last lived independently. Ordinarily the person in question had to be present at such a hearing, but when Robert received a summons to appear on March 23, 1934, Hinrichsen successfully petitioned the Bern magistrate's office to have the requirement waived, noting the destabilizing psychological effect the hearing would have on his patient, the expense of sending him on such a long journey with an attendant, and the risk that once in Bern, the patient would refuse to return to Herisau. Robert was declared incompetent in absentia and charged 41.80 francs (around $350 in today's dollars) for the hearing.[42]

As he now resided in Appenzell Ausserrhoden, the responsibility for his affairs was transferred from the Municipal Guardianship Office in Bern to the Teufen Municipal Council along with all his assets, amounting at the time to 6,242.60 francs (roughly $50,600 in today's dollars). This was a substantial enough sum at the time to signify that he was in no immediate danger of becoming an impoverished ward of the canton. He was assigned a guardian as of May 31, 1934: one Jakob Walser (no relation), a curtain manufacturer who was both president of the Teufen Chamber of Commerce and a Teufen Municipal Council member.[43]

Jakob Walser experienced his ward as competent. The annual report on Robert's condition and holdings filed in 1937 stated, "The possibility must be considered of eventually releasing the patient from the institution and returning him to his previous occupation." Jakob Walser's report from 1938 spoke of the possibility of release even more emphatically, observing, "writer colleagues who are his friends are making great efforts to return him to society." (He must have been referring to Carl Seelig, whose entry into Robert's life will be discussed shortly. Walser had told Seelig he thought he could survive on a yearly income of 1,800 francs [around $13,700 in today's dollars].) Jakob Walser also noted that Hinrichsen continued to oppose Robert's release on the grounds that he "still suffers from delusional ideas," though "not severely," and that he "would not be able to resume his career as a writer with any success." Jakob Walser concludes that it is "very unlikely" that Robert will "be released in the foreseeable future." By 1940, his report describes it as "unimaginable" that his ward will ever return to his writing or any other career, "as he is now over 60 years old and no longer possesses this capacity."[44]

Patients like Robert—calm and cooperative, requiring no special accommodations or treatment—were desirable for an institution like Herisau. He paid his fees without incident (now via his guardian) and, through the little labors he performed daily, contributed to the institution's functioning and sustainability. The cost of his "third class pensioner" accommodations and board in Herisau (including occasional modest surcharges for mending or cobbler services) amounted to approximately 1,000 francs per year (around $6,800 in today's dollars). In 1941, Jakob Walser reported that he had succeeded in "getting together a sum of 4,000 francs from the sums collected from his [Robert's] friends and benefactors," enough to cover several more years in the asylum. (Much of the collecting was done by Seelig, who, for example, solicited a contribution of 1,000 francs from the Martin Bodmer Foundation in 1937.) Without this intervention, the 6,242.60 francs Robert held in 1934 would have been depleted. That would have put him in danger of being transferred to an institution where his maintenance would cost the canton less. Jakob Walser wrote in 1940 that he had considered recommending a transfer to the Alpstein retirement home but decided against it out of concern that his ward would refuse to cooperate with Alpstein's administration. In 1941, Jakob Walser stepped down as Robert's legal guardian and was replaced by Alfred Hungerbühler, a Teufen supermarket proprietor.[45]

Not writing continued to be a theme in Robert's life. In January 1937, when Lisa was visiting, he told her he hadn't "so much as picked up a pen" (her words) in Herisau, "so as not to cause a stir" (his words). He did at some point try out the writing room Hinrichsen continued to leave at his disposal: he mentioned this room to Seelig that same month, noting that every time he went into it, he would "simply sit there as if nailed to my seat, writing nothing." He had "started to write something but couldn't get working properly among all the lunatics and half-lunatics in the asylum." For Hinrichsen, Robert's continued "failure" to write only confirmed his beliefs; he wrote to Lisa in February 1937 that Robert was "consistently lacking the élan required for creative production," while the patient declared it "unreasonable" that he should be expected to write in the absence of freedom, while confined to an asylum. Hinrichsen had already predicted this outcome two years earlier, when he wrote to Lisa that Robert "displays no inclination to write," an activity that would require "a certain surplus of energy" that Robert, in Hinrichsen's estimation, lacked.[46]

A more sympathetic literary colleague than Hinrichsen entered Robert's life in 1935: critic and editor Carl Seelig. The wealthy scion of a Zurich family, Seelig, who was sixteen years Robert's junior, passionately desired to befriend the writers he admired; his correspondents included Hermann Hesse, Stefan Zweig, Robert Musil, Hermann Broch, and both Heinrich and Thomas Mann. When he reviewed a book, he would mail the author a clipping as a conversation starter. None other than Hesse wrote the foreword to the translation of *Gulliver's Travels* Seelig published in 1925.[47]

When writers began to flee Germany and Austria in the 1930s, Seelig used his networking skills to find income and publishing opportunities for Musil, Alfred Polgar, Joseph Roth, Kurt Tucholsky, and others. And when he heard about a Swiss writer he greatly admired living in exile of a different sort in Herisau, "I felt a need," he wrote, "to do something for his work and for him personally." Seelig had previously corresponded with Robert about a publishing project Seelig had tried to launch in Leipzig before the German mark collapsed in 1923. In 1935, inspired by reading *Jakob von Gunten,* he wrote to Robert in Herisau saying he wished to publish an anthology of Robert's earlier writings.[48]

An entry in Robert's medical record from September 1935 indicates that he discussed this letter with a doctor. His first impulse was to refuse: he was still alive, after all; why should his work be edited by someone else? And if so, why not by someone more distinguished, like Eduard Korrodi? In the end, he replied to Seelig by requesting a 500-franc fee. This exchange led to a meeting that would mark the start of a twenty-year association, with Seelig regularly visiting Robert in Herisau. After each meeting, Seelig wrote down everything he remembered of their conversation—and published his notes in book form after Walser's death. *Walks with Walser* (*Wanderungen mit Robert Walser*) provides an important window into the last two decades of Walser's life.

Seelig's first visit, on July 26, 1936, was arranged in consultation with Lisa. Meeting alone with Hinrichsen on his arrival, Seelig asked how ill Robert was and whether Hinrichsen saw any possibility of his being released. As Seelig reported in a letter he wrote to Lisa that evening, Hinrichsen said a release would not be advisable. Then he sent an attendant to fetch Robert. In *Walks with Walser,* Seelig writes of being "astonished by his appearance":

A round childlike face that looks as if it's been split down the middle by a thunderbolt, with a hint of red in the cheeks, blue eyes, and a short golden mustache. His hair already graying at the temples; his collar frayed, and tie a little crooked; teeth not in the best condition. As Dr. Hinrichsen moves to fasten the top button of Robert's vest, he fends him off: "No, it must remain open!" He speaks in [. . .] the same Bernese dialect he had spoken in his youth in Biel.[49]

Going out together for a long walk, as Seelig proposed, was an inspired choice. Being in motion helped Robert shake off the habitual sluggishness and uncommunicativeness he had developed in the asylum. Even under these perambulatory circumstances, it took a while for him to warm up to his visitor. "Robert's older sister Lisa had warned me that her brother was uncommonly mistrustful," Seelig wrote. "What am I to do? I'm silent. He is silent. Silence is the narrow path on which we approach each other." They left the asylum grounds and set off for the larger town of St. Gallen several miles to the northeast. Seelig reports that Robert let down his guard only after a beer and then a glass of local (Berneck) red wine at a restaurant on the town's main square. Robert started telling stories about his past, retracing his beginnings as a writer in Zurich and the outlines of his career. He discussed some favorite books (Dostoevsky's *Idiot,* Eichendorff's *Memoirs of a Good-for-Nothing,* Gottfried Keller's poetry, Jeremias Gotthelf's *Uli the Farmhand* and *Uli the Tenant Farmer*) and criticized one writer he disliked: Rilke ("bedtime reading for old maids").[50]

Seelig's published account emphasizes his patience and skill at drawing out the reserved older writer. However, he told a different story about their visit in the letter he wrote to Lisa that evening: "Robert was in fact astonishingly unreserved and talkative from the first minute on. We marched to St. Gallen on foot, and on this march he told many stories and asked me many questions. He talked to me about his life, and I told him stories of my travels." (Seelig had undertaken a journey around the world in 1929–1930.) When the topic of the Walser anthology Seelig wanted to publish came up, Seelig told Lisa, Robert said that even "winning a prize of 1,000 or 2,000 francs for this book" wouldn't do him any good: "the time for finding readers for such a book has passed."[51]

Despite these reservations, Robert agreed to Seelig's anthology. *Big Little World* (*Grosse kleine Welt*), a selection of both published and unpublished Walser texts, appeared in 1937 with the Eugen Rentsch publishing house in Zurich. The book's reviewers included Alfred Polgar, who pronounced it "a masterpiece of German prose," and Stefan Zweig, who called Walser a "miniaturist par excellence" and praised his "flawless prose-gems, each as self-contained and pure as a poem."[52]

During the forty-four walks Robert and Seelig took together between 1936 and 1955, Robert cast off the taciturn persona he inhabited within the walls of the asylum. He rediscovered the pleasure of conversing with a younger, deferential writer, as he had enjoyed in Biel during his years of friendship with Emil Schibli. It was much easier for him to open up to Seelig than to Hinrichsen; whereas Seelig approached him with respect and admiration, Hinrichsen's questions revealed his belief in Robert's literary inconsequentiality as demonstrated by his illness. Though Robert could still become standoffish at times, he clearly enjoyed reminiscing in Seelig's company.

Robert's rapport with Seelig—with whom he engaged in long, impassioned conversations about books, history, and his life punctuated with witty, incisive remarks—demonstrates that the portrait of him presented in his medical record was at best incomplete and at worst wildly inaccurate. How was the label "catatonic" ever applied to this tireless storyteller and wanderer who often exhausted his younger companion with his energetic uphill sprints? Robert apparently kept abreast of world news and would debate politics with Seelig, railing, for example, against the United States' 1950 military intervention in Korea. To be sure, Seelig did sometimes find Robert irritable or glum, and even distrustful after Seelig met privately with asylum staff. And Seelig occasionally records Robert sounding paranoid, as when he speaks of "conspiracies to keep out vermin like myself" that force him to remain "on the periphery of bourgeois existence."[53]

But some pretense must have underlain the silent, recalcitrant resistance Robert continued to show Hinrichsen, even at the risk of being defined by his diagnosis. To act crazier than he was by withdrawing into the interior of his own personality was perhaps a form of self-defense against the injustice he felt his confinement to be, even if he lacked the confidence to pursue a life outside the asylum's walls. His taciturnity extended to other staff members as well, even after Hinrichsen's death in 1941. In 1954 a young resident from Waldau, Theodor Spoerri, who was studying "psychiatrically interesting ingenious personalities," came to interview Robert. Dr. Steiner, the psychiatrist now overseeing his care, reported surprise at seeing Robert open up more to this stranger than Steiner was used to seeing, though even with Spoerri he remained "on the whole rather monosyllabic."[54]

Walser's conviction that he had failed as a writer frequently surfaces in his conversations with Seelig. It seemed to him in retrospect that he "possessed too little social instinct," "performed too little for society's sake," and "lost himself in subjectivity," appearing to thumb his nose at the upright citizens he hoped would be his readers. "One should never reject

society," Robert now declared, "one must live in it and either fight for or
against it. That is the error of my novels. They are too whimsical and too
reflexive, their composition often sloppy." He also regretted having written
so openly about his siblings. The longer work of his he remembered with
the most pleasure was his "poetic fantasy" *Jakob von Gunten*.[55]

Robert spoke in a similar vein about his literary career to his post-
Hinrichsen doctors, contending that his novels' modest reception proved
their limited worth. Several times he reiterated that thinking about his
books gave him no pleasure, and once, during a long conversation with
new Herisau director Heinrich Künzler in 1949, he explained that his
years in the asylum had given him time to think clearly about his career. It
seemed to him in retrospect that he hadn't written well enough and was
just one of many justifiably unsuccessful writers. When Künzler asked
whether there was really nothing in all his work he was proud of, he said,
"maybe some of the smaller pieces, the short prose or feuilleton texts."[56]

Robert's medical record continued to report that he "read only old
magazines," "did crossword puzzles," and spoke only of the bureaucracy
of publishing when discussing his career. Meanwhile, his conversations
with Seelig show that he was regularly reading and thinking about
literature—mostly the nineteenth-century authors he'd always loved—and
forming critical aesthetic judgments about what he read. This part of his
inner life remained invisible to the asylum staff.

Perhaps not wanting to be seen as ill, he hid parts of his life from Seelig
too—never mentioning his hallucinations, for example. Early on, when
Seelig asked Robert whether he knew why he was in the asylum, Robert
replied, "Because I'm not a good essayist."[57] Seelig left this remark out of
Walks with Walser; perhaps it didn't serve his purpose to suggest in print
that Robert sometimes toyed with him. A more famous—and likely apocry-
phal—Walser quote that can be traced back to Seelig, though it too appears
nowhere in *Walks with Walser,* is, "I'm not here to write but to be mad."[58]

In all the conversations Seelig recorded, "hearing voices" comes up
only a single time. Describing in 1938 his final years in Bern, Robert told
Seelig he was "plagued by wild dreams—thunder, shouting, strangling
hands at my throat, hallucinatory voices"—from which he "often awoke
screaming." There's no indication that any of the symptoms described
were still ongoing. In short: to his doctors Robert consistently showed
himself as sicker than he was, and to Seelig as healthier. Hinrichsen felt

that Seelig underestimated the severity of Robert's condition; in a 1940 letter, he asked him to stop encouraging Robert to leave the asylum, emphasizing that his patient was still afraid to sleep alone. Seelig's transcripts indicate that he did subsequently stop speaking with Robert about the possibility of his release.[59]

Robert didn't like to discuss his physical ailments with Seelig either, though Seelig was sometimes alerted to them by Robert's doctors. In 1943, Robert was briefly hospitalized when doctors suspected that a cancerous tumor in his lower colon was causing a bowel obstruction. Against the doctors' advice, Robert categorically refused surgery—and eventually the problem resolved itself to the point that a doctor described it as an "intestinal ulcer" (which Robert was also not eager to discuss). On another occasion, he came out for a walk sneezing incessantly after having caught "the flu" (or at least a bad head cold) from a fellow patient. And on Good Friday 1955, just before his seventy-seventh birthday, he insisted on taking a proper walk despite his doctor's warning that his heart was still weak after a recent pulmonary infection severe enough to require hospitalization. Robert remained suspicious of every attempted medical intervention, but Seelig reports that he confessed enjoying one aspect of his hospital stay: being able to just lie there as one's desires "sleep like a child weary from playing."[60]

The walks with Seelig were a little like that, too. Walking and talking, Robert forgot for a while that he was a patient at a psychiatric clinic. Seelig brought him cigarettes and dark chocolate and thought nothing of picking up the tab as they ate and drank all day, including a great deal of alcohol.[61] They sometimes started an outing with breakfast, washed down with beer and coffee, or else drank a quick vermouth as fuel. Lunch invariably included a bottle of wine, and they would refresh themselves after their afternoon peregrinations with more beer or wine.

Despite being permitted to go on outings with Seelig any day of the week, Robert felt uncomfortable doing so on a day other than Sunday. He didn't want to "take a day off" from his work at the asylum. He explained to Seelig that this was out of consideration for his fellow patients, and, another time, said that taking a workday off was an "extravagance" he could no longer afford since he was no longer writing; in any case, he remained attached to his daily routines. A former attendant at the asylum, Josef Wehrle, who was assigned to Walser's ward for fifteen months beginning in 1948, described him as pedantically aware of the schedule (work from 1:30 to 4:30 p.m., bedtime at 7:30) and impatient with staff members who weren't punctual. He also had a ritualistic way of eating his bread: he would tear it into a little heap of pieces about one centimeter across, then dunk half the bread in his coffee, pressing it down with a spoon. After eating all the coffee-soaked bread, he would ask for a second cup of coffee and repeat the process. Seelig, too, observed Robert "dip[ping] his bread crusts in coffee."[62]

There was something comforting about submitting to a routine and external decisions about the shape of a life. "I am convinced," Seelig reports Robert saying, "that Hölderlin was not nearly so unhappy in the last thirty years of his life as the literature professors make him out to be." Walser's medical record shows that he consistently approached seriously and with professionalism every "work therapy" task he was assigned. It seems no task was too slight for him to take pride in performing it well. Along with his fellow patients, he sorted wastepaper (for example, separating the sheet of tinfoil from chocolate bar wrappers to be recycled while the tissue paper was saved to be burned in the asylum's heating system); sorted pieces of twine for the post office; teased wool; picked over dried lentils, beans, or chestnuts; folded and glued together paper bags; tidied rooms; and swept floors. His record notes the skill and speed with which he handled the particularly delicate task of gluing together electrical housings.[63]

When a doctor asked him whether he found paper-bag fabrication tedious, Robert responded, "I always liked doing it, every sort of work is meaningful." He refused, however, all clerical assignments, such as preparing a ledger book for the clinic's office by drawing parallel lines down each page. He also rejected the job of library assistant that came open in 1944 and even refused a task in the asylum's gardens that recalled his work at Waldau. By 1950, his primary work assignments were paper-bag manufacture and cleaning.[64] He preferred work that had nothing to do with his past.

Some of the "therapy" tasks performed by Herisau patients replaced work that otherwise would have been performed by paid staff; and some of their labor, such as manufacturing paper bags, fulfilled the paid contracts the hospital maintained with outside firms. A note in Robert's medical record indicates that the clinic secured a long-term contract for paper-bag production in 1943. Internal clinic discussions considered whether patients should be paid for their labor, given regular pocket money, or rewarded in other ways, such as outings. Notes by Seelig in 1945 and 1950 indicate that Robert received no salary for his work in the asylum. Wehrle confirmed this, saying that Robert had received from Seelig the little pocket money he had and that the clinic paid its working patients only in the form of the coarse tobacco known as "asylum tobacco," along with a weekly pack of cigarette papers.[65]

Frieda Mermet told an interviewer in 1967 that she used to visit Robert around twice a year, almost as often as Seelig did, though no record of these visits exists. (In Robert's medical record, visitors were sometimes noted but often went unidentified.) Once Mermet had retired from Bellelay and moved to Basel to be near her son, the journey to Herisau wasn't as long. Robert would always meet her train. "Then," she said, "we would go to a restaurant for lunch; he enjoyed that enormously. Later we would have coffee and cake, and if I then asked: Herr Walser, would you like anything else? he would ask for a beer, and we would drink a glass of beer, and then he would say: 'Now I have had everything I am fond of.' " Once her son joined her on a visit, and after listening to Robert talk politics as they walked, he remarked: "you could see that he was well informed and had a good understanding of what was going on in the world. Above all he had such healthy views that I asked myself why this man was in the asylum."[66]

Robert was allowed to go for walks on his own and made ample use of this privilege, often setting out between lunch and the start of the afternoon work session to stroll around the surrounding hills. While walking her family's German shepherd as a child, Herisau native Marlies Schoch recalls that she often encountered Robert ("a tall, dark figure") sauntering up and down the Wachtenegg or poking around the ruins of Rosenberg Fortress. The first time they met, he quickly said hello and asked her not to be afraid. He would greet her on subsequent encounters but never say much—at most a remark about the weather. She recalled thinking he didn't seem ill despite the shabbiness of his clothing. Another such report comes from Hans-Rudolf Merz. Encountering Robert on a path near his childhood home in Herisau, he was struck by the strange appearance of this walker, with his waistcoat and umbrella: "His face revealed an awe-inspiring sternness, his eyes seemed to gaze into some far-off expanse."[67]

Throughout his years in Herisau, Robert insisted to clinic personnel that it was impossible for him to write because of the voices he heard. He was convinced they were a foreign, often threatening presence, and this did not change between his arrival in Herisau in 1933 and the end of his life. In 1939, he described the voices as "command[ing] him to strive for success" and making huge demands on him. They would fall silent when he sat down to write but afterward would "start to act angry if they [weren't] satisfied with what he [had] written."[68]

Interviewed by a psychiatrist in 1951, he "answer[ed] in the affirmative when asked whether the voices spoke scornfully about his person and his writing" and vehemently denied the suggestion that these voices might represent his own internalized self-criticism: "No, that has nothing to do with me," he replied, "it comes from the outside."[69] At this point it had been eighteen years since Robert had last submitted anything for publication, but his feelings of failure remained so nakedly immediate as to fill his brain with a racket of self-loathing. The psychotropic medications that might have brought relief were not yet available.

As for other recently developed therapeutic modalities, Hinrichsen had been too conservative to experiment with them, seeing these new techniques as bringing as many dangers as benefits. He made one concession to the times in 1937, when he hired a new doctor who was an expert in insulin therapy; but electroshock therapy and leucotomy remained off-limits in Herisau until Hinrichsen's death in 1941. His successor, Hans Oscar Pfister, who would direct the clinic for two years, quickly added sleep therapy (keeping patients drowsy with narcotics) and electroshock therapy to the clinic's offerings.[70] But Robert's condition, though described as "chronic," was not considered particularly severe, especially as he remained a "quiet" patient, displaying little agitation. So he was never a candidate for these more extreme treatments.

On September 28, 1943, Karl Walser died of heart disease in Bern at the age of sixty-six. He'd been painting a series of four large frescoes for the city's Municipal Theater when illness forced him to interrupt the work with only three paintings completed. After a period of hospitalization, he traveled to a spa in Glion, outside of Montreux, to recover, but his condition quickly worsened and he was rushed back to the hospital, where he died. When newly appointed asylum director Heinrich Künzler informed Robert of his brother's death, Seelig says he gave only a monosyllabic response, apparently displaying no emotion; though he *was* moved, Künzler reported, by the news that his sister Lisa was ill.[71]

Lisa was in fact terminally ill, and three months after Karl's death she sent word through Seelig from the hospital in Bern that she wanted Robert to visit her one last time. When Seelig informed Robert of this request on January 2, 1944, Robert immediately refused, making various excuses, but he kept returning to the subject, obviously distressed. The thought of Lisa, who for years had cared for him, lying helpless in a hospital bed was unbearable. "We'd stand there like two idiots with poor Lisa," he said to Seelig, "maybe we'd even make her cry." It just wasn't something he could make himself do. "Such is human fate," he declared. "I too will have to die alone one day. I'm sorry about Lisa, of course. She was a wonderful sister to me. But her sense of family borders on the pathological, the immature."[72] She died five days later.

Karl's and Lisa's deaths set bureaucratic gears turning in the section of the Teufen Municipal Council responsible for guardianship affairs. As Robert Walser's legal representative, the council had a financial interest in seeing to it that his account was credited with an appropriate share of whatever he inherited from his late siblings. To verify this, the office began to look more closely into the details of Karl's and Lisa's finances than Oscar, now living in Lugano, found appropriate. He sought to end this bureaucratic prying by petitioning to have Robert's incompetence revoked, arguing that his brother had always been of sound mind.

Oscar's petition was considered by the council in Teufen. But changing Robert's legal status required an attestation from the clinic that his condition had improved, which Künzler was unwilling to provide, finding Robert's condition the same as when he first came to Herisau. Seelig offered a solution to the impasse by volunteering to take over as Robert's legal guardian and personally guaranteeing his future solvency. The council agreed, and in March 1945 a contract was signed regulating the division of Karl's estate, with a flat sum of 3,000 francs (roughly $15,200 in today's dollars) going to Robert. That same month, he also received 4,035.80 francs from Lisa's estate.[73] With these inheritances, along with the funds previously raised by Jakob Walser and Seelig, Robert was now financially secure.

Like so much in Robert's institutionalized life, the change of guardian happened against his will. A note from Künzler to Oscar on May 22, 1944—two months after the new arrangements were finalized—remarks, "Your brother does not wish to have another guardian and specifically not

Mr. Seelig."[74] Inclined toward suspicion in the best of times, Robert did not trust Seelig nearly as fully as Seelig's portrait of their relationship implies. After Seelig's essay on the occasion of Robert's sixtieth birthday appeared in *Neue Zürcher Zeitung*, Robert told a doctor Seelig had fabricated quotations attributed to him and sarcastically referred to Seelig as "clairvoyant."[75]

Three days after assuming Robert's guardianship, Seelig visited him. Seelig's account of their conversation notes only that Robert—"unshaven, with gray stubble on his sullen face"—was engaged in a "silent struggle to overcome his suspicion because of my conference with the doctor [that morning]." The only mention anywhere in *Walks with Walser* that Seelig had become Robert's guardian in 1944 comes in a 1953 entry noting that Seelig had been referenced in an *Appenzeller Zeitung* article as Walser's "legal guardian and only friend." He feared Robert would react with fresh distrust and reports being relieved when he didn't. But for all these suspicions, and despite Robert once explaining to a doctor that Seelig was a "colleague" rather than a "friend," he did say in 1946 that he enjoyed Seelig's visits and their literary conversations.[76]

Over their two decades of walking together, Robert Walser and Carl Seelig crisscrossed much of the territory between Herisau and Lake Constance. They walked in all weathers, with Robert usually carrying his big umbrella and never wearing an overcoat though he typically had a hat. They visited (and drank in) many of the towns scattered across Canton Appenzell Ausserrhoden, and some neighboring cantons as well: Appenzell Innerrhoden and St. Gallen. Some of their outings involved trains or post buses, but many were on foot, with Robert leading the way at a breakneck pace. Only after he had reached his mid-seventies could he be prevailed upon to slow down, as on July 17, 1955, when he was beset with such severe cramps in both legs that he suggested—completely out of character—that they cut short their walk and take a bus or train home.[77]

Seelig's book is the only surviving record of their peregrinations. And so Robert Walser's last great walk story was written not by but about him. Perhaps the most memorable outing the two of them undertook was their June 1, 1942, trip to the Säntis, the Alpine peak Robert saw in the distance from the asylum grounds. Being walkers rather than mountain climbers, they took the new aerial tramway from Schwägalp, enjoying the ten-minute ascent that swept them up to the summit eighty-two hundred feet above sea level. "We find the ride wonderfully dramatic," Seelig reports. "Pieces of ice and snow begin to crash into the windows like a wild hailstorm. When we press our noses to the cold glass, we see snow-covered limestone crags looming toward us like threatening cyclopean breasts."[78] They visited the weather station, whose keeper invited them into his parlor to warm up, then took some refreshment in a tavern perched high on the mountaintop, peering across the peaks to Italy, Austria, Germany, and France and surveying the Appenzell countryside far below.

Beyond Seelig's activity as Robert's guardian and walking companion, he was of service in another way: shepherding new collections of Walser's writings into print. Besides publishing *Big Little World* in 1937, Seelig also arranged for a reprint edition of *The Assistant* that appeared in 1936 with a small publishing house in St. Gallen, Verlag der Schweizer Bücherfreunde (Swiss Bibliophiles Publishing), bringing in 200 francs (around $1,600 in today's dollars). This was supplemented by an additional 100 francs from the Swiss Writers' Association, intended as an advance against the fee for the translation of the book into French, which fell through.[79] Seelig also established a bank account at the Schweizerische Kreditanstalt for Robert's professional earnings.

In 1944, the year Seelig became Robert's guardian, he oversaw the publication of four new collections of Walser's work. *The Walk* was reprinted by Bühl in Herrliberg-Zurich, and *Poems* (with Karl's illustrations) by Benno Schwabe & Co. in Basel with a new foreword by Seelig full of Walser quotations about poetry-writing. Two slender anthologies followed, containing both previously published and unpublished texts. *Quiet Joys (Stille Freuden)* appeared with Vereinigung Oltner Bücherfreunde (Association of Olten Bibliophiles), which published it in time for Christmas in both luxury and standard editions. And Benno Schwabe & Co. published a book of aphorisms edited by Seelig titled *On the Happiness of Unhappiness and Poverty (Vom Glück des Unglücks und der Armut)*, subtitled "The Most Beautiful Contemplative Passages from Walser's Books: Quiet Wisdom of a True Poet." Seelig's foreword to this book—another Christmas volume—dubs its author a "virtuoso of poverty" who "lives uncompromisingly on the periphery of bourgeois existence," the latter phrase a quote Seelig attributes to Robert in *Walks with Walser*. The "aphorisms" themselves were all excerpted from longer texts. The book ended with Jakob von Gunten's declaration, "I can only breathe in the lower regions."

This spate of publications reflected a newly romanticized literary identity curated by Seelig. We don't know whether Robert approved these book projects; as Robert's legal guardian, Seelig was able to sign contracts in his name. In any case, Seelig did more than anyone else during Walser's lifetime to ensure that his name and work endured in Switzerland's literary consciousness. Starting in the late 1930s, Seelig authored approximately forty newspaper articles on Walser, making a point of marking round birthdays with a flurry of publications. And between 1953 and 1961, he published a five-volume edition of Walser's selected prose writings with the Holle and Helmut Kossodo publishing houses in Geneva. Even if an element of self-interest motivated these projects—lifting up his own reputation along with Walser's—Seelig was largely responsible for Walser enjoying belated literary recognition in his old age.[80]

To be sure, Seelig was not the only one promoting Walser's work. Walter Muschg included *The Walk* in an anthology in 1939, and Otto Zinniker published the monograph *Robert Walser the Poet,* yet another romanticized portrait of Walser, in 1947. But it was above all thanks to Seelig's efforts that publishing income began to flow into Robert's bank account again. Seelig also collected overdue royalties from existing contracts with other publishers. Robert received fees totaling 720.50 francs (around $3,600 in today's dollars) in 1944, including 300 francs for the reprint of *The Walk* and 343 for the book of aphorisms. In Seelig, Robert finally found the literary agent he'd so desperately desired during his Biel years. Seelig's business acumen and literary-social savoir faire demonstrated there was still a place for books by Robert Walser in the literary marketplace, even for individual stories. "The Battle of Sempach" (1908) was reprinted in 1950 as a pamphlet by Tschudy in St. Gallen. Thanks to this new income, more than 10,000 francs (roughly $43,000 in today's dollars) would remain in Robert's accounts at the time of his death.[81]

Nonetheless, Robert's belief that he had failed as a writer appeared to persist. Whenever his doctors mentioned new editions or appreciations of his work—or, in 1942, an invitation to appear at an event in his honor in Bern—he brushed off the news as if it held no interest for him. His typical response was a taciturn "*So, so!*" ("I see" or "You don't say"); he gave the same response to Seelig when informed in 1955 that a young English poet named Christopher Middleton had begun to translate his work.[82]

While *Walks with Walser,* published the year after Walser's death in 1956, remains a valuable source of stories about Walser's life (and is quoted from in nearly every chapter of this biography), the image of Walser that Seelig presents is carefully controlled and to some extent manufactured. Earlier versions of at least one Seelig encounter with Robert printed in *Neue Zürcher Zeitung* contained lines of purported dialogue cribbed from published Walser stories. Such quotations do not figure in the book itself without attribution, but a comparison of Seelig's accounts of his conversations with Robert in the book to the letters he wrote to Lisa after their walks reveals notable differences. Following Walser's death, Seelig emphasized Robert's resignation and his renunciation of writing, raising Seelig's profile as a channeler of his thoughts.[83]

Seelig reports, for example, that in 1939 Robert told him it would be "absurd and brutal" to expect him to write while still a patient in the asylum: "The only basis on which a writer can produce is freedom. As long as this condition remains unmet, I will refuse to write ever again." Decades later, several witnesses emerged who claimed they did in fact see Walser writing in the 1940s, years after he rejected Hinrichsen's offer of a private room and pointedly turned his back on literary work. Otto Knellwolf, who staffed the post office counter in Herisau for a decade beginning in 1942, reported in a 2001 interview that "a tall man dressed in dark clothing" used to come into the post office, especially during the winter months, sometimes spending as much as an hour or two standing at one of the two writing areas for customers, which were supplied with ink, pens, and a little box of deposit slips. Knellwolf remembered the man well because "he came often and often stayed for a long time," occasionally buying a stamp and mailing a letter. He said the visitor sometimes wrote on the backs of the deposit slips. Once, the post office staff decided to inspect the contents of the wastepaper basket to see what the visitor had left behind and found "crumpled white scraps of paper on which something had been scribbled, illegible." Knellwolf knew the visitor was a patient in the clinic because one of the letter carriers recognized him, but he wouldn't learn he was a celebrated author until 1962, when a fountain in Robert and Karl Walser's honor was unveiled in Herisau.[84]

According to two former staff members, Robert wrote in the asylum as well, but not in the special room set aside for him. He did his writing standing up at a window ledge after meals. Former attendant Wehrle, interviewed in 1998, reported that Walser would often rise while others were still eating, roll a cigarette, lay it to one side until everyone else finished, and sometimes take out a piece of paper and start writing. He would turn his back to the dining tables and, if anyone approached, immediately hide what he was doing. Walser kept a stash of slips of paper in his vest pocket, Wehrle said, along with a very short pencil. He would break his pencils into three pieces (knives and scissors were not allowed on the ward) and sharpen the point with sheets of glass paper (similar to emery paper) supplied by patients who worked in the wood shop. Jochen Greven reports that when writer Peter Hamm visited Herisau to collect materials for a 1980 book, he met a retired clinic attendant (Wehrle?) who gave him a fair copy of an unpublished manuscript he claimed to have received as a gift from Walser. Margrit Meier, a psychiatric nurse who worked in Herisau between 1946 and 1965, recalled in 2001 that Robert often stood at the window, writing; she never saw anything he wrote.[85]

In any case, continuing to write privately, subtracting this activity from the general economy of literary production, was consistent with the way Walser had lived up to and continuing into his time in the institution. Perhaps Otto Hinrichsen's death allowed him to feel less scrutinized in his surreptitious return to his life's work, which he kept hidden from Seelig as well. Standing up at a windowsill in full view and writing on slips of paper in miniscule script legible only to himself was a way to write publicly in secret. Like the final novel he wrote in Bern, this writing was for himself alone. Whether he destroyed these secret manuscripts or whether they met some other fate is unknown.

The few letters Robert wrote during his years in Herisau—to Lisa, Fanny, and Frieda Mermet—were much shorter and to the point than his earlier ones. He thanked them for gifts and visits. Many letters simply went unanswered. Even when Hermann Hesse wrote to him in 1943, he did not write back. Aside from a handful of letters and a brief, dutiful biographical note written for inclusion in his medical record in 1946, he indulged in one last form of writerly activity: solving crossword puzzles. According to Wehrle, the clinic library contained bound volumes of old magazines, and Robert made his way through tome after tome, solving each of the puzzles.

A handful of hand-drawn crosswords and acrostics was found among his surviving papers.[86]

There is no such thing as an uneventful year from the perspective of the person living it, even when the life in question appears from the outside relatively uniform. An entire book could be devoted to Robert Walser's asylum years, which constitute a full third of his lifetime. In Herisau, Robert experienced at a distance—through newspaper and radio reports—the vast destruction wrought throughout Europe and other parts of the world as the scourge of National Socialism spread and grew, touching even neutral Switzerland. This time Robert wasn't among the Swiss men called up to defend the border, but he must have been affected by the nationwide rationing and the brutal headlines proclaiming the destruction of the German cities he'd once loved along with the crumbling of that nation's moral and cultural fabric. In conversations with Seelig, who sometimes visited him in uniform, Robert would reminisce about those early-twentieth-century years when Berlin seemed to lie at the very heart of all artistic and cultural achievement. "My world was shattered by the Nazis," he told Seelig. "The newspapers I wrote for are gone; their editors have been chased away or are dead. And so, I've become practically a fossil."[87]

The heart disease that felled Robert's brother Karl may have run in the family. Dr. Steiner had warned Robert against overtaxing himself after the severe lung infection he suffered in March 1955. Steiner had even informed Seelig that Robert's heart was weak now, emphasizing that strenuous exercise could put him at risk of a heart attack.[88] This information seemed of no interest to Robert himself. He was seventy-seven years old in 1955; why should it surprise anyone if a seventy-seven-year-old's heart was weak? He had met Seelig at the train station as usual that April, despite Steiner's overcautious carping, and then the two of them took a leisurely stroll up to the nearby Rosenberg ruins because Seelig, too, was acting solicitous now.

He continued taking walks on his own, of course—short ones after lunch on weekdays, sometimes just a stroll around the clinic grounds or a cigarette standing in the garden, and went for longer Sunday rambles on the hills ringing the town. His habitual walk led north from the asylum, across the hills, and then down into the lip of the valley. He descended to a footbridge that crossed the railroad tracks, then turned back uphill, steeply now, into the little wood called Rosenwald crowning the Wachtenegg, after which a brief dip into a mountain valley marked the crossing to the Rosenberg proper. Then he would circle down into Herisau itself, walking through the town and back up the hill on the other side to return to the asylum. The landscape here, with its huge sky and green rolling hills on all sides, their colors constantly changing with the seasons and weather, offered a lovely panorama: gentle, unassuming, quietly radiant. On clear days when he crested the peak of the Wachtenegg and emerged into the clearing to the east, he would see, far in the distance, the waters of Lake Constance glimmering like a gateway to another world.

When his weak heart finally caught up with him—giving out quite suddenly in the middle of his habitual after-lunch stroll on Christmas Day, 1956—the shock of it knocked him over backward. He'd walked as usual up the Wachtenegg, now blanketed in snow, his overcoat unbuttoned and swinging free, vest pockets stuffed with letters and pay stubs.[89] He'd just emerged from the woods and was descending the steep slope toward the farmhouse on the far side of the hill, stamping the soles of his heavy boots into the ground for traction, when he stopped short and fell. He died gazing up at the sky, one hand resting on his abdomen, the other outstretched, clutching a handful of snow.

ROBERT WALSER'S BODY WAS FOUND by two boys out sledding that Christmas afternoon. His hat lay upside-down in the snow some six feet up the hill behind him. At first, thirteen-year-old Erwin Brugger thought, "Here's another one who drank too much." The boys were afraid to touch or address the man lying there, so they raced back down the slope to hammer at the door of the Manser farm. A visitor to the farm who'd arrived not long before with her Appenzeller Sennenhund said the dog had grown agitated as they arrived, barking and trying to slip its collar to dash uphill. The Mansers sent the boys to a neighbor who had a telephone. The police came quickly, documented the scene with a camera, loaded the body onto a wooden sled, and set off again. A local physician placed the time of death between 1:30 and 2:00 p.m.[1]

Decades later, as the Robert Walser mystique began to crystallize, these striking police photographs became part of his legend. One, taken from above by examining magistrate Kurt Giezendanner, reveals a line of dark footprints leading down to where the body lies cradled in snow; the wanderer's final footprints end some distance away, as if the recumbent figure had somehow floated the last few yards.

Robert Walser's solitary death in the snow recalled the episode in his first novel, *The Tanners,* when Simon Tanner happens upon the body of young Sebastian, frozen to death in the snowy woods with a sheaf of poems in his pocket. Like Sebastian, Walser left behind a literary estate, albeit a more mysterious one: his cache of tiny manuscripts. Carl Seelig mythologized this legacy when he reproduced a microscript in the October 1957 issue of the journal *Du,* describing the tiny pencil script as an "indecipherable secret code of the writer's own invention that he employed in the 1920s and later at the beginning of his mental illness."[2] This mode of writing, Seelig wrote, "can only be interpreted as a fearful retreat from the public eye and a calligraphically bewitching camouflage that he used to conceal his thoughts from the public." One small section of the image was enlarged to highlight the script's illegibility.

Most of the 526 microscripts that survive today date from the years 1924–1928, with some written as late as 1933. A stack of them was found in a shoebox when Lisa collected Robert's effects from the Luisenstrasse apartment after his precipitous admission to Waldau. She sent the contents of this box, along with all the other manuscripts and newspaper clippings in her possession, to Seelig in 1937. When he asked her about the "tiny writing" in the pencil manuscripts, she replied that Walser's handwriting in his letters to her had shrunk over the years, but she believed this "[wasn't] actually writing." In 1957, Seelig received another bundle of Walser papers—stashed in yet another shoebox—from psychiatrist Hans Steiner in Herisau; it's unknown what exactly this bundle contained, but in any case the microscripts Walser wrote at Waldau came into Seelig's possession at some point.[3]

After publishing the microscript facsimile in *Du,* Seelig received a letter from a doctoral student in Cologne, Jochen Greven, who was writing the first German-language dissertation on Robert Walser's work. Studying the enlarged portion of the microscript reproduced in the magazine, Greven had found it legible, which he demonstrated by transcribing part of the text. Seelig did not answer this letter. Instead, several weeks after receiving it, he added a provision to his will, stipulating that after his death, all of Robert Walser's manuscripts were to be burned "at his [Walser's] request." "It is my will," he added, "that none of them be published." What was he afraid these manuscripts might contain?[4]

Seelig had consistently tried to exercise control over both Walser's image and his person. According to Greven, Seelig refused to allow Joseph Breitbach and Theodor Heuss to visit Walser in Herisau in the late 1940s (though he accepted contributions from both for Walser's financial support). Seelig also became incensed after Theodor Spoerri's visit in 1954 and prevailed upon the clinic's administration to inform Spoerri that follow-up visits were out of the question. Surrendering to Seelig's control was the price Walser paid for his support.[5]

In the years following Walser's death, Seelig began to collect information about his life and work, writing to whomever he could think of who'd known him. He was preparing to write Walser's biography, modeled, perhaps, on the Albert Einstein biography Seelig had published in 1954. In early 1962, he wrote to Greven that the Tschudy publishing house in St. Gallen would publish the first volume of his Walser biography that fall, with the second volume appearing in 1964. Less than a week after sending this letter, Seelig tried to leap onto a moving tram at Bellevue in Zurich, slipped, and was fatally injured. He survived his ward by little more than five years.[6]

Walser's unpublished manuscripts were not destroyed. The executor of Seelig's will, Elio Fröhlich, was also Max Brod's lawyer and as such already familiar with the genre of the immolation request. The manuscripts weren't Seelig's to burn in any case; they were the property of Fanny, who became Robert's last surviving heir after Oscar's death in 1959. Before he died, Seelig had shepherded a five-volume collection of selected works by Walser into print: *Prose Writings*, published by the Holle and Kossodo publishing houses. This was followed by a twelve-volume *Collected Works* (Kossodo) edited by Greven between 1966 and 1975. And in 1978, in honor of Walser's one-hundredth birthday, the major German publisher Suhrkamp issued a revised edition of *Collected Works* as a softcover boxed set, marking Walser's belated entry into the German-language canon.

In 1967, Fröhlich engaged Greven to catalogue Walser's microscripts. The first of these to appear in book form, in 1972, were Greven's transcription of the "Felix Scenes" and his cotranscription with Martin Jürgens of the novel *The Robber*. Another six volumes' worth of microscripts—all the texts for which no published or fair copies survive—were transcribed by Bernhard Echte and Werner Morlang and published between 1985 and 2000. The remaining microscripts are currently being transcribed and published as part of a new critical edition, the *Kritische Robert Walser-Ausgabe,* in progress since 2008. A second new edition—the *Berner Ausgabe*—launched in 2018 with a three-volume edition of Walser's complete letters. In short, the work of Robert Walser is still being investigated, discovered, and presented to the reading public.[7]

The unpublished biographical materials Seelig gathered were preserved by the Carl Seelig Foundation in Zurich (created and overseen by Fröhlich) at the behest of Fanny Hegi-Walser. After her death in 1972, the foundation also became the first institutional home of the Robert Walser Archive. The archive is now part of the Robert Walser Center in Bern, with the manuscripts themselves housed in the Swiss National Library. Much of Seelig's research found its way into Robert Mächler's 1966 biography, *The Life of Robert Walser,* as well as the present book.

A solitary death in the snow, mysterious penciled runes, and decades of institutionalized seclusion combined to produce a romantic image of Robert Walser as a writer who turned his back on the world of human activity. Since many of his texts make a point of asserting their author's unknowability, it was perhaps inevitable that the afterlife of his work would involve, among other things, an insistence on his mysteriousness, his inscrutability.

The idea of the literary hero, the romantic loner suffering for the sake of Art, remains seductive. Robert Walser loved the notion too and wrote about many such figures in his stories, essays, poems, and novels. But his work cannot be reduced to his championing of outsiders and outsiderdom. The marginality he celebrates is that of secretly magnificent complexities hiding in plain sight all around us under the guise of the ordinary and small. Studying Walser's life and work, I discovered that his own outsider status was less the product of volition and more a corner he found himself painted into again and again. But did this not, in the end, serve him as an artist? Could his great short prose of the 1920s have been written without the endless frustrations and agony of failure? Like so many questions about Robert Walser's life, these, too, must go unanswered.

Appendix: Robert Walser's Known Addresses

Each residential address is given along with the dates Walser was formally registered at that address, where known; otherwise, the information is based on return addresses in letters and other documents. There are occasional overlaps as well as gaps. Roman numerals indicate floor number, where known, European-style, counting only the stories above the ground floor.

Biel

Dufourstrasse 3 / (born) April 15, 1878
Nidaugasse 36 / autumn 1879–winter 1884/1885
Brühlstrasse 69c / 1889
Zentralstrasse 40 / early 1890s
Zentralstrasse 52 / 1893–March 1895

Basel

Bäumleingasse 10 / April 1, 1895
Theaterstrasse 22 / June 8, 1895–August 26, 1895

Stuttgart

Gerbergasse 2a/2b / August 1895–September 1896

Zurich

Zeughausstrasse 3 / September 30, 1896–April 5, 1897
Zeltweg 64/II / March 1897
Zurlindenstrasse 49/I / April 5, 1897–mid-October 1897
Neumarkt 3/V / October 14, 1897–November 23, 1897
Ämtlerstrasse 106 / December 13, 1897
Lindenbachstrasse 9 / March 1, 1898
Hinterbergstrasse 31 / March 19, 1898–early June 1898
Grossmünsterplatz 6 / June 1, 1898–July 1898
Schrägweg 93 / July 25, 1898
Rothstrasse 22 / August 17, 1898
Vogelsangweg 1 / September 14, 1898
Vogelsangweg 1 / October 25, 1898–January 1, 1899

Thun

Obere Hauptgasse 39/I / January 28, 1899–autumn 1899

Solothurn

Gurzelngasse 34 / October 13, 1899–May 14, 1900

Munich

Unteranger 18/II / November 28, 1900–early December 1900
Amalienstrasse 48/II / early December 1900
Oberanger 38/IV / July 3, 1901–August 6, 1901
Schellingstrasse 43/II / September 14, 1901–October 14, 1901

Zurich

Trittligasse 6 / November 1901

Berlin

Pestalozzistrasse 92a/II / from around New Year's until late January 1902

Täuffelen

Täuffelen schoolhouse / February 1902–April 1902

Zurich

Spiegelgasse 23/II / May 1902–February 1903

Winterthur

Obergasse 17 / March 1903

Zurich

Froschaugasse 18/II / July 1903

Wädenswil

Villa zum Abendstern / July 28, 1903–January 5, 1904

Zurich

Froschaugasse 18/II / January 1904

Trittligasse 6 / January 1904–May 1904
Frankengasse 24/III / June 1904
Schipfe 43/V / July 1904—March 1905

Biel

Quellgasse 17 / March 1905

Berlin

Kaiser-Friedrich-Strasse 70 / March 1905–May 1905

Zurich

Neumarkt 3/V / June 1905–presumably until July/August 1905

Berlin

Kaiser-Friedrich-Strasse 70/IV / presumably July/August 1905

Dambrau (Dąbrowa, Opole Voivodeship, Poland)

Dambrau Castle / October 1905–late December 1905

Berlin

Kaiser-Friedrich-Strasse 70/IV / late December 1905–summer 1907
Wilmersdorfer Strasse 141 / rear building IV / late 1907
Schöneberger Ufer 40 / April 1908–early September 1908
Kaiserdamm 96 / September 1908
Kurfürstendamm 29 / spring 1910
Spandauerberg 1 / summer 1910–early 1913
Hohenzollernstrasse 14 / mid-January 1913–mid-February 1913

Bellelay

Schoolhouse, Bellelay Asylum / February 1913–April 1913

Biel

Hotel Blaues Kreuz, Unterer Quai / April 1913–December 30, 1920

Bern

Murifeldweg 14 / January 4, 1921
Manuelstrasse 72 / November 8, 1921

Murifeldweg 3/IV / February 1, 1922
Kramgasse 19/IV / April 1, 1922
Fellenbergstrasse 10 / May 3, 1924
Gerechtigkeitsgasse 51/III / November 3, 1924
Junkerngasse 29/III / December 2, 1924
Thunstrasse 21/I / February 2, 1925
Gerechtigkeitsgasse 29/III / April 1, 1925
Thunstrasse 20/III / September 1, 1925
Elfenauweg 41/I / December 2, 1925
Junkerngasse 26/II / May 1, 1926
Gerechtigkeitsgasse 50/III / June 1, 1926
Kramgasse 32/II / August 2, 1926
Luisenstrasse 14/III / August 17, 1926–January 24, 1929

Notes

Abbreviations

AdB   Robert Walser, *Aus dem Bleistiftgebiet,* edited by Bernhard Echte and Werner Morlang, 6 vols. (Frankfurt am Main: Suhrkamp, 1985–2000).

BA   Robert Walser, *Werke (Berner Ausgabe),* edited by Lucas Marco Gisi, Reto Sorg, Peter Stocker, and Peter Utz, vols. 1–3, *Briefe,* edited by Peter Stocker and Bernhard Echte with Peter Utz and Thomas Binder (Berlin: Suhrkamp, 2018–).

KWA   Robert Walser, *Kritische Ausgabe sämtlicher Drucke und Manuskripte,* edited by Wolfram Groddeck and Barbara von Reibnitz (Frankfurt am Main: Stroemfeld, Schwabe, 2008–)

RWA   Robert Walser-Archiv, Robert Walser Center, Bern.

SW   Robert Walser, *Sämtliche Werke in Einzelausgaben,* edited by Jochen Greven, 20 vols. (Zurich: Suhrkamp, 1985–1986).

Introduction

1. W. G. Sebald, "Le promeneur solitaire: On Robert Walser," in *A Place in the Country,* trans. Jo Catling (New York: Random House, 2013), 125–64, 139; Robert Walser, "A Little Ramble," translated by Tom Whalen, in *Selected Stories,* trans. Christopher Middleton and others (New York: Farrar, Straus & Giroux, 1982), 30–31, 31.

2. Max Brod, "Kafka liest Walser," in *Über Robert Walser,* vol. 1, ed. Katharina Kerr (Frankfurt am Main: Suhrkamp, 1978), 85–86.

3. Robert Walser, "Swine," in *Microscripts,* 2nd ed., trans. Susan Bernofsky (New York: New Directions/Christine Burgin, 2012), 35–36.

4. Robert Walser, "There exist drunken geniuses . . ." and "All those who like to laugh while crying . . . ," in *Masquerade and Other Stories,* trans. Susan Bernofsky (Baltimore: Johns Hopkins University Press, 1990), 171–75.

5. Robert Walser, "Das Kind," SW 8:74–79, 78; Kay Redfield Jamison, *Robert Lowell: Setting the River on Fire, A Study of Genius, Mania, and Character* (New York: Knopf, 2017), 7.

6. "Ich-Buch" can also be translated as "first-person narrative." From "Eine Art Geschichte," translated by Christopher Middleton and quoted in Walser, *Selected Stories,* xi.

7. Catherine Sauvat, *Robert Walser* (Paris: Plon, 1989); this French-language work appeared in German as *Vergessene Weiten: Biographie zu Robert Walser,* trans. Helmut Kossodo (Zurich: Bruckner & Thünker, 1993).

8. BA 2:289–91; Robert Walser, "Fritz Kocher's Essays," in *A Schoolboy's Diary,* trans. Damion Searls (New York: NYRB Classics, 2013), 13.

9. Bernhard Echte, ed., *Robert Walser: Sein Leben in Bildern und Texten* (Frankfurt am Main: Suhrkamp, 2008). Echte's book in turn draws on materials earlier collected in Elio Fröhlich and Peter Hamm, eds., *Robert Walser: Leben und Werk in Daten und Bildern* (Frankfurt am Main: Insel, 1980).

Chapter 1. Behind the Toy Shop (1878–1894)

1. Robert Walser, "Die Kindheit," SW 20:296–99, 296–97; Walser, *The Tanners*, trans. Susan Bernofsky (New York: New Directions, 2009), 147–48.
2. Letter from Lina Marty-Hauenstein to Carl Seelig, June 30, 1943, RWA, Nachlass Carl Seelig, B-04: Robert Walser.
3. Robert Walser, "Tagebuchblatt," SW 16:400–401, 401; letter from Lina Marty-Hauenstein to *Neue Zürcher Zeitung*, April 18, 1938, RWA, Nachlass Carl Seelig, B-04: Robert Walser.
4. Her name is sometimes spelled "Elise" in extant documents. It was customary in Switzerland for a woman's surname to be appended to her husband's upon marriage.
5. Robert Walser, "Das Bild des Vaters," SW 7:152–72, 154, 162.
6. Elisa Walser revealed the cause of her father's early death in a letter to her son Hermann in 1889, when she herself had contracted the same illness—from which she recovered. Letter reproduced in D[orothea]. E[lisabeth]. Walser, *Elise Walser-Marti, Die Mutter von Robert Walser* (self-published brochure, 1976), 6–7, 9 (no printed page numbers; hereafter, numbering is per the author of the present book). Dorothea Elisabeth Walser, the great-granddaughter of Adolf Walser's brother Jakob, gathered stories circulating in the extended Walser family as well as doing original research for her self-published pamphlets on family history. It was her father who had the Walser family tree researched and drawn up in 1959. D. E. Walser, "Vorwort," in *Robert Walser: Aus seiner Familie* (self-published brochure, no page numbers, 1977); Kopulationsbescheinigung (marriage certificate), RWA, Sammlung Robert Walser, E: Sammlung Adolf und Elisa Walser.
7. Bernhard Echte, *Walsers Kindheit und Jugend in Biel: Ein biographischer Essay* (Wädenswil: Nimbus, 2002), 15–16; D. E. Walser, *Elise Walser-Marti*, 9.
8. Letter from Claire Zahler to Carl Seelig, October 29, 1953, RWA, Nachlass Carl Seelig, B-04: Robert Walser.
9. Robert Walser, "Ein Dichter," SW 16:216–19, 216; Gabriel Walser, *Neue Appenzeller Chronick oder Beschreibung des Cantons Appenzell* (St. Gallen: Ruprecht Weniger, 1740), quoted in Echte, ed., *Robert Walser*, 11; Johann Baptist Homann, *Atlas novus Reipublicae Helveticae* (Noribergae: [Sumptibus Homannianis heredibus], 1769).
10. Johann Ulrich Walser, *Das Ladenbüchlein im Lande Utopia* and *Sonnenklarer Beweis, daß der Hundt-Radowsky der in der Offenbarung Johannis beschriebene Antichrist oder das Tier aus dem Abgrund mit sieben Häuptern und zehn Hörnern sei*, both quoted in Echte, ed., *Robert Walser*, 12.
11. Walser, *The Tanners*, 238; Walser, "Parisian Newspapers," translated by Tom Whalen and Carol Gehrig, in Walser, *Selected Stories*, 141.
12. "Biel," *INSA: Inventar der neueren Schweizer Architektur* 3 (1982): 27–126, 33; Zukunftstadt (City of the future), Zukunftsstrasse (Future Street), Phantasiestrasse (Imagination Street).

13. Echte, ed., *Robert Walser,* 18.
14. Walser, "Das Bild des Vaters," SW 7:156.
15. D. E. Walser, *Elise Walser-Marti,* 11. The shop at Nidaustrasse 21 was joined at the rear to their home at Schulgasse 3; both buildings were torn down in 1926. Echte, *Walsers Kindheit und Jugend,* 26–27.
16. Robert Walser, "Felix-Szenen," AdB 3:153–91, 154.
17. Robert Walser, "Fidelio," SW 17:210–13, 211; Walser, "Felix-Szenen," AdB 3:154, 165–66.
18. Letter from Marie Schaetzle-Ehrensperger to Carl Seelig, October 18, 1953, RWA, Nachlass Carl Seelig, B-04: Robert Walser.
19. Walser, *The Tanners,* 60.
20. Walser, "Felix-Szenen," AdB 3:171.
21. BA 2:328.
22. Bernhard Echte gives the cause of young Adolf's death as "consumption"; Dorothea Elisabeth Walser describes it as "the result of a minor injury," D. E. Walser, *Elise Walser-Marti,* 10. According to the death notice published by the family at the time, he died "after a three-month painful illness." Reproduced in Echte, *Walsers Kindheit und Jugend,* 33; Robert Walser, "Wenn du kannst, Herrin meines Herzens, so verzeih mir, dass ich gestern abend Rehpfeffer aß . . . ," AdB 1:256–59, 257; Walser, "Fidelio," SW 17:211; letter from Elisa Walser-Marti to her niece Elise, January 6, 1885, RWA, Sammlung Robert Walser, E: Sammlung Adolf und Elisa Walser.
23. Letter from Lina Marty-Hauenstein to *Neue Zürcher Zeitung,* April 18, 1938.
24. Walser, *The Tanners,* 147.
25. Walser, "Das Bild des Vaters," SW 7:154.
26. Hermann's studies were facilitated by a loan from a school principal in nearby Grenchen. Robert Mächler, *Das Leben Robert Walsers,* 2nd ed. (Frankfurt am Main: Suhrkamp, 2003), 23; letter from Elisa Walser to Hermann Walser, 1889, quoted in D. E. Walser, *Elise Walser-Marti,* 11–13.
27. Robert Walser, "Der Handelsmann," SW 16:180–84, 181.
28. Walser, "Das Bild des Vaters," SW 7:160, 163.
29. Walser, "Das Bild des Vaters," SW 7:168–69.
30. Echte, *Walsers Kindheit und Jugend,* 41.
31. Robert Walser, *The Assistant,* trans. Susan Bernofsky (New York: New Directions, 2007), 101–2.
32. Walser, "Felix-Szenen," AdB 3:179.
33. Todesanzeige (death notice) Elise Walser née Marti, October 22, 1894, RWA, Sammlung Robert Walser, E: Sammlung Adolf und Elisa Walser; BA 1:20; "Heditäre Belastung," Krankengeschichte Robert Walser, Heil- und Pflegeanstalt Herisau, StAAR: Pa.057-07. The note reads, "reportedly apoplectic five years long."

Chapter 2. From the Bank to the Stage (1885–1896)

1. Robert Mächler, *Das Leben Robert Walsers,* 25.
2. Walser, *The Tanners,* 142; Walser, "Der Poet," SW 16:219–22, 219; Walser, "Der junge Dichter," SW 16:213–16, 214; Echte, ed., *Robert Walser,* 31.
3. Robert Walser, "Für das Lebensbild des Kaisers Wilhelm . . . ," AdB 5:36–40, 38; Walser, *The Tanners,* 143.

4. Robert Walser, "Grausame Bräuche, Sitten, Gewohnheiten . . . ," AdB 4:178–81, 179–80.
5. Robert Walser, *The Tanners*, 257.
6. Robert Walser, "Knocking," translated by Tom Whalen and Carol Gehrig, in *Selected Stories*, 133–34, 133; Walser, "Im Progymnasium . . . ," AdB 5:90–92, 91; Echte, *Walsers Kindheit und Jugend*, 69; Walser, "Die Buben Weibel," SW 15:95–100.
7. Quoted in Echte, ed., *Robert Walser*, 41.
8. Walser, *The Tanners*, 345–46.
9. Robert Walser, "Meine Vergangenheit blitzt im allgemeinen wie ein sauber geputztes Silberbesteck . . . ," AdB 5:89–90, 89; Walser, "Felix-Szenen," AdB 3:184.
10. Theater brochure reproduced in Bernhard Echte, "Karl und Robert Walser: Eine biographische Reportage," in Bernhard Echte and Andreas Meier, eds., *Die Brüder Karl und Robert Walser* (Stäfa: Rothenhäusler, 1990), 150–203, 156.
11. Robert Walser, "Wenzel," SW 2:81–91, 84.
12. A March 1895 handbill from the Biel Municipal Theater confirms that the Biel Drama Club mounted three performances of *Klaus Leuenberger* that year, with a cast of more than one hundred. There's no evidence Robert was a member or served as a copyist. Echte, "Karl und Robert Walser," 157.
13. Walser, "Wenzel," SW 2:88–89.
14. Walser, "Felix-Szenen," AdB 3:176.
15. Robert Walser, "Die Brüder," SW 5:101–5, 102; Echte, ed., *Robert Walser*, 51.
16. Walser, "Die Brüder," SW 5:103; Flora Ackeret, who corresponded with Hermann Hesse in the nineteen-teens, sent him a long reminiscence about the members of the Walser clan; letter from Flora Ackeret to Hermann Hesse, December 13, 1918–March 5, 1919, Deutsches Literaturarchiv Marbach, D: Hesse, Hermann.
17. Echte, ed., *Robert Walser*, 53.
18. Friedrich Schiller, *Wilhelm Tell*, translated by Theodore Martin, in *The Works of Frederick Schiller*, vol. 2 (London: Henry G. Bohn, 1847), 449–553, 529; Robert Walser, "Tell in Prosa," SW 3:36–38, 36.
19. Carl Seelig, *Walks with Walser* [Wanderungen mit Robert Walser], trans. Anne Posten (New York: New Directions, 2017), 128.
20. The Royal Court Theater (Königliches Hoftheater) burned to the ground in 1902; Echte, ed., *Robert Walser*, 52; Mächler, *Das Leben Robert Walsers*, 41; Seelig, *Walks with Walser*, 128, 135.
21. Robert Walser, "Die Talentprobe," SW 2:67–69, 67–68.
22. Walser, "Wenzel," SW 2:91.
23. In German: "Auf den Brettern, die die Welt bedeuten," from the poem "An die Freunde," Friedrich Schiller, *Werke*, 3rd ed., vol. 1, ed. Robert Boxburger (Berlin: G. Grote, 1891), 105; Mächler, *Das Leben Robert Walsers*, 41.
24. Walser, "Die Brüder," SW 5:103.

Chapter 3. The Young Poet (1896–1899)

1. Robert Walser, "Lebenslauf (I)," SW 20:433–34, 433. Walser wrote this biographical note for *Der Lesezirkel* (8:2 [1920], 20f) to accompany a selection of his poems and prose (cf. SW 20:457).

2. Echte, ed., *Robert Walser,* 32, 58.

3. Robert Walser, "Johanna," SW 4:29–30, 29. The salary of 125 Swiss francs per month is also assigned to the narrator of the somewhat later (1917) story "Luise," which relates events similar to "Johanna" (SW 5:192–207, 193).

4. Real-life Senn had three sons: Heinrich, Emil, and Theodor; Walser, "Johanna," SW 4:29; Echte, ed., *Robert Walser,* 61; Echte, "Karl und Robert Walser," 160.

5. Robert Walser, *Jakob von Gunten,* trans. Christopher Middleton (New York: Vintage, 1983).

6. BA 1:11.

7. BA 1:12–13.

8. BA 1:14.

9. Seidel used Roman script to dedicate to fellow socialist Julius Vahlteich a copy of *Aus Kampfgewühl und Einsamkeit,* now in the collection of the University of Chicago Library.

10. Robert Seidel, *Aus Kampfgewühl und Einsamkeit: Gedichte* (Stuttgart: J. H. W. Dietz, 1895), 2, 20.

11. Robert Walser, "Zukunft!," SW 13:48.

12. Seidel, *Aus Kampfgewühl und Einsamkeit,* 3.

13. Robert Walser, "Luise," SW 5:192–207, 194–95. Meyer's *Encyclopedia* was a respected German-language reference work.

14. Walser, "Luise," SW 5:195–96.

15. BA 1:16–17.

16. BA 1:17; letter from Heinrich von Kleist to Ulrike von Kleist, in *Sämtliche Werke und Briefe* 2, 9th ed., ed. Helmut Sembdner (Munich: Carl Hanser, 1993), 725. A volume of Kleist's letters had been published by Robert's employer Cotta in Stuttgart around 1893.

17. Walser, "Luise," SW 5:194.

18. Echte, "Karl und Robert Walser," 159.

19. Echte, "Karl und Robert Walser," 158.

20. Echte, "Karl und Robert Walser," 160–62.

21. Other texts inspired by Louisa Schweizer's history include "Weihnachtsgeschichte I," "Der Gute schrieb," "Festzug," and the poem "Der fünfzigsten Geburtstag," cf. Echte, "Karl und Robert Walser," 160; Walser, *The Assistant,* 133–35; Walser, "Luise," SW 5:206.

22. Bernhard Echte, "'Etwas wie Personenauftritte auf einer Art von Theater': Bemerkungen zum Verhältnis von Biographie und Text bei Robert Walser," *Runa* 21:1 (1994): 31–60, 37; other texts inspired by Rosa Schätzle's history include "Rosa," "Luise," "Weihnachtsgeschichte I," and "Ich weiß zur Stunde nicht recht," cf. Echte, "Karl und Robert Walser," 161; BA 2:194.

23. Renfer would die tragically young, at age twenty-six, cf. Echte, ed., *Robert Walser,* 66. Friends of Schätzle's whom Robert met in Zurich included art dealer Otto Ackermann and his girlfriend, painter Maria Slavona, whom Walser would recall decades later in conversation (Seelig, *Walks with Walser,* 59), and perhaps also Emanuel von Bodman, then a student but later a noted German author, whom the narrator of Walser's 1921 "Festzug" claims as an acquaintance (Robert Walser, "Festzug," SW 17:29–32, 31–32); Anne Gabrisch, "Robert Walser und die Fee," *Akzente* 38:3 (1991): 250–65, 257.

24. Internal memo reproduced in Echte, ed., *Robert Walser,* 58; Arbeitszeugnis der Transport Versicherungsanstalt "Schweiz" (certificate of employment), November 22, 1897, RWA, Sammlung Robert Walser, C: Dokumente zur Biographie.

25. Walser, "Fidelio," SW 17:212; Walser, "Die Gedichte (II)," SW 16:254–60, 254; Mächler, *Das Leben Robert Walsers,* 53. (A Roman numeral following a title in Walser's collected works is used to differentiate between pieces that share a title, as he sometimes reused titles.)

26. Walser, "Die Gedichte (II)," SW 16:254.

27. BA 1:19–20.

28. Fritz Nußbaum, "Professor Hermann Walser," *Geographische Zeitschrift* 26:3 (1920): 65–67; Katja Zellweger, "Familie Walser," in *Robert Walser Handbuch,* ed. Lucas Marco Gisi (Stuttgart: Metzler, 2015), 16–18, 16; Werner Morlang, *Robert Walser in Bern: Auf den Spuren eines Stadtnomaden* (Oberhofen: Zytglogge, 2009), 160–61.

29. Joseph Viktor Widmann, "Lyrische Erstlinge," in *Über Robert Walser,* 1: 11–12, 11.

30. BA 1:409.

31. Robert Walser, "Ein Landschäftchen," SW 13:20.

32. Robert Walser, "Am Fenster (II)," SW 13:22.

33. Franz Blei, "Robert Walser," *Prager Presse,* April 21, 1935. This is one of a series of similar portraits Blei wrote of Walser. See Anne Gabrisch, "Robert Walser und Franz Blei—Oder: vom Elend des literarischen Betriebs," accessed June 30, 2020, https://www.robertwalser.ch/fileadmin/redaktion/dokumente/jahrestagungen/vortraege/Gabrisch-1999.pdf, 12.

34. Robert Walser, "Doktor Franz Blei," SW 5:212–23, 213–14.

35. Walser, "Doktor Franz Blei," SW 5:219.

36. Echte, ed., *Robert Walser,* 78–81. Echte's discovery of these poems in Blei's diary is a valuable find, as some of the poems Blei copied are otherwise unrecorded.

37. Walser, "Beiseit" (original title: "Spruch"), SW 13:22 (Ich mache meinen Gang; / der führt ein Stückchen weit / und heim; dann ohne Klang / und Wort bin ich beiseit).

38. Editor's note, Robert Walser, "Gedichte," *Wiener Rundschau* 3:18 (1899): 422–23, 423.

Chapter 4. Drama (1899–1900)

1. Echte, "Karl und Robert Walser," 166.

2. Gabrisch, "Robert Walser und die Fee," 252–53; Seelig, *Walks with Walser,* 59.

3. Mächler, *Das Leben Robert Walsers,* 24.

4. Gabrisch, "Robert Walser und die Fee," 254–55; Echte, ed., *Robert Walser,* 82.

5. Letter from Flora Ackeret to Hermann Hesse, December 13, 1918–March 5, 1919, Deutsches Literaturarchiv Marbach, D: Hesse, Hermann. Passing references in Ackeret's reminiscence about the Walser siblings suggest that Hesse had asked her to explain an earlier remark describing Robert as sometimes "spiteful" and "unjust." She also wrote that she "instinctively saw in E. W. [Ernst] one who'd gone astray, even though everyone teased me a little, both my own family and even Lisa, declaring him quite simply an absent-minded professor."

6. Gabrisch, "Robert Walser und die Fee," 255.
7. Gabrisch, "Robert Walser und die Fee," 256.
8. Karl even gave Ackeret a present, a book about the painter Karl Stauffer-Bern, that he'd previously given to Schätzle and then demanded back. Stauffer-Bern's affair with his married benefactor, Lydia Welt-Escher, had produced an explosive scandal that rocked Swiss society to its core. As the daughter of a major Swiss industrialist and the daughter-in-law of a government minister, Welt-Escher had been very much in the public eye. The scandal culminated in the suicides of both lovers in 1891. Robert wrote about this story several times in his later work; letter from Flora Ackeret to Hermann Hesse, December 13, 1918–March 5, 1919; Bernhard Echte, "Warum verbarg sich Robert Walser in Thun? Ein Dokument von Flora Ackeret," in *"Immer dicht vor dem Sturze . . .": Zum Werk Robert Walsers,* ed. Paolo Chiarini and Hans Dieter Zimmermann (Frankfurt am Main: Athenäum, 1987), 331–47, 339, 341.
9. Robert Walser, "Damals war es, o, damals . . . ," AdB 1:277–79, 277.
10. Robert Walser, "Der Kamerad," SW 16:260–63, 263; Walser, "Freundschaftsbrief," SW 16:397–99, 398.
11. Echte, "Warum verbarg sich," 335.
12. Letter from Flora Ackeret to Hermann Hesse, December 13, 1918–March 5, 1919; a schoolmate of Fanny's recalled Lisa as one of the prettiest girls in Biel, with "indescribable charm," letter from Marguerite Chavannes to Carl Seelig, May 11, 1953, RWA, Nachlass Carl Seelig, B-04: Robert Walser.
13. Letter from Flora Ackeret to Hermann Hesse, December 13, 1918–March 5, 1919.
14. Letter from Flora Ackeret to Hermann Hesse, December 13, 1918–March 5, 1919.
15. Helmut Sembdner, "Das Delosea-Inseli," in *In Sachen Kleist. Beiträge zu Forschung,* 3rd ed. (Munich: Hanser, 1994), 9–17, 10.
16. Robert Walser, "Kleist in Thun," translated by Christopher Middleton, *Selected Stories,* 17–25, 23; Walser, "The Battle of Sempach," in *Masquerade,* 37–42.
17. Besides Walser, "Kleist in Thun" (1907), these include "Porträtskizze" (1907), "Was braucht es zu einem Kleist-Darsteller?" (1907), "Auf Knien!" (1908), "Kleist in Paris" (1922), "Kleist" (1927), "Heinrich von Kleist" (1928/1929), "Kleist-Essay" (1936), and "Weiteres zu Kleist" (1936).
18. Walser, "Kleist in Thun," 25; Walser, "Apollo und Diana," SW 4:35–36, 35; Walser, "Damals war es, o, damals," 277; Walser, "Notizbuchauszug," SW 18:162–65, 163. This must have been the Spar- und Leihkasse Thun, founded in 1866. Cf. Manuel Berger, "Die Anfänge der Spar- und Leihkasse," *Berner Zeitung,* June 27, 2016, https://www.bernerzeitung.ch/region/thun/die-anfaenge-der-spar-und-leihkasse/story/20231105. The brewery was the Aktienbrauerei Thun. In a biographical note Walser submitted to accompany poems published in *Wiener Rundschau* (August 1, 1899), he describes his workplace as a fashion boutique, though he may have been joking (Mächler, *Das Leben Robert Walsers,* 60).
19. Robert Walser, "Widmann," SW 6:16–18, 16.
20. Echte, ed., *Robert Walser,* 96–97; Kurt Ifkovits, "'Guten Tag Herr Dichter der Tapetenfabrik': Franz Blei und *Die Insel,*" in *Franz Blei: Mittler der Literaturen,* ed. Dietrich Harth (Hamburg: Europäische Verlagsanstalt, 1997), 172–87, 172–73.
21. Robert Walser, "Helle," SW 13:12.

22. Quoted by Jochen Greven, "Nachwort," SW 13:268–79, 270.

23. Untitled poem, SW 3:6 (Es kommt mich Lachen / Und Lächeln an. / Was liegt daran! / Das sind so Sachen . . .); cf. Paul Keckeis, "Lyrik (frühe Gedichte, *Saite und Sehnsucht*)," in *Robert Walser Handbuch*, 94–95, 95.

24. Ifkovits, "Guten Tag Herr Dichter der Tapetenfabrik," 174.

25. Jochen Greven dated this notebook by analyzing the handwriting (Jochen Greven, "Nachwort," SW 13:268–79, 270). Since four of the poems from this notebook appeared in *Die Insel*, we know its contents overlapped with the shorter volume sent to Blei. It's unclear whether Books One and Two of this three-book sequence were the notebooks sent to Widmann and Blei (neither is extant) or whether there were other notebooks too that no longer survive.

26. Elio Fröhlich, "Nachwort," in *Robert Walser, Saite und Sehnsucht: Faksimile-Ausgabe im Auftrag der Carl-Seelig-Stiftung* (Zurich: Suhrkamp, 1979), 111–16, 112.

27. Robert Walser, "Winterregen," SW 13:37.

28. Robert Walser, "Welt," SW 13:11.

29. Echte, "Karl und Robert Walser," 204; Walser, BA 1:24.

30. Robert Walser, "Lake Greifen," in *Masquerade*, 3–4, 3.

31. Walser, "Lake Greifen," 3. The personification is easier in German, since the word for "description," *die Beschreibung*, is a noun of feminine gender and therefore takes the pronoun "she."

32. Robert Walser, "The Aunt," in *Masquerade*, 105–8, 105. This story first appeared in *Neue Zürcher Zeitung* on January 24, 1915.

33. Walser, "The Aunt," 105–7.

34. Robert Walser, "Eindruck einer Stadt," SW 17:93–95, 94.

35. Gurzelngasse has been renumbered since Walser's time; the house number was originally 17.

36. BA 1:24.

37. Robert Walser, "Die Knaben" (feuilleton text), SW 16:263–66, 263; Walser, *Die Knaben* (short play), SW 14:7–17, 7.

38. Walser, *Die Knaben* (short play), SW 14:12–13.

39. Walser, *Die Knaben* (short play), SW 14:9.

40. Robert Walser, *Dichter,* SW 14:18–28, 23–24.

41. Walser, *Dichter,* SW 14:21.

42. Walser, *Cinderella,* translated by Walter Arndt, in *Robert Walser Rediscovered,* ed. Mark Harman (Hanover: University Press of New England, 1985), 62–100, 80.

43. Walter Benjamin, "Robert Walser," translated by Mark Harman, in *Robert Walser Rediscovered,* 144–47, 146.

44. Robert Walser, *Snowwhite,* translated by Walter Arndt, in *Robert Walser Rediscovered,* 101–35, 130.

45. Lucas Marco Gisi, "Otto Hinrichsen als erster Rezensent Robert Walsers?," in *Mitteilungen der Robert Walser-Gesellschaft* 18 (April 2011), 20–22, 21.

46. BA 1:27; BA 2:228, 379.

47. The dating of *The Pond* is uncertain; it's assumed to have been composed either during Robert's 1899–1900 sojourn in Solothurn or in 1902 in Täuffelen. The 1902 dating is based on a fair copy of the manuscript; the first draft is no longer extant. Fröhlich, "Nachwort," 112; Seelig, *Walks with Walser,* 23; Walser, *Der Teich,* trans.

Raphael Urweider and Händl Klaus (from Swiss German to German), ed. Reto Sorg (Berlin: Insel, 2014), 25.

48. BA 1:467, 468.

Chapter 5. The German Cities (1900–1903)

1. These were followed by the Neue [New] Pinakothek, the world's first museum for contemporary art.

2. Rainer Metzger, *München, die grosse Zeit um 1900: Kunst, Leben und Kultur 1890– 1920* (Vienna: Brandstätter, 2008), 118; Gerhard Neumeier, *München um 1900: Wohnen und Arbeiten, Familie und Haushalt, Stadtteile und Sozialstrukturen, Hausbesitzer und Fabrikarbeiter, Demographie und Mobilität: Studien zur Sozial- und Wirtschaftsgeschichte einer deutschen Großstadt vor dem Ersten Weltkrieg* (Frankfurt am Main: Peter Lang, 1995), 24.

3. Orphaned as a child, Heymel grew up in Schröder's family and inherited several million marks when he turned twenty-one; Schröder later distinguished himself as a poet and Shakespeare translator, Echte, ed., *Robert Walser,* 108–9.

4. Franz Blei, "Prolog über Walser," *Die Literarische Welt* 1:1 (October 9, 1925), in *Über Robert Walser,* 1:64–66, 66; Robert Walser, "München," SW 16:269–70, 270; Walser, "Diesen Aufsatz über Frank Wedekind . . . ," AdB 4:222–23; Franz Blei, *Erzählung eines Lebens* (Leipzig: Paul List, 1930), 274.

5. Letter from Rudolf Alexander Schröder to Otto Julius Bierbaum, undated, quoted in Echte, ed., *Robert Walser,* 112.

6. Quoted in Mächler, *Das Leben Robert Walsers,* 65.

7. Walser, "München," SW 16:269.

8. Robert Walser, "Würzburg," SW 6:35–50, 36; *Die Insel der Blödsinnigen* is reproduced in Echte, ed., *Robert Walser,* 111.

9. Walser recalled years later someone saying the new clothes turned him from a traveling journeyman into a prince (BA 2:329).

10. Statistics from Brian Ladd, *The Ghosts of Berlin: Confronting German History in the Urban Landscape* (Chicago: Chicago University Press, 1997), 96, 116; Anthony Read and David Fisher, *Berlin: The Biography of a City* (London: Hutchinson, 1994), 128–29; Walser later wrote about one such restaurant: "Aschinger," in *Berlin Stories,* ed. Jochen Greven, trans. Susan Bernofsky (New York: New York Review Books, 2012), 14–16.

11. Quoted in Georg Brühl, *Die Cassirers: Streiter für den Impressionismus* (Leipzig: Edition Leipzig, 1991), 71.

12. Robert Walser, "Renoir," SW 13:170–71, 170. Sold to a German collector by Cassirer, this painting is now held by Museum Folkwang in Essen, Germany.

13. As told to Jochen Greven by Roland Kuhn, whose mother was a childhood friend of Lisa Walser. Jochen Greven, "Nachwort des Herausgebers," SW 1:111–22, 118.

14. Robert Walser, "Fritz Kocher's Essays," in *A Schoolboy's Diary and Other Stories,* trans. Damion Searls (New York: New York Review Books, 2013), 3–38, 11–12.

15. Walser, "Fritz Kocher's Essays," 16–17, 26; Walser, "Autumn," in *Masquerade,* 5–10, 6 ("Wenn alles so weiß ist, weiß man alles viel besser in der Stunde," Walser, "Der Herbst," SW 1:10–12, 11); an alternate translation, "When everything outside is so

white, everything in class is so right," is found in Walser, "Fritz Kocher's Essays,"
6; the boy who inspired the name Fritz Kocher also makes a cameo appearance—as
class clown—in Walser, "Tagebuch eines Schülers," SW 2:104–13, 110. This story
mentions several of Robert's teachers by name, though not all their attributes are
accurately reported. Cf. Echte, ed., *Robert Walser*, 28–29.

16. By comparison, he'd received 50 marks for the last of the shorter pieces published
   in the magazine *Die Insel*, BA 1:34.

17. BA 1:37; in a 1927 prose piece, a Walser narrator reports that "at the age of 24, [he] cheerfully, i.e. in a businesslike manner, hit [this respected critic] up for money," Walser,
   "Brief an Alfred Kerr," SW 24–26, 26; Greven, "Nachwort des Herausgebers," SW 1:115.

18. Robert Walser, "A Painter," translated by Susan Bernofsky, in *Looking at Pictures*,
   trans. Susan Bernofsky, Lydia Davis, and Christopher Middleton (New York:
   Christine Burgin/New Directions, 2015), 11–39, 11, 13.

19. Letter from Fritz Probst to Carl Seelig, undated, RWA, Nachlass Carl Seelig, B-04:
   Robert Walser.

20. Classified advertisement, *Neue Zürcher Zeitung,* April 4, 1902, 2nd evening ed.,
   quoted in KWA III.3:326; BA 1:42.

21. Seelig, *Walks with Walser*, 17, 36.

22. BA 1:38; production delays prevented this book from appearing until 1904; Robert
   Walser, "Two Strange Stories about Death," translated by Christopher Middleton,
   Selected Stories, 12–13.

23. BA 1:51.

24. BA 1:55–56, 3:138.

25. Echte, ed., *Robert Walser*, 142.

26. For photographs documenting military exercises in this period, see Hans Rudolf
   Kurz, *100 Jahre Schweizer Armee* (Thun: Ott, 1978), 64–65.

27. Letter from Fritz Probst to Carl Seelig, undated; for Militärgarten's history, see the
   website of Hotel Restaurant Jardin, accessed September 30, 2020, https://www.
   hotel-jardin.ch/de/hotel/geschichte/.

28. Hans Rudolf Kurz, *100 Jahre Schweizer Armee*, 272.

29. Echte, ed., *Robert Walser,* 147.

30. Robert Walser, "Der Wald," SW 1:91–107, 91.

Chapter 6. The First Published Book (1903–1905)

1. BA 1:55–56.

2. Population as of 1900, *Meyers grosses Konversations-Lexikon: ein Nachschlagewerk
   des allgemeinen Wissens*, 6th ed. (Leipzig: Bibliographisches Institut, 1908–1909),
   vol. 20, 291, https://babel.hathitrust.org/cgi/pt?id=njp.32101064063256;view=1up
   ;seq=361.

3. Echte, ed., *Robert Walser*, 152–56.

4. Walser, *The Assistant*, 186–87.

5. BA 1:59.

6. The manuscript of "Gräfin Kirke, Eine Phantasie" was later lost or destroyed. The
   others are "Brentano, eine Phantasie" (SW 15:78–86); "Simon, eine Liebesge-
   schichte" ("Simon: A Love Story," in *Masquerade*, 15–19); "Der Mehlmann"

("Mehlmann: A Fairy Tale," trans. Susan Bernofsky, *Review of Contemporary Fiction* 12:1 [Spring 1992]: 22–23); and "Seltsame Stadt" (SW 2:29–32); BA 1:61.

7. Echte, ed., *Robert Walser*, 157; Walser, *The Assistant*, 284; Mächler, *Das Leben Robert Walsers*, 75.

8. BA 1:69; Echte, ed., *Robert Walser*, 160–61; André Zinggeler, "Prof. Hermann Walser: Leben und Werk—eine Analyse seiner Notizbücher," master's thesis, Geographisches Institut, Universität Bern, 1987, 8; Walser, "Lebenslauf (1920)," SW 20:433–34, 434.

9. BA 1:64–65.

10. Echte, "Karl und Robert Walser," 204; Claire Badorrek-Hoguth, *Der Buchkünstler Karl Walser. Eine Bibliographie* (Bad Kissingen: Manfred J. Badorrek, 1983), 88.

11. BA 1:69, 70.

12. BA 1:72.

13. BA 1:86–88.

14. Joseph Viktor Widmann, "Gebrüder Walser," in *Über Robert Walser*, 1:13–16.

15. F.M., "Literarische Festtagsgeschenke," *Neue Zürcher Zeitung*, December 22, 1904; Johannes Schlaf, "Neue Bücher," *Das Neue Magazin* 20:3 (January 21, 1905): 87f.

16. Echte, ed., *Robert Walser*, 165.

17. BA 1:117n7.

18. BA 1:90.

19. BA 1:100n17; letter from Marguerite Chavannes to Carl Seelig, May 11, 1953; BA 1:99.

20. BA 1:118.

21. BA 1:90, 2:191.

22. Flora Ackeret, "Der Konfirmandenanzug," *Zürcher Post*, March 9, 1904, 1.

23. Robert Walser, "Marie," translated by Susan Bernofsky and Tom Whalen, in *Masquerade*, 55–68, 56–57, 64. The double-suicide theme is an echo of Heinrich von Kleist's biography.

24. Robert Walser, "A Painter," 37.

25. BA 1:123.

26. BA 1:127.

27. Franz Deibel, "Fritz Kochers Aufsätze," *Die Freistatt* 7:16 (April 22, 1905): 256; Albert Geiger, "Fritz Kochers Aufsätze," *Das Literarische Echo* 7:11 (1905): 772–73.

28. Heidi Kräuchi, "Karl Walser. Sein Beitrag zur Entwicklung des Bühnenbilds," PhD diss., University of Vienna, 1976, 47–52.

29. BA 1:129–30.

30. BA 1:130.

31. BA 1:68.

Chapter 7. A Berliner and a Novelist (1905–1906)

1. Tilla Durieux, *Meine ersten neunzig Jahre* (Munich: F. A. Herbig, 1971), 107.

2. Robert Walser, "Leben eines Dichters. Wandverzierungen von Karl Walser (1905)," SW 5:261–65, 261, 265.

3. Max Hochdorf, "25 Jahre Schauspielschule des Deutschen Theaters," in *Fünfundzwanzig Jahre Schauspielschule des Deutschen Theaters zu Berlin* (Berlin: Richard Labisch, 1930), 9–19, 12.

4. G. Manthei, *Der herrschaftliche Diener. Lehrbuch zum Selbstunterricht nebst praktischer Anleitung zum Serviettenbrechen*, 3rd ed. (Berlin: Verlag der Herrschaftlichen Dienerschule, 1903); Oscar T. Schweriner, "Berliner Dienerschulen," *Welt-Spiegel* 1:97 (December 5, 1901).

5. Robert Walser, "Tobold (II)," in *Masquerade*, 80–100, 82.

6. Seelig, *Walks with Walser*, 26–27; Walser, *The Tanners*, 198.

7. Letter from Karl Walser to Fanny Walser, undated, RWA, Sammlung Robert Walser, E-03: Sammlung Fanny Walser.

8. BA 1:135.

9. Franz Blei, "Prolog über Walser" and "Robert Walser," in *Über Robert Walser*, 1:64–69, 65, 69.

10. Walser, "Tobold (II)," 91. Hochberg's sister-in-law was Daisy, Princess of Pless (née Mary Theresa Olivia Cornwallis-West), but there's no evidence she passed through Dambrau during Robert's time there. W. John Koch, *Daisy Princess of Pless 1873–1943: A Discovery* (Edmonton: W. John Koch, 2003), 86; von Heyking's book was titled *Letters That Never Reached Him;* Walser, "Tobold (II)," 90; Seelig, *Walks with Walser*, 16.

11. Walser, "Tobold (II)," 85–87, 94–95.

12. Kräuchi, "Karl Walser," 75. Komische Oper, located just south of the Friedrichstrasse bridge over the Spree, was destroyed during World War II and is unconnected with the theater that now bears this name, which at the time was called the Metropol-Theater.

13. BA 1:137; letter from Karl Walser to Fanny Walser, February 8, 1906, and a second undated letter sent soon thereafter, RWA, Sammlung Robert Walser, E-03: Sammlung Fanny Walser.

14. Walser, "Tobold (II)," 86.

15. Walser, *The Robber*, 55, 57.

16. Robert Walser, "Rathenau war von etwas melancholischem Gemüt," KWA VI.2:238–39, 238. The text was deemed too risqué and potentially slanderous in the 1980s, cf. AdB 2:625, n480a/b; Hochdorf, "25 Jahre Schauspielschule," 10.

17. Walser, *The Robber*, 13. ("Islands" is perhaps a reference to the journal/publishing house *Die Insel* [The Island].) Rathenau, who would die a bachelor, is also believed to have had intimate friendships with women. Cf. Shulamit Volkov, *Walther Rathenau: The Life of Weimar's Fallen Statesman* (New Haven: Yale University Press, 2012), 31–32.

18. Robert Beachy, *Gay Berlin: Birthplace of a Modern Identity* (New York: Knopf, 2014), xvii, 46–47.

19. Beachy, *Gay Berlin*, 97–99; Robert Deam Tobin, *Peripheral Desires: The German Discovery of Sex* (Philadelphia: University of Pennsylvania Press, 2015), 1–2.

20. Walser, *The Tanners*, 223–25.

21. Seelig, *Walks with Walser*, 11; Walser, *The Tanners*, 256.

22. Walser, *The Tanners*, 278–79, 284.

23. Robert Walser, "The Tanners" (short prose text), in *Berlin Stories*, 101–2.

24. Walser, "Simon," 17; Walser, *The Tanners*, 131.

25. BA 1:139–40; Seelig, *Walks with Walser*, 17; Sigrid Bauschinger, *Die Cassirers: Unternehmer, Kunsthändler, Philosophen: Biographie einer Familie* (Munich: C. F. Beck, 2015), 119.

26. Letter from Christian Morgenstern to Bruno Cassirer, April 8, 1906, BA 3:86.
27. BA 1:146.
28. Seelig, *Walks with Walser*, 41; letter from Christian Morgenstern to Bruno Cassirer, October 8, 1906, BA 3:86; Christian Morgenstern diary entry quoted in Echte, ed., *Robert Walser*, 193.
29. After earning a high school diploma in the Austro-Hungarian Empire, Simon Agapalian enrolled at the University of Zurich in 1898 and departed mid-semester in November 1899. Matriculation records, Universität-Zürich, accessed July 31, 2017, http://www.matrikel.uzh.ch/active//static/772.htm; Walser, *The Tanners*, 311–12; Robert Walser, *Geschwister Tanner* (Berlin: Bruno Cassirer, 1907), 281. Flora Ackeret's copy of the novel is in the collection of NMB Neues Museum Biel, Depositum Bundesamt für Kultur, Gottfried Keller-Stiftung, Bern. The maidservant's name was Marie Rickli (previously unpublished research, personal archive of Bernhard Echte, Wädenswil).
30. Walser, "The Tanners," 101; *The Tanners*, 163, 241, 244.
31. Walser, *The Tanners*, 92, 102; letter from Georg Kolbe to Hermann Schmitt, January 8, 1908, quoted in Echte, ed., *Robert Walser*, 206.
32. Wolfram Groddeck and Barbara von Reibnitz, "Editorisches Nachwort" (afterword) KWA I.2:318–19. A third edition printed in 1933 by Rascher & Cie. was labeled "third to fifth thousand."
33. KWA I.2:321–28; Joseph Viktor Widmann's article was published anonymously: "Schweizerische Dichter und österreichische Rezensenten," *Sonntagsblatt des Bund*, April 28, 1907, 135f.

Chapter 8. The Balloon Ride (1907–1908)

1. BA 1:153; Walser, *The Tanners*, 131.
2. Walser, *The Tanners*, 273; BA 1:153.
3. Mächler, *Das Leben Robert Walsers*, 100; Jochen Greven, "Nachwort des Herausgebers," SW 11:167–79, 172; Seelig, *Walks with Walser*, 72. Robert had not yet visited Poland, as Silesia at the time was part of the German Empire.
4. BA 1:155–56, 155, 159.
5. BA 3:87–89.
6. BA 1:164–65, 3:93.
7. BA 1:167; letters from Christian Morgenstern to Enno Quehl, July 21, 1907, and to Fega Frisch, September 28, 1907, in Christian Morgenstern, *Werke und Briefe: Kommentierte Ausgabe* 8, ed. Reinhardt Habel and Katharina Breitner (Stuttgart: Urachhaus, 2011), 338, 368; despite some ambiguity, I am convinced by the argument put forth by KWA I.3 (*Der Gehülfe* [Erstdruck]) editors Angela Thut and Christian Walt that in this letter to Frisch, Morgenstern is referring to this first *Assistant* manuscript, "Editorisches Nachwort" (afterword), in KWA I.3:269–304, 277–79; a nostalgic prose piece Walser published in 1929 contains the line "Once, because of a scornful remark, I tore up a two-hundred-page manuscript"— the line preceding it concerns a prince combing a chambermaid's hair, however, so this can hardly count as documentary evidence; Robert Walser, "Fragment," SW 12:100–110, 104.

8. BA 1:159.
9. Walser, "Kleist in Thun," 23.
10. Hans Joachim Kreutzer, *Heinrich von Kleist* (Munich: Beck, 2011), 25; Robert Walser, "The Battle of Sempach," in *Masquerade*, 37–42.
11. Seelig, *Walks with Walser*, 54.
12. Walser later recalled the invitation to submit as having been issued in connection with one of Scherl's novel contests, but Scherl didn't run one that year, so he must have misremembered. Seelig, *Walks with Walser*, 54, 79; on the editing of *The Assistant*, cf. Thut and Walt, "Editorisches Nachwort," KWA I.3:281; and Wolfram Groddeck and Barbara von Reibnitz, "Editorisches Nachwort," in KWA IV.1:369–82, 379.
13. Seelig, *Walks with Walser*, 54; letter from Christian Morgenstern to Bruno Cassirer, February 18, 1908, in Morgenstern, *Werke und Briefe*, 8:450–51; Christian Morgenstern, diary entry, February 1908, quoted in KWA I.3:314; BA 1:182.
14. Thut and Walt, "Editorisches Nachwort," KWA I.3:286; Kurt Aram (pseudonym for Hans Fischer), "Neue deutsche Erzählungsliteratur," *Frankfurter Zeitung und Handelsblatt*, September 9, 1908, first morning edition, 1.2,2; Wilhelm von Wymental, "Robert Walser: *Der Gehilfe* [*sic*]," *Die Zeit*, June 14, 1908, 23–24; Fritz Marti, "Belletristische Spaziergänge," *Neue Zürcher Zeitung*, August 14, 1908, first morning edition, 1; and Hans Bethge, "Der Gehilfe" [*sic*], *National-Zeitung*, June 7, 1908, morning edition, Sunday supplement 23:4; all quoted in Thut and Walt, "Editorisches Nachwort," KWA I.3:291–92, 295–96.
15. Joseph Victor Widmann, "Robert Walsers Schweizerroman *Der Gehülfe*," in *Über Robert Walser*, 1:25–29. First published in *Der Bund*, July 10–11, 1908, 1–2, and July 12, 1908, 1–3.
16. Anon. [Fanny Johnson], "Two German Novels," *Times Literary Supplement*, August 13, 1908, 262.
17. Robert Walser, "Der Hausfreund," SW 20:41–43, 42.
18. Walser, "Aschinger," 14–15; Walser, "Katzentheater," SW 4:56–57; Walser, "Theater News" ("Theaternachrichten"), appeared in Walser's collection *Essays* (*Aufsätze*) in 1913 under the title "Four Scherzos" ("Vier Späße"), SW 3:33–36.
19. Robert Walser, "Mountain Halls," in *Berlin Stories*, 69–70, 69.
20. Walser, "Mountain Halls," 69.
21. Max Brod, "Kafka liest Walser," in *Über Robert Walser*, 1:85–86; Max Brod, *Streitbares Leben: Autobiographie* (Munich: Kindler, 1960), 393–94.
22. Echte, ed., *Robert Walser*, 210.
23. BA 1:175.
24. Robert Walser, "The Secretary," in *Berlin Stories*, 103–5; Walser, "Frau Bähni," in *Berlin Stories*, 106–10; Sigrid Bauschinger, *Die Cassirers*, 95; Tilla Durieux, *Meine ersten neunzig Jahre*, 82.
25. Mächler, *Das Leben Robert Walsers*, 107–8. Fega Frisch's stories about Walser were communicated to Carl Seelig, who took notes on them that were later used by Mächler (cf. Mächler, *Das Leben Robert Walsers*, 109); the visitor was fellow Berner and fledgling novelist Albert Steffen, who recorded his impressions in his review of *Große kleine Welt* in *Goetheanum*, Dornach, December 26, 1937, reprinted in *Über Robert Walser*, 1:146–47.

26. Letter from Karl Walser to Fanny Walser, December 21, 1907, RWA, Sammlung Robert Walser, E-03: Sammlung Fanny Walser; Walser, "An eine angehende Tänzerin," SW 15:44–45.

27. Robert Walser, "Potpourri," SW 18:214–20, 214. This monthly allowance is noted by Mächler without stating his source. Mächler's biography predates the transcription and publication of Walser's novel *The Robber* that speaks of such an allowance. Mächler, *Das Leben Robert Walsers*, 92.

28. Mächler, *Das Leben Robert Walsers*, 107.

29. Mächler, *Das Leben Robert Walsers*, 107; Seelig, *Walks with Walser*, 78; BA 2:180–81.

30. BA 1:160.

31. Durieux, *Meine ersten neunzig Jahre*, 107–8.

32. Bauschinger, *Die Cassirers*, 83–84, 119–20.

33. Paperwork described in Durieux, *Meine ersten neunzig Jahre*, 108.

34. Seelig, *Walks with Walser*, 48; BA 1:185; Robert Walser, "Balloon Journey," translated by Christopher Middleton, in *Selected Stories*, 14–16.

Chapter 9. The Fall (1908–1913)

1. Echte, ed., *Robert Walser*, 231.

2. Carl Seelig's Notes on a Conversation with Fega Frisch, October 23, 1944, in "Robert Walser Biographie II," RWA, Nachlass Carl Seelig, D-03-a-13: Walser, Robert.

3. BA 1:184.

4. Karl mentions the etchings in a letter to Fanny, promising her he'll send them to her when they're finished. Letter from Karl Walser to Fanny Walser, December 21, 1907, RWA, Sammlung Robert Walser, E-03: Sammlung Fanny Walser; Echte, ed., *Robert Walser*, 243.

5. Seelig, *Walks with Walser*, 12; Robert Walser, *Jakob von Gunten*, trans. Christopher Middleton (New York: Vintage, 1983), 24.

6. Walser, *Jakob von Gunten*, 24, 27.

7. Walser, *Jakob von Gunten*, 47–48, 141.

8. Walser, *Jakob von Gunten*, 96, 136, 141, 153.

9. Walser, *Jakob von Gunten*, 139; Jochen Greven, "Anmerkungen," SW 2:129–33, 132–33n104.

10. Hermann Hesse, "Robert Walser," in *Über Robert Walser*, 1:52–57, 55–57.

11. BA 2:276.

12. Robert Walser, "Was macht mein Stück?," SW 15:41–44, 42.

13. Robert Walser, "Der Schriftsteller," SW 3:129–34, 129, 133; in 1920, Walser responded to a query from Kleist scholar Georg Minde-Pouet, saying that he'd written his essay on Kayssler's performance in *Prince Friedrich of Homburg* on the basis of second-hand reports and hadn't seen the performance; BA 1:618; Walser, "Abschied," SW 15:100–104.

14. Robert Walser, "The Little Berliner," translated by Harriett Watts, in *Selected Stories*, 44–51, 44, 48.

15. Reviews quoted in Hans-Joachim Heerde, "Editorisches Nachwort," KWA I.4:141–63, 154–55.

16. Joseph Victor Widmann, "Jakob von Gunten," in *Über Robert Walser*, 1:33–38, 37–38; review by J.E.P. [= Jacob Elias Poritzky], *Berliner Börsen-Courier* 42:337 (July 22, 1910), morning edition, first supplement, 6, quoted in KWA I.4:160.

17. The size of the print run for *Jakob von Gunten* is unknown; possibly it was one thousand copies, as with the two previous novels, or maybe more. It can't have been three thousand copies, because books that sold that many copies got added to a special list in Cassirer's papers, and this one wasn't. The novel was still listed as "in print" in Cassirer's 1926 catalogue. Cf. Heerde, "Editorisches Nachwort," KWA I.4:146–47; cf. Echte, ed., *Robert Walser*, 249.

18. Robert Walser, "Food for Thought," in *Berlin Stories*, 93–96, 93.

19. BA 1:186; Robert Walser, "An Actor," in *Berlin Stories*, 56–57, 57.

20. Robert Walser, "Über eine Art von Duell," SW 17:166–71, 167; Mächler, *Das Leben Robert Walsers*, 108; Seelig, *Walks with Walser*, 62; "A Homecoming in the Snow," in *Berlin Stories*, 136–39, 138.

21. BA 2:299.

22. Walser, *The Robber*, 58, 53; Walser, "Sommerfrische," SW 4:15–16, 15.

23. Efraim Frisch, "Ein Jüngling," *Die Neue Rundschau* 22:3 (March 1911): 416–20; Echte, ed., *Robert Walser*, 251; Max Brod, "Kommentar zu Robert Walser," *Pan* 2:2 (October 1911): 53–58.

24. Letter from Egon Erwin Kisch to Max Brod, April 20, 1913, quoted in Echte, ed., *Robert Walser*, 268.

25. Robert Walser, "Drama," SW 15:121–22; Walser, "Frau Wilke," translated by Christopher Middleton, in *Selected Stories* 118–22, 120–21.

26. BA 2:300; Bernhard Echte, "Anmerkungen und Nachweise," in Walser, *Feuer: Unbekannte Prosa und Gedichte* (Frankfurt am Main: Suhrkamp, 2005), 129–41, 130.

27. Robert Walser, "Birch-Pfeiffer," SW 3:107–8, 108; Walser, "Lenz," SW 3:109–14.

28. Bauschinger, *Die Cassirers*, 334; "A Note on Van Gogh's *L'Arlésienne*," translated by Christopher Middleton, in *Looking at Pictures*, 48–49, 48.

29. Otto Pick, "Z moderni prozy nemecke," *Novina* 5:12 (May 10, 1912): 374–75; Robert Walser, "Ovation," SW 3:62–63; cf. Elizabeth Boa, "A Young Man Plays the Ringmaster: Reply to J. K. Hawes," *Deutsche Vierteljahrsschrift für Literaturwissenschaft und Geistesgeschichte* 69:2 (1995): 337–43, 41n10; Franz Kafka, diary entry from October 8, 1917, quoted in Susan Bernofsky, "Preface," in *Masquerade*, xxi–v, xxi; Kafka's words are translated as "his use of vague, abstract metaphors" by Martin Greenberg with Hannah Arendt in *The Diaries of Franz Kafka 1910–1923* (New York: Schocken Books, 1976), 388; cf. Hans Dieter Zimmermann, *Der babylonische Dolmetscher: Zu Franz Kafka und Robert Walser* (Frankfurt am Main: Suhrkamp, 1985), 20–26.

30. Robert Walser, "Frau Scheer," in *Berlin Stories*, 121–33; Echte, ed., *Robert Walser*, 258; Walser, "Rückblick," SW 16:244–47, 245; related by Fega Frisch to Seelig, in Mächler, *Das Leben Robert Walsers*, 109–10; *Adreßbuch für Charlottenburg*, 1912, reproduced in Echte, ed., *Robert Walser*, 260.

31. Robert Walser, "Der neue Roman," SW 6:93–95, 95.

32. Walser, *The Robber*, 3; Walser, "Rückblick," SW 16:244, 246; Walser, "Cowshed," in *Berlin Stories*, 54–55; Bernhard Echte, "Anmerkungen und Nachweise," in Walser, *Feuer*, 131.

33. BA 2:181; AdB 1:232.

34. The book is dated 1913 but appeared in December 1912.
35. Echte, ed., *Robert Walser*, 269; Walser, "Frau Scheer," 125.
36. They were now living at Hohenzollernstrasse 14.
37. He later told Seelig—apparently misremembering over twenty-five years later—that he'd had only "a hundred francs to my name" when he left Berlin. What had stuck with him was the sense of defeat. Seelig, *Walks with Walser*, 21.

Chapter 10. The Return to Switzerland (1913–1914)

1. Robert Walser, "Die Einsiedelei," SW 3:146–47.
2. Mächler, *Das Leben Robert Walsers*, 114.
3. Seelig, *Walks with Walser*, 37; Bernhard Böschenstein, "Erinnerungen an Lisa Walser," lecture held on October 11, 2009, in Bellelay, RWZ N(R) 009.28.
4. Robert Walser, "Der nächtliche Aufstieg," SW 4:81–82; Walser, "Das Gebirge," SW 4:103–5.
5. Frieda Mermet, "Frau Frieda Mermet erzählt," *Neutralität* 5:3 (May 1967): 15–19, 16.
6. Mermet, "Frau Frieda Mermet erzählt," 16; Mächler, *Das Leben Robert Walsers*, 115; Louis Mermet, quoted in Mermet, "Frau Frieda Mermet erzählt," 16; BA 1:214n13.
7. Robert Walser, "Meta," SW 4:19–22; Walser, "Fußwanderung," SW 4:22–24.
8. BA 1:210.
9. Echte, ed., *Robert Walser*, 286; Mermet, "Frau Frieda Mermet erzählt," 15.
10. Mermet, "Frau Frieda Mermet erzählt," 15.
11. Seelig, *Walks with Walser*, 21; Robert Walser, "Der Kuss," SW 4:24–26.
12. Robert Walser, "The Dream (I)," translated by Susan Bernofsky, in *Looking at Pictures*, 53–56.
13. Max Brod, "Kleine Prosa," *Die Neue Rundschau* 24:2 (1913): 1043–46, 1043; 1043–45; Peter Panter (= Kurt Tucholsky), "Der Dreischichtedichter," *Die Schaubühne* 9 (17): 478–79.
14. There are conflicting accounts of how long Walser remained in Bellelay, but according to a pair of postcards to Brod postmarked in Bellelay (May 31, 1913) and Biel (July 31, 1913), he must have relocated to Biel in June or July, BA 1:210, 211; Seelig, *Walks with Walser*, 21.
15. Seelig, *Walks with Walser*, 17.
16. Ernst Hubacher, "Der letzte Poet," *Der Kleine Bund* 314 (July 8, 1955), quoted in Echte, ed., *Robert Walser*, 283; Robert Walser, "Poets," translated by Christopher Middleton, in *Selected Stories* 115–17, 115–16; Seelig, *Walks with Walser*, 70; BA 1:211.
17. Robert Walser, "Brief eines Vaters an seinen Sohn," SW 4:73–76; Walser, "Der Vater," SW 4:109–11, 109–10.
18. BA 1:224; Walser, "Das Bild des Vaters," SW 7:152–72.
19. Robert Walser, "Helbling's Story," translated by Christopher Middleton, in *Selected Stories*, 32–43, 33; 42–43 (translation slightly amended).
20. Robert Walser, "Nervous," translated by Christopher Middleton, in *Selected Stories*, 52–53.

21. Robert Walser, "Der Knabe (I)," SW 4:32-34; Walser, "Das Götzenbild," SW 4:34-35.

22. Robert Walser, "Der Traum (II)," SW 4:105-7.

23. BA 1:214, 216, 217.

24. BA 1:217.

25. BA 1:218.

26. BA 1:221-22.

27. Robert recapped this conversation in a letter to Mermet, BA 1:223; BA 1:224.

28. Wolfram Göbel, *Der Kurt Wolff Verlag 1913-1930* (Munich: Buch & Media, 2000), 1320, 1324; Kurt Wolff, "On Publishing in General," translated by Deborah Lucas Schneider, in Michael Ermarth, ed., *Kurt Wolff: A Portrait in Essays and Letters* (Chicago: University of Chicago Press, 1991), 8-20, 11-12.

29. Robert Musil, "Die *Geschichten* von Robert Walser," *Die Neue Rundschau* 25:2 (1914): 1167-69, quoted in Wolff, "On Publishing in General," 12 (translation slightly amended).

30. Robert Musil, "The Stories of Robert Walser," translated by Mark Harman, in *Robert Walser Rediscovered,* ed. Mark Harman (Hanover: University Press of New England, 1985), 141-43, 142; Joachim Benn, "Thomas Mann und 'Der Tod in Venedig,' " *Die Rheinlande* 23 (1913): 307-11; Benn, "Robert Walser," *Die Rheinlande* 24 (1914): 131-34, 131.

31. BA 1:226, 232.

32. Sabine Brenner, "Hermann Hesse und der 'Frauenbund zur Ehrung rheinischer Dichter,' " in *"Beiden Rheinufern angehörig": Hermann Hesse und das Rheinland,* ed. Sabine Brenner, Kerstin Glasow, and Bernd Kortländer (Düsseldorf: Heinrich-Heine-Institut, 2002), http://www.literatur-archiv-nrw.de/sonderausstellung/ Beiden_Rheinufern_angeh_rig/Sabine_Brenner__Hermann_Hesse_und_der___ Frauenbund_zur_Ehrung_rheinischer_Dichter__/seite_1.html, accessed March 21, 2018; the prize sum was reported in *Berliner Tageblatt* 44:163 (March 30, 1915), morning edition, quoted in KWA III.3:353n13. The fee for *Little Fictions* was also 300 marks, according to the contract signed on January 27, 1914.

33. BA 1:229.

34. BA 1:230-31.

35. BA 1:230.

36. Mermet, "Frau Frieda Mermet erzählt," 16.

37. F. A. Kuenzli, *Right and Duty, or Citizen and Soldier: Switzerland Prepared and at Peace, A Model for the United States* (New York: National Defense Institute, 1916), 81, 86, 94.

38. General U. [Ulrich] Wille, *Bericht an die Bundesversammlung über den Aktivdienst 1914/18* (Zurich: Arnold Boll & Cie., 1919), 1.

39. Werner Bourquin and Marcus Bourquin, *Biel Stadtgeschichtliches Lexikon von der Römerzeit (Petinesca) bis Ende er 1930er Jahre mit Ergänzungen für den Zeitraum bis 1999* (Biel: Büro Cortesi, 1999), 472; all information presented here and in Chapters 11 and 12 about troop movements and activities is taken from the war diaries pertaining to Walser's regiment in the collection of the Swiss Federal Archives (Bundesarchiv Bern), in this case: *Tagebuch, Infantrie Regiment 41 (Grenzbesetzung), August 5, 1914-April 27, 1915,* Swiss Federal Archives, signature 27:14109, vol. 1439, "Front-Rapport," August 7, morning.

40. Kuenzli, *Right and Duty*, 70, 84.
41. Jon Mettler, *Festung Schweiz: Ein Projekt der Berner Zeitung*, https://www.bzgrafik. ch/multimedia/festungschweiz/#kapitel1, accessed April 28, 2018; "Front-Rapport," August 12, 1914, April 16, 1915, and April 22, 1915, *Infanterie Regiment 41 (Grenzbesetzung), August 5, 1914–April 27, 1915*.
42. "Front-Rapport," August 29 and August 31, 1914, *Infanterie Regiment 41 (Grenzbesetzung), August 5, 1914–April 27, 1915*; BA 1:239.
43. Memo from Colonel Heusser dated September 3, 1914, Bern, clipping pasted into "Front-Rapport September 2, 1914," *Infanterie Regiment 41 (Grenzbesetzung), August 5, 1914–April 27, 1915*.
44. BA 1:240.
45. Sabine Brenner, '*Das Rheinland aus dem Dornröschenschlaf wecken!': Zum Profil der Kulturzeitschrift* Die Rheinlande *(1900–1922)* (Düsseldorf: Grupello, 2004), 169.
46. The bearded man appears to be Hedwig's jilter from *The Tanners* in a cameo. "Zwei Frauen," SW 16:128–30, 129–30.
47. Mermet, "Frau Frieda Mermet erzählt," 16.
48. Robert Walser, "Der Soldat," SW 16:333–34, 333.
49. Robert Walser, "Denke dran," SW 16:376–77; in 1911, for example, Korrodi had published an essay titled "Berlin and Swiss Literature" in which he'd written admiringly about Walser's work; quoted in KWA III.3:342. The story about Walser's aunt appeared in *Neue Zürcher Zeitung* on January 24, 1915, under the title "Ramble" ("Wanderung") and was reprinted in Walser's 1918 collection *Poet's Lives* (*Poetenleben*) under the title "The Aunt" ("Die Tante").
50. BA 1:241, 242.
51. Bernhard Zeller, "Der Verleger Kurt Wolff," in *Kurt Wolff: Briefwechsel eines Verlegers 1911–1963*, ed. Bernhard Zeller and Ellen Otten (Frankfurt am Main: Verlag Heinrich Scheffler, 1966), vii–lvi, xxviii; Göbel, *Der Kurt Wolff Verlag*, 684n17. This Iron Cross recipient, being Jewish, had to flee Germany in the 1930s and in 1942 founded the publishing house Pantheon in New York City with his wife, Helen Wolff.
52. *Berliner Tageblatt* 44:12 (January 7, 1915), morning edition.
53. BA 1:159.

Chapter 11. A Walk in Wartime (1915–1917)

1. At least as per his own report, as cited in Seelig, *Walks with Walser,* 30.
2. Swiss Federal Archives, 27-14109-1439, *Tagebuch, Infanterie Regiment 41 (Grenzbesetzung), Aug. 5, 1914–April 27, 1915*.
3. BA 1:261.
4. Swiss Federal Archives, 27-14109-1439, *Tagebuch für Infanterie Regiment 41 im 4. Ablösungsdienst vom 6. Oktober 1915 bis 4.12.15*; 27-14109-1440, *Tagebuch für Füs. Bat. 134 vom 6. Oktober 1915 bis 7. Sept. 1917*.
5. Entry for December 1, 1915, *Tagebuch für Infanterie Regiment 41 im 4. Ablösungsdienst*.

6. Eduard Korrodi, "Bericht über den Vortrag von Hans Trog über Karl und Robert Walser," *Neue Zürcher Zeitung* 136 (January 28, 1915), morning edition, 103, quoted in "Dokumentarischer Anhang," KWA III.3:325–490, 348–52; Hans Trog, "Die Brüder Walser," in *Schweizerland: Monatsheft für Schweizer Art und Arbeit* 1:11/12 (August/September 1915): 645–52, excerpted in KWA I.4:162.
7. Korrodi, "Bericht über den Vortrag von Hans Trog," KWA III.3:350.
8. Robert Walser, "Der Pole," SW 4:112–14.
9. Robert Walser, "Ich wanderte und wandre noch," SW 4:6.
10. The second work distributed by the Women's League was Herbert Eulenberg, *The Morning after Kunersdorf;* BA 1:255; Jochen Greven, "Nachwort des Herausgebers," SW 4:175–77, 76, cf. BA 1:569n11; Karl Wagner, "Robert und Karl Walser im Kurt Wolff Verlag," in *Kurt Wolff: Ein Literat und Gentleman*, ed. Barbara Weidle (Bonn: Weidle, 2007), 76–82, 80; Göbel, *Der Kurt Wolff Verlag,* 1324; Lucas Marco Gisi, "Bieler Zeit (1913–1921)," in *Robert Walser Handbuch,* 141–45, 141.
11. BA 1:247.
12. In his letter, Walser mistakenly calls the journal *Kriegs-Echo* (War Echo), perhaps confusing it with a weekly of the same name published in Berlin, BA 1:247; Robert Walser, "Phantasieren," SW 16:97–99, 98–99.
13. Robert Walser, "Aus Tobolds Leben," SW 6:83–91; Walser, "Etwas über den Soldaten," SW 16:334–37; Walser, "Beim Militär," SW 16:337–39, 337–38.
14. BA 1:245; Lisa would confirm this years later in an interview at the psychiatric clinic where Robert became a patient in 1929, Krankengeschichte Nr. 10'428, Irren-, Heil- und Pflegeanstalt Waldau (Psychiatrische Universitätsklinik Bern), 7.
15. BA 1:253, 258.
16. BA 1:253.
17. BA 1:257–58.
18. Fanny was now free of moody Mühlestein, who'd found someone richer to marry in Munich, BA 1:440; BA 1:254.
19. BA 1:270, 271.
20. BA 1:280, 282.
21. Letter from Emmy Ritz-Hirschburger to Carl Seelig, November 12, 1953, RWA, Nachlass Carl Seelig, B-04: Robert Walser; BA 1:282.
22. BA 1:283–84; Robert Walser, "Hans," SW 7:173–206, 206.
23. BA 1:287–88; Wiedmer's circular is described in "Schenkungen: Briefe," in *Zentralbibliothek Solothurn: 26. Bericht über das Jahr 1955* (Solothurn: Union, 1956), 11–15, 12.
24. Robert Walser, "The Walk," translated by Christopher Middleton, in *Selected Stories,* 54–104, 54, 59.
25. Walser, "The Walk," 62. Translation amended.
26. Walser, "The Walk," 85–87.
27. BA 1:292; Robert had published four short pieces in the December 1915 issue of *Die weissen Blätter;* two months earlier, the journal had published Kafka's novella *The Metamorphosis.* A shorter version of "The Brothers" ("Die Brüder"), the one previously published text in *Prose Pieces,* appeared that same month in *Vossische Zeitung,* cf. Walser, "Die Brüder," SW 5:101–5, cf. BA 1:303n10.

28. The other two were "Das Ehepaar" ("The Married Couple," SW 16:131–34) and "Eine verflixte Geschichte" ("A Bollixed Up Story," SW 16:126–28), cf. Jochen Greven, "Anmerkungen," SW 5:273–78, 274n109.

29. Robert Walser, "Das Seestück," SW 5:81–83, 81; Walser, "Zahnschmerzen," SW 5:116–18.

30. Robert Walser, "Die Wurst," SW 5:111–14.

31. BA 1:302, 304, 303.

32. *Börsenblatt für den Deutschen Buchhandel* 83:280 (December 2, 1916), 8568. Reproduced in KWA I.8:334. Rascher issued the book in four formats: as hard- and soft-cover editions; as volume 55 of Rascher's series Writings on Swiss Ways and Art; and as part of an anthology published around the same time, *Swiss Book of Stories and Sketches,* edited by Konrad Falke, cf. KWA I.8:229.

33. BA 1:307.

34. Robert Walser, "Tobold," in *Masquerade,* 80–100.

35. Robert Walser, "Fräulein Knuchel," translated by Susan Bernofsky and Tom Whalen, in *Masquerade,* 69–70, 69. *Masquerade* also contains "The End of the World," "Fritz," and "Basta," while "Nothing at All" and "So! I've Got You" can be found in *Selected Stories.* "Helbling" (SW 5:162–66) appears loosely related to "Helbling's Story," discussed above. For whatever reason, Walser chose not to include "Nervous" (published in *Neue Zürcher Zeitung* in June 1916) in *Little Prose.*

36. BA 1:348.

37. BA 1:377–78, 386–87.

38. BA 1:329, 3:101, 1:322.

39. BA 1:381; Seelig, *Walks with Walser,* 124.

40. BA 1:319, 321–25, 335–36, 337, 339–40, 349-50, 353.

41. BA 1:369n6.

42. Eduard Korrodi, "Schweizerische Erzähler," *Neue Zürcher Zeitung* 138:1224 (July 4, 1917), first evening edition, 1, quoted in KWA I.8:271; mb [= Hans Müller-Bertelmann], "Die zweite Reihe," *Thurgauer Zeitung* 157 (July 7, 1917), second daily edition, 1, quoted in KWA I.8:271; additional praise appeared in *Der Bund, Züricher Post, Berner Tagblatt,* and the magazine *Das Werk.*

Chapter 12. The Aftermath of War (1917–1920)

1. "The Walk," 54.

2. Bread prices in Zurich rose 82.5 percent between 1914 and 1917; the price of pork rose 255 percent nationwide between 1914 and 1918; and the price of eggs rose around 50 percent between 1916 and 1919, Peter Moser, "Mehr als eine Übergangszeit: Die Neuordnung der Ernährungsfrage während des Ersten Weltkriegs," in *14/18: Die Schweiz und der Grosse Krieg,* ed. Roman Rossfeld, Thomas Buomberger, and Patrick Kury (Baden: Hier und Jetzt, 2014), 172–99, 174, 177; Ismael Albertin, "Die Massnahmen des Zürcher Stadtrats zur Verbesserung der Lebensmittelversorgung 1914–1921," in *"Woche für Woche neue Preisaufschläge": Nahrungsmittel-, Energie- und Ressourcenkonflikte in der Schweiz des Ersten Weltkrieges,* ed. Daniel Krämer, Christian Pfister, and Daniel Marc Segesser (Basel: Schwalbe, 2016), 211–33, 224–26; "Pädagogisches Material, 1918: Krieg und Frieden, Zum

Workshop, 'Für oder gegen den Streik' " (Biel: Neues Museum Biel, 1918), 12–13, https://www.nmbiel.ch/files/Kunstvermittlung/Aktionswochen_Fruehling_2018/ PD_Fuer_gegen_Streik_NMB.pdf, accessed July 15, 2019; BA 1:431.

3. BA 1:389.

4. Swiss Federal Archives, 27-14109-1440, *Tagebuch für Füs. Bataillon 134 vom 6. Oktober 1915 bis 7. Sept. 1917*, July 16, 1917–September 5, 1917; BA 1:388.

5. BA 1:390, 392.

6. Seelig, *Walks with Walser*, 94; BA 1:405.

7. BA 1:392–93, 398. He would later quip to Hesse that in Ticino he and the other soldiers drank the red wine "like milk, one and a half or two liters a day," BA 1:419.

8. BA 1:434; Swiss Federal Archives, 27-14109-1440, *Tagebuch für Füs. Bataillon 134 vom 18. Februar 1918 bis 16. März 1918*.

9. BA 1:436.

10. Walser, "Hans," SW 7:206; Walser, *The Assistant*, 210–13.

11. BA 1:397, 402, 406, 408–11.

12. BA 1:410.

13. BA 1:410.

14. The date printed inside the book was 1918.

15. Matthias Sprünglin, "Editorisches Nachwort," KWA I.9:129–58, 142–43.

16. "Letter to Hermann Hesse, November 15, 1917," trans. Christopher Middleton, *Review of Contemporary Fiction* XII:1 (Spring 1992): 28–29, 29.

17. Hermann Hesse, "Poetenleben," in *Über Robert Walser*, 1:57–58; BA 1:422–23.

18. Sprünglin, "Editorisches Nachwort," KWA I.9:142, 144–52; Hans Müller-Bertelmann, "Neue Schweizer-Prosa II," *Die Schweiz* 21:11 (November 1917): 669–73; "Für den Weihnachts-Büchertisch I," *Burgdorfer Tagblatt* 87:296 (December 15, 1917): 2; BA 1:591.

19. Walser, "Frau Wilke," in *Selected Stories*, 118. Cf. Walser, "Frau Wilke," KWA III.3:41–44, 41.

20. BA 1:418.

21. For a more detailed description of Walser's revisions of "The Walk," see Susan Bernofsky, "Introduction," in *The Walk*, trans. Christopher Middleton with Susan Bernofsky (New York: New Directions, 2012), 3–11.

22. BA 1:427–28.

23. Gustav Adolf Frick, "Die schweizerische Papierfabrikation unter besonderer Berücksichtigung des Standortes," Schweizer Industrie- und Handelsstudien 14 (Paris, Weinfelden; Constance: A.-G. Neuenschwander'sche Verlagsbuchhandlung, 1923), 38; BA 1:442–43, 447–48.

24. BA 1:473–74, 476n15.

25. BA 1:464, 465.

26. BA 1:484, 487; Walser first mentioned having been ill—long enough to read two or three books in bed and still not having recovered—in a letter to Mermet on August 7 (BA 1:481), and it wasn't until August 24 that he was back to regular letter-writing.

27. Years later, he mentioned in a letter getting "dizzy spells" that he speculates were "after-effects of the flu," BA 2:384; Catherine E. Ammon, "The 1918 Spanish Flu Epidemic in Geneva, Switzerland," *International Congress Series* 1219 (2001): 163–68, 164–65; BA 1:509n41.

28. Monika Schönenberger, "Munition für den Ersten Weltkrieg kam auch aus der Schweiz," Schweizer Radio und Fernsehen, September 28, 2014, https://www.srf. ch/kultur/gesellschaft-religion/der-1-weltkrieg/munition-fuer-den-ersten-weltkrieg-kam-auch-aus-der-schweiz; Christian Pfister, "Frieren, kalt essen und zu Fuss gehen. Die Energiekrise 1917–1919 in der Schweiz," in *Woche für Woche neue Preisaufschläge,"* 113–32, 113.

29. BA 1:514.

30. BA 1:512, 470, 478.

31. BA 1:491, 477, 438, 440.

32. BA 1:440, 480–81.

33. BA 1:487, 486, 497, 501, 500, 530, 560.

34. Mächler, *Das Leben Robert Walsers,* 131.

35. Letter from Marguerite Chavannes to Carl Seelig, May 11, 1953, Nachlass Carl Seelig, B-04: Robert Walser; reminiscences of Ruth Gygi, quoted in Echte, ed., *Robert Walser,* 315; BA 1:516n40.

36. Mächler, *Das Leben Robert Walsers,* 130; Dr. [Ernst] Bärtschi, "Hermann Walser," *Korrespondenzblatt der Studentenverbindungen Halleriana bernensis und Manessia turicensis* 17:3 (November 6, 1919), 32–34; cousin twice removed D. E. Walser writes that a former student of Hermann reported decades later that Hermann had been losing his hearing and was occasionally teased by his students, D. E. Walser, *Robert Walser: Eine Auslegung* (self-published, 1980), 12–13.

37. BA 1:560, 561, 564.

38. Mermet, "Frau Frieda Mermet erzählt," 18; Margrit Kistler, "Erinnerungen an Robert Walser," *Poesie: Zeitschrift für Literatur* 2:5/6 (1973): 44–49, 49.

39. This story is recorded in a "memory protocol" set down by Guido Stefani, former director of the Robert Walser Archive in Zurich, documenting a conversation with Dr. Walter Hugelshofer, the executor of Karl Walser's estate, whom Stefani had asked to question Hedwig "Trude" Walser about the rift between the brothers. "Gedächtnisprotokoll über ein Telefon mit Herrn Dr. Hugelshofer," January 5, 1981, RWA collection; Krankengeschichte Nr. 10'428, Irren-, Heil- und Pflege-anstalt Waldau (Psychiatrische Universitätsklinik Bern), 2.

40. Emil Schibli, "Erinnerung an Robert Walser," in *Reife und Abschied: Aus dem Nach-lass von Emil Schibli* (Bern: Benteli, 1962), 93–96, 93.

41. The old practice of indenturing children (*Verdingkinder*) in Switzerland continued into the twentieth century; Echte, ed., *Robert Walser,* 334–35; Mächler, *Das Leben Robert Walsers,* 139; Charles Linsmayer, "Emil Schibli," Historisches Lexikon der Schweiz, https://www.hls-dhs-dss.ch/textes/d/D12253.php, last updated July 26, 2011.

42. Emil Schibli, essay in *Seeländer Volksstimme,* August 27, 1927, quoted in Mächler, *Das Leben Robert Walsers,* 138; Frieda Schibli, as reported to Robert Mächler, in Mächler, *Das Leben Robert Walsers,* 139.

43. Undated newspaper clipping in Emil Wiedmer's literary estate, quoted in Echte, ed., *Robert Walser,* 337.

44. Claire Zahler, as reported to Robert Mächler, in Mächler, *Das Leben Robert Walsers,* 135; Ernst Hubacher, "Der letzte Poet," *Der Bund,* July 9, 1955, quoted in Mächler, *Das Leben Walsers,* 135–36.

45. Lydia Rihs, as reported to Bernhard Echte, October 4, 1991, quoted in Echte, ed., *Robert Walser,* 336.

46. Letter from Klara Schlup-Wolf to Carl Seelig, September 26, 1953 ("Erinnerungen an Robert Walser"), and October 13, 1953, RWA, Nachlass Carl Seelig, B-04: Robert Walser; BA 2:31.

47. Schibli, essay in *Seeländer Volksstimme,* quoted in Mächler, *Das Leben Robert Walsers,* 138; Seelig, *Walks with Walser,* 17, 70; BA 1:558.

48. Seelig, *Walks with Walser,* 41.

49. At least one of these books was accepted but never published; BA 1:484–85, 597, 559, 573, 601.

50. BA 1:464; he'd written to Mermet in late June 1918 that he was about to take up "a new sort of task" that he was "convinced will make me sweat," BA 1:472.

51. BA 1:517, 558; "Freiburg," in *Alemannenbuch,* ed. Hermann Hesse (Bern: Seldwyla, 1919), 76–77, 76, also SW 16:310–13, 310.

52. Robert Walser, "Pencil Sketch," in *Microscripts,* 29–32, 31–32.

53. BA 2:299; Seelig, *Walks with Walser,* 21.

54. BA 1:517; he sent this description of the novel's subject matter to Efraim Frisch on January 5, 1919; Walser, "Der fremde Geselle," SW 3:144–46, 145; BA 1:518.

55. BA 1:547, 552.

56. In 1923, the mark would be worth only one-*trillionth* of its prewar value; this may also have been why the Hermann Meister publishing house never published the Walser work(s) they'd accepted; BA 1:552.

57. BA 1:552, 329, 452, 519–20.

58. For example, he asked Efraim Frisch to use his Düren account for payments from *Der Neue Merkur* on September 2, 1919, BA 1:586.

59. BA 1:518, 506, 557.

60. His application—with which he enclosed a bank statement—was supported by a letter from Hans Schuler, former secretary of the Swiss Union of Commerce and Industry, who'd proposed Robert for the Swiss Schiller Foundation grant, and also by Bodmer, BA 1:569, 570, 588, 616; Echte, ed., *Robert Walser,* 332; United States Council of National Defense Reconstruction Research Division, *Readjustment and Reconstruction Information* 1: *Readjustment and Reconstruction Activities in Foreign Countries* (Washington, DC: Government Printing Office, 1919), 12.

61. BA 1:557, 570, 577.

62. Mächler, *Das Leben Robert Walsers,* 145. Mächler believes he'd amassed debts that needed to be repaid. According to archivist Lukas Gloor of the Robert Walser-Archiv, each of the five surviving Walser siblings received the same sum in a combination of cash payments and bonds: Robert received 3,833.60 francs in cash and another 1,000 in bonds (Lisa received 2,833.60 in cash and 2,000 in bonds), email correspondence from March 20, 2019.

63. Emil Schibli, *Die Vorlesung, Der kleine Bund* 108:77 (February 15, 1957), reprinted in *Über Robert Walser,* 1:174–78, 176–77.

64. Bernhard Echte, "Die Spur auf dem Vorsatz. Robert Walsers Biographie im Spiegel seiner Widmungsexemplare," *Librarium: Zeitschrift der Schweizerischen Bibliophilen Gesellschaft* 51:2 (2008): 135–47, 144; Mächler, *Das Leben Robert Walsers,* 140; Echte, ed., *Robert Walser,* 340; BA 1:632, 639.

65. Robert Walser, "Der Leseabend," SW 16:69–75, 75; Walser, "Der Vortragsveranstalter. Der Dichter," AdB 4:338–40.

66. Matthias Sprünglin, "Editorisches Nachwort," KWA I.11:193–217, 195; according to Rascher's records as of 1931, quoted in Sprünglin, "Editorisches Nachwort," KWA I.11:212, 215.

67. He also perhaps took inspiration from seeing actor Alexander Moissi—an old Berlin acquaintance—who performed on tour in Biel and went out drinking with Walser after the show, at least by Walser's own report: "Moissi in Biel," SW 16:318–20; "Der Taugenichts," SW 14:135–42; "Das Liebespaar," SW 14:143–66; "Dornröschen," SW 14:167–76; "Das Christkind," SW 14:177–89.

68. BA 1:534, 558, 609, 616, 628–29; Seelig, *Walks with Walser*, 62.

69. BA 1:632, 635, 603–4.

70. BA 1:641.

Chapter 13. The Secret Novel (1921–1925)

1. Seelig, *Walks with Walser*, 18.

2. Document of the Governing Council of Canton Bern concerning the appointment of Robert Walser as assistant archivist, reproduced in Echte, ed., *Robert Walser*, 344.

3. The Rathaus today is more austere in appearance following a renovation in 1940–1942.

4. BA 2:9; Robert Walser, "Neueste Nachricht," SW 17:7–8, 7.

5. Seelig, *Walks with Walser*, 17–18; Mermet, "Frau Frieda Mermet erzählt," 17; Echte, ed., *Robert Walser*, 344.

6. Robert Walser, "Die Elfenau," SW 17:19–21, 19.

7. BA 2:10; Walser, *The Robber*, 32.

8. BA 2:9, 1:605.

9. BA 2:9; Walser, "Neueste Nachricht," 7.

10. Walser, *The Robber*, 32–33.

11. BA 2:10, 12–13; Robert Walser, "Reise ins Emmental," SW 17:16–19, appeared in *Leipziger Tageblatt* in April 1921; "Nachricht Drei," SW 17:10–12, appeared in *Die Weltbühne* in June 1921.

12. BA 2:90.

13. Seelig, *Walks with Walser*, 17–18.

14. Walser distrusted Faesi—whose novella *Füsilier Wipf* had appeared alongside *The Walk* in 1917—for reasons no longer clear. He'd declined invitations from Faesi to read his work in Zurich (BA 1:432, 529) and in early 1920 refused to allow poems of his to be included in an anthology Rascher was planning—apparently because Faesi was the editor, BA 1:607–8, 611–12.

15. BA 2:38, 65n12, 363.

16. BA 2:63–64; Curt Hauschild, letter to the Swiss Writers' Association, April 4, 1924, BA 3:120.

17. Mächler, *Das Leben Robert Walsers*, 158. The same story is recounted—described as hearsay and without the name Caesar—by Franz Blei, *Erzählung eines Lebens* (Leipzig: Paul List, 1930), 273; Walser, *The Robber*, 68; BA 2:65.

18. Gerald E. Brennan, "The Rowohlt Verlag GmbH," in *International Directory of Company Histories* 96, ed. Tina Grant (Detroit: St. James Press, 2009), 356-61; Seelig, *Walks with Walser,* 124. Presumably the manuscript remained in Rowohlt's archive, destroyed during World War II when an Allied bomb struck a storage building in Stuttgart, "Dokumentarischer Anhang," *Die Rose,* KWA I.12:135; Robert Walser, "Das 'Tagebuch'-Fragment von 1926," SW 18:59-110, 78; BA 2:287.

19. Robert Walser, "Theodor: Aus einem kleinen Roman," SW 17:345-69.

20. Walser, "Theodor," 351.

21. Lisa Wenger, "Reader's Report on Robert Walser, *Theodor, ein kleiner Roman,*" reproduced in Echte, ed., *Robert Walser,* 353.

22. Ernst Morgenthaler, "Wie ich den Dichter Robert Walser kennen lernte," in *Ein Maler erzält* (Zurich: Diogenes, 1957), 73-78, 73-76.

23. "Literarischer Club," under the rubric "Kleine Chronik," *Neue Zürcher Zeitung* 370 (March 20, 1922), evening edition, d1-d2; BA 2:51.

24. *Lesezirkelheft,* quoted in Carl Seelig's manuscript notes for a biography of Robert Walser, page titled "Fritz Kochers Aufsätze," and Dr. Werner Lauber, telephone conversation with Carl Seelig on January 3, 1954, quoted in Seelig's manuscript notes, page titled "Fritz Kochers Aufsätze," both in "Robert Walser Biographie II," RWA, Nachlass Carl Seelig, D-03-a-13: Walser, Robert.

25. Morgenthaler, "Wie ich den Dichter Robert Walser kennen lernte," 73-76.

26. BA 2:42, 50, 51; Morgenthaler, "Wie ich den Dichter Robert Walser kennen lernte," 76.

27. Morgenthaler, "Wie ich den Dichter Robert Walser kennen lernte," 76.

28. BA 2:52; Morgenthaler, "Wie ich den Dichter Robert Walser kennen lernte," 76-77; BA 2:60; Seelig, *Walks with Walser,* 48.

29. Conversation with Hermann Hubacher (October 1944), recorded in Seelig's manuscript notes, page titled "Karl," RWA, Nachlass Carl Seelig, D-03-a-13.

30. Conversation with Anna Hubacher-Tscherter (undated), recorded in Seelig's manuscript notes under "Biographie II," RWA, Nachlass Carl Seelig, D-03-a-13; Echte, ed., *Robert Walser,* 351-52.

31. Hermann would later sculpt the Ganymede that stands beside Lake Zurich at Bürkliplatz; Anna Hubacher-Tscherter, quoted in Echte, ed., *Robert Walser,* 351-52.

32. "Cad" and "dog" are somewhat less colorful than the Swiss expressions *Lümmel* and *Saucheib,* BA 2:45.

33. The friend was one "Miss Wannenmacher," BA 2:23.

34. BA 2:81; "N'est ce pas, je suis un vrai vagabond, parceque [*sic*] je change si rapidement mes pensions?," BA 2:58.

35. Robert Walser, "The Green Spider," in *Masquerade,* 139-40; Walser, "Das 'Tagebuch'-Fragment," 101-2; Walser, *The Robber,* 12.

36. Walser-Hindermann, a pupil of the great Gottfried Semper, enjoyed a successful architectural career, building among other things the Allgemeine Gewerbeschule in Basel. "Nekrologie F. Walser," *Schweizerische Bauzeitung* 79:20 (May 20, 1922), 260-61.

37. As usual playing with ambiguity and irony, he says he can always return to his "traditional" employment of beating rugs, BA 2:35.

38. Forty francs per month was the rent of the room he stayed in longest, at Luisenstrasse 14, starting in 1926. Seelig, *Walks with Walser,* 17; BA 2:246. He did publish a prose piece in March 1925, "Erich," whose narrator visits a splendid room that "cost 40 francs; he never spent more than eighteen francs monthly on a room." Walser may have wished to emphasize his thriftiness in this printed text, since the room he paid 40 for in 1926 sounds unexceptional. Walser, "Erich," SW 8:43–46, 44.

39. Letters from Lisa Walser to Carl Seelig from March 9, 1937, and April 24, 1937, RWA, Sammlung Robert Walser, E-02: Sammlung Lisa Walser; cf. Mächler, *Robert Walser,* 148; *The Robber* mentions a life-changing inheritance from an uncle, but Lisa never saw that novel, Walser, *The Robber,* 4; Friedrich Walser's remark about the starvelings was communicated by Ruth Pfander-Walser, conversation on July 20, 2019; D. E. Walser, *Elise Walser-Marti,* 11.

40. BA 2:58, 99; Walser, "Das 'Tagebuch'-Fragment," 74; Walser, "Erich," 44; Walser, "Am I Demanding?," translated by Christopher Middleton, in *Selected Stories,* 148–51.

41. Electrician: Mr. Vogt, Gerechtigkeitsgasse 51; greengrocer: Arnold Brügger, Junkerngasse 29; merchant: Adolf Hummel, Thunstrasse 21; warehouse supervisor: Rudolf Lehner, Gerechtigkeitsgasse 29; laundress: Elisabeth Vollenweider, Thunstrasse 20, was a laundress like Mermet, except that she was also the proprietress of her own business, located just next door (at Thunstrasse 18). Elisabeth Vollenweider's business is listed under laundries (*Glättereien*) in the forty-fourth edition (1926) of *Adressbuch der Stadt Bern,* ed. Fritz Haller-Blon (Bern: W. Michaelsen, 1926). All we know of his landlord and/or landlady at Elfenauweg 41 is the family name Kilchmann; Morlang, *Robert Walser in Bern,* 24; Seelig, *Walks with Walser,* 75.

42. Helen Münch-Küng, *Der Literaturkritiker Eduard Korrodi,* Zürcher Germanistische Studien 18 (Bern: Peter Lang, 1989), 45–47, 50.

43. BA 2:61, 62–63.

44. In particular, Robert reported displeasure with what he saw as revanchist, German nationalist sentiments expressed in essays by Ernst Robert Curtius and Otto Flake that Frisch had published, BA 2:18–20, 42.

45. Letter from Alfred Fankhauser to Robert Mächler, September 7, 1964, reprinted in Mächler, *Das Leben Robert Walsers,* 155–57; cf. BA 2:92.

46. Seelig, *Walks with Walser,* 75; BA 2:82; Walser, "Jean Paul," SW 17:157–62, 157; BA 2:128.

47. BA 2:11; Robert Walser, "Die Ruine," SW 17:126–42, 132–34; BA 1:487.

48. BA 2:56.

49. BA 2:70, 78–79, 123–24.

50. Peter Stocker, "Literaturbetrieb, Verlage, Zeitschriften und Zeitungen," in *Robert Walser Handbuch,* 40–48, 47; BA 2:45, 46n33.

51. Letter from Gustav Kilpper to Efraim Frisch, April 25, 1925, quoted in BA 2:122n10; letter from Curt Hauschild to the Swiss Writers' Association, April 4, 1924, BA 3:121.

52. BA 2:93.

53. Robert Walser, "Fünfuhrtee," SW 17:195–96, 195; Walser, "A Little Ramble," translated by Tom Whalen, in *Selected Stories*, 30–31, 31.

54. Robert Walser, "Napoleon und die Gräfin Valewska," SW 17:52–54, 52 (the spelling "Valewska" was standardized to "Walewska" in a later printing); Emil Schibli, *Die Vorlesung, Der kleine Bund* 108:77 (February 15, 1957), reprinted in KWA III.3:488–90, 489.

55. Robert Walser, "Mäntel," SW 17:196–97, 197.

56. Robert Walser, "All those who love to laugh while crying . . . ," in *Masquerade*, 173–75, 173; cf. "Alle diejenigen, die gern lachen und zugleich weinen," AdB 4:95–98, 95.

57. Robert Walser, "Ophelia: Eine Novelle," SW 17:279–95, 283–84.

58. Robert Walser, "Ich ging wieder einmal ins Theater," SW 17:38–41, 39; Walser, "Robert the Rascal," in *Masquerade,* 125–26, 125 (translation altered), "Der Schurke Robert," SW 17:208–10, 208. The first sentence of the version of this text printed in the November 1924 issue of *Der Basilisk,* the Sunday supplement of the newspaper *National-Zeitung* (Basel), contains the adjective "spider-web-like" (*spinnwebartige*), either a typo for or an edit of the word "spider-web-delicate" (*spinnwebzarte*) originally contained in the manuscript, KWA VI.1:128–29, 128, cf. Wolfram Groddeck, Angela Thut, and Christian Walt, "Editorisches Nachwort," KWA VI.1:379–91, 384.

59. In the poems Walser wrote during this period, he employed elaborate, often comical, rhymes to similarly destabilizing effect, cf. Samuel Frederick, "Robert Walser as Lyric Poet," in *Robert Walser: A Companion,* ed. Samuel Frederick and Valerie Heffernan (Evanston, IL: Northwestern University Press, 2018), 65–86, 74–76.

60. Echte, ed., *Robert Walser,* 228, 370; Paul Mayer, *Ernst Rowohlt in Selbstzeugnissen und Bilddokumenten* (Reinbek bei Hamburg: Rowohlt, 1968), 76; other writers Hessel would recommend to Rowohlt would include his friend Walter Benjamin, with whom he would also cotranslate three volumes of Proust's *In Search of Lost Time* and whose *Origin of German Tragic Drama* and *One-Way Street* he would shepherd into print in 1928. Only two volumes of the Benjamin/Hessel Proust translations (vol. 2: *Im Schatten der jungen Mädchen,* and vol. 3: *Guermantes*) saw print before the National Socialist seizure of power prevented the publication of further Proust volumes. The manuscript of their translation of vol. 4 was destroyed or lost, cf. John T. Hamilton, "The Task of the Flâneur," in *A New History of German Literature,* ed. David E. Wellbery, Judith Ryan, Hans Ulrich Gumbrecht, Anton Kaes, Joseph Leo Koerner, and Dorothea E. von Mücke (Cambridge, MA: Harvard University Press, 2004), 748–53, 751–52.

61. Robert Walser, "Der Onkel," SW 8:33–34, 34; "Wer vormals demütelte, der herrschelte jetzt," Walser, "Lehrer und Dienstmann," SW 8:32–33, 33; Walser, "Eine Ohrfeige und Sonstiges," SW 8:49–65, 63; such portmanteaux push the boundaries of the translatable, cf. "A Slap in the Face et cetera," translated by Mark Harman, in *Robert Walser Rediscovered: Stories, Fairy-Tale Plays, and Critical Responses,* ed. Mark Harman (Hanover, NH: University Press of New England, 1985), 34–46, 45, where the word is translated "stretch a leg in the park"; "Letter to

Edith," translated by Susan Bernofsky and Tom Whalen, in *Masquerade* (translation amended), 162–64, 163.

62. Robert Walser, "A Lump of Sugar," in *Masquerade,* 154–55; Walser, "Das Kind," SW 8:74–79, 75.

63. Walser, "Das Kind," SW 8:78.

64. Walser, "Das Kind," SW 8:79.

65. Other examples discussed in Chapter 7 were written in 1925 or after and for the most part went unpublished; Robert Walser, "Schwäche und Stärke," SW 8:95–98, 96–97.

66. BA 2:101, 126, 111, 114.

67. Hermann Hesse, "Erinnerung an Lektüre," *Die Neue Rundschau* 36:9 (September 1925): 964–72, 970–71, quoted in Wolfram Groddeck, Hans-Joachim Heerde, and Caroline Socha, "Editorisches Nachwort," *Die Rose,* KWA I.12:109–34, 129, 117–19.

68. Walser, *The Robber,* 19, 16, 11; the character Selma was apparently inspired by two of Walser's former landladies, Emma Lenz-Gräub, described earlier in this chapter, and Bertha Winter, a retired nurse from whom he rented a room with desk and balcony starting in May 1924, Morlang, *Robert Walser in Bern,* 13; at the news of Foreign Minister Rathenau's assassination, the Robber utters a cry of "Bravo" (echoing a key turning point in Lessing's *Emilia Galotti*)—an act of disrespect for which Edith later punishes him, Walser, *The Robber,* 11.

69. Walser, *The Robber,* 100.

70. Walser, *The Robber,* 103–4, 106; Walser, "Sacher-Masoch," SW 8:68–70, 69.

71. Robert Walser, *Der 'Räuber'-Roman,* SW 12:129 (cf. "little-girlishnesses," *The Robber,* 94); Walser, *The Robber,* 96. "Im allgemeinen bin ich gegenwärtig freilich wohl fast etwas zu diplomatisch aufgelegt, als daß ich eine solche Mission leicht übernähme," Walser, *Der 'Räuber'-Roman,* SW 12:131.

72. Walser, *The Robber,* 129.

73. The pages on which *The Robber* was composed measure 13 by 21.6 centimeters (approximately 5 1/8 by 8 7/16 inches); the term *Mikrogramm* ("microscript"), referring to an individual pencil draft manuscript, was coined by Jochen Greven in 1967, Lucas Marco Gisi, Peter Stocker, and Reto Sorg, "Nachwort," in *Mikrogramme* (Berlin: Suhrkamp, 2011), 203–13, 208.

74. BA 2:220.

75. "Letter to Max Brod, October 4, 1927," translated by Susan Bernofsky, *Review of Contemporary Fiction* 12:1 (1992): 35–36, 36.

Chapter 14. The Unraveling (1925–1929)

1. Robert Walser, "Meine Bemühungen," quoted in Susan Bernofsky, "Unrelenting Tact: Elements of Style in Walser's Late Prose," in *Robert Walser and the Visual Arts,* ed. Tamara S. Evans, Pro Helvetia Swiss Lectureship 9 (New York: City University of New York, 1996), 80–89, 81.

2. The work of Stein, whose *Tender Buttons* appeared in 1914, had not yet been translated into either German or French; Joyce's *Exiles* was published in German in 1919, but *Ulysses* (Paris, 1922) would not be translated until 1927; Joyce isn't mentioned in Walser's extant letters or texts.

3. Hermann Hesse, "Poetenleben," in *Über Robert Walser,* 1:57–58, 58; BA 2:118. Walser later mentioned this letter to Seelig, saying Mann had called him "a clever child" (*Walks with Walser,* 19).

4. BA 2:250n7.

5. W. G. Sebald, "Le promeneur solitaire: A remembrance of Robert Walser," in *A Place in the Country: On Gottfried Keller, Johann Peter Hebel, Robert Walser, and Others,* trans. Jo Catling (New York: Random House, 2013), 125–64, 139; Walser, "A Little Ramble," 31; Seelig, *Walks with Walser,* 12.

6. Robert Walser, "A Sort of Cleopatra," in *Microscripts,* 107–9, 107, 109.

7. BA 2:136–37; BA 2:117n4.

8. BA 2:299.

9. BA 2:262–63; "Letter to Max Brod October 4, 1927," 35; BA 2:297n19.

10. Samuel Fischer, "Bemerkungen zur Bücherkrise" (1926), Signaturen der Epoche," in *Geschichte des deutschen Buchhandels* 2:1 (Munich: K. G. Saur, 2007), 5–28, 20; Kurt Wolff, quoted in Ernst Fischer, "Marktorganisation," in *Geschichte des deutschen Buchhandels* 2:1, 265–304, 274.

11. Mermet, "Frau Frieda Mermet erzählt," 17; BA 2:79–80.

12. BA 2:192.

13. Hans-Joachim Heerde and Barbara von Reibnitz, "Editorisches Nachwort," KWA III.4:2, 675–713, 703–4; this *Novina* (as opposed to the earlier Prague journal of the same name) was the former literary supplement of the newspaper *Čas* that had folded during the war, Kurt Ifkovits, "Robert Walsers Prager Spuren," in *Robert Walsers 'Ferne Nähe': Neue Beiträge zur Forschung* (Munich: Wilhelm Fink, 2007), 107–24, 113–14, 116–17; BA 2: 183, 133; Seelig, *Walks with Walser,* 11.

14. Ralf Lienhard, "Einleitung," in *Der Kreis der "Individualität"* (Bern: Haupt, 2003), 9–42, 24–27, 29; BA 2:392, Seelig, *Walks with Walser,* 11.

15. Bernhard Echte, "Hölderlin'sche Schicksalsfortsetzungen," *Recht und Psychiatrie* 21:2 (2003): 85–97, 91; Ifkovits, "Robert Walsers Prager Spuren," 118; BA 2:210, 216, 222; Seelig, *Walks with Walser,* 61–62.

16. BA 2:210, 210–11n15, 286.

17. BA 2:83–84, 84n3; Roman Bucheli, "Rychner, Max" in *Neue Deutsche Biographie* 22 (2005), 309–10, https://www.deutsche-biographie.de/pnd118750526.html.

18. BA 2:85, 76n10, 106; Robert Walser, "Kurt," translated by Susan Bernofsky and Tom Whalen, in *Masquerade,* 157 (translation amended); Rychner had declared his displeasure with the way contemporary Swiss literature was dominated by the reflections of the solitary male—brooding, introverted dreamers turned away from the world—with too little interest in writing female characters ("Über den Entwicklungsroman," *Almanach des Verlages Grethlein 1899–1924* [Zürich: Grethlein, 1924], 71–77).

19. BA 2:198. The topic of the relationship between intellect and creativity also figured in an another article from the journal Robert took issue with: a piece by Ernst Robert Curtius about Charles de Saint-Evremond.

20. BA 2:199.

21. Walser's use of the Swiss diminutive *Prosastückli* ("little prose piece") is humorously self-deprecating; BA 2:142, 289–91.

22. By 1917, more than forty agencies specialized in placing short prose in newspaper feuilleton sections, Andreas Graf, "'Ehrliche Makler' oder 'Ausbeuter der Schrift-

stellerwelt'? Die Anfänge der Literaturagenturen in Deutschland," in *Literarische Agenturen—die heimlichen Herrscher im Literaturbetrieb?*, ed. Ernst Fischer, Mainzer Studien zur Buchwissenschaft, vol. 11 (Wiesbaden: Harrassowitz, 2001), 85–99, 90–92; Walser's use of literary agents was first discovered by Bernhard Echte, cf. "Nachwort" in Robert Walser, *Feuer: Unbekannte Prose und Gedichte,* ed. Bernhard Echte (Frankfurt am Main: Suhrkamp, 2005), 117–27, 124–25.

23. Gregor Ackermann, "Wiederentdeckte Walser-Drucke," *Mitteilungen der Robert Walser-Gesellschaft* 15 (2008): 9–13, 9–10.

24. Hans-Joachim Heerde, "Robert Walser und der Allgemeine Schriftstellerverein (ASV)," *Mitteilungen der Robert Walser-Gesellschaft* 17 (April 2010): 16–24, 18–19; BA 2:285.

25. This letter from *Berliner Tageblatt* is no longer extant, but Walser wrote to Rychner about receiving it, BA 2:295; Seelig, *Walks with Walser,* 21; BA 2:292.

26. BA 2:302, 411; Seelig, *Walks with Walser,* 10.

27. BA 2:317, 336–37.

28. "The Ruin" ("Die Ruine") from 1925 is one such composite text. Cf. BA 2:136; on Microscript 116, Walser also changed the printed address to "Little Fool Street" and added the note "published by Magical Publishing," cf. *Microscripts* 134, note to pages 89–90.

29. BA 3:138.

30. BA 2:146; Robert Walser, "A Letter to Therese Breitbach" (undated, between September and November 1925), translated by Christopher Middleton, in *Selected Stories,* 164–66, 165–66; Seelig, *Walks with Walser,* 26.

31. BA 2:174, 179.

32. Walser, "A Letter to Therese Breitbach," 165–66; BA 2:341; Mermet, "Frau Frieda Mermet erzählt," 18; Walser, "New Year's Page," in *Microscripts,* 129–31, 131; Seelig, *Walks with Walser,* 18.

33. BA 2:328, 408.

34. BA 2:79, 81, 90; Mermet, "Frau Frieda Mermet erzählt," 17; Seelig, *Walks with Walser,* 10, 62.

35. Walser boasts of his "tightrope-walkerish" stunt on the bridge railings in a letter to Mermet (BA 2:78); Walser, *The Robber,* 36, 42–43, 60; BA 2:293.

36. BA 2:326, 346, 365.

37. BA 2:272, 288.

38. Echte, ed., *Robert Walser,* 401.

39. BA 2:379.

40. BA 2:265, 381.

41. Robert Walser, "Wenn Autoren krank sind," SW 19:265–68, 266.

42. Mermet, "Frau Frieda Mermet erzählt," 17–18; BA 2:209, 237–38, 213, 229n1.

43. BA 2:141; letter from Frieda Mermet to Carl Seelig, January 14, 1954, RWA, Nachlass Carl Seelig, B-04: Robert Walser; BA 2:162; BA 2:96.

44. BA 2:251, 255, 297, 383, 398, 400.

45. BA 2:164n27.

46. Mermet, "Frau Frieda Mermet erzählt," 17–18.

47. Letter from Lisa Walser to Otto Hinrichsen, July 10, 1937, quoted in Echte, ed., *Robert Walser,* 276.

48. BA 2:312; Isabella Kammacher, "Er hätte mein Onkel werden können," *Mitteilungen der Robert Walser-Gesellschaft* 2 (March 1998): 5.

49. BA 2:94, cf. D. E. Walser, *Robert Walser: Aus seiner Familie,* n10; BA 2:408; Hans Marty's business card became "Microscript 389," in *Microscripts,* 127–28.

50. Seelig, *Walks with Walser,* 62, 103; BA 2:189–90; to Seelig, Walser also mentioned an associate Seelig notated as "A.F." (Alfred Fankhauser?), whom Walser described as "completely shameless," saying he "should have socked him."

51. Kistler, "Erinnerungen an Robert Walser," 44–46.

52. BA 2:411–12.

53. Walser's letter about the woman in Murten violently describes her as a "sow," a "she-dog," and a "cat fit for drowning," BA 2:190–91; 205, 246; Walser, *The Robber,* 1.

54. BA 2:208.

55. BA 2:385–86, 226, 234, 139, 183; Robert Walser, "Wenn ich bei mir von einer Sehnsucht reden darf . . . ," AdB 2:482–87, 485.

56. BA 2:239, 384; Seelig, *Walks with Walser,* 18.

57. Walser, "Die Elfenau," SW 17:21; Robert Walser, "Wohnungswechsel," 80–83, 81.

58. BA 2:188–89, 212–13, 224; Frieda Gall lived with her husband and five children at Elfenauweg 41, *Adressbuch der Stadt Bern* (1927), 224.

59. Schweizerische Nationalbibliothek, Zf 967, *Anzeiger für die Stadt Bern,* April 30, 1926.

60. Martha Häberlin was born in 1884; BA 2:246, AdB 5:21.

61. Letter from Hermann Hubacher to Carl Seelig, September 16, 1953, RWA, Nachlass Carl Seelig, B-04: Robert Walser.

62. Conversation with Hermann Hubacher and his wife Anna Hubacher-Tscherter (October 1944) recorded in Carl Seelig's manuscript notes for a biography of Robert Walser, page titled "Berner Zeit," RWA, Nachlass Carl Seelig, D-3-a-13: Walser, Robert. The "bear pit" housing several live bears, the city mascot, was a popular attraction in Bern—the bears now inhabit a more comfortable enclosure; Karl had previously told Seelig that Robert had fallen in love with a circus artiste who kept a monkey and that he had taken 1,000 francs out of the bank to give to her, Seelig, notes from a conversation with Karl Walser on March 1, 1937, RWA, Nachlass Carl Seelig, D-3-a-13: Walser, Robert.

63. BA 2:331, 333, 337, 369.

64. Adolf Schaer-Ris, "Flüchtige Begegnung mit Robert Walser," *Der Kleine Bund,* April 4, 1943, quoted in Morlang, *Robert Walser in Bern,* 136–40, 140.

65. Emil Stumpp, "Bei Robert Walser," *Annalen: Eine schweizerische Monatsschrift* 2:4 (April 1928): 310–12.

66. Mermet, "Frau Frieda Mermet erzählt," 18.

67. Krankengeschichte No. 10.428, Irren-, Heil- und Pflegeanstalt Waldau (Psychiatrische Universitätsklinik Bern), 2.

68. Krankengeschichte No. 10.428, Irren-, Heil- und Pflegeanstalt Waldau (Psychiatrische Universitätsklinik Bern), 7; Margrit Kistler learned of Walser's hallucinations from one of the Häberlin sisters when she came looking for him several weeks after his hospitalization, Kistler, "Erinnerungen an Robert Walser," 47; Seelig, *Walks with Walser,* 21.

69. Seelig, *Walks with Walser,* 21.

Chapter 15. The Quiet Years (1929-1956)

1. This is the first of many notes throughout this chapter taken from Robert Walser's medical records from the Irren-, Heil- und Pflegeanstalt Waldau (Psychiatrische Universitätsklinik Bern) (Krankengeschichte No. 10.428), hereafter "Krankengeschichte Waldau," and the Heil- und Pflegeanstalt Herisau (Krankengeschichte No. 3561, StAAR: Pa.057-07), hereafter "Krankengeschichte Herisau." The Waldau records are archived at the Museum of Psychiatry, Bern. The Herisau records are in the collection of the Staatsarchiv des Kantons Appenzell Ausserrhoden. They are consecutively numbered, with the Herisau record beginning on page 13; Fritz Walther, "Wilhelm von Speyr 1852-1939," *Verhandlungen der Schweizerischen Naturforschenden Gesellschaft* 120 (1940/41): 494-502, 497; Seelig, *Walks with Walser,* 66.

2. Walther, "Wilhelm von Speyr," 494-97; Martina Wernli, *Schreiben am Rand: Die "Bernische kantonale Irrenanstalt Waldau" und ihre Narrative (1895-1936)* (Bielefeld: Transcript Verlag, 1914), 22.

3. Krankengeschichte Waldau, 1-2.

4. Krankengeschichte Waldau, 2.

5. Krankengeschichte Waldau, 2-4.

6. Dr. W. [Walter] Morgenthaler, *Die Pflege der Gemüts- und Geisteskranken* (Bern: Verlag Hans Huber, 1930), 101-2.

7. Morgenthaler, *Die Pflege,* 101-2; another celebrated patient at Waldau during this period was the artist Adolf Wölfli—to whose illness and work Morgenthaler devoted a monograph in 1921, *A Mental Patient as Artist.* Wölfli and Walser overlapped at Waldau by almost two years but probably never met. Repeatedly violent to asylum staff and fellow patients, Wölfli was kept in isolation. Walter Morgenthaler, *Ein Geisteskranker als Künstler* (Bern: E. Bircher, 1921).

8. Krankengeschichte Waldau, 4.

9. Krankengeschichte Waldau, 5.

10. BA 2:413, 415, 417; his letter to the Häberlins, no longer extant, is mentioned in their letter to Lisa on February 22, 1929, RWA, Sammlung Robert Walser, E-02: Sammlung Lisa Walser.

11. BA 2:414-15; Krankengeschichte Waldau, 5.

12. Krankengeschichte Waldau, 5-6.

13. Seelig, *Walks with Walser,* 66; Krankengeschichte Waldau, 6.

14. Krankengeschichte Waldau, 7.

15. Krankengeschichte Waldau, 8.

16. BA 2:424; Robert Walser, "April," SW 13:119, written in 1930 or 1931 and unpublished.

17. SW 13:126.

18. SW 13:237-38.

19. Angela Thut, Christian Walt, and Wolfram Groddeck, "Editorisches Nachwort," *Prager Manuskripte,* KWA V.2:489-96.

20. BA 2:427-28, 440. Cf. Microscript 9, *Microscripts,* 37-38.

21. Krankengeschichte Waldau, 8-9.

22. Wernli, *Schreiben am Rand,* 288; Krankengeschichte Waldau, 9-10.

23. Krankengeschichte Waldau, 9.

24. Wernli, *Schreiben am Rand,* 214; *Jahresbericht der bernischen kantonalen Irrenanstalt Waldau* 1933, quoted in Wernli, *Schreiben am Rand,* 219; K[onrad] Alt, "Über ländliche Beschäftigung der Kranksinningen in Anstalt und Familienpflege," *Compte Rendu des Travaux du 1er Congress International de Psychiatrie, de Neurologie de Psychologie et de l'Assistance des Aliénes,* ed. G. A. M van Wagenburg (Amsterdam: J. H. de Bussy, 1908), 2:777–88, 778. In later years, Waldau would be criticized for not remunerating patients for their labor, Max Müller, *Erinnerungen: erlebte Psychiatriegeschichte, 1920–1960* (Berlin: Springer, 1982), 440, quoted in Wernli, *Schreiben am Rand,* 221.

25. Krankengeschichte Waldau, 10.

26. BA 3:51–52.

27. Oscar had proposed in June 1929 that he would cover half Robert's fee at Waldau, with Lisa and Karl each covering one-quarter. But later he and Karl both stopped contributing when they became convinced that Robert was living it up at their expense. Letters from Oscar Walser to Lisa Walser, June 13, 1929, June 6, 1930, and June 8, 1930, RWA, Sammlung Robert Walser, E-02: Sammlung Lisa Walser; letters from Lisa Walser to Carl Seelig, March 3, 1937, and March 9, 1937; Frieda added—at least this once in 1937—a contribution of 25 francs to the 100-franc sum Lisa sent Seelig for Robert every month, letter from Lisa Walser to Carl Seelig, June 12, 1937, RWA, Sammlung Robert Walser, E-02: Sammlung Lisa Walser.

28. This conversation is described in a letter from Lisa Walser to Carl Seelig, March 9, 1937, RWA, Sammlung Robert Walser, E-02: Sammlung Lisa Walser.

29. Lucas Marco Gisi, "Otto Hinrichsen als erster Rezensent Robert Walsers?," *Mitteilungen der Robert Walser-Gesellschaft* 18 (April 2011): 20–22; in a diary entry from July 1933, Hinrichsen recalls having shown Blei Walser's first poems in *Der Bund* in 1898, reproduced in Echte, ed., *Robert Walser,* 433; Lucas Marco Gisi, "Das Schweigen des Schriftstellers: Robert Walser und das Macht-Wissen der Psychiatrie," in Martina Wernli, ed., *Wissen und Nicht- Wissen in der Klinik: Dynamiken der Psychiatrie um 1900* (Bielefeld: Transcript Verlag, 2012), 244n39.

30. "Aerztliches Zeugnis" addressed to the Director of Herisau Sanatorium by Jakob Klaesi, dated June 18, 1933 (Krankengeschichte Herisau); letter from Lisa Walser to Carl Seelig, March 1, 1936, RWA, Sammlung Robert Walser, E-02: Sammlung Lisa Walser.

31. Krankengeschichte Waldau, 10.

32. Otto Hinnerk [Hinrichsen], *Triumph der Wissenschaft* [Triumph of Science]: *Komödie in 3 Akten* (Zurich: Rascher, 1932); Lisa had asked Hinrichsen whether Robert might be upgraded as a courtesy, as had been the case at Waldau, letter from Lisa Walser to Otto Hinrichsen, June 22, 1933, reproduced in Echte, ed., *Robert Walser,* 429; letter from Otto Hinrichsen to Lisa Walser, June 26, 1933, RWA, Sammlung Robert Walser, E-02: Sammlung Lisa Walser.

33. Livia Knüsel, "Robert Walser in der Arbeitstherapie," in *Robert Walser: Herisauer Jahre 1933–1956,* 2nd ed. (Herisau: Appenzeller, 2013), 39–55, 44.

34. Walser's resistance to Hinrichsen and the long history of Hinrichsen's beliefs about the connection between mental illness and creativity are described in detail in Gisi, "Das Schweigen des Schriftstellers."

35. Otto Hinrichsen, diary entry from July 1933, reproduced in Echte, ed., *Robert Walser*, 433.

36. Robert Walser, "Mutter Natur," SW 20:79–80, 80.

37. Seelig, *Walks with Walser*, 24, 28 (translation amended), 25; letter from Otto Hinrichsen to Carl Seelig, September 11, 1940, RWA, Nachlass Carl Seelig, B-04: Robert Walser; Krankengeschichte Herisau, 14–15.

38. Seelig, *Walks with Walser*, 21.

39. Krankengeschichte Herisau, 13–15, 17, 19, 25.

40. Krankengeschichte Herisau, 14, 18.

41. Otto Hinrichsen, petition submitted to the Municipal Guardianship Office, Bern, on January 19, 1934, reproduced in Echte, ed., *Robert Walser*, 434.

42. Echte, ed., *Robert Walser*, 435; BA 2:450.

43. On July 1, 1933, Walser's assets had amounted to 7,244.55 francs, meanwhile diminished by the expenses of his move to Herisau and the first nine months of his care there; handwritten transcription of letter from Lisa Walser to Oscar Walser from July 1, 1933, RWA, Sammlung Robert Walser: E-02: Sammlung Lisa Walser; Peter Witschi, "Unter Vormundschaft," in *Robert Walser: Herisauer Jahre*, 83–91, 84.

44. "Vermögensbestand 1937," "Vermögensbestand 1938," and "Vormundschaftsbericht 1940," RWA, Sammlung Robert Walser, C-02 Dokumente aus den Heil- und Pflegeanstalten Waldau und Herisau; Seelig, *Walks with Walser*, 11.

45. Witschi, "Unter Vormundschaft," 89. In 1942, the charges for room and board came to 2.75 francs per day (= 1,003.75 per year); "Vormundschaftsbericht 1940," "Bericht 1941," and invoice attached to "Bericht 1943," RWA, Sammlung Robert Walser, C-02 Dokumente aus den Heil- und Pflegeanstalten Waldau und Herisau; letter from Martin Bodmer to Carl Seelig, February 11, 1937, RWA, Sammlung Robert Walser, B-04: Robert Walser.

46. Letter from Lisa Walser to Carl Seelig, January 18, 1937, RWA, Sammlung Robert Walser, E-02: Sammlung Lisa Walser; letter from Carl Seelig to Lisa Walser, January 7, 1937, RWA, Sammlung Robert Walser, E-02: Sammlung Lisa Walser, referring to the same meeting with Walser on January 3, 1937, as described in Seelig, *Walks with Walser*, 9–13; letters from Otto Hinrichsen to Lisa Walser, October 14, 1935 (quoted in Gisi, "Das Schweigen des Schriftstellers," 250n65, 251) and February 24, 1937, RWA, Sammlung Robert Walser, E-02: Sammlung Lisa Walser; Seelig, *Walks with Walser*, 11.

47. Ulrich Weinzierl, *Carl Seelig, Schriftsteller* (Vienna: Löcker, 1982), 59.

48. Echte, ed., *Robert Walser*, 436; Seelig, *Walks with Walser*, 7; BA 2:48; Hermann Hesse had recommended that Seelig invite Robert to expand his essay "Brentano" into a book-length piece; Robert wasn't interested, letter from Hermann Hesse to Carl Seelig, December 20, 1921, in Hesse, *Die Briefe* 3, ed. Volker Michels (Berlin: Suhrkamp, 2015), 428.

49. Seelig, *Walks with Walser*, 7–8, translation amended.

50. Seelig, *Walks with Walser*, 9.

51. Letter from Carl Seelig to Lisa Walser, July 26, 1936, reproduced in Echte, ed., *Robert Walser*, 438.

52. Stefan Zweig, "Große kleine Welt," and Alfred Polgar, "Robert Walser's *Große kleine Welt*," in *Über Robert Walser*, 1:139, 141.

53. Seelig, *Walks with Walser*, 30, 105.

54. Wernli, *Schreiben am Rand*, 324–25.

55. Seelig, *Walks with Walser*, 11–12, 36.

56. Krankengeschichte Herisau, 26.

57. This comment of Walser's was related by Carl Seelig to Jochen Greven and recorded in Greven's notes on their conversation, quoted in Gisi, "Das Schweigen des Schriftstellers," 241.

58. The provenance of this famous quotation is spurious. It was first recorded by Christopher Middleton in his introduction to his 1969 translation of *Jakob von Gunten* and exists in German only as a back-translation from Middleton's English. Fifty years later, Middleton could no longer recall where this quotation had come from. It was most likely communicated to him by Seelig the one time they met, in late January or early February 1955. Middleton reports that Seelig, upon learning that the young English poet had begun to translate Walser's stories, invited him over and poured him a glass of cognac that he joked was "in lieu of an honorarium" (author's phone conversation with Christopher Middleton on November 28, 2014). Cf. Christopher Middleton, "Translation as a Species of Mime," *Review of Contemporary Fiction* 12:1 (Spring 1992): 50–56, 50.

59. Seelig, *Walks with Walser*, 18 (translation amended); letter from Otto Hinrichsen to Carl Seelig, September 9, 1940, RWA, Nachlass Carl Seelig, B-04: Robert Walser.

60. Seelig, *Walks with Walser*, 16, 38, 40, 51, 131.

61. Walser wasn't a fan of milk chocolate, BA 2:463.

62. Seelig, *Walks with Walser*, 44, 49, 114; "'Er war anders wie die andern': Ein Gespräch zwischen Catherine Sauvat und Josef Wehrle," *Mitteilungen der Robert Walser-Gesellschaft* 2 (March 1998): 6–9, 7.

63. Seelig, *Walks with Walser*, 40; Barbara Auer, "Geschrieben, aber nicht gedruckt," in *Robert Walser: Herisauer Jahre*, 33–37, 35; Knüsel, "Robert Walser in der Arbeitstherapie," 41.

64. Krankengeschichte Herisau, 24; Knüsel, "Robert Walser in der Arbeitstherapie," 45, 47, 52.

65. Knüsel, "Robert Walser in der Arbeitstherapie," 48, 52.

66. Mermet, "Frieda Mermet erzählt," 18–19.

67. Schoch later served in the Cantonal Council for Appenzell Ausserrhoden, quoted in Peter Morger, "Wandern statt Dichten," in *Robert Walser: Herisauer Jahre*, 11–17, 12; Merz later served on the Swiss Federal Council, Hans-Rudolf Merz, "Ein fremder Wanderer: Zum 60. Todestag von Robert Walser," *Neue Zürcher Zeitung*, December 25, 2016, http://www.nzz.ch/feuilleton/zum-60-todestag-von-robert-walser-ein-fremder-wanderer-ld.136637.

68. Krankengeschichte Herisau, 19.

69. Krankengeschichte Herisau, 27.

70. Margit Gigerl, "Weshalb Robert Walser nicht geheilt wurde," in *Robert Walser: Herisauer Jahre,* 57–71, 67–68.

71. Echte, ed., *Robert Walser,* 466; Echte and Meier, eds., *Die Brüder Karl und Robert Walser,* 206.

72. Seelig, *Walks with Walser,* 59–60.

73. Witschi, "Unter Vormundschaft," 87, and Echte, ed., *Robert Walser,* 466.

74. Letter from Heinrich Künzler to Oscar Walser, May 22, 1944, quoted in Witschi, "Unter Vormundschaft," 87.

75. Krankengeschichte Herisau, 16. Seelig's article quoted Walser saying, "To this day, I've never been short on unsuccessfulness, but life can be delightful even without success!" The article also reports that Seelig asked Robert what he would do if he "had money" and received the answer: "go for a walk. Be happy. Observe Nature and people." Carl Seelig, "Robert Walser zum 60. Geburtstag am 15. April," in *Über Robert Walser,* 1:188–93, 188.

76. Seelig, *Walks with Walser,* 65, 116–17; Krankengeschichte Herisau, 22–23.

77. Seelig, *Walks with Walser,* 134.

78. Seelig, *Walks with Walser,* 31–32. In his book, Seelig dates the Säntis excursion May 11, 1942, but his correspondence with Walser and Walser's medical record indicate it took place on June 1, 1942, BA 2:495, 496n8.

79. BA 2:461n5, 462.

80. The last extant contract signed by Walser himself was for *Big Little World* in 1937, BA 3:52–54; Lucas Marco Gisi, "Im Namen des Autors," in *Medien der Autorschaft: Formen literarischer (Selbst-)Inszenierung von Brief und Tagebuch bis Fotographie und Interview,* ed. Lucas Marco Gisi, Urs Meyer, and Reto Sorg (Munich: Wilhelm Fink, 2013), 139–51, 146; Robert Walser, *Dichtungen in Prosa,* ed. Carl Seelig (Geneva: Holle/Kossodo, 1953–1961).

81. Walter Muschg, ed., *Schweizer Novellenbuch* (Zurich: Schweizer Bücherfreunde, 1939); Otto Zinniker, *Robert Walser der Poet* (Zurich: Werner Classen, 1947); Muschg was also the editor of the Benno Schwabe & Co. series in which the 1944 reprint of *Poems* appeared; Rascher's edition of *The Tanners* sold 933 copies between 1942 and 1948, producing royalties of 335.88 francs that Seelig had paid out along with the outstanding balance of 187.20 francs that had meanwhile accrued; royalty statement reproduced in Witschi, "Unter Vormundschaft," 89; Robert Walser, *Die Schlacht bei Sempach: Eine Geschichte,* appeared as volume 3 in the series Der Bogen (St. Gallen: Tschudy-Verlag, 1950); Witschi, "Unter Vormundschaft," 91.

82. Krankengeschichte Herisau, 21, 27; Seelig, *Walks with Walser,* 132.

83. Lucas Marco Gisi, "'Uns ist es nun einmal beschieden, spazieren zu gehen': zu Carl Seeligs *Wanderungen mit Robert Walser,"* in *"Spazieren muss ich unbedingt": Robert Walser und die Kultur des Gehens,* ed. Annie Pfeifer and Reto Sorg (Paderborn: Wilhelm Fink, 2019), 199–211, 205–6.

84. Seelig, *Walks with Walser,* 21; Auer, "Geschrieben, aber nicht gedruckt," 33–34.

85. "Er war anders wie die andern," 8; Auer, "Geschrieben, aber nicht gedruckt," 37; the manuscript Wehrle gave Hamm, "Etwas vom Handkuß" ("Something about

the Kiss on the Hand"), dates from 1930 or 1931 and was first published in 1986, SW 20:402–4, email from Jochen Greven to Susan Bernofsky, November 21, 2008. Hamm coedited (with Elio Fröhlich) *Robert Walser: Leben und Werk in Daten und Bildern* (Frankfurt am Main: Insel, 1980).

86. Seelig notes in 1943, "He has not responded to any of my letters or packages in the last six months," *Walks with Walser,* 51; Hesse sent his letter through Seelig, who wrote to Hesse a month later saying there'd been no response; Hesse had written to Robert, "We have grown old now, and working is no longer possible. I can't even read much anymore. But now and then, when I want to read something beautiful, I take out one of your dear books and read a little, I go walking with you through the beautiful world and take pleasure in this. I've just done so once again and wanted to tell you so," BA 2:504; "Er war anders wie die andern," 8; a note in Walser's medical record confirms his interest in crossword puzzles, Krankenge-schichte Herisau, Pflegerapporte, January 14, 1952.

87. Seelig, *Walks with Walser,* 63.

88. Seelig, *Walks with Walser,* 63.

89. The contents of his vest pockets included letters and postcards from Seelig, the Morgenthalers, Fanny, and Frieda Mermet, Mächler, *Robert Walser,* 258; the final note in his medical record reads: "Today when Mr. Walser was on his outing he died of a heart attack."Krankengeschichte Herisau, Pflegerapporte, December 25, 1956.

Epilogue

1. Mächler, *Robert Walser,* 257–58; Michael Allmaier, "Welt ohne Kanten," *Die Zeit,* December 20, 2006, https://www.zeit.de/2006/52/Schweiz-Walser; "Unheimliche Begegnung im Schnee," *Neue Zürcher Zeitung,* December 24, 2006, https://www.nzz.ch/articleERGNN-1.85647.

2. Caption by Carl Seelig (signed "C.S.") beside an image of an unidentified micro-script page (in fact Microscript 300). "Robert Walser" (dossier), *Du* 17:10 (October 1957): 42–52, 46.

3. Walser's effects also included a large stash of pornographic photographs, according to Carl Seelig's lawyer and literary executor, Elio Fröhlich. This is perhaps why Lisa complained so indignantly to Robert's doctors about his irregular erotic hab-its when she was interviewed at Waldau in April 1929 shortly after clearing out his Luisenstrasse room. Werner Wüthrich, "Die letzte Habe des Schriftstellers Robert W.," *Mitteilungen der Robert Walser-Gesellschaft* 24 (April 2017): 5–8; Angela Thut, Christian Walt, and Wolfram Groddeck, "Editorisches Nachwort," KWA VI.1:379–91, 381; letter from Lisa Walser to Carl Seelig, April 28, 1937, RWA, Sammlung Robert Walser, E-02: Sammlung Lisa Walser; letter from Hans Steiner to Carl Seelig, August 11, 1957, quoted in KWA VI.1:381.

4. The first English-language dissertation on Walser, by George Avery, was in prog-ress at the same time. It was defended in 1959, one year before Greven's; letter from Jochen Greven to Carl Seelig, October 23, 1958, RWA, Nachlass Carl Seelig, B-04: Robert Walser; testament, Carl Seelig (photocopy), RWA, Nachlass Carl Seelig, C-01: Persönliche Dokumente.

5. Jochen Greven, *Robert Walser—ein Außenseiter wird zum Klassiker,* 2nd ed. (Lengwil: Libelle-Verlag, 2003), 29–30.

6. Carl Seelig, *Albert Einstein: Eine dokumentarische Biographie* (Zurich: Europa, 1954); Greven, *Robert Walser,* 35.

7. Greven, *Robert Walser,* 148; "Felix Scenes" and *The Robber* first appeared in the twelfth volume of the Kossodo *Collected Works* edition.

Acknowledgments

IF I HAD UNDERSTOOD, when I first began thinking about writing a biography of Robert Walser, how many years of labor it would entail, I surely never would have begun. The project began with a grant proposal submitted in 2004 to the American Council of Learned Societies, which funded my initial work on the book. Subsequent support came from a Lannan Foundation Residency Fellowship in 2008, a National Endowment for the Humanities Fellowship in 2008–2009, and a fellowship from the Leon Levy Center for Biography at the Graduate Center of the City University of New York in 2012–2013, where under the expert guidance of director Gary Giddins, I discarded all my chapter drafts and started writing the book again from scratch. A grant from the Guggenheim Foundation provided more writing time and funded a research trip to Berlin. The manuscript was finalized during a year spent as a fellow at the Dorothy and Lewis B. Cullman Center for Scholars and Writers at the New York Public Library. I am immensely grateful for this support, as I am to the School of the Arts and the Division of Humanities at Columbia University as well as the Robert Walser Foundation Bern.

I am also indebted to Mark Ineichen LL.M. and the Pro Scientia et Arte Foundation in Switzerland for generous supplementary research support.

Many individuals helped me at various stages of the project. Above all, I am grateful to the present and former staff of the Robert Walser Center and Robert Walser-Archiv in Bern. This includes first and foremost director Reto Sorg, without whom it would be difficult to imagine this project coming together, and current and recent archivists Lukas Gloor and Lucas Marco Gisi, as well as Peter Stocker, Gelgia Caviezel, Stefanie Nydegger, Pino Dietiker, Margit Gigerl, and Livia Knüsel. I am also deeply indebted to past archivists from the Walser-Archiv's Zurich years: Werner Morlang† and Bernhard Echte, who opened his private archive to me, sharing decades of research. And I have many grateful memories of Jochen

Greven,† who patiently answered more questions than I even knew to ask, and of Christopher Middleton,† whose masterful translations first made Walser's work come alive for me.

Enormous thanks are due as well to Samuel Frederick, Paul North, and Ruth Meyer Schweizer, who read and painstakingly commented on my draft manuscript, as well as to Valerie Heffernan for editorial help with Chapter 3, Robert Tobin for a consultation on Chapter 7, Max Lüscher-Marty for assistance with historical currency conversions, and Robin Jacobson, MD, FRCPsych, MRCP, who helped me understand Walser's medical history. Any errors, of course, are my own.

Thanks also to Katia Frey, Yvonne Studer, and Sophie Stäger for kind archival assistance; Christine Burgin and Barbara Epler for editorial advice; Ian Beilin, Columbia University Research Collections and Services Librarian; Salvatore Scibona, Lauren Goldenberg, and Paul Delaverdac of the Cullman Center for Scholars and Writers at the New York Public Library; Michael Gately at the Leon Levy Center and its founder Shelby White; Petra Hardt and Nora Mercurio at Suhrkamp Verlag; Dörthe Perlenfein, Julia Maas, and Gunilla Eschenbach of the Deutsches Literaturarchiv, Marbach; Stefan Emmenegger of the Hermann Hesse-Stiftung; staff of the Stadtbibliothek Biel/Bienne, Zivilstandsamt Seeland, Zentralbibliothek Solothurn, Zentralbibliothek Zürich, Bibliothek am Guisanplatz, Bern, Schweizerisches Bundesarchiv, and Schweizerische Nationalbibliothek; Jutta Hafner of the Staatsarchiv Appenzell Ausserrhoden; and PD Dr. phil. Andreas Altorfer, director of the Psychiatrie-Museum Bern.

I am also indebted to my tireless editor at Yale University Press, Jennifer Banks, who shepherded this project into existence with wisdom and grace, my stalwart agent, Chris Calhoun, Jessie Dolch for meticulous copy editing, Jeffrey Schier for project management, Robin Charney for proofreading, Andrew Lopez for the index, and J. A. Hopkin and Robert Rubsam for invaluable help with the page proofs.

And with warmest thanks to my beloved partner, Richard Gehr, who accompanied me through most of the writing of this book and read every one of its pages with an astute editorial eye.

Credits

Grateful acknowledgment is made to the following for permission to reproduce previously published and archival materials:

Deutsches Literaturarchiv Marbach and Hermann Hesse-Stiftung: Letter from Flora Ackeret to Hermann Hesse, December 13, 1918–March 3, 1919.

NMB Neues Museum Biel, Depositum Bundesamt für Kultur, Gottfried Keller-Stiftung, Bern: Flora Ackeret's annotations in her personal copy of *Geschwister Tanner* by Robert Walser.

Psychiatrie-Museum Bern, Universitäre Psychiatrische Dienste Bern (UPD) AG: Robert Walser's medical record from Waldau Asylum.

Robert Walser-Stiftung Bern: All texts by Robert Walser copyright © Robert Walser-Stiftung Bern and Suhrkamp Verlag, Berlin.

Staatsarchiv des Kantons Appenzell Ausserrhoden: Robert Walser's medical record from Cantonal Sanatorium of Appenzell Ausserrhoden, Herisau, StAAR, Pa.057-07.

Suhrkamp Verlag, Berlin: Excerpts from Robert Walser, *Sämtliche Werke in Einzelausgaben* copyright © Suhrkamp Verlag Zurich 1985; excerpts from Robert Walser, *Aus dem Bleistiftgebiet* copyright © Suhrkamp Verlag Frankfurt am Main 1985–2000; excerpts from Robert Walser, *Werke (Berner Ausgabe)* copyright © Suhrkamp Verlag Berlin, 2018.

Farrar, Straus and Giroux: Excerpts from *Selected Stories* by Robert Walser, translated by Christopher Middleton and others, with an introduction by Susan Sontag. Translation and compilation copyright © 1982 by Farrar, Straus and Giroux. Reprinted by permission of Farrar, Straus and Giroux.

New Directions: Excerpts from *The Assistant* by Robert Walser, translated by Susan Bernofsky. Copyright © Suhrkamp Verlag Zurich 1978 and 1985. License edition by permission of the owner of rights, Carl-Seelig-Stiftung, Zurich. Translation copyright © 2007 by Susan Bernofsky. Reprinted by permission of New Directions Publishing Corp.

New Directions: Excerpts from *The Tanners* by Robert Walser, translated by Susan Bernofsky. Copyright © Suhrkamp Verlag Zurich 1978 and 1985. License edition by permission of the owner of rights, Carl-Seelig-Stiftung, Zurich. Translation copyright © 2009 by Susan Bernofsky. Reprinted by permission of New Directions Publishing Corp.

University of Nebraska Press: Excerpts reproduced from *The Robber* by Robert Walser, translated by Susan Bernofsky, by permission of the University of Nebraska

Index

clothes, 84–86, 108, 110–11; in author
photo, 81–82; "better dressed now than
before," 221; in care packages, 168, 179;
frivolous-looking, 86–87; hats, 71, 187,
209–10, 221, 268, 300, 307; long walks
in funny clothes, 78; mending of, 184,
204, 261; rag slippers, 164, 210; shabby,
185, 209–10, 269, 297; slips of paper in
vest pocket, 304; and stays with
friends, 228–29; in youth, 40, 58–59.
See also appearance
"Coats," 236
Collected Works (1966-1975), 309
Comedy (1919), 210–11, 252
"Comedy Evening," 251
"Comrade, The," 67
"Concerning a Sort of Duel," 150
copying: as bank clerk, 100–101, 103; Blei
copies poems, 60; Copyists' Office for
the Unemployed, 92–93, 97–98;
editing and revising, 200, 235; for
insurance work, 41–42, 50; labor of,
235, 244, 255; and microscripts, 256;
and pencils, 153, 200, 235, 244, 255; for
The Robber, 244, 258–59; for *Tobold*,
211–13; in "Wenzel," 32. *See also*
handwriting; transcription
Corinth, Lovis, 88
"Countess Kirke: A Fantasy," 99
crossword puzzles, 294, 304–5
Czarnetzki, Hedwig Agnes ("Trude"), 141,
158, 207–8, 150

Dambrau (Germany), 113, 117, 177, 181, 183
Dauthendey, Max, 85–86
Dear Little Swallow (book proposal), 211
death of RW, 306–7
Dehmel, Richard, 93, 181
Deibel, Franz, 107
depression. *See* mental illness
Dernburg, Bernhard, 127
Deutsche Allgemeine Zeitung (newspaper),
214
Deutsche Monatshefte (journal), 161–62,
164, 166–67
"Diary," 224, 231

"Diary of a Pupil," 146
Dickens, Charles, 33, 152, 155, 200
"Discussion," 257
Dohnal, Jaroslav, 251
Dostoevsky, Fyodor, 73, 131–32; *The
Brothers Karamazov*, 234; *The Idiot*,
292
"Dostoevsky's Idiot," 239
"Dr. Franz Blei," 59–60, 198
"Drama," 153
drama. *See* plays; theater
"Dramatist, The," 9
"Drawing Lesson," 135
"Dream, The," 167
"Dreams," 72
drinking. *See* alcohol
Du (journal), 307–8
Dubler-Grässle, Carl, 98–100, 136, 259
DuMont Schauberg publishing, 254
Durieux, Tilla, 108, 137, 139, 257
Dürrenmatt, Friedrich, 3–4

Echte, Bernhard, 8, 51, 309, 315; *Robert
Walser: Sein Leben in Bildern und
Texten*, 10
editing, 122–23, 128, 131–32, 192–93,
200–201, 212–13, 235, 238, 256. *See also*
copying; handwriting; manuscript
destruction
education. *See* school
Eichendorff, Joseph von, *Memoirs of a
Good-for-Nothing*, 125, 199, 217, 292
"Elfenau," 220, 267
Eltze, Erich, 155
employment, 36, 55–56, 59, 70, 90, 92, 94,
218; arts over, 39, 42, 54–55; assistant,
97–100; asylum life as work, 295; bank
clerk, 1–2, 30, 33–34, 78, 100–101, 103,
165; Copyists' Office for the Unemployed, 92–93, 97–98; failure to seek,
283; financial difficulties of writing,
92–94, 96–97, 103, 111, 136, 158, 167,
184, 210, 215, 218, 224, 248–51, 255, 277;
insurance work, 40–43, 50, 53; labor in
asylums, 282, 296–97; and literary
agencies, 254–55, 302; longing for

Hinrichsen, Otto, 58, 284–91, 293–95, 298,
303–4; death of, 293, 298, 304;
incompetence of RW, 288; mentally ill
cannot produce creative works,
286–87, 290; reviews, 81, 284; on
Seelig, 295; work therapy, 286; writing
room for RW, 285–86, 290, 303–4. *See
also* Cantonal Asylum in Herisau;
medical record

Hirschfeld, Magnus, 118

Hiss, Hugo, 262

Hitler, Adolf, 283

Hochberg, Konrad von, 114

Hofmannsthal, Hugo von, 72, 110, 130, 135,
138

Hofmiller, Josef, 149

Hölderlin, Friedrich, 250, 296; and mental
illness, 198, 269, 286

home, 229, 257, 267

"Homecoming in the Snow, A," 150–51

homosexuality. *See* sexuality and gender
identity

Hotel Blaues Kreuz, 64, 184, 195, 205, 208,
211; cost of, 163, 210, 230; routine at,
185–87; temperance hotel, 163–64, 234

Hottingen Readers' Circle. *See* Literary
Club of the Hottingen Readers' Circle

Hubacher, Ernst, 164, 209, 226, 269

Hubacher, Hermann, 226; RW shows up
unannounced at summer home,
228–29; RW's strange behavior
towards, 268–69

Hubacher-Tscherter, Anna, 228–29

Huber, Rudolf, 186, 190–93, 199–200,
213–14, 217

Humperdinck, Engelbert, *Hansel and Gretel*, 265

Hundt-Radowsky, Hartwig, 16

Hungerbühler, Alfred, 290

Huttenlocher, Ferdinand, 34

Hyperion (journal), 135

"I Have Nothing," 189–90, 247

"Idol, The," 166

"Imaginings," 182–83

"In Junior High," 29

"In the Army," 183

Individualität (periodical), 251, 259–60

inflation, 182, 195, 201–2, 213–15; and
publishing, 223, 235; workers strike
against, 202–4

influenza pandemic (1918), 202–3, 267

innocence. *See* naiveté

Insel, Die (journal), 71–73, 157–58;
complete works offered, 90; design, 72;
end of, 99; establishment of, 71; fairy
tales, 81; parody of, 86; pay rate, 93;
pieces in, 101; visit to, 83–86

Insel publishing, 90, 99, 101–3, 108, 114;
not accepting RW's manuscripts, 107,
128, 132, 142, 201–2, 235

Institute Benjamenta (film), 1

irony, 3, 10; critics overlook, 103, 286;
detached irony, 236; quintessentially
Walserian, 49; three-layer writing, 152.
See also naiveté

Jacobsen, Jens Peter, *Niels Lyhne*, 260

Jacobsohn, Siegfried, 134, 147, 153–54

Jakob von Gunten (1909), 1, 112, 143–49,
146–49, 152–53, 155, 176, 294

Jean Paul, *Life of the Cheerful Little
Schoolmaster Maria Wutz*, 233

"Johanna," 40, 166

Johnson, Fanny, 133

"Journey to a Small Town," 256

Joyce, James, 246

Jugend (journal), 83–84

Jürgens, Martin, 309

Kafka, Franz, 1, 3, 42, 246, 251; *Contemplation*, 158, 163, 167, 169–70; influence
on, 135–36, 155; "The Judgment," 161;
The Metamorphosis, 334n27; "The
Stoker," 163

Kainz, Josef, 37

Kämmerer, Gustav, 34–35

Kandinsky, Wassily, 83

Kayssler, Friedrich, 134, 148

Keller, Gottfried, 55, 132, 200, 232, 278,
292; *Green Henry*, 125, 131; as model of
narrative structure, 130–31

residences: (*continued*)
226–31; male-headed households, 231;
in Munich, 83–86; relocated often, 4,
19, 23, 25, 28, 54, 65, 229–31, 267, 274;
in Solothurn, 78; in Stuttgart, 34–38; in
Täuffelen, 91–92; in Winterthur, 94; in
Zurich, 47, 92–93, 97, 100, 104–5,
108–9

Rheinlande, Die (journal), 132, 150, 157,
159, 161, 175; reviews, 170

Rheinverlag publishing, 223

Richthofen, Bernard von, 118

Rilke, Rainer Maria, 72, 83, 292

Ringelnatz, Joachim, 279

Robber, The (1925), 6, 28, 32, 116–17, 152,
220–21, 224–25, 241–46, 255–59, 265,
304, 309

The Robbers (Schiller), 31–32, 70, 89

Robert Guiskard (Kleist), 69–70

Robert Walser (Sauvat), 9

*Robert Walser: Sein Leben in Bildern und
Texten* (*Robert Walser: His Life in
Images and Texts*, Echte, 2008), 10

Robert Walser Archiv, 7–8, 10, 31, 309

Robert Walser Center, 309

"Rocking," 72

Rodin, Auguste, 88

romance: amorous adventures, 116–20;
with au pair, 227–28, 234; Fanny and
Mühlestein, 105, 109, 116, 334n18;
flirtation, 120, 176, 204–5; inflated
prospects, 205, 221, 229–30, 232, 234,
263, 265; KW's, 52–53, 66–69, 91, 121,
137, 141; Lisa's troubles, 104, 123–24;
with Mermet, 167–69, 171–72, 183–85;
in *The Robber*, 116–17, 242, 256;
romantic interests listed, 256; with
shopgirl, 40–41. *See also* marriage;
sexuality and gender identity; women

romanticism: literary hero, 310; nineteenth-century style rejected, 191;
romantic tropes, 4; RW as romantic
outsider, 1–2, 6, 302, 307, 310; and *The
Tanners*, 125

Rose, The (1925), 6–7, 239–41, 243–44, 247,
251, 258

Roth, Joseph, 134

Rothenhäusler, Oskar, 262

Rousseau, Jean-Jacques, 278

Rovzoj (journal), 251

Rowohlt, Ernst, 155, 161, 224, 239, 241, 249,
251, 254; RW becomes a Rowohlt
author, 157–58

Rudolf, Alfred, 219

"Ruin, The," 234, 253

Rummel, Johann David (uncle), 14

Russian literature, 122, 131, 137, 277

Rychner, Max, 212, 226, 249; important
editor for RW, 252–53

Sacher-Masoch, Leopold von, 243

Salten, Felix, 125

Samstag, Der (weekly), 107, 135

Saturn (journal), 217

"Sausage, The," 189

Sauvat, Catherine, *Robert Walser*, 9

Schaer-Ris, Adolf, 269

Schaetzle-Ehrensperger, Marie, 20–21, 29

Schäfer, William, 132, 150, 170; nominates
RW for literary prize, 170–71

Schaffner, Karl, 229

Schätzle, Rosa, 51–53, 64, 66

Schätzle family, 63

Schaubühne, Die (journal), 129, 134–35,
138, 147, 149–50, 153–56, 163

Scheer, Anna, 155, 158

Scheerbart, Paul, 72

Scherl publishing, 131, 146

Schibli, Emil, 208–10, 215, 232, 234, 236,
293

Schibli-Furrer, Frieda, 208–9

Schiele, Egon, 202

Schiller, Friedrich, 37, 247; *The Robbers*,
31–32, 70, 89; *William Tell*, 36

Schiller Foundation, 214, 216, 222

schizophrenia: and eccentricity, 276; Ernst
diagnosed, 65, 275, 286; RW
diagnosed, 5–6, 275–76, 286

Schlaf, Johannes, 103

Schmid, Rosa, 263

Schmidt publishing, 224

Schneider, Hedwig, 227–28